Jonathan Littman

REVISED AND EXPANDED EDITION

ONCE UPON
A TIME IN
COMPUTERLAND

The Amazing
Billion-Dollar Tale
of Bill Millard

A TOUCHSTONE BOOK
Published by Simon & Schuster Inc.
NEW YORK   LONDON   TORONTO   SYDNEY   TOKYO   SINGAPORE

Simon and Schuster/Touchstone
Simon & Schuster Building
Rockefeller Center
1230 Avenue of the Americas
New York, New York 10020

Published by arrangement with the author.
SIMON AND SCHUSTER, TOUCHSTONE and colophons
are registered trademarks of Simon & Schuster Inc.

Designed by Carla Weise/Levavi & Levavi
Manufactured in the United States of America

1   3   5   7   9   10   8   6   4   2
1   3   5   7   9   10   8   6   4   2   Pbk.

Library of Congress Cataloging in Publication Data

Littman, Jonathan, 1958-
Once upon a time in ComputerLand : the amazing billion-dollar
tale of Bill Millard / Jonathan Littman.— 1st Touchstone ed.
        p.   cm.
Reprint. Originally published: Tucson, AZ : Knight-Ridder Press, © 1987.
"A Touchstone book."
1. ComputerLand (Firm)—History.   2. Millard, Bill.   3. Computer industry—
United States—History.   4. Businessmen—United States—Biography.   I. Title.
        [HD9696.C64C655   1990]
        338.7′6100416′0973—dc20   89-48785
                                                             CIP

ISBN 0-671-70218-1
0-671-69392-1 Pbk.

For Waldo

Acknowledgments

Writing a book is an act of faith, and friends help to make the faith constant. There was my father, whose belief and able editing guided me through the early months when the book was taking shape. My mother, who listened. My brother Jeremy, who introduced me to my editor-to-be and read early drafts. My editor, Ted DiSante, who took a chance on my idea, encouraged my first efforts, and then patiently and skillfully fine-tuned the manuscript. Patty Morris, who diligently typed thousands of pages of interview transcripts, accelerating the agonizing process of assimilating the words and opinions of many. Dave Nelson and Jim Leeke, who generously read the book in its early form and shared ideas. Jerry Dougherty, who gave superior legal guidance. Steve Rosenthal, without whose sage advice I might have written myself out of an interview with Bill Millard and missed the heart of the story. Lily McFadden, who encouraged me to quit my job to write the book.

And finally to the Philadelphia lady, and the stories yet to be told.

• • •

Like most books, this one began with basic research: It started with thousands of pages of court proceedings and transcripts. Added to that snakepit of contradictions were several computer searches that heaved up hundreds of articles on the subject. Later, I examined financial sheets, state filings, bankruptcy hearings, indictments, in-house magazines, résumés, advertisements, memorandums, letters, telexes, hand-scrawled notes, and the diaries and calendars of two men. Stuffed with facts, I took tape recorder and notebooks and began tracking down the men and women of whom I had read so much.

My interviews took me from Los Angeles to Boston, Washington, D.C., Manhattan and Albany, New York, out west to Arizona, and then finally to my hometown of San Francisco. Some interviewees liked to meet for breakfast at seven A.M. in San Jose; one preferred $12 double Chivas Regals at the Fairmont in San Francisco; another made me tea and fed me as long I let his wife beat me at pool. I picked some up at airports, drove others to catch flights, and spent nearly an entire day talking by phone to Saipan, at about $100 an hour. There were, of course, the months when it seemed nearly every other day I would drive over the Hayward Bridge to ComputerLand; the workers at the cafeteria were convinced I was a new employee.

For me, the book was in those interviews, most of which ran two to three hours, and were often piled one on top of another from early morning until late at night. There is something precious about watching the tape slowly spin on the recorder while a stranger tells secrets. An interviewer is in many ways a priest without the power of absolution. It almost seems that a person will tell his interviewer things he would confess to no one else.

Only a handful of people, out of fear for the millions of dollars involved, refused months of requests for an interview. One was convinced that the "other side" had paid me as a spy, not to write a book, but to gather intelligence on the enemy. Another declined on the possibility that I might be one of those wearing a "black hat." Another feared that if he talked, worse could happen to him than just a lawsuit.

But these were the exceptions; the overwhelming majority were eager to talk, despite real or imagined risks. And some had waited ten years to tell their story. Without that openness and trust this book would not have been possible. I would like to express my appreciation to all of the people who graciously consented to interviews, but especially those who posed—as well as answered—questions and helped me inch closer to the amazing story of ComputerLand and Bill Millard.

Contents

Prologue

In 1983 an article in *Forbes* gave William Millard a new name: "The Instant Billionaire." Only two years before, when IBM introduced its first personal computer, Millard's franchising chain, ComputerLand, had begun three heady years of phenomenal sales and growth. Sales exploded from $61 million in 1981 to over $1.4 billion in 1984. Stores mushroomed all over the country. By the end of 1984, more than 783 ComputerLand franchises operated in 24 nations. *Forbes* declared Millard the 27th richest man in America, and Millard boasted, "I am the biggest winner of all in the microcomputer industry."

Some said Millard was simply in the right place at the right time. The following year a popular book would describe his good fortune in a section entitled "Lucky Ducks."

But suddenly Millard's luck seemed to run out. By 1985, *Forbes* had a new tag for Millard: "The Beleaguered Billionaire." A tragic flaw appeared to be his undoing. Through a strange twist of fate a $250,000 promissory note threatened Millard's vast empire.

Players

THE ENTREPRENEURS

William H. Millard
Son of railroad clerk. Disciple of Werner Erhard's human-potential movement est. Founder/owner of IMSAI and ComputerLand.

Philip Reed
Harvard-educated son of Loring Reed. New Mexico auto dealer. Millard's first major investor, business partner, and friend.

John Martin-Musumeci
High-school dropout. Also known as John Martin. Independent businessman and car salesman. Franchise consultant who developed the concept of ComputerLand.

THE WORKERS

Joseph Killian
Computer engineer and inventor of the IMSAI microcomputer, forerunner to the Apple computer and key product for fledgling ComputerLand.

Edward Faber
Ex-Marine and ex-semipro baseball player. Former IBM employee. President of ComputerLand.

Bruce Van Natta
Berkeley poet, bohemian, and computer scientist. Millard's early first lieutenant at IMSAI.

THE SPECULATORS

Bruno Andrighetto
Produce baron. Gold-mine owner. Stock-market investor.

Loring Reed
Father of Philip Reed. As president of Marriner & Co., holder of the $250,000 note to Millard.

THE LITIGATORS

Herbert Hafif
Successful personal-injury lawyer. Onetime candidate for governor of California. Nightclub owner and emcee. Legal challenger to Millard's empire.

Terry Giles
Criminal lawyer and businessman. Defender of William Millard.

Chronology

1973 Millard founds IMS, predecessor to ComputerLand.

1975 IMS develops the IMSAI 8080 microcomputer.

1976 Philip Reed obtains $250,000 loan for IMS from Mar-
riner & Co. in exchange for promissory note convertible
into 20 percent of IMS stock.

Millard promises IMS stock to Killian and Van Natta.

John Martin sells the concept of ComputerLand to Millard.

ComputerLand incorporated. IMS becomes IMSAI.

Millard's Panamanian tax scheme.

1977 Marriner note modified to include 20 percent of ComputerLand.

John Martin leaves ComputerLand.

1978 Millard completes reorganization of IMS, IMSAI, and
ComputerLand.

Killian and Van Natta receive IMSAI stock.

1979 IMSAI goes bankrupt.

1980 Millard rejects offer to buy back Marriner note.

Philip Reed goes to work for Martin's new company,
Micro/Vest.

1981 Marriner note purchased by Micro/Vest.

Micro/Vest sues Millard for 20 percent of ComputerLand stock.

IBM PC introduced to popular acclaim. ComputerLand is the main retail outlet for the computer.

1982 Martin gives Philip Reed 25 percent of the Micro/Vest note.

1983 Killian and Van Natta sue Millard for ComputerLand stock.

1984 ComputerLand tops $1 billion in sales.

1985 *Micro/Vest* v. *ComputerLand* trial.

1986 Millard moves to the island of Saipan and puts ComputerLand up for sale.

Killian/Van Natta v. *Millard* trial.

Saipan tax laws change.

1987 Millard tells FBI of alleged Saipan corruption and is subpoenaed to appear before a grand jury.

Death threats.

Millard testifies before Saipan investigative committee and grand jury.

ComputerLand sold.

Saipan murders.

1988 ComputerLand fails to go public.

Island billion-dollar bankruptcy.

Oral appeal of *Micro/Vest* v. *Millard*.

Martin threatens nun, speaks with spirits, channeler.

1989 *Martin* v. *Micro/Vest, Herb Hafif*.

If this were play'd upon a stage now, I could condemn it as an improbable fiction.

—*Twelfth Night*

PART I

1

West

In the summer of 1970, Philip Reed III said good-bye to his young wife and daughter in Racine, Wisconsin, threw a small suitcase into the back of his Chevrolet Impala, and began a journey west. The young Harvard graduate was not leaving his wife or going on vacation. By the time he returned he hoped to have his own General Motors dealership.

It certainly wasn't necessity that sent Reed packing. His father, P. Loring Reed, had married money, or more precisely Elizabeth Reece. More buttons are put on shirts by Reece machines than any other button-sewing devices. That is a lot of button-sewing, and the Reece Co., though largely family-owned, has been traded on the New York Stock Exchange for many years.

Bright, tall, and extremely handsome, young Reed knew that one day an executive position in the successful $35-million company would be waiting. But that was not all. Reed's father was president of Marriner & Co., a wool processor once valued at $10 million.

Although Philip Reed was born and raised near Boston, a case of rheumatic fever had sent him off to the dry, hot climate of the Southwest. It was a different world. Reed attended Orme, a ranch school with just one hundred students, seventy miles north of Phoenix. The shy, sickly, retiring boy eventually became captain of the football team and class president. But Harvard had never heard of Orme, and so Reed spent a fifth year at the prestigious Massachusetts prep school Andover, taking courses in the hope of getting accepted by an Ivy League college.

At Andover, Reed had switched from football to pole vaulting, and the big meet that spring was against the Harvard freshman team. On his last jump he cleared the winning height but fell out of the pit, almost breaking his ankle. While he lay in pain in the locker room, the Harvard track coach talked him into sending in an application, although the deadline had passed. He applied, was accepted, and just as his father before him, Reed became a Harvard man.

Reed studied economics and psychology at Harvard, and his grades were only average. Halfway through his sophomore year, in 1967, he married the beautiful daughter of Don Hutson, the All-Pro Green Bay Packers football star of the 1940s and 1950s. Soon a baby was on the way. School seemed esoteric and unimportant and Reed was anxious to get out in the real world. After his sophomore year he took a year off from Harvard and went to work for Frank Gerrity, his father's close friend and also a board member of Marriner & Co.

Reed drove a forklift and hoisted icy boards at Gerrity Lumber. He loved the hard work and mixed easily with the blue-collar workers and their families. The rough, physical labor gave him an opportunity to work on something real, something that wasn't intellectual.

During his year in the lumberyard, Reed grew to respect Gerrity as a bright, serious businessman. A director of the Bank of New England and the trade consul to Ireland, Gerrity was an inspiration to Reed, a successful executive who took time out to encourage young men to go into business. Reed might very well have kept working for Gerrity Lumber, the largest lumber company in New England. There had once even been a standing joke between Gerrity and Reed's father that Reed would one day marry Gerrity's daughter. The two older men had been classmates at Harvard and were like brothers.

But Reed returned to Harvard and after graduating, decided that he wanted to learn the car business. He went to work at his father-in-law's thriving Cadillac dealership in Wisconsin. Not long after, his father-in-law offered him a partnership. But Reed wanted his own dealership, one where he would be the boss, and so he set out to find the right location.

. . .

Colorado, Utah, California, Arizona, New Mexico, and Texas—
they all rolled past him on a stretch of asphalt, cheap hotels, and
greasy food. Reed was only twenty-six, and most of the General
Motors dealers he talked to didn't take him very seriously. Tired
and discouraged after a couple weeks on the road, Reed ended up
at the regional GM office in Dallas, where he was told that he was
going about his search the wrong way. He needed to find a dealership that "wanted out." He remembered a small town in southern
New Mexico that looked just the right size and had a dealership
that seemed available.

Las Cruces was six hundred miles from Dallas, and Reed figured if
he drove all night he'd be there by morning. The bleary-eyed young
man's enthusiasm was rewarded. The owner of the new Las Cruces
Chevrolet dealership had suffered a series of heart attacks during construction of the building and wanted nothing more than to sell. Reed
talked a couple of banks into some loans, his parents pitched in the
down payment, and he had his dealership.

In 1970, Las Cruces was growing right along with the rest of the
Sun Belt, and Phil Reed Chevrolet-Oldsmobile grew with the town.
A year later Reed became the youngest approved Cadillac dealer in
the nation; the next year he added a Honda dealership. By 1973, his
company had doubled in size. Reed paid back some of the bank loans
and bought another dealership in Roswell, New Mexico. A family
holding company was formed to own the booming businesses. After
pondering the name for a while, they settled on Liz Corp., named
after Philip's mother, Elizabeth.

Yet, as his business grew, Reed saw his control slipping away. He
had hired a lot of young people to work for him and his operations
were becoming strained. He wondered if a machine could monitor
the work of his new, untrained employees. At the time, Wang Labs
made a big, clunky computerlike device that was being used in auto
dealerships for finance and insurance calculations. Salesmen could
punch in the price of the car, the down payment, and the number of
months of financing. The Wang machine would grind away for a few
minutes and spit out the monthly car payment. What if, Reed wondered, you could install these devices throughout the dealership to do

other things, too, such as inventory, accounts receivable, and payables?

Not willing to wait for innovation, Reed founded a new company called Auto Power, with a mission—writing the software to make the Wang computer help run his dealerships. Auto Power, owned entirely by Liz Corp., soon had four programmers and an office in Albuquerque. But as the project began to come together, Reed realized it would be necessary for the machines in each of the dealerships to "talk" to one another.

Reed didn't know much about computers, but he packed his suitcase and all of his computer manuals and flew to Boston to see Dr. An Wang of Wang Labs. It just so happened that Dr. Wang was doing research on what would one day be known as networking—the technology that allows distant computers to share common resources such as printers, storage devices, and information. But after two weeks at the labs, including a couple of days with Dr. Wang himself, Reed felt he had exhausted Wang's knowledge of this new field. Somebody at Wang suggested he contact IMS Associates, a consulting firm in northern California run by a fellow named Bill Millard.

After the session at Wang, Reed had expected that IMS would be a big, professional company. Perhaps that was why the second-story office in the little Wells Fargo Bank in San Leandro (a blue-collar community between Oakland and San Jose) struck him as especially small. He was greeted in a tiny reception area by a kind woman who, he would later find out, was Millard's wife. On the right was the work room. The whole office was not much bigger than a small apartment.

Reed was led into what seemed to be the only office. There was nothing on the plain desk, no paperwork at all. Only a little coffeepot on a credenza in the corner broke the spartan atmosphere. The two men shook hands. Millard was a bit older and more mature than Reed had expected and had a robust appearance.

As they talked, Reed felt himself drawn toward Millard. There was something appealing about his openness. Millard shared his recent bad experiences in business and talked about his goals for the future. He had started a company called System Dynamics to sell a software program called "Faster" for large IBM mainframe computers. Short of money, he'd been forced to sell equity in the company to venture capitalists to keep the project alive. Soon, his share had dwindled to less than 30 percent of the company. The investors demanded greater sales and faster profits. Millard described how he felt that he was "tied up to the post and beaten" for things over which he had no control.

Reed had never heard anyone speak in such a personal, powerful way about business. It struck Reed that this was probably a unique organization. Here was a guy, thought Reed, who had been to the school of hard knocks most of his life and was ready to do something great. They talked for hours and not once was Reed distracted from Millard's intense gaze.

Reed was intrigued by Millard's tales of business failure. Millard continued his story, sharing with Reed the painful bankruptcy of System Dynamics, which had wiped out Millard's life savings and forced him to remortgage his house.

Nothing was off limits in their open dialogue. The two men felt a need to know each other because Reed was proposing no ordinary deal. Even Millard's more recent financial troubles caused by a soured consulting project had a strange attraction for Reed. Millard seemed to have learned from his tough breaks.

In Millard's penetrating green eyes Reed saw ambition, but he also thought he saw gentleness and traits of a man who appeared to care about the way he did business. Reed knew then that he would do business with Millard. It was more of a feeling than a conscious decision. Millard was somebody you wanted to do business with, even if it was risky.

Struggling to meet the payroll for System Dynamics had been partly responsible for pushing Millard into bankruptcy. But Millard didn't want to make the same mistakes twice. Now he hired people on an hourly basis. When there was no work, as was the present case, there was also no payroll to meet. In the small, paperless office, with Millard's wife sitting outside, Reed and Millard negotiated an agreement to develop a network that would tie the Wang computers together in a powerful sharing of computer resources never before accomplished. It was an unusual arrangement—one that set Millard apart in Reed's mind as a special person. The two strangers took each other's side.

Millard told Reed that if Reed funded the project he would pay Reed royalties, and Reed would have the exclusive right to sell the product to auto dealers. Millard would retain the right to sell to others. But Reed thought Millard was being too generous, offering him too high a royalty. Millard, however, wouldn't budge. Paying Reed any less just wouldn't be fair.

It was not the normal, tough negotiating that Reed had expected. The two acted more like friends than businessmen. And by the end of the day Reed had taken the first small step toward what would soon become the closest business friendship of his life.

For several months a young, unemployed physicist named Joe Killian had called IMS Associates every few weeks looking for a programming job. But there was no response. He decided to call Bill Millard one more time.

"Well, you know, I *am* meeting with these customers. I'll probably need an electrical engineer," Millard told him on the phone.

Killian was surprised. The résumé he had sent Millard emphasized Killian's computer programming skills. Physics had been his major at Harvey Mudd College, although he had studied electrical engineering while taking Ph.D. courses in atmospheric physics at the University of Nevada. But Killian had built radio receivers as a boy and worked with computers in college. Become an electrical engineer? "Sure, why not?" he thought. It sounded interesting enough.

Killian was supposed to just listen and watch at that first meeting, but that was plenty. Philip Reed, the president of Auto Power, the "customer" who might be offering a contract to design a computer networking device, had flown out in his prop plane with his pilot. At that meeting, Reed pulled out a box full of electrical pieces and wires. Killian remembered wondering whether it was some kind of joke as they all sat shaking their heads at the ratty contraption. There was no way to salvage the original design. The only way to do it right, they decided, was to start all over again with IMS Associates handling the design and manufacture.

Reed advanced Millard $3,200 to start the project. A couple of months would pass before Millard signed a formal contract, acknowledging the advance. Reed also agreed to have Liz Corp. lend Millard $10,000 a month for up to twelve months so Millard wouldn't have to wait until he fulfilled the contract to get paid. The agreed-upon price of one working system was $60,000.

Killian was officially hired as the project's electrical engineer when

Millard took him out for a hamburger after the meeting. "You've taken est, haven't you?" asked Killian as they drove. Millard hadn't mentioned it, but Killian, who had also taken "the training," read the signs clearly. "If he was inclined toward me for any other reason, that probably cinched it," remembered Killian.

Killian had never wired a single logic chip before, but the $12.50 per hour Millard offered was reason enough to try. Though Killian would only be paid, as Millard wrote in his diary, "When, as & if paid by IMS client," it seemed a lot of money to a married man whose only prior work had been teaching flying part-time and building a house for a friend.

Killian may not have had the credentials of an electrical engineer, but he certainly had the ability. In a few months he had an ungodly looking contraption that actually seemed to work. Reed thought Killian was a brilliant engineer. He was amazed at the way Killian could look at a piece of electronic equipment and intuitively figure out how it worked or where the problems lay.

The prototype network devices were cased in wood instead of the traditional metal boxes, but when they were plugged in, the electronics worked nearly flawlessly. Killian flew to Las Cruces to spend a week hooking up the machines at Reed's dealerships. Reed was amazed. It looked like the Atlantic telephone cable, but it worked. Reed gladly paid Millard $60,000. The line-driver/multiplexor, known affectionately as MUXLIU, *seemed* to be networking, a capability thought to be years in the future.

Reed took the machine on the road to a group of car dealers in Kansas City. Eighty percent of them signed up for the system on the spot. "We were just ecstatic," remembered Reed. "We put up a demo, and jeez, it works or appears to work." Before installing any of the networking devices, however, they decided it might be a good idea to set up a system in Reed's dealerships under day-to-day conditions.

Four months later they were still trying to get some real work done. The Wang computer they were using had disk drives slower than a turtle. A Wang engineer came out and concluded that he wasn't sure Wang could "adequately support the system." They would be happy, however, to take all the Wang equipment back. Work ground to a halt. By then Reed had put more than $100,000 into the project. His plan to buy additional dealerships was on hold. The computer networking project was at a dead end.

In the meantime, Killian had an idea. All those new integrated circuits that were coming out—tiny circuitry, squeezed on little chip-like pieces of silicon—were hard for hobbyists to keep track of. What if IMS produced a book describing how integrated circuits worked? Millard wasn't too keen on paying his engineer to write a book. But if he drafted something, maybe they could work out an agreement.

Killian didn't have anything better to do—Millard wasn't paying him for any other work—so he gathered all the information he could find from the various integrated chip manufacturers. The little book he patched together explained how to use the chips to build your own computer. Reluctantly, Millard agreed to place a few lines in the regular IMS advertisement in *Popular Electronics* to announce the "TTL Pin Out Handbook." Millard made an oral agreement to give Killian 10 percent of the profits from sales. The book, the first of its kind, sold well, and the resulting thousands of dollars of profits kept IMS going during the long, slow summer and fall of 1974.

But the book was only a temporary solution to the troubles at IMS. New hope arrived in the form of a bright young man Millard had plucked out of graduate school at the University of California at Berkeley and hired for $1,250 a month. Bruce Van Natta had responded to the IMS ad for a part-time programmer mainly because his wife, knowing they needed the money, had cut the two-line ad out of the paper.

UC Berkeley had one of the best computer-science schools in the country, and Van Natta didn't intend to leave before completing his degree. But after a couple of hours of talking to Millard, he decided to join the three-person company. IMS seemed headed straight for microprocessors, the wave of the future. And Van Natta hadn't overlooked the way Millard had pulled his folder from a stack of résumés more than a foot high. "At the time it didn't seem like a big step," remembered Van Natta. "It seemed like the most natural thing in the world. You wanted to work for Bill."

It was Thursday afternoon and Millard asked Van Natta when he could show up for work. "I said, and I thought I was being really eager, 'What about Monday? Monday morning!'" recalled Van Natta.

"What about tomorrow morning?" said Millard.

"I can't. I'm taking a final."

"What about noon?"

"I don't have time to get here."

"What about one o'clock?"

It was settled. Without even withdrawing from school, Van Natta would show up for work the day after the interview. Millard gave him plenty of incentive. Ten percent of the profits made on the Auto Power deal would be his. The agreement, however, was oral.

Van Natta was quickly put to work on the software. It was hoped that improving the software's performance would compensate for the slow disk drives. But that wasn't good enough, and Millard proposed one last idea to Reed. Perhaps with the latest economy-priced mini-computer from Digital Equipment, the LSI 11, they could achieve the speed the Wang computer lacked. They were coming to the end of the line. Reed told Millard that this was the last infusion of cash. He couldn't spend any more. "We can do it!" Millard proclaimed.

They threw themselves into the task. Reed provided a letter of credit to help Millard obtain a $158,000 loan from the Bank of America. But the money didn't solve anything. As the expenses mounted, so it seemed did the enormousness of the problem. Finally, as if things were not bad enough, the delivery of the Digital computer was delayed. And just as the last-ditch effort floundered, the competition heated up. Several other companies were offering accounting systems for automobile dealers, and their pricing didn't seem to leave much room for IMS.

Meanwhile, Reed's dealership had fallen below General Motor's required capital level. Reed was told nicely that he was taking too much money out of the dealership, wasn't paying attention to the car business, and was "out there fooling around with these computers."

The chicken was good at Jake's Lion in San Leandro. Jake's had Chicken Jerusalem and Chicken Avocado and Chicken Jack Cheese. Every Monday night the cooks seemed to conjure up a new way to prepare chicken. The waitresses were pleasant, and it was comforting the way the tables were so close to the bar, so close that you could hear every roll of the dice and watch the patrons stare into each other's blurry eyes.

Jake's was a favorite meeting place for Millard, Killian, and Van Natta. They liked it because the food was good and they could order as late as ten or eleven P.M. and sit drinking coffee until two or three in the morning. They also liked it because it was the place where they asked big, crazy, unanswerable questions, the place where they scratched their heads, said, "Why not?" and madly scribbled impossible inventions on the back of napkins.

Millard liked to have meetings. At first they were really just question-and-answer sessions. Killian would come to Millard and say, "Gee, I don't know if we can do that." Millard would say, "Why not?" Killian would tell him the reasons and then Millard would ask questions about each reason, and Killian was soon convinced to go ahead and do it anyway. Millard would ask the question, and Killian would do the thinking. And they were very good questions. One of the best was "Why can't you do that?"

Soon, they began having formal meetings. They started at six or seven or eight or nine P.M. or whenever the day's work ended. The format was simple: "Here's the problem. What are the solutions?" Nothing was impossible to Millard. There was always a crack in the wall, one loose brick that would bring the last obstacle tumbling down. Killian didn't know about a lot of things he was doing, but he just went ahead and did them anyway. The important thing was that they were not afraid to try.

Their meetings usually started at the office. Sometimes the three would forget the time and have to hurry to get to Jake's before the kitchen closed. Without ever mentioning it, even the couple of miles to Jake's became part of the game. You couldn't speed. It was no good to cheat. That would have been winning without integrity—the crude, cheap way to win.

One night Millard and Killian drove together, leaving Van Natta alone in his Dodge. Van Natta tried every way to beat them to the restaurant, but even a couple of neat shortcuts didn't make any difference. Only a few blocks from the restaurant, the two cars waited side by side at a red light.

As his engine idled, the small frustration of the moment was symbolic to Van Natta. There was no hope of winning in any significant way. Accelerating as the light changed would be a shallow victory. But wait, maybe there was a chance. What if he turned right—even though it was the opposite direction from the restaurant—made a U-turn in the middle of the block (legal in San Leandro) and then cruised through the green light as the others sat pinned behind their red one? Millard and Killian watched in amazement. Van Natta had turned a seemingly sure draw into an outrageous victory. His miraculous effort became a metaphor for their positive thinking, a force that would loosen the restraints of reason.

Over chicken and sweet Rhine wine they bubbled over, around, below, and through the impossible. Inventions tripped off their tongues. Geodesic domes were in vogue, and they figured they could take hard Styrofoam, design molds for triangle shapes with double-sided sticky tape, and voilà! Portable, instant homes! Hydroponic farms was another of many ideas investigated at Jake's. Home energy controllers. * Sprinkler controllers. Just about every gadget or gizmo of the 1970s spun by in some shape or another. They were true believers pursuing a dream. Where the dream took them didn't matter. And they never stopped to think whether the dream was necessary. When you're a true believer, the dream takes care of itself.

The time they spent at Jake's was also a time of simple friendship. Millard talked proudly about his bicycle racing, and he and Killian talked endlessly about flying. They were good old days in the making, with the three people in the business sitting down to their weekly meeting.

Perhaps it happened early one morning, after the last cup of coffee at Jake's. If not, the seed of their future success was certainly sown in that rare atmosphere of hope. Of all the ideas that exploded from that raucous corner table, this one is the hardest to track. Of the three, only Killian made no claim to what became the truest dream, a dream that would outgrow buildings, spread beyond states and across oceans, and then die, only to be reborn in a success story beyond their wildest imaginations.

An outsider might have considered their plight impossible. The Digital Equipment computer they needed for the networking project was not only late, but just when they thought it might actually become a viable product, they discovered another problem. As they started pricing the parts, they were faced with the realization that maybe they had underbid the project.

Even the always optimistic Millard began to despair of ever reaching the goal. Almost two years had passed since Reed offered him the contract that promised to end his seesaw consulting existence. More than $200,000 of Philip Reed's development money had brought them no closer to the goal.

*Christened the Widget Interface.

Meanwhile, Intel had come out with a couple of new microprocessors: the 8008 and the 8080. A company called Omron was making display terminals that used the 8008. IMS met with Omron's marketing director, Ed Faber. Could they strike a deal? Perhaps the 8008 was powerful enough to do the job. But just when they were about to get some of the terminals, Killian took one of the machines apart and saw that the chips had been altered and would be incapable of the job. Yet another solution had proved inadequate. Nonetheless, they had all liked Faber's straightforward demeanor, and he wasn't forgotten.

Nobody in the computer business had missed the January 1975 issue of *Popular Electronics* with the MITS Altair microcomputer on the cover. Readers were not quite sure what to make of a hobbyist computer sold only in kit form, but they knew it was bound to be important. In those days computers consumed whole rooms, or parts of whole rooms, and required special reinforcement and air-conditioning. Ordinary people and even not-so-ordinary people hardly ever saw computers at work. Computers were in corporate basements and lorded over by a "technical priesthood" who turned them on and made sure the disks were spinning right. Engineers dreamed of having their own computer, but a computer that fit on a desk and cost less than $500? It was too absurd, too ridiculous, to be true. Still, an engineer who had done some consulting for Millard had actually bought an Altair and by now had received the parts, soldered them together, and gotten the thing to work.

Soon after the *Popular Electronics* cover issue, a thousand Altairs a month were selling, according to the magazines in which MITS advertised. Killian and Van Natta came to the conclusion that perhaps there was something to the MITS Altair. Maybe they could use it to solve Reed's problem. The idea began to crystallize: develop a network for Reed using the Altair, but retain the rights to sell it outside the automotive dealer business. Van Natta phoned MITS and ordered some kits. Everything was fine until he got down to the finer details. MITS wouldn't give IMS thirty days to pay, and IMS didn't have the money to pay up front. Delivery time was also a long way off. So much for that solution.

But things happened quickly in those days—they had to. About two days later, Killian and Van Natta were talking in the hallway. The hell with MITS, they decided. Why couldn't they create a copy of the Altair? They went to Millard with the idea of building their own microcomputer. Millard tossed in the idea of making sure it was rugged and commercial. And so Killian called up one of Millard's part-time engineers, Jesse Boothe, and asked if they could use his Altair to help design their own. Boothe agreed, and Killian started designing the first MITS-compatible microcomputer. Killian defined the structure of the Altair, laid out the accessory boards that would slip inside, designed the front panel, sketched all the chassis drawings, and wrote the 4K BASIC software programs that the thing would run on.

Time was running out. The summer of 1975 was almost over and although Killian had done three-quarters of the work, the well was dry back at Las Cruces. The banks and General Motors were worried. Reed had not only siphoned off the profits of his dealerships but had taken out personal loans for Auto Power. Everything he owned was "up for grabs," and he still hadn't paid back his father or Liz Corp. It started to look like "a huge hit" was necessary to pay everybody back.

In Van Natta's mind it was simple. MITS Altair was selling a thousand machines a month. We have money problems, right? Well, why don't we put an ad in *Popular Electronics?* If we can sell just fifty a month, take 5 percent market share away from Altair, take a look at what that will do. That's fifty a month at $500 each. Say we make $200 on them. That's $10,000 a month to cover our cash flow.

The numbers were appealing. The goal, which by now could be counted on to change as regularly as the seasons, had changed again. Millard and Reed came up with another plan, one last chip, one final spin of the wheel.

2
Miracles

Each day the mailman brought a sack of hope. At first it was just a trickle—perhaps two or three a day. A few innocent-looking envelopes bearing hand-scrawled return addresses. But each day the sack grew. Millard opened the letters excitedly. Real checks and money orders fell like fruit, rich and full before his eyes.

People were actually sending in money for their computer kit. Not promises, not inquiries, but money! Millard had been patient. He had suffered. He had lost one business to the same investors he thought would fuel its growth. He had remortgaged his house and seen his savings disappear, but he had never given up. His failure only hardened his determination to succeed. Now, after all the years of scraping, his dream of a manufacturing company was taking shape.

IMS had done nothing much, simply placed the ad in *Popular Electronics*. The ad was small, the print was fine, but it included all the ordering information. Prices for several computer products were given. No one at IMS worried that the products weren't available, or that Killian hadn't even finished the design for the computer, because all of a sudden their funding problems were over. They took deposits and set up to ship their first products in November 1975.

In October, Philip Reed moved into the San Leandro Islander Motel on 14th Street. Millard had phoned him in Las Cruces to ask him to answer the phones that were ringing off the hook and hire somebody to run the daily operations. Millard asked if he could come out to San Leandro for just a couple of weeks to get things off the ground. Reed stayed for six months.

During the summer, IMS had outgrown the little bank office. Its new address, 1922 Republic Avenue in San Leandro, seemed more appropriate for a budding computer company. Now they had plenty of space, a small warehouse, a shed filled with junk and one of Millard's old boats in storage. Reed and Millard shared an office.

As a boy, Reed had enjoyed starting projects. Working with Millard, he suddenly realized that he had found his niche. There was something tremendously exciting about the early stages of companies, the explosive time when ideas, people, and money jelled as one new, powerful force. Reed was put in charge of developing sales, and he and Millard planned manufacturing. Suddenly everything was fresh. They had to figure out what parts to order, set up manufacturing, hire a manufacturing manager, and decide what and when they would ship. It was fun. Reed began to see how a dream could become reality.

Only weeks before, in late September 1975, Reed's father had attended one of Millard's company meetings at which the future of IMS was discussed. Loring Reed was impressed by Millard and IMS. He had met Millard several times before on regular visits to see his son, but this was the first time Millard really had anything to show that was more than a dream. Loring Reed's company, Marriner & Co., had originally been in the wool textile manufacturing business. Manufacturing was close to his heart. Though he knew little about computers, Loring Reed could understand the potential for a company manufacturing computer kits.

His father's support meant everything to Philip Reed. Money from his father had been behind virtually every business deal he had made. It was reassuring to know that should he fall, his father was there to catch him.

When Reed and Millard revised their agreement once again and pinned their hopes on the sales of the still-uncompleted microcomputer kit—abandoning their original plan to develop a computerized accounting system for auto dealers—Reed knew it was a gamble. In their previous agreement, Millard had agreed to pay him a 15 percent royalty on any sales IMS generated outside of the auto-dealer business. After talking it over, they had decided that 15 percent would stifle the company's growth and that it would be to their mutual benefit to reduce that royalty to 5 percent of gross sales. By that time, Reed had already invested close to a quarter of a million dollars in IMS.

No one had to tell anybody at IMS to get to work. Work was fun. Excitement was in the air. As the checks and orders rushed in, the staff built up. Millard's wife, Pat, was there practically every day now, and their daughters, Barbara, Ann, and Elizabeth, came in regularly after school. It wasn't long before ten to twelve children were working after school and on weekends. They were paid $1.50 an hour, and although word went round that it was a technical violation of the law, nobody seemed to worry. They needed every pair of hands they could find. Besides, they were children of employees, and for many parents it meant not having to pay a baby-sitter.

Millard hired the new people and made sure they were enthusiastic. He preferred est people. People "who had taken the training." People who understood that this was more than a job. People who understood that he wasn't talking about work or wages, but life. It was true that every new employee got Millard's talk about profit sharing and equity participation, but that really wasn't why people worked for him and worked so hard. Millard had a vast well of trust. He thought that people were capable of doing whatever they set their minds to. His trust and optimism were contagious. When he hired people, they seemed to shine in his trust.

There was something magnetic about Millard. He talked about his vision, how IMS would be much more than just another computer company. He was looking for those who shared his vision. There was nothing reasonable about his dreams. He believed he could create miracles, and that was the appeal of his unreasonableness. In a reasonable society, miracles just happen. You can't cause a miracle. But at IMS, it seemed, miracles were *created*.

Impossible things simply had to be done. In just a few weeks Killian designed the memory and peripheral boards they would sell along with their computer kits. Then they assigned half a day to check the boards for problems. Freshly hired engineers plugged the boards in, checked them out, changed the wire list and moved on to the next one. It wasn't thought of as a miracle at the time. It was simply what needed to be done.

"I want to be the source," Millard began to say to people. Not a resource, but *the* source. And in a sense he was. Millard became the source of power, the source of miracles, the fountain at the center. When he came out of his office at lunchtime, he often physically touched people, gently. There seemed to be magic in his touch.

When Killian butted up against an engineering impossibility, he turned to Millard. Millard would calmly break the problem down into its parts and ask his simple questions. The next thing he knew, Killian would have the answer and wonder why he hadn't seen it sooner. Was it really a miracle? Or was it just Millard's attitude that if you believed, anything was possible?

People worked hard at IMS not just because they believed in Millard's dream but also because they believed in Millard. Many were convinced that Millard was a genius or a prophet. There was something inspiring about him. It was hard to put your finger on it, but you could catch reflections of it in his eyes and his intense gaze. Whatever Millard suggested, people did. Somehow he always seemed to have reason on his side.

Millard was convincing. He persuaded Dennis Holeman to quit his job at Westinghouse and take a 25 percent pay cut to run IMS's manufacturing operations. Other than the Millards, IMS then had only a few employees, not counting the kids: Van Natta and his wife, Killian, and Kathy Matthews, Millard's sister. Millard told Holeman during his initial job interview that he would create a stock plan for the founding employees. The promise, however, was not in writing. Holeman was so enthusiastic that he offered a week of his services without pay. A week later he was hired.

Earlier in the year, Millard had asked Killian if he'd like to end his $12.50-an-hour part-time position and join the company full-time at $1,500 a month. With the hours he was logging, Killian would have made a lot more by sticking to the hourly wages. But Millard could be persuasive. It was the way Millard presented things. "He usually thought it out very carefully, and if you wondered about something, he could explain his logic, and you'd find yourself agreeing with him by the time he'd finished," remembered Killian. "You'd say, 'Well, I have to agree with that, and so there is no real choice to be made. Let's just go along with what you suggest.' And you know, it felt fine, absolutely fine all the way."

There were also the personal touches. Van Natta worked late most nights. Often he and Millard would leave the building together. Sometimes they would walk first to Millard's car, but Millard would never leave until Van Natta had reached his car, started his engine, turned on the lights, and started rolling. It was a little thing, a question of waiting just a few seconds, but no matter where they were or how late it might be, Millard repeated the ritual. "I think he did it just because he cared about me," said Van Natta.

As the November 15 shipping date approached, Killian and Van Natta found themselves staying even later at the office. So did Millard. Somehow he always found something to do. He'd clean up his office or do some paperwork. He was working as hard as anyone. That always impressed Killian. It felt good that Bill was there.

Van Natta remembered one time that he and Killian had to work all night to meet a deadline. When Millard discovered what they were doing, he stayed, too, though he couldn't help in any technical way. Most of the night he sat watching his two engineers in silence. Van Natta didn't know if it actually helped at all, but Millard was always there.

Millard was good with people, if not with numbers. Numbers got in the way of dreams, and Millard's dreams were big. Reed knew that rapid growth required outside capital. He had learned that lesson at his auto dealerships and was learning it in the computer business. If in the first month you ship 50 computer kits, and in the second month you plan to ship 250, you will need outside capital. The deposits on the first 50 kits simply wouldn't pay for the parts you needed for the next month's 250. It was basic economics, but Reed also knew that Millard didn't really believe in economics.

Personal experiences were more important to Millard. Reed knew that Millard hadn't forgotten his bad experience with outside capital in his former company, System Dynamics. When IBM stepped in and stripped away the market for System Dynamic's software product, Millard had been kicked out of his own company in a struggle for control. The wounds hadn't healed.

Still, Reed kept trying to convince Millard that acquiring outside capital was essential to the company's growth. He began developing preliminary business plans. IMS was getting some local press, and by late 1975 the venture capital community had begun calling. It was Reed, with his financial background, who fielded those calls, but Millard kept putting the inevitable decision off.

Millard had never found financial decisions easy. Two semesters was the extent of his college education, and he had not been much of a student in high school. Rumor had it that Millard was the only person ever to have flunked the IBM salesman school and yet still be allowed to continue in the company's employment. He was simply a born salesman.

A few years earlier, Millard had taken a self-improvement course from another born salesman, a former used car and Grolier Encyclopedia salesman once called Jack Rosenberg. After changing his name to Werner Erhard, he went into the seminar business. Est—an acronym for Erhard Seminar Training—was one of the most popular self-improvement seminars that swept through California in the early 1970s. Millard latched onto est. It seemed to be everything he wished he'd had in a formal education.

Many of the principles of est can be found in a little, tan, untitled pamphlet by Werner Erhard known as "Up to Your Ass in Aphorisms" that Millard always kept nearby. One of the central sayings of the slim book, printed on fine paper with orchid leaves embossed on the cover and signed "I love you, Werner," was

If you keep saying it
   the way it really is
eventually your word
   is law in the universe.

Millard believed that saying, and the thirty-two others in the book. "It wasn't even a religion to Bill," recalled Van Natta, who two years later also took the training. "It was the simple truth."

One of the ways you got your word to be "law in the universe" was by doing what est followers called "making an agreement." Agreement went something like this: If people agreed long enough that men could go to the moon, then men would go to the moon. Millard applied the concept of agreement to IMS. If they agreed that IMS could survive with minimum outside capital, then it would survive. All they had to do was simply agree to design and ship a microcomputer kit faster than it had ever been done before. The kit would be built; outside capital would be unnecessary. In the world of est, intention was everything.

Millard made lots of agreements in those early days, and so it was not surprising that in October he made new agreements with Killian and Van Natta. Sales of Killian's "TTL Pin Out Handbook" were dwindling, and the 10 percent profits Millard had promised Van Natta in the Auto Power network project was an agreement made in a deal that had changed. Millard wanted to provide his friends with something new. He offered his engineers each 1 percent of the gross sales of the company. Killian and Van Natta gratefully accepted the new deal.

Killian knew that the strength of an est agreement was that it bound its makers tighter than a written contract. If you didn't live up to your half of an agreement, it was a stain on your honor. But sometimes Millard employees who hadn't lived up to their agreements were given another chance. They could, as a Millard employee would later say, "recreate the agreement," accomplish what they had said they would in the first place, "clean themselves out" in an est version of the confessional.

Killian designed, talked to Van Natta, and designed some more. They seldom left the office before eleven at night and they worked every day. Coming down the home stretch of the development for what would soon be known as the IMSAI 8080, they added up the hours and realized they'd worked forty-two consecutive days, averaging more than twelve hours a day.*

After one day's efforts, the two drove home together. Killian was driving his 1967 Volvo station wagon in the direction of San Francisco. It was Sunday, about eight in the morning, and Killian reflected, "You know, if this were a regular workday, we'd be caught in a traffic jam." Van Natta laughed, punchy after working all night. Driving home from work at eight A.M. wasn't that unusual. There was work to be done. There wasn't anything else in the world.

---

*One night at Jake's they created the name IMSAI by spelling out the initials of IMS Associates, Inc. Soon the company would be known as IMSAI, although the name would not formally change for nearly a year.

Time was precious. Time was like food or money and was not to be wasted. How it started nobody quite remembers, but Van Natta noticed that in a long hallway in the Republic Avenue building, as people moved from one office to another, they were picking up the pace. One day as he trotted down the hall, he noticed somebody else trotting by him. "What in the world is that person running for?" he thought. Only then did Van Natta realize that he, too, was running. The travel time "was an interruption," he remembered. "It was no-time."

Lunch was also no-time. It helped that Killian, Van Natta, and Reed didn't eat much lunch. Millard always kept peanut butter and soda crackers in his lower-right desk drawer. If anybody was hungry, Millard would dole out a cracker topped with peanut butter. Millard loved peanut butter, and the desk drawer always provided a ready supply. One day an old refrigerator appeared. And then a redwood picnic table. Jelly was added to the menu, and there was milk to wash it down. Later, cold cuts were provided. It was another example of Millard's special touch. Despite the shaky financial condition of the company, he would still supply lunch. The enthusiastic Van Natta saw a practical reason for the free lunch: "If we kept good food in there, people wouldn't wander out for lunch, and you'd get more work out of them."

The first fifty customers had been told the kits would be shipped in November of 1975. Halloween passed, and it didn't look like they were going to make it. People began to be concerned about the mail-order laws. You couldn't take somebody's money and sit on it for too long. Not wanting to be on the wrong side of the law, Reed spearheaded the effort to write a letter to those who had ordered kits, informing them that they couldn't make that November shipping date, but were going to shoot for December. Reed offered to refund any deposits to customers not willing to wait. Nobody asked for their money back.

The new shipping goal slipped a month to December 15. There wasn't much time to write documentation for the computer kits or the various computer boards they were offering. Killian went into his office and started dictating into a tape recorder. Van Natta stood guard over his door, making sure he wasn't interrupted. On the afternoon of December 15, printers were standing by. But as evening fell, documentation was still being typed and edited by Millard. At about three

A.M. on December 16, Millard walked up to Van Natta and said they were not going to make it—they had to stop.

Students from a nearby junior college who were supposed to be working part-time had been there since noon, collating paper, sorting parts, and putting them in plastic bags. When Van Natta told them they were not going to make the deadline, many of them cried. The company had worked for a year to ship on the fifteenth. Nothing else counted. Van Natta refused to go home, and in the morning a few hours later they found him sleeping on the floor with plastic bubble wrap drawn over him. Later that day, December 16, United Parcel Service picked up the first shipment of fifty IMS computer kits for delivery to customers.

Christmas Eve came, but the pace hardly slowed. Millard had announced that the next month's shipment would be huge—250 units. Around noon Van Natta went into Millard's office and suggested that they send everyone home early for Christmas. Millard agreed. Van Natta made his rounds, encouraging people to start celebrating the holiday a few hours early. They told him no, they had work to do. What business did he have telling them to quit! Nobody would go home. Finally, Van Natta told Millard they wouldn't leave. Millard ordered everyone out of the building. One by one they filtered out. Even so, Millard didn't trust them to go home. Later, after everyone had left, Millard and Van Natta circled back and checked on the building, just to make sure no one had sneaked back in.

Christmas was bountiful for Bill Millard and IMS. They had met their first challenge, and the future seemed rich with opportunity. They had shipped 50 computer kits, more or less on time, and Millard projected they would ship 250 in January. He rewarded himself with a nearly $5,000 raise to $48,000 per year. But the best present of all didn't come wrapped and didn't arrive on Christmas morning. One day late in December 1975, Ed Faber showed up on the IMS doorstep. Killian, Van Natta, and Reed knew Faber was someone special. Millard had tried to hire him once before.

It wasn't only that Faber had been a captain in the Marine Corps and had played semipro baseball. Faber, too, had done the est training, and he had toiled for mighty IBM for twelve years—another sort of training. And now, after stints with three other high-technology companies, he was ready for something brand-new. Faber was an experienced professional who knew sales and business as well as he once knew how to hit a curve ball. If Millard was the vision, perhaps Faber would be the arms and legs. With his dour, leathery face, bowl-shaped hair and friendly waddle, Faber was everything Millard was not. And they sensed that he was just the man they needed to turn the dream into reality.

3
The Note

On the afternoon of January 23, 1976, Millard called Killian, Van Natta, Reed, and a few others into his office. The list of employees to be fired had been drawn up. There wasn't much argument. Only Marvin Walker, an old friend and former employee of Millard's, recently made head of manufacturing, put in a successful plea to keep someone—Richard Desman, IMS's ace parts purchaser. In return for that favor, Walker agreed to defer his own salary.

At three P.M. the next afternoon, seventeen employees, nearly half of the IMS work force, were told that their services would no longer be required by the end of the day. They were given two hours to say good-bye and gather their belongings. Millard liked these things crisp. As long as he was going to fire so many, why let them stay around and infect morale? By Monday morning it didn't seem that bad. People were missed, of course, but there wasn't much talk. There was work to do.

On January 22, 1976, the day before what became known as "Black Friday," Millard wrote in his inexpensive, paperback diary:

I don't know if IMS can last another 60 days. This a.m. I didn't see how we could make the 2/1 payroll . . .
Current income may be "below critical mass."

IMS has no equity—and a $50K negative net worth. No cushion exists.
The 5% royalty to Liz Corp + 2% (Joe & Bruce) wipes out anything the
company is able to do in the short run.
Plan to cut staff from 44 to 27 tomorrow. . . .

Millard's officers were surprised, even shocked, as he outlined the dire
situation they faced. Most had assumed that the company was booming. How could they be so short on money when the orders just came
pouring in? But Millard was running the business end of the company, and so they believed him. Those employees probably *did* have
to be let go. And Millard was right to do it fast.

It helped that people were paid only up until that last Friday. You
didn't have to give notice at IMS, and Millard didn't give severance
pay. "Bill Millard's theory was that the books had to be balanced every
day," said Van Natta. "There wasn't a debt that was growing between
you and Bill Millard." As another employee remembered, "Millard
was always even." Still, eliminating employees didn't remove the
Bank of America loan problem.

Perhaps some of the other problems they were experiencing were
due to overly optimistic sales projections. Millard had hired about
thirty people since December, but IMS had shipped just 100 computer kits in January, not the 250 Millard had anticipated. The company was losing money fast. It was expensive to set up production,
buy parts, and ship computer kits. By the end of January 1976, IMS
would have lost nearly $100,000 selling the marvelous IMSAI 8080.
How could it be?

Reed had tried to get Millard to overcome his aversion to venture
capital, but it seemed that the scars from his previous failure went too
deep. "My reaction to that was negative," Millard would later say on
the witness stand. "I wanted the company to be as big as it could
be—and I intended it to be very, very big—and what I wanted it to
be is no bigger than I could self-fund it from within."

Millard's theory of self-funding had one small problem. IMS was
losing more than $1,000 a day, and the Bank of America had given
Millard a "final, final decline" to extend an additional loan to the
company.

"You're right, Phil. We've got to have money in here next week,"
Reed recalled Millard suddenly saying a few days later. Although he
was relieved that Millard finally understood the need for capital, Reed

wondered whether it was too late. He couldn't put a business plan together and get funding in three days with venture capitalists. They would have to go to people they already knew and raise the money on their personal reputation.

According to Philip Reed, that requirement eliminated "almost everybody that Bill knew." But he felt there was one chance—his father, Loring Reed. As president of Marriner & Co., Loring Reed was interested in diversifying. Philip Reed thought he, or somebody he knew, might have some money to invest. He called his father and discovered that, indeed, he was interested. Loring Reed had been following the project since its inception.

Loring Reed suggested that if his company was going to invest the money, they would like to do it in the form of a convertible note. It was not an easy decision for Millard. The last time he parted with equity in his company, he eventually lost control. But Loring Reed was not interested in an investment that wouldn't eventually give Marriner the option of a share in Millard's company. "They weren't willing to make a straight loan," said Philip Reed. The reason was, as his father recalled, "It [IMS] was very promising and very risky."

Before Millard would give up stock in his struggling company, however, he wanted to make sure of certain conditions. He reminded Philip Reed that IMS was a closely held corporation and that any stock issued in the company would be subject to a permanent right of first refusal by IMS. Millard was only following the bylaws of IMS, a provision "Restricting the Transfer of Shares." Millard also told Reed that he was not willing to give away more than 20 percent of his company—no matter what the price.

Everything now depended on Philip Reed. Millard needed at least $125,000 to pay off IMS's bank loan, and the company could not buy parts or meet the next payroll without outside money. Privately, however, Millard seemed fatalistic about the outcome of Reed's mission. He wrote in his diary that he would leave on a huge cross-country marketing trip regardless of whether Reed met with success. Nothing, not even financial disaster, could stop him from taking to the skies to promote the marvelous IMSAI 8080.

Killian went to the hardware store and bought a couple of suitcase handles. The screws twisted easily into the aluminum casing. It wasn't the most elegant solution, but he thought it would do the trick. All Killian knew was that Philip Reed would be demonstrating the IMSAI 8080 and would need some way to carry the thirty-pound machine.

On January 28, Reed took his seat on the San Francisco flight to Boston. In all the commotion, the readying of the computer and the quick gathering of something vaguely resembling a business plan, he hadn't bothered to bring winter clothes.

The temperature was around zero when Reed arrived in Boston, and the howling gusts topped thirty miles an hour. Reed had no overcoat, no gloves—only his California suit. The IMSAI 8080 felt heavier than thirty pounds, and his hand began to stick to the wooden handle.

The sign that shook in the wind read FRANKLIN STREET, named after the man who discovered the electricity that breathed life into the machine upon which Reed's hopes lay. They were waiting for him at 100 Franklin Street, in the fine, warm offices of Powers & Hall, the law firm that represented both Marriner and Loring Reed. The meeting was held in the office of Bill Gulliver, Marriner's attorney. The entire board of Marriner was there: Philip Reed's father, Frank Gerrity, and another man, Albert Creighton. Creighton was another very successful businessman, president and founder of Devcon, a pioneer in industrial-repair compounds, a company he would later sell for millions of dollars. Many years before, like his two lifelong friends Gerrity and Loring Reed, Creighton had graduated from Harvard.

Of the three men, only Loring Reed had much personal or financial interest in Marriner. His 40 percent family holdings in Marriner gave him more stock than either of his partners. Gerrity and Creighton played no daily role in the company. They received occasional stockholder's reports from Loring Reed and once or twice a year met with him at Powers & Hall for stockholder meetings. Reed ran the company. It was his only job.

Reed had been the president of Marriner since the early 1960s. When cheap, foreign imports threatened Marriner's profits, Reed had gone to Washington to lobby for protectionist measures. But there was little Reed could do. It was the end of an era. Marriner's revenues skidded from $10 million in the 1960s to $1.5 million in 1974. Eventually only Reed drew a salary from Marriner. And by the mid-1970s, Marriner had sold off its manufacturing plant, warehouses, and equipment. It could hardly be called a manufacturing company any longer.

There were some real estate holdings in Louisville, in Texas, and in Philip's adopted home of Las Cruces, New Mexico, as well as some interests in car dealerships (including Philip's), but the value of the investments, few of which were successful, had dwindled. Loring Reed, however, had no intention of presiding over the demise of Marriner. His commitment to the company was clear. More than once he had tried to buy the stock of his two partners. As recently as 1974 he made an unsuccessful offer of $3.50 per share for their Marriner stock.

Gerrity and Creighton's other business interests dwarfed the now ailing Marriner. But Gerrity respected Loring Reed's dogged determination. Loring Reed didn't have to work. His wife was worth millions, yet still Loring Reed did all he could to keep Marriner going. If his investments for Marriner weren't always profitable, perhaps he was unlucky. No one doubted that Marriner was Loring Reed's company. He presided over what was left of the money, and his friends largely gave him free rein. By now Gerrity's holdings in Marriner were valued at only a few hundred thousand dollars. It was a small price to pay to give his old friend a chance to reestablish his once thriving enterprise.

As Philip Reed peeled his numb fingers off the suitcase handle, he hoped they would see the same future he envisioned. The machine he was about to demonstrate bore little resemblance to what we now call a personal computer. The IMSAI 8080 microcomputer had no tape drives, no screen, not even a keyboard. Reed can't even remember if he turned the machine on, because if he had, "you would have seen just a couple of lights [glowing]." The strange-looking device, lined with colored switches on its front panel, had virtually no software and certainly not any that Reed would have known how to operate.

Philip Reed gave the Marriner board members a simulated demonstration of how the IMSAI 8080 would work. "We think there is a good market for smaller computers," he said as he unscrewed the cover, exposing the machine's intricate wires and circuits, and pointing to where the planned accessory boards would fit in the back.

The four men, all in their late fifties or sixties, had never seen anything like it, and Reed figured his odds for success were good.

Besides his father, he knew Gerrity from the year he spent working in his lumberyard, and had met Gulliver once or twice before while accompanying his father to Powers & Hall on some family legal matters. Philip Reed was asked to leave the room.

"Could you stay another day?" the board of directors asked after he returned. There was a computer expert at the State Street Bank whom they wanted to inspect the machine. Reed didn't argue, but he began to worry. Millard wouldn't have asked him to fly across country if he hadn't needed the money desperately.

The next morning Philip Reed walked into the bank with his blue box. The man he was scheduled to see was an expert in large mainframe computers who, according to Reed, "had never seen anything smaller than a battleship." When Reed pulled the cover off the IMSAI 8080, the man was enthralled with the intricate wires and switches.

His recommendation was glowing, and the decision of the board of directors was unanimous. Marriner would invest $250,000 in a five-year convertible note. Interest would be at 12 percent, due monthly. Anytime before the five years were out, Marriner would have the option of converting the note into 20 percent of IMS, instead of receiving the $250,000 back. The terms were not a surprise to either party; several phone calls had been made ironing them out.

On January 30, 1976, Millard wrote in his diary: "Phil returned from Boston with an offer from his dad's company for a 5-year convertible debenture @ 12% for $250,000—convertible to 20% of the company stock. . . . I accepted the offer." The next morning Millard and Reed's pilot took off from Oakland at nine-thirty. They stopped in Ogden, Utah, for lunch and gas and then continued to Scottsbluff, Nebraska, where they stayed the night at a motel. Five days later, well into his trip, Millard wrote, "IMS has $250,000 now. Used 125K to pay off our loan, and 125K for savings + 14K in cash."

Before leaving on his trip, Millard explained the note to Killian and Van Natta. Killian remembered Millard describing it as "a loan without voting control," but recalled that Millard said, "Yes, there was an option for stock in the future, but not enough to control the company if they [Marriner] took the option."

Did Millard accept the Marriner money because he was comfortable dealing with the Reeds, people he knew and trusted, or was it simply the first deal that jelled? Killian couldn't tell. Van Natta recalled Millard saying that they needed to be careful with the money because it was all the money that they were going to get, but concedes that he and Killian were largely ignorant of the deal. "We relied on Bill to take care of the business end of things."

The money was an injection of hope. On January 14, IMS had only $17,700 in cash to pay the overdue loan, bills, and payroll, but by February 5, after the money had been securely transferred to IMS, the company had $270,932. Only days after being let go, laid-off employees began calling back, looking for work. In a few weeks many would be rehired. Attention turned to the next month's shipping. Philip Reed, recently made executive vice president of IMS, would be running the company while Millard traveled the country. Everything appeared to be back on schedule.

Faber, who had started as just another salesman, was running the sales department after a few weeks on the job. People liked him. He seemed to have all the positive traits of someone who had taken "the training" without the pushiness that often characterized est graduates.

Faber exuded integrity. He was a salesman who never seemed to be selling. The Marine Corps veteran, twelve-year IBMer began doing what he had done many times in the last decade—building a team.

Millard had looked forward to the marketing trip for some time. He had asked Philip if he could hire his pilot and plane to fly him around the country. During the three- to four-week trip, Millard would visit numerous cities in Philip's twin-engine Piper Seneca, demonstrating the IMSAI 8080 to anybody he thought might promote or buy the new technology: magazines, dealers, resellers, corporations, and computer clubs. And when he returned from the exciting trip, Millard would be rewarded with something he had always wanted—a beautiful Cadillac Seville with "IMSAI 1" license plates. He had ordered it for himself, with IMS money, on the same day he wrote in his diary, "Don't know if the company can last another 60 days."

4
Stock Option

Philip Reed was enjoying his new role. After working several months for IMS without compensation, he had become executive vice president and earned a modest salary. Neither he nor Millard thought it necessary to formalize their arrangement. Spoken agreements had always sufficed between the two friends. Besides, Reed was sure that Millard would be impressed by what he had accomplished in his absence. Certainly Millard would be impressed by Bob Smith, IMS's new chief financial officer. Smith had graduated from Dartmouth, earned an MBA from Stanford, and received his CPA certificate while at Arthur Young. But it wasn't just his credentials that impressed Reed. Smith was more than a bright "numbers man." He possessed an abundance of that essential ingredient necessary to employment at IMS—enthusiasm. He also had something in common with Reed; neither had taken the est training.

The welcoming party for Millard at the Oakland Airport in late February 1976 consisted of Philip Reed, Millard's wife, and their daughters. Reed's pilot brought the plane down gently, completing the final leg of their journey. The IMSAI 8080 had been a success. Millard had traveled cross-country, proudly demonstrating the IMSAI 8080 version of the future. Chicago, New York, and Washington, D.C., had all been stops on the whirlwind tour. Presentations had been made to the *Chicago Tribune*, the Goddard Space Flight Center, the Army, and the Navy. The IMSAI 8080, Millard had said again and again in countless presentations, would be the control center for tomorrow's space station, office, and wherever else it was needed. Millard was a true believer, and his enthusiasm was catching.

When Millard began his trip, Killian happened to be on vacation, visiting in-laws in New Hampshire. Millard had sent Reed's pilot up to New Hampshire to fly Killian back to New York City. Killian remembers being impressed when they walked into the Time-Life building. Even better, the demonstration seemed to spark the interest of the editor of *Time*, who loved the tic-tac-toe game. Killian accompanied Millard on a few more demonstrations—including one at Bell Labs—and then Millard joined him for the flight back to New Hampshire. Millard lunched with Killian and his in-laws before leaving to visit the next city on the schedule.

The trip was an ideal opportunity for Millard to dive into his new hobby in earnest. Killian had been teaching Millard to fly in his Mooney Super 21 four-seater plane. Many a weekend Killian, a licensed instructor, had taken Millard for spins up to the mountains and across the rugged peaks into Nevada. Millard's marketing trip was a chance for yet more intensive instruction. Reed's pilot, a flight instructor as well as an accomplished pilot, gave Millard daily flight instruction for free. The pilot would do the takeoffs and landings and handle the rough weather. Most of the way, however, Millard took the wheel. It was a great trip, and for Millard it was only the beginning of his travels.

Returning home had to be a bit of a letdown. The problems back at San Leandro were not as exciting as visits with *Time* or Bell Labs. Millard had barely got settled in when Philip Reed asked him to sign a temporary note, acknowledging that he had received the $250,000 from Marriner. Millard hesitated. The agreement was barely a page long and didn't include the rights of first refusal and closely held provisions they had discussed earlier. "When I got back, I had this document to sign, and it wasn't the document I was expecting. And he [Philip Reed] told me that [it] was going to take longer to develop than he had expected and this was to simply be in the file until the other document got developed," Millard said later.

More than anything, Millard wanted to preserve the closely held nature of his company. The temporary note didn't mention the clause that concerned Millard most: If before the end of the five-year life of the note Marriner decided to convert its interest into 20 percent of IMS, Millard wanted the right of first refusal before Marriner would sell any of the stock to outsiders.

Philip Reed was flabbergasted by Millard's attitude. He had traveled across the country on a moment's notice, miraculously secured the money Millard so desperately needed, and now that Millard had Marriner's money he was squabbling about what Reed viewed as an inconsequential detail. "I told Bill that if he had any questions on it to talk directly to Marriner," remembered Reed, who didn't want to be the man in the middle. "The relationship really needed to be between Bill and Marriner."*

Philip Reed couldn't understand Millard's position. During his marketing trip, Millard had spent a day at Loring Reed's beautiful home near Boston, met Loring's wife, Elizabeth, and their daughters and granddaughters. Millard had brought along the tic-tac-toe game for the IMSAI 8080, which the girls found delightful. Besides treating Millard to a feast of roast goose and "loads of wild rice," Loring Reed had put him up for the night. The next morning, after his wife fixed Millard a hearty breakfast, Loring Reed loaned him one of his cars and arranged for him to meet with an executive of a large company. Why had Millard not straightened out any problems then, when he was face-to-face with his father? Philip Reed wondered.

Loring Reed was also surprised. Why wouldn't Millard at least confirm that he had received the money? "We put up a quarter million bucks and we just wanted someone to acknowledge that he'd received it." Subsequently, Loring Reed said, "We would write up the agreement." Millard's desperate need for money had made a more complete document impossible. The initial agreement was "nothing," Loring Reed said. "One paragraph as I remember . . . a five-year note, convertible into twenty percent of the stock." In the words of Loring Reed, it was all "very simple."

Reluctantly, Millard agreed to fill in the blanks of the makeshift document. After some discussion, he began to see the logic of Reed's position: "Marriner is sitting back there—I mean, missing $250,000 which they had just sent to a California company—and there is

*Through his 50 percent ownership of the Liz Corp., Philip Reed held shares in Marriner & Co., in addition to his small personal holdings.

nothing in their files to justify where the money is and why it's not at Marriner." But it was trust, Millard would later say, that really convinced him to sign on the dotted line. In more than two years of business with Philip Reed, there had never been an agreement they couldn't later smooth out or adjust. As Philip Reed himself would say, they agreed "on the fly all the time" and worried about writing things down only when they had a chance to catch their breath. Bill Millard did business by building relationships: "the relationship between Phil Reed and I [sic] and his father at this point in time was blind, absolute trust, friendship, and even love."

But actually Millard did not agree to the terms until more than a full week after his return, when Loring Reed flew out to IMS. Wrote Millard in his diary: "Phil's Dad was here [at IMS]. I agreed to convertible debenture—no dilation [sic] terms. He agreed that he will support my control of the company for better or for worse when it comes to making final decisions."

Perhaps there was another reason why Millard felt cautious about the agreement. IMS might have money, but the company's success was by no means insured. Walker, his new operations manager, didn't show up for work one day because of a personality conflict he had with Bruce Van Natta.

Fifteen years before, in 1961, Walker and Millard had competed for the same position, director of the Alameda County Computer Center. When Millard won the job, he hired Walker to become his operations manager. Later, when Millard headed up the computer center across the bay in San Francisco, Walker came to work for his favorite boss again. Walker had also toiled for System Dynamics, Millard's first company.

Loyalty had brought Walker to IMS just a couple of months before in January. Millard had called Walker up and asked if he'd be willing to help. Millard had talked about giving his old friend 5 percent stock just as he had given him and others 5 percent stock in System Dynamics. But that wasn't why Walker was willing to try again. Walker respected Millard, enjoyed his energy, and was looking for a challenge. Walker had close to three-quarters of a million dollars socked away in investments. Money was not the reason he worked.

A skilled manager at the San Francisco computer center, Walker had monitored the work of nearly a hundred people. But Bruce Van Natta was more than he could handle. Sometimes Van Natta wore shoes; sometimes he didn't. One day he'd shave; another he didn't. Walker would ask him a question about inventory or an order, and Van Natta might reach in his breast pocket or somewhere in his pants and pull out the crumpled paper. The orders could be literally anywhere on Van Natta's body. "It was insanity," Walker recalled. "He was a wild man." Walker was struggling to bring some order to IMS's bursting production, and Millard could not afford to let him go.

Bob Smith was another matter. Smith didn't seem to understand that, in Millard's eyes, he was turning things upside down with his talk about bringing in venture capital and motivating key employees with an equity plan. Millard told Smith again and again that the company didn't need the outside capital Smith insisted was necessary. Millard asked Smith to "get in touch with his feelings," and consider whether the company really needed the money or did the money just represent power. Smith was encouraged to apply for one of the company scholarships for est. Apparently, after a seminar he would understand. It was the kind of talk that Millard gave to many employees, but Reed remembered Smith replying, "No, Bill, you need the cash to buy the parts."

When the employee equity plan was not even discussed, Smith became frustrated. The accounting manager was Millard's sister, Kathleen Matthews, and Millard wouldn't even let his own finance man see the payroll. Walker said there were other reasons for Smith's frustrations with Millard. "Bill always had a thing about the Eastern establishment." Young and bright, Smith had gone to an Eastern college. And if that wasn't reason enough, Walker noted another intangible strike against Smith: "He saw Bob Smith as sort of being Phil's man."

On February 26, 1976, Millard had both good and bad news. He wrote in his diary: "Marvin Walker changed his mind about leaving the company today and asked to stay on. Hooray! . . ." But after documenting that boyish excitement, Millard carefully noted his first cause for suspicion: "Bob . . . told me he wants equity in the company if he's going to do his best. . . . I'm beginning to feel uneasy about Bob and the relationship between Phil & Bob." A few days later Smith was no longer with the company.

There were other problems besides personnel. Paying off loans and suppliers had further drained the company's cash position. By March 1976 the balance sheet would show only $68,427. Among other things, it was clear that IMS needed a higher profit margin. Millard knew they needed to boost profitability, but as his January 22 diary entry had recorded, there were other obstacles to that goal: "The 5% royalty to Liz Corp. + 2% (Joe + Bruce) wipes out anything the company is able to do in the short run."

Millard sat down with Killian and Van Natta and calmly explained the situation. The 2 percent was diminishing the company's cash flow, he said, making it difficult to buy parts and supplies. Killian and Van Natta were glad Millard was telling them about the problem. The last thing they wanted to do was hurt the company. They had worked hard to make it successful, and nothing was more important in their lives.

Millard offered a solution. He could give them each 5 percent equity in IMS, and their fortunes would rise or fall with the company. Killian and Van Natta were happy. They liked the idea of owning part of the company. To them it seemed a tremendous offer. It was reassuring the way Millard always had an answer. When they seemed to be faced with a real dilemma, Millard had a solution that was fair for everybody.

Millard made the decision easier. By September 1976 (six months away), their royalty fees (1 percent each) would be terminated, but if they converted to stock now, they could become part owners in IMS immediately. No written agreement was made. They trusted each other implicitly. On March 3, 1976, Millard, however, left behind a record of the agreement in his diary:

> Joe, Bruce and I agreed to terminate our 1% of the gross agreement today and I agreed to cause them to procure 5% equity (each) in IMS with "closely held" provisions for 5 years, plus company buy-back provisions should they leave IMS voluntarily within next two years. Stock not subject to buy-back is 1% plus 1/24 of 4% for each month employed—commencing 3/1/76.

If Killian and Van Natta had each kept their 1 percent interest, each would have earned $21,000 in the six-month term from March to September 1976. Instead, they agreed to transfer their royalties for stock ownership and celebrated by joining Millard and his wife for dinner and a belly-dance show.

5

High on est

By March of 1976, IMS had taken on the persona of its main product, the IMSAI 8080, and was known by customers and employees alike as IMSAI.* Having outgrown the Republic building, the company moved into a new facility on Wicks Avenue in San Leandro. Despite having grown exponentially from just four employees to about seventy-five, IMS retained its small-company feel. Est and something as simple as the free lunch seemed to keep them together.

By now the lunch menu included cold cuts, cheese, milk, juice, and of course the house specialty—peanut butter and jelly. Twenty or more people would lunch each day. Tablecloth-covered picnic tables were set up in the warehouse. One person was put in charge of buying the food, and all the employees were responsible for keeping the lunch area clean.

Employees played checkers and dominoes during lunch hour. One of the regulars was Millard's wife, Pat, who continued to help out when work got busy. At lunchtime, many people would talk about the latest est seminar they attended, or the latest est project they were involved in.

*No formal name change, however, had taken place. Legally the company was still IMS Associates, Inc.

There were lots of est projects going on at the time. The tens of thousands of est graduates were encouraged to donate their time and services to est founder Werner Erhard and his organization. Typically, est projects involved asking your friends to take est seminars, and then your friends would ask their friends to take seminars. It was sort of like a chain letter. Est considered these hundreds of thousands of unpaid hours as "empowering." The 160 people whom Erhard paid worked long hours, six or more days a week and for little pay, but their small financial rewards were no deterrent. There was no shortage of volunteers or poorly paid employees working late into the night on one est project or another. Millard himself had been generous with his time, donating hundreds of hours to setting up a computer data base to help Werner (as his disciples called him) keep track of a rapidly growing flock.

The more he saw him in action, the more Millard revered Werner. People would do anything for Werner. But not for money. The man commanded. When Werner walked into a room, it grew quiet. People hung on his words. Millard began to look for his new top employees from Werner's organization. They were just what he needed. IMS's help-wanted ads stated a preference for est graduates. As IMS grew, however, many employees, especially in the production and manufacturing department, were not est graduates. It couldn't be helped; sometimes there simply wasn't time to find any.

Most est graduates wanted nothing more than to share their revelation. At lunchtime, on break, in the parking lot, everywhere at IMS, the pitch was "Why don't you come to the seminar tonight?" Est had free guest seminars, which the uninitiated could attend for several hours. Essentially these were "advertisements" for the $300, four-day, three-night, full-scale training. Graduates would rise at the guest seminars and testify how est had changed their lives, made them more productive, focused, and happy. Then, inevitably, many guests would sign up for the real thing. Enrolling in the next seminar required prepayment. Van Natta, when invited to his first guest seminar, took the precaution of not bringing his wallet.

IMS employees in production and manufacturing often thought est a little strange. They noticed how people who took the training seemed to change. They spoke a peculiar jargon, known as "estianese," and seemed to pay more attention to appearance and dress. The more abrasive, enthusiastic converts came to be known as "estholes." They seemed to adopt a haughty attitude, not much different from people who might have graduated from elite universities or grown up in certain polished neighborhoods.

Stories about the "esties" became a favorite topic in production and manufacturing. One of the production department's eavesdroppers returned one afternoon to relate the latest absurdity. The wife of one of Millard's top employees had something she wanted to "share" with the company. She was having trouble with her husband. It seemed his performance at home wasn't matching his achievements in the office; he didn't satisfy her in bed! "That was what they talked about in management meetings, and we would just die," said one production employee.

Mostly, however, employees laughed away their differences. Sitting around at lunch together made it easier. Crazy as they might seem, people couldn't be bad if they'd split peanut butter and jelly sandwiches with you.

With or without est, IMS remained a family. Many wives of key IMS employees volunteered their services, and Millard gladly accepted their help for free. Later they were often hired, as they came to realize it was the only way to see their husbands. "Everybody's husband or wife worked there—their kids, their wives, their husbands," remembered Sheri Sorick, a secretary. At times IMS resembled a daycare center, with children running and screaming down the halls. Kathy Matthews's brood was the stuff of IMS legend; she had six children working at IMS.

Shipping time was when the IMS family really pulled together. When there was a big order, every available body would go to the warehouse and help package the computer pieces together. Long tables were set up like an assembly line. Little cupcake tins were used to keep everything separate. People would file up and down, counting out the bolts, screws, nuts, and 4K memory chips, and putting them in little plastic sandwich bags bought at the supermarket. To measure out wire for the computer boards, they wrapped it around three-foot-long wooden boards notched at the end.

They could gather all the parts for one kit in less than ten minutes. Games were played to see who could assemble a kit the fastest. The kids always won. They would race down one side of a table, slip underneath, pop up the other side, grab the plastic bag, and pick out the nuts and bolts with their tiny fingers. "We were too big to get under the table," laughed Sorick. When the kids won, the adults had to stop work to buy them ice cream cones or make them peanut butter sandwiches.

Lots of ice cream was bought that spring; shipments were up and sales were booming. Faber and two others manned the phones. It was the reverse of telephone solicitation. Hobbyists, engineers, and other "techies" called in, itching to buy the IMSAI 8080. IMS was selling a lot of kits, but Faber noticed that they were selling them just one at a time.

Faber had started talking to a southern California businessman in late December 1975 who wanted to buy several IMSAI kits at once— at discount—and then sell them through his storefront. "Well, that was a silly idea," recalled Faber. "Just silly enough so that I said, 'Yeah, let's see if we can make that one work.'"

Soon after, Faber found it easy to sell ten or fifteen machines at a time. The only problem was that with the kit priced at $439 there wasn't room for more than a 10 percent discount. So Faber and Millard talked it over and raised the base price to $499. Up went the discount to 15 percent. And lo and behold, a couple of other guys wanted to get in on the action. "This is a great idea," recalled Faber. "So I talked to Bill some more and we raised the price again in March, to I think $599, and passed along another ten percent." By now the discount was 25 percent.

What had started out as a gamble now seemed a sure thing. Each time they *raised* the price, the phones rang off the hook. People were calling and wanting to open stores. Faber watched monthly gross sales expand from $35,000 in December 1975 to several hundred thousand dollars in April 1976. By early April, Faber himself was selling thousands of dollars of equipment a day. He couldn't handle all the orders coming in over the telephone lines. He converted Sorick, his secretary from his two previous jobs, into a saleswoman.

Faber was a strict boss. Work began at seven or eight in the morning, and except for a short lunch break, his sales staff was expected to stay on the phones until seven at night. He set high goals for his expanding sales department and expected his staff to surpass those goals. But when a month was slow or an individual was having a rough time selling, he never let that person fail. He would walk over and gently say in his low voice, "Why don't you write this one up?" Faber would give away an easy sale—one of his regular customers who put in an order every month—because he wanted everyone to make the goals. They were a team.

Outside of Faber's tight-knit sales group, however, signs of strain were starting to show. Beneath the atmosphere of unity and hope, something bad was happening, something that had to be stopped. On March 22, 1976, Millard wrote in his diary: "IMS's first Steering meeting tonight (Bruce, Ed, Marvin, Joe, Phil and I) low for the year; Marvin reported that he is certain that about $2,000 of parts were stolen in one fell swoop last week! I'm stunned, disappointed, angry, worried, furious, bitter. . . ." No longer were they one vision, one goal. Some were on the other side.

In the spring of 1976 the meetings began. Employees who had taken est didn't find them unusual. They were set up very much like est seminars; employees sat in little chairs and Millard stood in front. Millard would talk about how many kits were shipped that month and how many would be shipped next month. The sales department and individual salesmen were congratulated for surpassing their goals. The news was always good. Then the real talk would begin. Millard had a vision. IMS would be more than just a successful computer company. And he was going to do whatever it took to make it a success. New IMS employees, and many were new, were often awed by Millard. The meetings began with Millard staring intensely at the group for a few seconds. "He seemed to be very, very clear and close to his intention as far as what he wanted to do," remembered Julie Banuelos, who had worked for Erhard before joining IMS. "He seemed really right on at first. He said all the right things, did all the right things, went through all the right motions."

In the style of est, people could raise their hands and "share" with the group. Banuelos remembers standing up and telling Millard that she was really glad she worked for him and couldn't think of a better place to be. The group clapped after she was finished. That was called "acknowledgment." You were always acknowledged after you "shared."

But not everyone was awed by Millard's presence. Many who had not taken est would leave the meetings scratching their heads, wondering what Millard had said for the last half hour. He must have been saying something important because the est section clapped and cheered after certain phrases.

Yet Millard's intensity and enthusiasm, powerful weapons of motivation in one-on-one encounters, seemed to fizzle in front of a group. "It was he [Millard] standing in front with everybody sitting around like in an audience," recalled Van Natta. "Bill came out very poorly." Millard was not a good speaker. He seldom prepared remarks beforehand, though he often spoke for thirty minutes or more. He strung together est concepts like "sharing," "space," "vision," and "acknowledgment," neglecting verbs, nouns, and other necessary parts of speech. Even some est graduates admitted to losing track of the point.

Philip Reed often missed those meetings. He'd leave early on Friday to fly home and see his family for the weekend. When he returned on Monday mornings after meetings, he began to hear more and more people criticize Millard. "He'd get up there and it would be like listening to Muammar Qaddafi ramble on," said Reed. "He'd just start talking about philosophy, and it would lead off into nowhere. It didn't bear much relevance to what people were doing or experiencing within the company."

Reed hadn't taken the training and didn't really understand. Meetings were about good news. An unwritten rule said that if problems were not dwelt on, they would, like bad moods, simply fade away. Acknowledging that a problem existed was the same as acknowledging the possibility of failure, and was somehow felt to make failure all the more likely. If everyone concentrated on the good and the positive, the company would succeed.

The est training was about making your life work. If you really wanted your life to be a success, you had to take complete responsibility for what happened to you. Winning in life was the goal. If you had a problem, you were being negative. It was your problem. Reed recalled times when employees were called down in front of the group and told by Millard, "That's your problem; the company doesn't have any problems!" And then, said Reed, Millard would deliver the scolding: "If you've got a problem with the way things are being done, you'd better take a good look at yourself!" IMS was a utopian company. It had no problems. There were only miracles. It was clear to his well-trained followers that Millard was the source of everything great and good, and everything was going perfectly.

There was one meeting, however, when Millard was not quite so great and good. Sometime in the spring of 1976, Millard announced that the plan for equity participation was canceled. There was only a stunned response. The promises of stock flashed before them—how

Millard had said that they were gentlemen and his word was a solid agreement. "I felt very much that I'd been had," remembered one key employee who had signed on at a low wage on Millard's word that stock would be forthcoming. There was nothing, short of quitting, that he or any of the other shocked employees could do. Millard had been careful not to make many promises in writing. Until further announcement, the plan to distribute stock was shelved.

Reed began to feel uncomfortable about the changes he saw in Millard. Accustomed to attacking problems, Reed found Millard increasingly evasive and unrealistic. As Reed colorfully noted in his diary, Millard no longer seemed to listen to others: "He resists even slight alterations to courses—he grazes the rocks and reefs and steers off course to who knows where and will not alter to give a measure of safety. One should sail alone if he will not consider the crew. . . ."

But Millard did consider at least one aspect of the crew. Less than a month after Bob Smith's replacement was hired, Millard began to complain. From what Reed could see, the new finance man was simply trying to install standard business practices. But that was the wrong approach to take with Millard. Reed could see that the new fellow, too, would quickly join the growing ranks of ex-IMS financial officers.

Six months had passed since Reed moved into the San Leandro Islander. The time had come to make a decision—commit to a full-time position at IMS and bring his family out to live with him, or return to salvage his now-strained car dealership. Reed began to question whether IMS could survive under Millard. He didn't know whether the company was going to run into trouble in 1976, 1978, or 1980, but he knew it wasn't going to survive under Millard's philosophy. Reed was torn between his growing reservations about Millard and the excitement of working in the dynamic microcomputer industry IMS was helping to forge. The automobile business had become stale in comparison to the new challenges at IMS.

It was not an easy decision. Reed and his wife, Jane, had picked out a house to rent in San Francisco's exclusive Pacific Heights. He had located a school for his daughter. Despite their business differences, in many ways Millard and Reed were still best friends.

Finally, Reed broached the subject with Millard. Reed remembered Millard telling him what an important part of the business he was. Reed wanted more concrete evidence of his contribution; he repeated his desire to convert his royalty agreement into significant equity. Reed's 5 percent of gross sales represented a huge chunk of profits. But he had the company's interests at heart: "I said to bring it [the royalty] down so that the company could get financing. I was just interested in a decent return, not raping the company."

Millard had a solution. Why not swap the 5 percent of gross sales for 5 percent of the stock? It was then that Reed understood Millard. "I suddenly got a clear picture then, and it wasn't the money or the amount of equity, but I got a very clear impression that Bill doesn't do anything that isn't to his advantage."

Reed had been prepared to reduce his royalty agreement—but not for what he viewed as a trivial amount of stock. Reed had sunk $230,000 of his own and his family's money into IMSAI, raised another $250,000 through the Marriner note, arranged for a letter of credit for another $158,000, and worked day and night for six months. The 5 percent stock offer stung Reed like a slap in the face. "He didn't want me there as much as he'd like to get rid of this royalty agreement and convert it into absolutely as little equity as he could!"

After talking it over with his wife, Reed decided that Millard was not the guy he wanted to "hitch his wagon to." He told a stunned Millard that he wouldn't be staying. "I'm going to get in your way more than I'm going to help you," he told Millard. "This is your company—go for it!" At first Millard resisted, but then he agreed that if Reed thought it was the right thing, so be it. Besides, Reed agreed to come back at least once a month. By the time he got around to logging the event in his diary, Reed seemed almost philosophical: "I am even with IMS: Money and time and effort = royalties, experience and knowledge."

Millard was good at good-byes. Before Reed left, Millard wanted to show his friend just how much he meant to him. Pat Millard had given her husband a limited-edition porcelain eagle made by a Japanese artist. "I want another one of those, and I want to give it to Phil because he'll know exactly what I'm saying," Millard told his wife. Millard and Reed had talked about eagles before—the symbol of excellence in the est culture. When Reed unwrapped the eagle in the privacy of Millard's office, the three cried and hugged each other. Said Reed, "It was the end of a very strong and meaningful time for all of us."

Philip Reed had already left the employ of Bill Millard when the May 1, 1976, draft of the Marriner note arrived. The drafting of the note had been delayed by the death of Marriner's attorney. Loring Reed had put a new man to work on the final agreement—Andrew Bailey, also of the Powers & Hall law firm and coincidentally, the attorney for Reed's wealthy wife. Once again Millard was surprised by the agreement. The four-page document was not at all what he expected. It did not spell out the right of first refusal. It did not spell out the closely held provisions. Millard was struck by what it didn't contain. But Philip Reed, Millard recalled, "Acknowledged by reminding me, 'Yes it was not complete. It was not intended to be complete.' He reminded me it did not contain this paragraph he and I were accustomed to putting in all of our agreements which stated that it was complete."

Millard was also concerned that the document was silent about his agreement to provide Marriner with monthly company financial reports, and Marriner's agreement to subordinate the $250,000 note to IMS's bank loans. Philip Reed reminded Millard that Marriner's attorney had died. "After all, Bill, we trusted you with the money. We sent you the money when you hadn't signed anything, and now it's several months later and it's been spent, and after all this is going to cost a lot of money and it's not necessary," Millard recalled Reed saying. "We know each other, we have done business all along. What's the problem? Why make us spend money that we don't have to spend?"

Millard said he had essentially the same phone conversation with Loring Reed. He sensed that Loring Reed was not entirely comfortable that he had agreed to pay for the drafting of the agreements. "How come you're being hard-nosed about having us spend money when we all know it's not necessary?" Millard remembered Loring Reed asking. Finally, Millard said, "It was just costing money, and I agreed to sign the document as it was. I agreed that [it] was all true." On May 1, 1976, Millard signed the Marriner promissory note.

There was one thing Millard would not remember—the time or date of his phone calls to Loring Reed. And his diary did not record the concerns he said he had voiced to his good friends the Reeds.

6

The Pitch

San Leandro is on the east side of San Francisco Bay. The thin, thirteen-mile Hayward bridge snakes over the stale, muddy waters; and there in the hazy distance loom the warehouses and coffee shops. Trucks, filled with produce from the south, pound back and forth, leaving their marks in the pavement, soft from the afternoon heat. Ten miles away on the crowded freeway was IMS.

Heat had never bothered Philip Reed. After living in Las Cruces, he wasn't bothered by San Leandro's summer temperatures, but he sometimes found the rough smell of diesel and the dreary, flat expanse of warehouses and empty, weed-ridden lots nauseating. Cheap rent seemed the only reason that IMS, or any other company, would be located in San Leandro.

It was July 1976 and Reed was back again in San Leandro. Although he had formally parted with IMS, every month or so, as promised, he had returned. Millard and Reed had remained in close contact. On May 26, Millard had renegotiated the royalty agreement with his former executive vice president. The last monthly 5 percent royalty payment had approached $14,000, and both agreed that such large payments threatened to strain the resources of IMS.

Millard proposed a fixed $8,903-a-month payment in exchange for the cancellation of Reed's royalty agreement. To sweeten the deal

Millard offered to pay a total of $500,000 by 1981. Millard also offered an immediate $47,000 down payment and another $43,000 down payment within a month. Soon after signing a "Novation of Sales Agreement," Reed would have second thoughts.* IMS's June gross sales were $478,000. Five percent of those sales under his old royalty agreement would have earned almost $24,000 for that month alone. Instead, he received just $8,903.

Nevertheless, Reed was putting that all behind him and looking to the future. Millard had invited him to join Ed Faber and Marvin Walker for a meeting with John Martin, a visitor from the East. Philip had never met Martin, but he had heard of Martin's idea and thought it had promise.

For a man just thirty years old, Martin had plenty of ideas. Martin got his first big start at the age of twenty-one as a department manager for the W. T. Grant Company. At twenty-two, he and his brother owned Tom Thumb Raceways, a slot car track, in Lowell, Massachusetts. Soon the brothers opened new miniature raceways in Nashua and Manchester, New Hampshire.

Martin quickly graduated to bigger and better cars. He sold Pontiacs and Chevrolets in Massachusetts and called himself an "ace salesman." He moved out to Riverside, California, to be near his daughter and worked for an employment agency as a counselor, placing salesmen in jobs. Martin liked that idea best, took it back East, and in late 1971 opened Empex Systems in Boston, franchising his own line of employment agencies. By the early 1970s he had eleven agencies in Massachusetts and New Hampshire, but by 1975 his "chain" had dwindled to just five outlets.

In late 1975, Martin received a phone call from Dick Brown of Burlington, Massachusetts. Brown ran The Computer Store, which owned about half a dozen outlets across the country. Although all of his stores were company-owned, Brown was excited by the idea of franchising. Brown heard of Martin's franchising experience through his landlord, who also happened to be Martin's landlord. When Brown first called him, Martin hesitated and stalled for months, but the persistent computer man followed him around from office to office. Initially "terrorized" by the concept of computers, Martin finally

*Webster's defines *novation* as "the substitution of a new legal obligation for an old one."

conquered his fear and decided there was money to be made in franchising retail computer stores.

And so Martin eventually accepted Dick Brown's offer and became a franchise consultant for The Computer Store. But he soon had a difference of opinion with the vice president of the company. Potential franchisees wanted to sell IMSAI 8080 computers, but Martin remembered that the vice president refused. "He would always answer, 'No, you're not allowed to sell that. You can only sell MITS Altair because a Ford dealership sells Fords and a Chevy dealership sells Chevies.'" Martin thought differently. "Unbeknownst to me then—I had very little legal sophistication—that was not only illegal but was an unsound business practice."

Martin realized that the heart of the computer market was technology. He didn't know anything about IMS and the IMSAI 8080. Like many people, he even thought it was a Japanese company. But he knew it would be a mistake to start a franchise based on just one untried manufacturer. "They [The Computer Store] were opposed to that. They felt that would strain and jeopardize their relationship with MITS Altair. It wasn't their perception of how a franchise should go, and we came to a parting of ways."

But Martin knew the potential of computer franchising, and he knew there was a way to do it right. The franchise idea wouldn't let him rest. At home in New Hampshire he started developing plans for a concept he called "Computer Shack." During the first three months of 1976, Martin developed franchise business plans, investment guides, and direct-sales systems. He even instructed his attorneys to start trademarking the Computer Shack name and create a corporation.

Martin began to realize that the idea was bigger than he was. He had not yet solved the problem he had when Brown first called him: "I had no knowledge of computers." Martin was discouraged because he didn't think he could pull it off. His plan had already been gathering dust for a couple of weeks when he went to Windsor, Connecticut, for the opening of the first franchised computer store in America. While there he bought one of the first copies of *Byte* magazine.

Three or four days later, Martin was home watching the dreary rain drizzle down. He thumbed through the magazine, trying to understand the computerese. On the back page he saw an ad that said, "Altair users step up to an IMSAI." "Son of a bitch, there's that name

IMSAI again!" Martin remembered thinking. Martin dialed the San Leandro number and asked for the president. The next day he flew out to San Francisco, took a helicopter to Oakland, and by two P.M. was talking to Bill Millard.

Martin's basic idea was to franchise computer stores much as McDonald's franchises hamburger restaurants. His first meeting was alone with Millard. When he heard about it, Philip Reed was optimistic. He thought that it might be just the opportunity IMS needed. Let others take the risks and put up the capital. IMS could sit back and get a cut of the stores' sales, while the franchises boosted sales of IMS's products. But would Millard bite? Reed could no longer predict or understand Millard's actions. As the company expanded, so it seemed to Reed did Millard's ego. No longer did he feel that he and Millard spoke as partners.

Millard's ego was not the only problem. Reed's intuition about Millard's difficulties with financial officers had been correct. His father agreed and sent Millard letters emphasizing the importance of attracting and maintaining good financial talent. Despite the advice, three financial officers shuttled through the offices of IMSAI in 1976. The fanfare that surrounded their abrupt hiring only served to underline their abrupt departures. Many officers were introduced at the monthly company party. "I'd like you to meet Mr. ——, the best financial man I've ever met," Todd Fischer of production recalled Millard saying on several occasions. Few lasted more than a few months. One was gone in thirty days. It became a bad joke. People would wonder how long the latest victim would last.

"Bill didn't really have a huge knowledge of accounting, controller concepts, or cash-flow planning," Walker remembered. "He would just interfere and try to run the show, and he just drove every one of them nuts."

"He was like the king in the old days," recalled Loring Reed. "When the messenger brought him bad news, he'd behead him." Loring Reed, however, had free run of the king's court during the spring and summer of 1976. One visit to IMS lasted for several weeks in May and June. He even helped with the bookkeeping. "They claimed they had all this backlog of orders," recalled Loring Reed. "But they didn't have enough to keep these people busy." Cancellations or changes in orders were not properly recorded. Nevertheless, Reed claimed to have "shuffled it all out in a couple of weeks."

Upon returning to Massachusetts, Loring Reed wrote a letter to Millard, dated July 9, 1976, thanking him "for that wonderful Sunday in the Napa Valley and the opportunity to meet your parents and your children." In the letter, Loring Reed made some suggestions that he hoped Millard wouldn't view as being critical. "I am, rather, trying to be helpful to you and your organization." He emphasized that "cash flow is vital to the company success," and that Millard was fortunate to have a person of the caliber of Curt Hawkins "heading up the financial end of your business." Loring Reed also suggested that since the company was developing international sales, Millard might want to consider offshore tax planning.

During his visit, Loring Reed had continued to give Millard what by now was the routine talk about bringing in outside capital. "He agreed with me [about the need for capital] when I was there," Reed said. "But nothing ever happened." And soon Hawkins, Smith's replacement, would also be gone.

Loring Reed had seen Millard paying less and less attention to the company's daily operations. Millard, however, viewed things quite differently. He always had. While others stumbled through the trees, Millard seeded the great forests of tomorrow.

John Martin's initial meeting with Bill Millard led to another meeting. Again it was held in Millard's office, but with IMS's four major decision-makers: Millard, Faber, Reed, Walker. No one questioned the fact that Martin's ideas were attractive. He had thought out the whole thing and presented a neat package. Sell franchises to dealers for $10,000 to $15,000 apiece. Sell them IMSAI computers and then collect 5 percent of everything rung up on their registers.

Something about the way Martin talked made Millard suspicious. Martin sounded like a stereotypical New Yorker, and he couldn't seem to open his mouth without exaggerating. He talked fast, maybe too fast. Faber also had reason to be suspicious. He realized that he had talked to Martin only recently. A few months before, Martin had called saying that he was representing a store in Windsor Locks, Connecticut, that was going to become a new franchise for The Computer Store and carry the MITS Altair computer. Martin had wanted to return the ten to twenty IMSAI 8080 computers the store had already paid for and received. When Faber refused to return the money, Martin's tactics grew rough, and Faber remembered what sounded like a threat: "I'll let it be known throughout the industry your attitude on this, and we'll make it clear that we're going to use the equipment as boat anchors!" Later, Martin said he was not threatening and was only joking about the anchors.

Regardless of what Martin actually said, it was enough to ruffle the stiff collar of Faber, who hung up and called Dick Brown, the president of The Computer Store, telling him he didn't appreciate that kind of "pressure being brought to bear and the insinuations or veiled threats." Brown apologized for Martin's behavior and would later say that this and smiliar incidents, along with Martin's tendency to "puff," were the real cause of their parting.

Gutsy and quick on his feet, Martin broached the delicate subject of their previous conversation. "You're the toughest guy I've ever tried to talk to and convince!" he complimented Faber in a humorous tone. Faber quickly brushed aside the previous telephone encounter. He believed in giving people second chances. Besides, the man's idea *was* attractive.

Millard was cautious and said little. He had always been a shrewd negotiator. Soon it was clear that the two men had reached a stalemate. Millard wanted the franchises to sell only IMSAI computers. Martin wanted the franchises to sell a variety of products. The IMSAI 8080 would be the catalyst, Martin emphasized, but to be really successful, franchises would have to be more than one-product operations.

Millard fought that idea, but Martin didn't give up easily. Martin tried what seemed every possible approach to convince Millard that selling other companies' products would be essential to success. Millard wouldn't budge. *

Reed offered to give Martin a ride back to the San Francisco airport. As Reed drove, Martin nervously questioned him: "What about this thing? Did we get anywhere?" Reed answered as best he could. He thought that Martin's idea was well received by Faber. With his IBM marketing background, Faber understood the wisdom of a varied product mix. Faber's approval was essential, for Millard listened to

---

*Millard, his daughter Barbara, and Ed Faber claim that it was Millard's idea to have franchises sell a variety of products. Marvin Walker and Philip Reed credit John Martin.

Faber and trusted his judgment. "What about this guy?" Martin continued nervously. "I just don't know where we are." Reed told Martin that he would keep him posted, that he thought Martin's idea had potential, but they needed a little time to think it all through and allow Millard to get comfortable with the concept.

Reed was surprised at how well things seemed to be going. He wrote in his diary, "Great excitement with Bill, Ed, and me over franchising sceme [sic]. Ed's observation that John Martin was and is a formitable [sic] weapon that needs to be aimed and fired is accurate. Bill and I talked and I got everything out there—we have a relationship that works. . . ."

Reed made sure the weapon stayed in range. In the next few weeks he and Martin stayed in touch, talking by phone. Despite their outward differences, the two men got along surprisingly well. It was the beginning of what would soon become Reed's second-strongest business friendship.

Only five months after Marriner had poured a quarter of a million dollars into his company, Millard was facing more money troubles. "IMS is really under the gun cash-wise," Millard wrote in his diary on July 22, 1976. The company needed a $100,000 loan to keep going.

With Loring Reed's help, Union Bank in Oakland agreed to lend IMS $100,000. The bank, however, was concerned about the Marriner note. It wanted to make sure that the Marriner note was subordinate to its loan, giving the bank first claim to any assets if IMS could not repay the bank loan. Loring Reed couldn't understand why the banker wanted the subordination agreement. It was clear to him that the Marriner note would be subordinated, but if the bank wanted the agreement he'd have his attorney write it up.

The loan and Loring Reed's agreement to subordinate his debt, however, did not solve Millard's problems. Some of the wild, crazy dreams Millard, Killian, and Van Natta had hatched at Jake's were now spinning out of control. One of the most ambitious, early projects was the IMSAI 108 intelligent hard disk. The plan was to allow several IMSAI computers to share the same high-capacity storage disks. It was a brilliant idea, ahead of its time, and the first customer was actually NASA, although they were subcontracting the project through a company in Huntsville, Alabama.

The only problem with the IMSAI 108 was that it didn't exist. Killian had a design, but no one had actually ever built this thing. Nevertheless, Millard liked the idea of designing equipment for NASA. The possibility of IMSAI computers one day collecting space data was exciting. He ordered engineering to give the project top priority.

As the company's slender technical resources were spent chasing space computers, glitches in more earthly endeavors began to appear. In July of 1976, IMSAI released its first, single-sided disk drive, the FDC 1. The power supply for the device had what the engineers jokingly referred to as a "design flaw." In effect, none of the units worked. In August, they were redesigned, but 99 percent of the devices were returned anyway. It wasn't until March of 1977 that a new release with an improved power supply was shipped. Loring Reed wrote Millard, warning that shipping dates were slipping, and that many products appeared to have serious design flaws. In August, Philip Reed wrote in his diary, "Floppy board errors on verge of disaster."

Marvin Walker wondered why more qualified engineers weren't hired. It seemed to him that Killian and Van Natta were being spread too thin. The presure and the long hours were taking their toll, and mistakes were cropping up in their work. A trend was beginning to emerge. Problems were considered to be like a virus and quite possibly contagious. It was best to turn them over to someone else. IMS began to rely on subcontractors to design some of the tricky parts of new products. "They [the subcontractors] were notorious, flamboyant, and many were less than talented," recalled Todd Fischer, who ran customer service. "IMSAI chose to let other people handle its problems."

By late summer enough work had been done to go to Alabama and attempt installation of the NASA project. Unfortunately, it didn't work. It seemed that one of the engineers had tried a shortcut on Killian's design. In doing so, he had overlooked the problem Killian's design had anticipated. Van Natta flew out to see if the work could be salvaged. It was no use. He returned, telling Marvin Walker that with the way the equipment was currently designed, the contract would be impossible to fulfill. Walker and Millard discussed their scarce options. "It was draining cash. It was draining employee resources and we decided to drop it," Walker recalled. "Sorry guys, good luck."

Many back at IMS wondered whether the company would be sued for defaulting on the NASA contract. Dennis Holeman, who had objected to the project from the beginning, began to question IMS's ethics. For the first, but not the last time, he considered leaving.

Others viewed the IMSAI 108 fiasco as only a minor setback. There was some truth to Millard's belief that if you didn't talk about problems, they ceased to exist. Soon, the failure was forgotten. "What did NASA care about a $75,000 contract?' Van Natta recalled. "I don't think we ever heard from them."

Not everything would so easily disappear. The specter of financial troubles had returned. Loring Reed wrote Millard, warning of a serious cash crunch that he predicted would strike on September 15. Millard, however, was not greatly concerned. He had hired a new chief financial officer. Hersh Mendelman, Werner Erhard's business manager, was taking over control of the numbers.

7

Panama

Shuffle

It had taken some doing, but Martin had finally figured out a way to convince Millard that the franchisees should carry other manufacturers' products. The idea came to Martin suddenly. He was in Gloucester, Massachusetts, when he rushed to a phone booth and called IMS collect. This time Martin had an answer for Millard's stubborn refusal to franchise stores that would sell other companies' products: "How would you like to be the only guy making a profit on your competitors?"

Millard suggested to Martin that he send something to indicate "how a business relationship between the two of us would work." Martin ordered his attorney in New Hampshire to draw up a contract between Martin's brand-new company, Expansion Systems, and IMS Associates.

On August 9, 1976, Millard responded to Martin's contract proposal by letter. Unwilling to sign a long-term contract, Millard preferred a temporary agreement with "no strings attached." He wrote:

During this interim period I am willing to pay you $1,000 for initial travel expense plus $1,000 per week including expenses thereafter for so long as we both desire that you be here. . . . It must be clearly understood that until or unless we enter into a signed agreement IMSAI reserves the unilateral right for any reason to stop the program, continue the program without you, terminate the interim relationship with, and use any and all materials or information procured from you for our benefit in any manner we see fit. . . .*

Despite the legalistic tone, Millard ended the letter on a warm "est-ian" note. "I look forward to making this interim relationship work to our mutual benefit and to it being the stepping stone to a subsequent agreement and relationship that would be mutually profitable and nurturing in the long term."

Martin was surprised by the letter. It seemed that Millard wasn't willing to trust him. The interim agreement Millard proposed was a polite way of saying, "We'll pay you a thousand bucks to fly out here and then see how it goes each week!" Martin added up the risks. He had tried to sell the concept to IMS's competitor, MITS, the maker of Altair, and they had turned him down. There were no other major manufacturers in the microcomputer market. If he waited, someone else would be sure to make a pass at IMS. Or even worse, maybe IMS would try it without him. Martin's reply a few days later was brief and positive.

They had a deal. Martin would create a standard franchise con-tract, file the appropriate papers with the various agencies, solicit the first franchise owners, and help them set up their stores. In return for those services, Martin would be paid $30,000.

Millard later demanded, however, that Martin sign an extensive contract, detailing more than a hundred things Martin had to accom-plish to fulfill the conditions of the contract. If at any time Millard was dissatisfied with Martin's performance, further $1,000 weekly payments would be canceled—including the $20,000 for completion of the job. Millard, of course, would be entitled to retain all the franchising materials Martin had created to that point.

Millard hadn't taken any chances. Faber had been sent to a fran-chising seminar in Los Angeles run by Aron Rothenberg & Asso-ciates. Papers had been filed in several states to reserve the Computer Shack name. When Faber returned, impressed by the seminar, Mil-lard arranged to hire Rothenberg on a consulting basis for a week or

---

*At the time, IMS and IMSAI were the same company.

two in September to get the project off the ground. IMS, of course, paid the bills.

On September 21, 1976, Millard incorporated a company called Computer Shack. On September 24, Millard took a $10,000 expense advance from IMS. Three days later, Millard's personal bank account recorded a deposit of $10,000. That same day, Millard deposited $10,000 in the new Computer Shack account. "I assume it was the same check," Millard later explained.

It was a busy summer and fall for Millard. Computer Shack was only one of many projects planned. Millard had been seeing a lot of Harry Margolis, then thought by some to be one of the country's leading tax attorneys. Margolis had done some rather astonishing things for Werner Erhard and est. Under Margolis's direction, the est company sold what they called "the body of knowledge" to corporations located in foreign countries. The knowledge was all of the techniques, as well as the content, of the est training. The distant corporations would then rent back the body of knowledge to est for use in the day-to-day activities in such a way that est's profits seemed minimal. There was nothing new or illegal about the basic method. Howard Hughes had avoided taxes in much the same way with Hughes Aircraft Company and the Howard Hughes Medical Trust. Still, Millard was impressed. He hired Margolis to reorganize his expanding circle of companies.

The elaborate reorganization Margolis laid out would pay Millard and his wife lifetime annuities, and somehow cut his companies' tax bills in half. The road to such a marvelous "end result," as Millard called it, would, however, have a few bumps and turns on the way. The plan would involve IMS first, and later on, Computer Shack.

On October 1, 1976, Harry Margolis, his partner, Robert Dunnett, and his Czechoslovakian paralegal, Ondrej Kojnok, would formally incorporate a company officially called IMSAI.* On November 1, Millard would resign as director of IMS and Kojnok would become its sole director. Kojnok would then sell the IMS stock to Presentaciones Musicales, S.A., a Panamanian company.

Margolis had created Presentaciones Musicales in 1960 for Nat King Cole. The tax savings Margolis and Presentaciones gained for

*IMS had unofficially been doing business under the IMSAI name since early 1976.

the famous singer were so great that they drew the attention of the IRS and led to a headline-grabbing tax court case. But Margolis had done his work well; technically, no laws had been broken. *

The plan for Millard was to have Presentaciones liquidate IMS and transfer its assets to IMSAI. IMS would disappear. One hundred percent of the stock of the new corporation, IMSAI, would be issued to Alexia Trust, a trust company on the Isle of Jersey, in the English Channel. Presentaciones would then sell to IMSAI the assets it had acquired from IMS and grant IMSAI a license for the know-how. In return for the license, IMSAI would pay royalties. To avoid a 30 percent withholding tax, the royalties were to be collected by Interlit, which only months before had gone by the name EST International Ltd (another corporation Margolis created in the British Virgin Islands). Free of taxes, but minus a 5 percent handling fee, the royalties would make their way south to Presentaciones.

The incredible logic behind this international money trail was perhaps best explained by one of Millard's most trusted lawyers: "This was the scheme Margolis used with his clients. When the money came out as royalties, that was a write-off. It took their tax down to zero. . . . That was the whole bag. This money didn't come out of midair. It was a circle jerk in saving taxes." And it was, apparently, permissible under the tax laws.

Once this international route was flowing smoothly, Presentaciones would enter into an agreement with the Alexia Trust company, transferring the obligation to pay the annuities to Alexia. Presentaciones would also disappear. IMSAI's royalties would be channeled to Interlit (formerly EST International) and then to Alexia. After several years, when the license finally expired, Interlit would also disappear. Alexia would have all the know-how and the right to the money.

Royalties were what made it all go around. IMSAI would have to pay for those licenses that gave them the know-how they needed to stay in business: 5 percent royalties on the first half-million of sales, 6 percent on the next half-million, 7 percent on the next million, and 8

---

*Singing money was one thing, basketball money was another. Charles Johnson of the Golden State Warriors attempted to shoot his basketball earnings through the Margolis tax-savings hoop. But Johnson's assets did not fare as well as the estate of the late Nat King Cole. Johnson would lose his case in tax court and have to pay taxes on the money that went to Panama.

percent on everything over two million. There were a couple of other catches. IMSAI would have no cash to run the business. All of the company's "cash on hand" would have gone south. Luckily, Presentaciones would be willing to lend IMSAI that money—the cash needed to stay in business—if IMSAI paid 10 percent interest. Only one more catch remained—Margolis's fee was 20 percent, or more, of the tax savings.

Eventually everything would disappear, except of course, those royalties, which would just keep pouring into that little company on the Isle of Jersey and back into Bill and Pat Millard's bank account. Millard wouldn't have long to wait for the cash to start flowing. Presentaciones recognized Millard's hard work and decided to reward him for his efforts. Margolis wrote a special clause into the agreement: "Annuitants may draw from the corporation as additional compensation for the corporate year ending October 31, 1976, the net profit of IMS for such fiscal year."

Millard, of course, was not planning on taking IMS's 1976 net profit and 5 to 8 percent of the gross of IMSAI for himself. The elaborate plan was part of Millard's dream, his vision for his companies. Millard would take the extra money and pour it back into his companies to make them bigger and stronger. Everyone would profit. One of Millard's lawyers would later declare that the ingenious scheme even helped improve the U.S. trade deficit: "We didn't have a trade deficit back then . . . because, as the evidence will show, there was a lot of incentive to encourage people to invest money outside the United States."

It would be a miracle. Millard would save thousands, perhaps millions, of dollars, guarantee himself and his wife lifetime income, fuel the expansion of his exploding companies, and improve the trade deficit—all without anything, except money, ever leaving the Bay Area. Even the stock certificates of Millard's companies would go no farther than Margolis's Los Gatos office. None of the buildings or equipment would be sent to Panama or the Virgin Islands or the Isle of Jersey. It was knowledge and money that were moving magically, circling the globe.

To make the transformation complete, Millard, too, would have to circle the globe. The Presentaciones deal only transferred to IMSAI the assets and knowledge to operate in the United States. Margolis wrote another clause to insure that someday Millard's empire would encompass the world. "The annuitants [the Millards] will immediately undertake on behalf of IMS in the name of PMSA a trip to foreign countries to introduce the IMS product line and to lay the basis for subsequent PMSA activities in all of the world other than the United States."

On October 1, 1976, Millard would leave on his seven-week "around the world trip." Millard's plan was to hold seminars to promote the IMSAI 8080 in foreign lands. One of his friends in the est organization was related to a high official in the Iranian government. Millard envisioned huge sales to oil-rich Iran. Tehran was one of the exotic cities to which Millard hoped to bring the IMSAI message.

Before leaving the country, Millard called a meeting to announce the formal name change of IMS to IMSAI. Soon, the sign out front would be taken down and a shiny new IMSAI Manufacturing Corp. sign put in its place. Outwardly, the company seemed to be booming. They were moving into a new building. The staff was well over a hundred employees. Sales were exploding. By the end of September 1976, in the eight months since the Marriner loan in February, the IMSAI 8080 had rung up $2,679,000 in sales. Limits didn't exist for IMSAI. The world was their market, and today's products were only the beginning. Their owner and president was once again flying off to yet another distant corner of the earth, searching out new markets for their marvelous computer. "We had negotiations for these things already all over the world," remembered Millard excitedly. "It was really incredible how much business was done around the world."

Before leaving on his trip, however, on September 29, Millard had dashed off a letter to Loring Reed. Millard wanted to insure that the matters they had discussed on the phone were clear:

Dear Mr. Reed:

. . . I have indicated to you the unusual opportunity that exists for me to dispose of the stock to a strong financial foreign corporation which would liquidate IMS and permit me to continue in the manufacturing end and to get into the franchise end of the computer field. I made it clear that there was continued and unquestioning acknowledgment of the support received from you at all times and of my desire to fulfill my responsibilities to you at all times and to see to it that the planned disposition of stock would not in any way limit your potential participation should you ever determine to convert the loan into stock as set forth within the Note. I also informed you that I considered the Computer Shack as quite independent of the manufacturing end and therefore something that would be perfectly appropriate for me to embark upon without any question of any interest therein on your part.

I am hereby giving you notice as required that I intend to dispose of the stock to Presentaciones Musicales, S.A., a Panamanian corporation, and it is my understanding that such corporation intends to liquidate. It is possible that my disposition of the stock will not actually take place as it is prospective only and it is possible that the corporation acquiring the stock would not liquidate since that would not be in my power to control. I intend that no step taken by me shall adversely affect your position under the promissory note. Indeed, it is both my intention and expectation that the steps contemplated will benefit all parties involved.

A new IMSAI Manufacturing Corporation, which should take over basically all of the responsibilities of IMS, is being set up and it is my intention to see to it that your interest in that corporation will remain the same as it is in IMS at the present time.

Please feel free to consult with either Harry Margolis or Ondrej Kojnok, from the Law Offices of Margolis, Chatzky & Dunnett, 16780 Lark Avenue, Los Gatos, California 95030, (408) 358-1961, at any time for any purpose during my absence. My confidence in their integrity, proficiency, and propriety in this matter is absolute. In my absence, you may consider and act upon any statement, request, or commitment made by them as having been made by me.

I appreciate your cooperation and support and look forward to having all matters cleared through your counsel to your satisfaction.

With all good wishes.

Very truly yours,

William H. Millard

Loring Reed promptly sent his reply. It was shorter, and when the October 6 letter arrived in San Leandro, Millard was several thousand miles distant.

Dear Bill:

. . . It seems to me that you are embarking upon a program which will have a substantial adverse effect upon Marriner's interest in the future of

IMS. Specifically, I am very concerned with your conclusion that the Computer Shack is an undertaking which you may personally own as opposed to IMS. The retailing and franchising of stores to distribute IMS products is a very logical extention of the IMS business operations and one that should belong to IMS.

I am somewhat confused with the reference in your letter to a 30-day notice. I assume that you are referring to the provisions of the Marriner-IMS promissory note which does require a 30-day notice in the event of liquidation or sale of the assets. Your letter, however, only notifies Marriner of your intention to sell your stock interset in IMS and no such 30-day notice is required in such event.

In view of my concerns and the apparent confusion, I have referred your letter to our counsel for his review and I know that you will have no objections if he contacts attorney Margolis directly to discuss more fully the subject matter of your letter.

Very truly yours,

Marriner & Co., INC.

P. Loring Reed, Jr.

President

cc/Harry Margolis, Esq.

Andrew C. Bailey, Esq.

Millard had left Marvin Walker in charge for what he expected would be a seven-week trip. There were a couple of contracts that Millard had instructed Walker to sign. The most important was a sales agreement with Computer Shack. Millard's new franchising company, which at this time officially had no employees other than president Ed Faber (and consultants Rothenberg and Martin), was putting in its first order—$3 million worth of IMSAI computers. Computer Shack had no stores and had not sold a single computer. That was why Millard told Faber and Walker to negotiate the terms. He wanted to make sure that everything between the two completely separate companies was clean and appropriate. Walker signed the $3 million contract Faber put before him. Because the order was the largest that IMSAI had ever received, Computer Shack was granted the largest discount IMSAI had ever offered—larger even than that extended to the United States government.

The other agreement was perfunctory. Computer Shack would be responsible for domestic sales and marketing of IMSAI products. A letter was sent, informing IMSAI's dealers of the change.

Millard had left his wife, Pat, behind to take care of some other financial matters. He spent the first three weeks abroad on his own to take care of business. On October 12, IMS made a shareholder's loan to Millard in the amount of $10,000. Pat Millard was there to deposit the money into her husband's account. The $10,000 would be used to buy the stock of Computer Shack. Added to the $10,000 loan Millard had made the fledgling company in September, Computer Shack now had $20,000. On October 22, Pat Millard joined her husband in Amsterdam.

Pat Millard would not be the only person charged with carrying out a critical mission for her husband that month. A large man with a foreign accent arrived at IMSAI one day. Walker was in Millard's office and asked if he could be of any assistance.

"I need you to sign these documents," the mysterious, Slavic-sounding man said. He then told Walker how Millard had arranged for him to transfer the company to a foreign corporation. Walker examined the strange documents. He couldn't sign them! He hadn't any knowledge of the documents. He'd have to be a fool to sign away the corporation to a stranger while the boss was out of town!

"I was told you would," Walker recalled the man protesting.

"Well, whoever told you that led you down the wrong path!" the ruffled Walker responded.

After the man left without the signature he sought, Walker telexed Millard in Europe. "Don't worry about it," Millard told his old friend by telex.

The next visitor would not be so easily handled. Walker remembered being in the accounting department when Loring Reed strode into the office. He was surprised at how quickly Loring Reed was on the scene. Only a day or so before Reed had called, demanding to know what the Panama deal was all about. Walker had confidence in Millard. He figured that Millard had just been too busy to discuss the matter fully and that Loring Reed was being picky. But it was hard to ignore Reed's anger. "He was livid. He threatened lawsuits," Walker recalled. "Loring Reed became unglued."

Reed demanded that they telex Millard and find out "what the hell's going on!" He then took the next step into his own hands. Accompanied by Philip, he drove south to Los Gatos to visit the offices of Harry Margolis. Father and son spent three hours listening to Margolis and Kojnok, but neither was sure what the tax attorney and paralegal were talking about. "You would have had to be a Chinese lawyer to have understood the damn thing," Loring Reed remembered. Loring Reed didn't like getting a song and dance. He had had just about enough. "Look, I don't understand even what you're saying," he told Margolis. "Now just give us the agreements. We can figure out what the hell they say."

Margolis couldn't do that. Millard was out of the country. "Call him up!" Loring Reed demanded. "He's told me I can see anything I want to see, and I want to see the agreements!" Margolis wouldn't budge.

A few weeks later in November of 1976, Millard returned from his fourteen-city trip. That week, *IMSIGH*, the company newsletter, noted his return with a reminder that employees' cars would be towed if they parked in Millard's marked parking place.

Loring Reed was one of the first to welcome Millard back. He flew out to California and gave him a scolding. "If you're going to go through with this, in the first place you're crazy! Hell, you're dealing with a bunch of companies and I'm asking questions: 'Who are these guys? What is this company? Who are the people behind it?' And you can't even tell me!" Then, Reed gave Millard a warning: "We'll take every damn means possible to stop you from doing it!"

Reed's warning didn't increase his popularity around IMSAI. "I remember Bill telling me in November when he came back from his trip that he thought I should be careful talking to Loring," remembered Walker.

Not until late November did Kojnok finally send the documents describing the Panama deal to Loring Reed. Bailey inspected them. It was just as Loring Reed suspected. Bailey told him that Millard was "trying to take the company right out from under Marriner. . . ."

According to Millard that was the farthest thing from his mind. It had never been his intention to damage Marriner's interest in the slightest. He wrote Loring Reed: "My intention has been that you should have all the rights and options appropriate to the Marriner note. . . . The liquidation and related matters, regardless of the form chosen by the attorneys, was not and is not intended at any time to get in the way of full, fair performance and acknowledgment of these responsibilities to you."

Philip Reed, however, concerned that the Panama liquidation might affect Auto Power's deal with Millard, also examined the documents. "Either Bill's a liar or he doesn't understand this deal," Philip remembered thinking after examining the documents. "Because it very definitely affects everybody." The way Philip saw it, the Panama deal would move all the assets out of the country, where they would be owned by somebody else. There would be no way to make any claims against some company in Central America.

But Philip Reed was also worried about his friend. Philip Reed and his father discovered that Margolis was under federal investigation for tax fraud.[*]

Philip Reed knew that Margolis had done extensive tax planning for the est organization. Reed also knew that Millard felt that Erhard could do no wrong. Reed was concerned that Millard's enthusiasm for Erhard was eroding his judgment, which Reed had never considered good when it came to numbers anyway. He wondered whether Millard understood the scope of the operation Margolis was setting in motion. After Marriner and Auto Power's attorneys had analyzed the documents, it was obvious to them that the South American deal was going to slip out of everybody's control.

For Millard's sake, not just their own, Philip Reed thought Millard should keep his operations north of the border. Millard needed to concentrate on running the business, and the Panama deal wasn't going to provide anything. "The problem was getting the business to the point where it was profitable," Reed remembered. "He had to make a lot of profit before he had to worry about taxes."

Philip Reed wrote to Millard, asking that the balance of the $500,000 obligation to Auto Power be paid. Despite his large request, Philip Reed ended the letter on a friendly note:

> . . . From what I can ascertain, it looks like you are embarking on another exciting phase of company growth. May it prove prosperous for both the Millards and the investors of PMSA.

[*]The Federal indictment naming Harry Margolis and involving Presentaciones was filed with the U.S. District Court of San Francisco nearly one year before, on December 23, 1975. Kojnok said it was "common practice in the office that when a client came through the office the first thing was to inform him about the indictment. The indictment also was published in the newspapers so at least I personally assume Mr. Millard knows about it." Margolis was eventually acquitted of that indictment.

I am as always available to assist in matters mutually beneficial.

Sincerely, Liz Corporation, Philip Reed

Loring Reed, however, did not appear to show the same good-natured concern about Millard's well-being. Telephone conversations and face-to-face meetings between the two men became increasingly combative. Loring Reed remembered telling Millard, "Look, why don't you get one of your friends [to invest in IMS], give us our $250,000 back, and then run the damn thing any way you want!"

The Reeds were not the only ones wondering what was going on. Killian and Van Natta had seen little of Millard since his return, and they hadn't seen much of him before he had left. Spring and summer of 1976 were one long series of trips. It wasn't just the traveling and the shiny new Cadillac. Millard had slimmed down, trimmed his hair, and taken to wearing suits. The two were concerned that perhaps Millard's success and the reorganization of the company had affected their friendship. They were also wondering how all these changes might affect their stock ownership. It seemed that Millard had not had the time to issue and actually hand them certificates. Van Natta wrote Millard a memo, laying out their stock agreement as he understood it. Killian read the memo and signed it "Me too, Joe" underneath Van Natta's signature.

But Millard had more immediate concerns than his stock agreement with Van Natta and Killian. Terrible misunderstandings had occurred in his absence. Margolis had given him drafts of documents and he had signed them assuming that he would still have the opportunity to approve final versions. Margolis had not understood his intention. While Millard was circling the globe, Margolis had created an exclusive agreement between Computer Shack and IMSAI—exactly the opposite of what Millard wanted!* Millard blew up. And when he found out about the IRS's interest in Margolis's previous work, Millard became worried. To make things worse, he heard rumblings of a tax change that would alter the rules of the game. As he wrote in his diary: "Excerpts indicated that new law required income

*Millard faced a revolt from IMSAI's dealers when he returned from his trip. Precipitating the revolt was a letter sent informing them of Computer Shack's new responsibility for IMSAI's domestic sales.

tax payments on foreign trust income as earned. This seemed to me to remove the 'key' element from the . . . tax plan."

Millard quickly canceled the exclusive agreement between IMSAI and Computer Shack. Then he talked to Margolis about whether he really wanted him to represent his companies in the future. But as Millard struggled with this dilemma, he realized that a lot had already happened. IMS was only a shell company. All of the assets had been transferred to IMSAI, and IMS was on its way to Panama. Stopping that seemed unlikely.

Try as he might, Millard was not able, as Loring Reed had suggested, to get one of his friends to help him pay back the note. Eleven days before Christmas, Loring Reed and Marriner's attorney, Andrew Bailey, sent Millard a different sort of holiday greeting:

December 14, 1976

IMS Associates, Inc.
1922 Republic Avenue
San Leandro, Ca. 94577

Attention: Mr. William Millard, President
Re: Marriner & Co., Inc.

Dear Sirs:

This office represents Marriner & Co., Inc. ("Marriner") in connection with a promissory note of $250,000 issued by IMS Associates, Inc. ("IMS") to Marriner under date of May 1, 1976. Marriner informs me that it has been notified recently that you orally informed Marriner that IMS is being liquidated and is in the process of dissolution. No written notice to that effect has been received by Marriner as required pursuant to the terms of the aforesaid promissory note.

The failure of IMS to give written notice of its intention to liquidate constitutes a breach of its agreement under the aforesaid promissory note. In addition the liquidation of IMS without notice to Marriner is part of a scheme to defraud Marriner of its rights as provided in the aforesaid promissory note and, in addition, is in violation of the provisions of Section 10 of the Securities Exchange Act of 1934.

Demand is hereby made for payment of all amounts owing under the aforesaid promissory note, including principal and accrued interest and, in addition, all damages accruing to Marriner, including attorneys' fees, arising from the fraudulent deprivation of the rights of Marriner under the aforesaid promissory note.

We have been instructed to commence appropriate legal action against IMS in order to protect the rights of Marriner unless these claims can be resolved to the satisfaction of Marriner within the next seven (7) days.

Very truly yours,

Andrew C. Bailey

ACB: ct
cc: Harry Margolis, Esq.

Millard had still not responded to the letter of his friend, Philip Reed. On the day after Christmas, Millard had Margolis write him a letter. He was upset that he had to use his lawyer to send his response, but Millard felt that "Phil was interjecting himself in between IMS and Marriner."
Margolis's letter read in part:

It is never pleasant to be placed in a position where one must assert rights in defense of clients when there has been a long, amicable, honorable relationship between the parties. Nevertheless, your letter of December 9th, addressed to Mr. Millard, is hardly defensible, given facts.

. . . It is clearly related to the position being urged by attorneys for Marriner and appears to be distinctly intended to intimidate or threaten. Both positions are unworthy of you and your father and are something that we would never have anticipated after our brief acquaintance. The fact is that there may be completely legal defenses to any obligations owed to you at all. . . . We expressly and unequivocally deny any liability to you of any kind, as suggested in your letter of December 9th.

We venture to suggest that the gentleman you were, or appeared to be, is the proper posture to assume so that lawyers can get out of the way and you and Mr. Millard can go on responsibly to settle your various relationships.

Abb Abley knew nothing about Panama. He was only a salesman at IMSAI, but Abley trusted his instincts, and they told him that IMSAI was headed for trouble. Abley listened to his fellow employees, and the word was that IMSAI didn't pay its bills; most were ninety days or more overdue. Vendors were complaining. Many suppliers would no longer do business with IMSAI, forcing the company to buy chips, computer boards, and other critical parts in parking lots and other locations of the evolving computer black market.

Abley also handled Millard's inventory and expenses. He knew exactly how much Millard spent on air fare, first-class hotels, and elegant dinners. Cabs were no longer sufficient. Limousines were required to chauffeur Millard when he arrived in a foreign city. Millard had barely touched down when the next foreign trip was planned.

It wasn't so much the expense, thought Abley, but the company was struggling for survival, and its president/owner was gallivanting around the world, jetting off on one trip after another. Ostensibly the company was booming. IMSAI's sales were $2,679,000 in the eight months from February to September 1976.

IMSAI was so successful that just two days before Christmas, Hersh Mendelman instructed Howard Samuels (another IMSAI finance man) to make an adjustment in the books. Samuels was to change the $20,100 that had been advanced to Millard and instead record a $28,000 bonus. Now, it seemed, the company owed him an extra $7,900. The company had intended the $20,100 to be a bonus all along.*

But there was something that Abley and many others at IMSAI sensed but did not know for certain. Big sales and big bonuses were one thing; profit was another. About $200,000 had been lost in 1976 in generating those impressive numbers.

---

*The two $10,000 checks, however, were marked "expense advance" and "shareholder's loan."

PART

II

8

Franchise

Man

In late August of 1976 John Martin packed his car and began the long cross-country drive to California. By the first of September he had arrived in San Leandro, checked into a nearby hotel, and started working for Ed Faber. Although Faber was technically president of Computer Shack, he was also still sales manager and director of marketing at IMSAI. It was all a bit confusing. Computer Shack didn't have any offices of its own, and so Faber worked out of his IMSAI office. Sometimes Faber would be working for IMSAI and sometimes he would be working for Computer Shack. Martin had an office next door.

In those first months in the fall of 1976, Martin was the only person working full-time for the fledgling company. He began by preparing the volumes of papers that needed to be filed with the different state and federal agencies. That was easy. The real trouble was trying to figure out whom to sell franchises to.

He went to Faber for help. As IMSAI's sales director, Faber was the keeper of the leads. He gathered his staff together and introduced them to Martin. Martin asked Faber whether he could have the files on all the people who *didn't* buy IMSAI dealerships. Faber's staff then picked the most promising files and provided Martin with the letters of inquiry that prospects had sent.

The first man Martin called was a nuclear scientist for an East Coast utility company. Ken Greene had tired of designing computer models to study accidents at power plants. He was looking for something different. While in San Jose on a business trip, he had wandered into a Byte computer store and was fascinated by the computer kits. When he found out there were two more stores in New York City, Greene was hooked. He wrote to the few manufacturers in business. John Martin's call couldn't have been more timely.

"We're getting into this really fabulous franchise concept of Computer Shack, and you're going to love it. It's wonderful. We've got lots of people interested," Greene remembered Martin saying. The day after their phone conversation, Greene flew out to California. Martin met him at the airport, and Greene spent the better part of the afternoon with Faber at IMSAI's offices.

"They pulled out these placards and said, 'This is what the graphics are going to look like. This is what the sign is going to look like. It's going to be wonderful,'" Greene recalled. "I mean it was one step removed from buying snake oil from a rented office of the salesman." Ed Faber was the man who convinced Greene that he wasn't buying snake oil. "If he had been another John Martin, as much as John and I became quite good friends, I would not have laid down money."

Greene's friendship with Martin got off to an inauspicious start. Greene later told Marian Murphy and Mike McConnell (Computer Shack executives) that he had once hired a private investigator to look into the franchise man. Greene said that the investigator found nothing serious, only something about a nasty custody battle preventing a man named John Musumeci from entering the state of New Hampshire.

As far as Greene was concerned, the investigation showed Martin was clean. Besides, he was a likable guy. The two men were about the same size and both were natural salesmen. Martin's proclivity for hyperbole was hilarious, his excitement and enthusiasm contagious. Greene was going to have a little fun with the cocky, confident little man.

Not long after, Martin flew into Newark, New Jersey, for the final negotiations of Greene's franchise agreement. The trip had been rough on Martin's stomach, and he was pale from having contracted either food poisoning or the flu. Greene welcomed him in his souped-up Pantara sports car "that does about 190 miles a hour." The nuclear scientist was in a hurry to negotiate. He had hardly left the airport when he employed his powerful bargaining ploy. As they got to issues that he was really hot on, he would accelerate. Soon, Greene was doing about 110 miles an hour on the interstate. To his credit, Martin never once protested as Greene sped through the New Jersey traffic. He did, however, sink yet lower and lower in the bucket seat. Over the years the story would be embellished considerably. It was one of the few times somebody at Computer Shack had ever put Martin in his place.

Greene was only the first of many franchisees Martin would woo with his smooth sales pitch in the next few months. Store number two was in Hayward and number three, West Los Angeles. In January, Greene came out for Computer Shack's first training class. Two of Computer Shack's trainers had been hired that day. Another wasn't officially hired yet because he was still under contract to another company. It was, as Greene remembered, "a phenomenal exchange of, we'll say, lack of knowledge." But Greene learned much from the Los Angeles owners. They had Ph.D.'s and MBAs and had done marketing, planning, and demographic studies. "Shoot, I didn't do that," Greene recalled. "I knew Morristown was a rich town. That's why I was there. I was going to sell computers to all those people."

The night before his store's opening, Greene's subconscious was running in circles. "All I could dream was that here all my friends and fellow associates from General Public Utilities [will be there] and we're going to open the doors to this store and nobody was going to come in. Nobody."

On February 18, 1977, the opening day of the first Computer Shack franchise, 112 people walked through the tiny, 450-square-foot showroom in Morristown. "Constantly flowing in," Greene remembered. "No advertising, and our sign wasn't even up."

Greene was fortunate to have a former IMSAI technician helping him out. The main product in Computer Shack's grand opening was an IMSAI 8080 with Vector Graphic memory boards. (Computer Shack stores couldn't sell the popular MITS Altair.) "Yes, it was a classy machine," Greene recalled lovingly. "It had 24K memory. I think I cooked eggs on it in the winter [because] it got so hot."

In those last twelve days of February, Greene had plenty of time to cook eggs. He produced just $832 in gross sales and sent Faber a royalty check for only $17. "Don't spend it all in one place," he joked in the accompanying letter. But by the second month, his sales had jumped to $17,000, and Greene began making a profit.

Around the first week in May 1977, Greene was standing in his store talking to two potential franchisees who were going to open a Computer Shack store on Long Island. A man walked in and asked if he was Ken Greene. After shaking his hand, the mysterious visitor handed Greene a large folder and left. In the folder was notification of a lawsuit naming him as defendant by the Tandy Corp. for encroaching on their Radio Shack trade name. When Greene turned around, the potential franchisees had gone.

Greene quickly called Computer Shack. "In two days my attorney will have me absolved of this, and it's all on your heads!" Greene told Computer Shack angrily. He remembered how he had warned Martin that Tandy's chain of Radio Shack stores would respond to the not-so-coincidental similarity of their names. "Not a problem in the world," he recalled John Martin saying. But there was a problem, and in a few weeks the new computer chain had a different name—ComputerLand. No one had really liked the name Computer Shack anyway. Maybe, in a manner of speaking, Martin had been right.

According to Ken Greene, it was John Martin who really helped his store to grow. "No grass grew under John's feet. I mean he was on the phone. I was talking to him. He was talking to me. Things happened," Greene remembered. "He was a negotiator. He talked to my landlords, trying to get a better deal on the lease, expediting things, assuring me the product was coming, assuring me the sign was coming, and the graphics were coming, and things were happening."

It was Martin who encouraged Greene to take a risk on more inventory. "I thought I needed extra cash, and John said, 'Get inventory! People want to buy product!' So I dumped $20,000 more in inventory, and he was right. That's probably why I did more business." Martin was the catalyst that made things roll, Greene said. "But he was a catalyst that didn't grow. He was still the proverbial pitchman. . . ."

When ComputerLand had registered as a franchiser, it had agreed not to use sales figures to induce people to purchase a franchise. But Martin was convinced that the projected sales figures he was using were low. He thought there was nothing wrong in what he was doing. The California Franchisee Department thought otherwise. They reviewed all the circulars and advertisements prepared by Martin. Faber told him to tone them down, but as he remembered, Martin insisted on learning the hard way that "just about every document we initially provided to the department was rejected, sent back with notations for things to be deleted or altered in some way to make them less offensive, or at least more in keeping with how they interpreted the law."

Every ComputerLand franchisee in the U.S., except one, met Faber, and for most that was the deciding factor in joining the unproven chain. "Here was a man who conveyed a real plan," recalled Greene. "A substantial signficant plan that made a whole heck of a lot of sense."

Whatever importance franchisees attributed to Faber's role, there was no doubt about Martin's dedication. Martin was flying all over the country selling franchises and assisting franchisees in their store openings. On one marathon trip, Martin flew to Cleveland, New Orleans, Miami, and New York, passing through Chicago on the way back, with a stopoff in Denver. As Martin later testified in court, his fear of flying added much to the strain of the heavy travel.

But the women at the office didn't think Martin feared anything. He certainly had no fear of rejection. Martin enjoyed flirting with the female employees of IMSAI, and later, ComputerLand. Martin's most common line was "How'd you like to go to Hawaii for the weekend?" Laura Marsh, like many ComputerLand and IMSAI employees, saw Martin as a typical New Yorker, "a fast mover, fast thinker. Some of it BS. He was a short man." Marsh was one of the few pretty women never asked to the Islands. "I think I was too tall for him," she remembered with a laugh.

Nothing seemed to deter Martin. Despite his masculine banter and seemingly endless supply of jokes, no one at ComputerLand or IMSAI really penetrated his confident front. Martin might share a few drinks at the Rare Steer (the local watering hole) with his co-employees, but he was unlikely to share much of himself.

Beneath Martin's chauvinistic, proud exterior was a young, sensitive man struggling with the pressures of his job and his personal life. Martin often lost his temper with his secretary, Millard's sister Joanne Zuniga. He would take her back into IMSAI's production facilities and scream at her at the top of his lungs. After several loud minutes, he would emerge as though nothing had happened. "John needed to go take care of personal affairs," recalled his friend Greene. Within Martin were secrets and troubles that others never saw, much less imagined. Few knew, for example, the tale behind John Martin's name.

It all began when he was working for the employment agency. "At the agency you had to change your name because they didn't want people dealing from their house. Everybody had what they call a professional name," Martin would tell a judge and jury years later, under oath.

Having a couple of different names was embarrassing at times. John would be taking a girl who knew him as Martin out for a date, and then just when things were going well, he would run into somebody who would call him Musumeci. "It got confusing. What I did was hyphenate it, and people who knew me very well call me John Martin, and people who don't know me very well call me John Martin-Musumeci," recalled Martin.

But the name on his driver's license stayed the same, Musumeci, and everybody at IMSAI and ComputerLand, and all of his friends, called him John Martin. Not until years later did they even hear of Musumeci. In 1979, at a computer show, Julie Banuelos would bump into her old friend from ComputerLand and IMSAI, John Martin. She would be surprised to see him accompanied by Philip Reed, but Banuelos would be even more puzzled by the "Martin-Musumeci" name tag her old friend wore. "He changed the name because he got married. He hyphenated his name with his wife's name," said Banuelos. "That's what he told me." How sweet, Banuelos thought, but he *was* that kind of guy.*

Back in the winter of 1977, however, after months of travel and ten-to-fifteen-hour days, Martin's sweetness was turning sour. Things weren't helped much during an IMSAI end-of-month party. According to *IMSIGH*, three of Martin's ribs and his nose were broken in the celebration. Martin had never paid much attention to his health, and now, under the stress of the work, his stomach was churning and he was running out of steam. Martin went to Millard and told him of his difficulties. Millard had an answer for his problems. "He told me to take est and to go without eating and sleeping," Martin recalled. And for a while it worked. "I thought est was the most powerful experience in my life."

*Banuelos and others never knew that their friend, born in 1946, began life with the name John Joseph Musumeci.

But est also taught Martin about the importance of keeping agreements. Millard had made one with him, and it was Millard's turn to live up to his promise.

"Look, my ten weeks are up," Martin told Millard as January 1977 rolled around. Originally, Martin had intended to just do a quick job: "Ten weeks, get in and out, take the thirty grand and run." But Martin didn't leave quite so fast. "The problem was that there were two or three problems," Martin said. "At the end of that ten weeks there was a hell of a lot more to do, and the company had a need for me."

There were other difficulties as well. Millard didn't want to pay the $20,000 balance on Martin's contract—or the 5 percent stock he had promised. "He had a couple of bases for my not having stock," Martin recalled. "It was his view that out of the two hundred or so items on that list of things I was supposed to provide, one or two of the things had not been fully done." Faber was present at the meeting, and according to Martin, ". . . at that point he [Faber] called him [Millard] an asshole and said, 'You know, *I'm* running the company! I think you're being real petty about this thing. I mean, John has overperformed the contract." Martin also remembered Faber telling Millard, "The truth is we're not here to talk about the ten weeks he did. That's completed. We're talking about him coming on board." By now, Martin was not surprised by Millard's response. "Fine, but I'm not going to give him any stock."

Martin decided that he would not descend to that level of pettiness. "Well, gentlemen, I'll see you later," he said. It was a Friday when Martin walked out. "You can do without me," Martin said. "Give me the rest of my money, I'm going home."*

At seven forty-five the following morning, Saturday, Millard called Martin at home. That phone call, Martin said, "was the beginning of the end of our relationship."

"I want to see you. I'll see you in a half hour," Martin recalled Millard saying. Martin got dressed and hurried down to the office. Millard's Cadillac was parked outside. Millard was sitting at his desk, waiting.

"You win. I'm going to give both you and Ed [Faber] five percent stock of the company," Millard said as Martin walked in the door. "It

---

*Faber did not recall such gentlemanly behavior. He testified later in court that Martin stormed out, slamming the door behind him.

was not something I had ever seen before or since," Martin would tell a jury eight years later. "He spoke with humility."

The offer was accepted. On February 14, 1977, Martin was hired as director of franchise sales. A couple of months later, Faber would log his 5 percent equity participation in a letter to Millard.* In the next few months, counting the few already signed, Martin would sign up a total of seventeen franchisees. Since each franchisee generally held an option to open three more stores, the seventeen franchisees represented a potential of more than sixty stores. But only a week after Martin became a full-time employee, Millard would question whether he had done the right thing on that Saturday morning. Perhaps his intuition about Martin had been correct. He wrote in his diary "almost lost the store due to Martin's approach to the franchise. Owners of Bldg didn't like Martin's approach."

---

*Faber's letter read in part, "I am offered 5% equity participation in ComputerLand Corp., formerly Computer Shack Inc. Such participation vests at ¼% per month beginning February 1977."

9
The
Ultimatum

In the closing days of 1976 Loring Reed's attorney, Andrew Bailey, had a rather disquieting phone conversation with Millard's attorney, Harry Margolis. Not the most diplomatic of fellows, Margolis led off the conversation by saying that he was calling on Millard's behalf, and that if they couldn't resolve the situation, then Marriner should sue. Bailey was also surprised when Margolis suggested that Marriner send accountants to examine the books and records of IMS because "the company is very near the brink of disaster and could go down the chute." Margolis then advised Bailey that if litigation was brought against IMS, the company would go bankrupt the next day.

Loring Reed just wanted out. On January 11, 1977, he sent a telex to Millard requesting $250,000 plus monthly $1,000 payments equaling $30,000. Once the money was paid, the two would never have to talk or see one another again. In the telex, however, Reed warned Millard that if he did not buy back the note by the April 1, 1977, deadline he set, "The failure of Marriner to commence litigation against IMS during the period April 1 will not prejudice the rights of Marriner against IMS." The message was clear. Ninety days to come up with $250,000 or Marriner's legal guns would fire.

Millard called up Kojnok and talked things over. Couldn't they just put everything back the way things used to be, before the Panama deal? Kojnok memorialized their conversation in a letter the next day: "You wish to be put in the position you were in before our tax planning work began except that you wish to utilize IMSAI Manufacturing Corporation in the place of IMS Associates. . . ." As the letter continued, it became apparent that as Millard's interest in the Panama deal had waned, so had the law firm's eagerness to defend Millard against Reed's claims: "We do not fully agree with your position and therefore we are not going to undertake any further steps in this area so long as we are not specifically asked to do so."

As the battle neared, Millard's legal forces retreated. He would have to face Loring Reed alone. No longer could he count on Margolis or Kojnok to write retaliatory letters. The difference was striking. There was no mistaking the Millard ring of authenticity in the communication he sent to Reed a few days later. The man whose attorneys had just politely told him to get lost fired off a telex to Reed in the posture of a samurai warrior:

> I am amazed at the contents of your Telex of 1/11/77. I have no desire to reward Marriner. . . . If IMSAI fails to exercise its option within the 90-day period, it seems appropriate to me that we proceed thereafter to do business or do battle. . . .

But as the phone calls from Loring Reed continued without relief, Millard found himself retreating. Reed seemed to be demanding that he "pay him off" or go out and find somebody who would be able to "buy out the note."

The note *was not* delinquent. Millard had made all the interest payments. ". . . This sounds like a demand, and the note is not past due, and I don't understand," Millard said to Loring Reed again and again. Still, bewildered or not, on February 3, Millard signed the option to purchase the note for $280,000 by April 15.

Less than two weeks later, on February 15, 1977, Millard logged a phone call from Kojnok into his diary: "Ondrej phoned. He received okay to liquidate from Franchise Tax Board. Wants to know if he should proceed with the liquidation." Three days later, on February 18, 1977, Ondrej Kojnok filed with the secretary of state the certificate of winding up and distribution of IMS Associates, which states that all of the known assets of IMS Associates Inc. had been distributed to Presentaciones, in Panama.

On February 23, Kojnok wrote a letter summarizing the work his firm had performed for Millard:

Based on the transfer of the stock from IMS to PMSA, PMSA commenced liquidation of IMS on November 1st, 1976. . . . Because of your desire to be returned to substantially the same position as if no transaction had taken place, the annuity agreement was rescinded and a provision made under which all assets and liabilities were returned to you from PMSA effective November 1st, 1976.

It seemed that the strange events of the last five months had not really happened. No transaction had taken place. The assets of IMS had not gone to Panama. It had all been some sort of absurd, surrealistic illusion. The provision changed the past, altered what had so recently been reality. Explained Kojnok, "Well, our intention was to satisfy Mr. Millard's request and put everything back where we started." Millard would soon discover it wasn't so easy to put everything back together again.

Millard had hired the accounting firm of Ernst and Ernst to perform an audit and a general review of the taxes of the corporations. While gathering and reviewing the relevant materials, David Kuhner, the CPA assigned to the task, became aware of the transfer of some assets to a Panamanian corporation.

Kuhner was worried that if the stock became worthless, Millard and his companies might suffer a loss they wouldn't be able to sustain. And there was something else Millard hadn't considered. Loring Reed and Philip Reed weren't the only ones at risk. Millard, too, was turning his fate over to a group of South Americans he had never met. They could control the annuities paid to the Millards, decide whether dividends would be paid, or raise the royalties he must pay.

After warning Millard of the danger, Kuhner phoned Margolis's office. How odd, he thought. Mrs. Felch, Kojnok's secretary, and Margolis's partner, Mr. Dunnett, were both officers of IMS. Kojnok was the sole director of IMS. No one, however, seemed to be in or able to answer Kuhner's calls: "We had difficulty getting ahold of Mr. Margolis on most occasions, so we wanted to put him on notice that this transaction was going to be rescinded. . . ." On March 4, 1977, Kuhner sent a letter to Margolis asking that the Panama transfer be halted.

Three days later, on March 7, 1977, the office of the secretary of state returned to Margolis's office the unfiled papers of IMS's proposed dissolution.

Perhaps Loring Reed sensed the strange events taking place. The next day he called Millard and demanded that Millard "pay me off!" Millard couldn't understand his insistence. He replied calmly, "The note is not due. I haven't defaulted on the note. It was a five-year note. All we have to do is pay the interest." Millard noticed that Reed seemed uncomfortable that the reorganization was still not complete. "How do I know you're going to do what you say you have done?" Millard recalled Reed asking.

Reed wasn't the only one puzzled by the reorganization. A week later, Kuhner wrote Millard, still unsure about IMS's status. He was concerned whether the reversal of IMS's liquidation had really been accomplished. He recommended to Millard a new attorney, Bob Randick.

Loring Reed always prided himself on being a professional. No matter how heated their phone conversations and threatening their correspondence might be, Loring Reed was not about to stop now, just because of Millard. Loring Reed was a gentleman first and a businessman second. He and Millard simply had a difference of opinion. That was what he kept telling himself, anyway. But Reed had not received a financial report since September 1976, the same month Computer Shack was incorporated. The truth was that he no longer trusted Millard. Reed was getting a closer look at the way Millard ran IMSAI, and he didn't care for it one bit.

Some of Millard's employees at IMSAI weren't too happy about it, either. A few months earlier, in October of 1976, before the ComputerLand name change, Computer Shack's Hayward pilot store had opened. Two of IMSAI's best technicians were sent over to the new facility for three to four weeks to get the demonstration store off the ground. At the time, IMSAI happened to be facing a nasty backlog of customer service repairs. IMSAI's customers would just have to wait.

IMSAI employees were often called on to do their bit for Computer Shack. Marian Murphy worked in IMSAI's receiving department and in late 1976 and early 1977 was also in charge of Computer Shack receiving. Because Murphy was fresh out of college, it didn't seem odd to her that she was doing work for another company. It only meant bringing in some equipment every couple of days. "I did some stuff for Computer Shack even though I was on the IMSAI payroll," she remembered. "Their [Computer Shack's] stuff was still shipped into our receiving department."

Employees in IMSAI's customer service and engineering, however, were concerned. Critical equipment they needed for development and testing was being diverted to Computer Shack. Even standard products, like the IMSAI 8080, tended to find their way to Computer Shack first. "If Computer Shack put an order in for perhaps fifty or a hundred IMSAI 8080 kits or assembled 8080s, generally the shipping schedule was shuffled to accommodate Computer Shack . . . ," recalled Todd Fischer, manager of IMSAI's customer service.

IMSAI employees looked at Computer Shack as just another company owned by Millard, the man at the top of the pyramid. Fischer viewed the new competition for resources as a squabble among siblings: "A tremendous internal row occurred among shipping and order control over the fact that IMSAI's inventory was being diverted to the Computer Shack division."

But these were only technicalities. Millard continued to tell Loring Reed that Computer Shack was a separate company, financed entirely out of hs own savings, and receiving no help from IMSAI. Reed listened to Millard's story about the division between the two companies and watched IMSAI give Computer Shack credit terms while other buyers were forced to pay on delivery. He listened to the story and heard phones sometimes answered "IMSAI" and other times answered "Computer Shack."

Did Millard think Reed was an idiot? For months the two companies worked out of the same building! "To try and say that it was a separate entity standing on its own feet didn't make any sense. It wasn't standing on its own feet!" said Loring Reed. IMSAI was subsidizing the growth of Computer Shack and Loring Reed was damned if he was going to let his investment slip away into Computer Shack before his eyes.

The six-month approval period with the Union Bank loan was nearing an end. Miraculously, Millard had paid off the $100,000 loan. If they could just "hold their breath for thirty days," the bank would give

IMSAI a new line of credit, perhaps as much as $250,000.

On March 25, 1977, with only ten days remaining until the new line of credit would be issued, Loring Reed wrote a letter to Union Bank, withdrawing his subordination agreement. Millard's proposed new line of credit disappeared.

Reed had at least two reasons for his untimely letter. The subordination agreement had a clause providing that if Marriner sold its note prior to its maturity, Marriner would have to cover any outstanding loans of IMS or IMSAI. "I withdrew the subordination agreement so . . . I wouldn't get $250,000 from Mr. Millard for the note and then turn around and have to pay the bank $150,000. That wouldn't be a very good deal," said Reed.

If that wasn't reason enough, Reed had an even better motivation: "We wanted to get out of the company and that would put more pressure on Mr. Millard to get us out." That same day in March, Reed phoned Millard, and as with many key points in his life, the event was logged into Millard's diary: "Loring Reed phoned at 1450. No use to co. [company] Not bullish in long run."

Millard was surprised and devastated by Loring Reed's sudden move: "I really think he did me, himself, our relationship, and the company wrong, you betcha." Never again would Millard trust Loring Reed. His callous action had put IMSAI in "immediate life jeopardy."

There were other pressures on IMSAI in March of 1977. Computer Shack's tab at IMSAI had blossomed to $129,000. As the bill expanded, IMSAI's cash to pay for parts and supplies and payroll disappeared. In January, when Computer Shack owed $47,000, IMSAI had $154,000 on hand. By February when Computer Shack owed $86,000, IMSAI's cash had shrunk to $86,000. By March, when Computer Shack owed $129,000, only $50,000 was left to pay the bills. As Computer Shack's debt rose, IMSAI's cash reserves sank. It didn't take a genius to figure out where that trend would lead.

Ed Gingrass, IMSAI's bright, new director of finance, interviewed by Harry Margolis and hired by Millard in January, did what any finance man would do in such a situation—he put Computer Shack on credit hold. The hold, however, didn't last a day. "He [Millard] told me it [the credit hold] was to be ignored," said Gingrass of his brief conversation with Millard. A couple of weeks later, Gingrass was gone. The Dartmouth graduate, with a master's degree in finance from Columbia University, was not leaving after just three months because Millard had decided not to offer him stock. Gingrass had received an attractive offer to work at another firm.

With the nearing of the April 15 Marriner note deadline, it became clear that Millard was not going to bite. Loring Reed was tired of being pushed around. This time, Reed decided that if Millard wanted to buy back the note, there would be a price: "If he didn't do it, and all the indications were that he wasn't very interested, I wanted it spelled out just exactly what our rights were."

Reed worked with Marriner's attorney, Bailey, to draft an agreement that would provide Millard a second opportunity to buy back the note. If Millard failed to purchase the note by the assigned date, however, Millard and IMS would be bound by an agreement that, as Reed recalled, "spelled out just exactly what our rights were."

It wasn't that the original document didn't protect Marriner's rights, Reed remembered, but who could have guessed that Millard "would set up all those damned companies." The new document, soon to be called the "Option and Modification Agreement," left nothing to the imagination. The document named every company Millard owned —including ComputerLand—provided for any future company Millard might incorporate, and declared that Marriner had the right to 20 percent stock in all of those companies. "We gave him all kinds of deals—two or three of them," Reed said. "We figured we were in bed with a wild man, and we wanted to sever the connection and get our money and forget it and go on to something else."

In early April of 1977, Loring Reed was visiting Philip in Las Cruces, as he had off and on for several years. On the night of April 8, 1977, he and Millard struck a deal on the telephone. Millard hung up the receiver and carefully noted the time. He then wrote in his diary: "At 10:03 P.M., Loring and I agree I have option until 7/1/77 for $250,000. $150,000 paid off at $2,500 per month for six months if I sign letter to become effective on July 1st if that note is not paid off."

Back in Las Cruces, Loring Reed was working on those things that would "become effective" if Millard didn't come up with the cash. He scrawled out the basics of their agreement on the stationery of his family's company, Liz Corp.:

Dear Bill:

The purpose of this letter is to confirm our agreement made on the telephone last evening, April 8th 1977.

I agreed on behalf of Marriner provided that you and Pat and all other IMS stockholders sign the enclosed agreement on or before April 22nd 1977, to grant you an option good until June 1, 1977 to purchase Marriner's $250,000 convertible note for $250,000 in cash and $2500 per month for a period of 60 months commencing July 1st 1977. (Total price of note $400,000.)

I am returning to the East on Monday. I would be interested in seeing some financial statements on Computer Shack when available. I expect to hear from you prior to April 22nd. I trust that your European trip will be successful.

Sincerely,

P. Loring Reed Jr.

Enclosed was the unsigned agreement, which basically stated that Marriner's option applied to IMS, IMSAI, ComputerLand, and any other company Millard started. The agreement included a couple of lines for Bill and Pat Millard to sign. Later, Reed couldn't remember whether his attorney, Bailey, actually wrote the document or told Reed what to write. But who wrote the draft soon became academic.

The next day Millard flew to London and then journeyed to the Continent. He had brought a few employees along to demonstrate the IMSAI 8080 at the Hanover Fair in Germany. The response from his around-the-world trip had been terrific. The international exposition was no different—the IMSAI 8080 was a hit. Millard knew the future. "There was no question about it; it was global absolutely," he recalled. "IMSAI was exploding, and literally, it was to get these footholds. Get them started and get a foothold. See, nobody had declared themselves global or really had taken a stand and said, 'We're number one!'"

Nobody, that is, until William H. Millard. While at the fair, Millard met a German who offered him a warehouse at a cheap rent. For a time, it looked like a small town near Frankfurt might be the headquarters for IMSAI's international operations.

Then Millard discovered some of the business advantages of Luxembourg. Taxes in Luxembourg were almost nonexistent and shipments could be flown directly into that tiny European nation. Operating out of any other country would have required a stop somewhere along the way. Luxembourg was centrally located, pro-business and pro-American. Millard also enjoyed the courtly treatment. "Arriving there with just my briefcase under my arm, I was able to get an appointment with a cabinet minister with a week's notice." IMSAI's international headquarters would be in Luxembourg.

But Millard's ambitions could not limit IMSAI to just Europe. At almost the same moment he was paving the way for IMSAI's international headquarters, he was creating a separate company at the other end of the world. Manufacturing operations were being set up in Singapore. Millard was confident that IMSAI Singapore would soon give them a competitive edge.

Business in San Leandro was not going as smoothly. Millard had declined to sign the rough document that Loring Reed had mailed. He instead had sent the document to his new attorney, Randick. Upon Millard's return from Europe, after Randick had made some revisions and added a few sections, Millard signed a new, professional-looking document and mailed it back to Reed.

But two could play at that. This late in the game, Reed was not about to overlook the paragraph Millard's new attorney had tried to add to the agreement:

> . . . nothing contained in this promissory note attached hereto as Exhibit A shall restrict the right of IMS or any other business corporation owned directly or indirectly by the Millards' to reorganize, consolidate, merge or transfer assets to any other such corporation.
>
> Any such reorganization, consolidation, merger or transfer shall not operate to accelerate the payments of the principal and its assignability.

For half a year Loring Reed had been fighting that very point. Under the name of reorganization, Reed was convinced that Millard had tried to throw the IMS/Marriner note to the four winds. Reed was not going to let some attorney insert a nice legalistic clause that would give Millard an excuse to do it all over again.

Bailey deleted the paragraph, made a few other changes, and sent the document back for round two. "They knew damn well what we wanted," remembered Reed. None of the basics of the agreement had changed in Reed's view. The only difference for Millard was that the price had gone up. Millard would have to pay $250,000 up front, and then $2,500 a month for five years for a total buyout of $400,000.

Not until late May of 1977 did Millard actually sign the Option and Modification Agreement (the agreement would bear the date May 11). To ensure that Marriner could not add a page he had not approved, Millard initialed and dated each of the four pages of the document. The clock began ticking again. He had until July 1, 1977, to raise the $250,000 for the initial payment. Soon after Millard signed the document, Reed let him know that it might be his last chance: "If you don't buy this, we want out of this company and I'm going to try and peddle it [the note] to somebody else!" They both knew the man who was taking the first step toward becoming that somebody else.

10

Dress
Rehearsal

One day the yelling stopped. Marian Murphy looked around, and sure enough, John Martin was gone. On May 1, 1977, Martin didn't show up for work. He never said good-bye or picked up his things. He was just gone.

Except for Millard and Faber, few really knew why Martin had left. Faber had been struggling with Martin for weeks. He had tried everything and finally decided that it was an impossible situation. Martin was not accustomed to working for someone else. Faber would keep telling Martin to stop making wild promises to prospective franchisees, and Martin would go on promising the moon.

Martin felt that was a "bunch of baloney." Things didn't get sold unless you were enthusiastic. He wasn't "puffing." He was just being John Martin, "ace salesman." But Martin recognized the contrast between what he called the "Faber and Martin styles." Once, while talking into a speakerphone with one of his franchise salesmen listening in, Martin told a prospective San Diego franchisee that he believed someday a computer store would sell $200,000 worth of products in a single month.* Faber, whose office was next door, couldn't help overhearing.

*At that point, the few in the business had barely sold more than $20,000 a month.

111

"Don't you tell people that someday a computer store will do $200,000 a month!" Martin recalled Faber saying. "The truth is a computer store has never done $200,000 a month."

Martin corrected Faber. He had never said it would do $200,000 a month. He had just said that he personally believed that someday it would. "You can't tell me not to tell people what I believe!" Martin shot back. "And the reason why I'm here, and why stock is important to me, is that I truly believe that's the kind of potential that's available!"

That was all Faber needed to make his decision. Faber had a business opportunity he was offering to people. Faber would provide businessmen with information about the franchises and then look for a match. He thought that Martin was selling too aggressively. In fact, Martin led the sales department in commissions. Five percent of every ($15,000 or more) franchisee fee went into his pocket. He also got a commission for the amount of inventory he could convince franchisees to stock. "He thought that was the way to do it, and I disagreed," Faber recalled. "He had to go, and the commission program went with him."

But Martin said there was more behind the split: "Millard was a great believer in what he used to call 'the going-up-in-price sale.'" Martin had watched the franchisee fee jump from $10,000 to $15,000 to $17,500. He didn't like what he was seeing, yet somehow the market withstood the price hikes. But when Millard threatened to raise the franchisee fee to $25,000 and raise the royalty rate to 8 percent, Martin had seen enough.

"Look, as a shareholder in the company, and as the franchise consultant who put the deal together, [I think] that's too violent a move," Martin remembered telling Faber just before leaving to close a couple of franchise deals. When he returned, it was too late. Letters had been sent informing potential franchises of the July franchise-fee hike.

Martin remembered the following exchange: "Ed, can't you go to the post office and recall them?"

"John, you don't make decisions here. I make decisions, and it's done."

Martin felt it was a mistake, perhaps a fatal mistake.

And so Faber felt he had no choice but to terminate Martin. He knew Martin would be upset, but once they talked about it, he thought the break would be amicable. Faber gave Martin some time to think about things and gave himself some time to see if he could find another place in the company for him. But after a couple of weeks it was clear that the man who needed to be "aimed and fired," as Philip Reed wrote, was not coming back. "We had already gotten all the value that John could contribute, and he could not grow," Faber recalled. "He had to go."

But Martin felt that he had not been paid what he deserved. He was trying to collect on some of the debts the company owed him when he made a startling discovery. Millard and Faber were denying that the stock agreement existed. Martin might have expected it of Millard, but Faber's denial came as a shock. He had always viewed Faber with high regard.

Fortunately for Martin, there was somebody in the company who knew about the agreement. Richard Bowman was Computer-Land's general counsel at the time, though he only had a license to practice in Georgia. "Bowman stepped in and they said, 'Okay, you're entitled to the stock, but you're not entitled to the full five percent, you're only entitled to one percent,'" recalled Martin. Millard claimed that the stock agreement, like virtually all his stock agreements, required two years to vest the full five percent. In the meantime, Martin became upset. "I threatened to sue. As a matter of fact, I hired a lawyer in San Francisco to sue." But Bowman calmly disarmed the conflict, and though Martin still didn't have his stock, he felt that he would eventually get his share.

The dispute and the hard work apparently ruined Martin's health, although he was just thirty years old. When Martin left Computer-Land, he was suffering from a nervous breakdown, bleeding from the stomach, and facing daily doctor visits for a year. Martin appeared to blame his ailments on the strain of working for Millard.

Millard would later say that Martin simply decided to leave. As evidence of their friendship, he would quote from a letter John Martin wrote to him after his departure saying, "Thank you for the contribution you have made to my life. I love you."

Martin was not without friends at ComputerLand. After he left, Abley visited Martin at his house. They lay out by the pool, dangled their feet in the water, and drank beer. Martin said little about ComputerLand. Abley could tell he was upset, but he also knew Martin wasn't likely to tell him how he felt. It was well known that Abley and Faber were friends, and despite Martin's sudden departure, there was little to indicate that Faber and Martin's friendship had soured. Shortly after leaving ComputerLand, Martin started his old consulting company, Expansion Systems, up again. Faber helped Martin with business plans, gave him good recommendations, and assisted him for over a year.

Other friends of Martin saw a different side to the breakup. Julie Banuelos of IMSAI had always been fascinated by John Martin. She wondered where Martin got his confidence. "How can you be so cocky?" she used to wonder. "You're just this little bitty short man."

Although Banuelos worked for IMSAI's customer services, Martin was in the next office. When Martin was away from his desk, Banuelos would often take his phone calls. After work, the two sometimes engaged in a favored IMSAI occupation—drinking. They would go to the Rare Steer, which after a few drinks they would affectionately call the "Bum Steer." It was at one of these cocktail encounters that Martin told Banuelos of Millard's promise to give him stock in ComputerLand. "He really felt he wasn't going to get it [stock], and he said he was going to go to the mat with the guy for the money," Banuelos recalled. At the time, Banuelos didn't think much of Martin's concern. Martin's confidence, she felt, was equaled only by his paranoia.

Perhaps Martin was not paranoid but merely fortifying himself for the battles he knew lay ahead. By September 1977, he had still not received his stock, and Millard owed him more than $3,000 in commissions and other fees. Martin met with Faber at his ComputerLand office. Faber had the checks. He also had something for Martin to sign—a one-year, noncompetition clause. "I was appalled. I thought it was illegal," Martin recalled of the noncompetition agreement. He left without signing and without the money.

Martin returned the next day and this time met with both Faber and Millard. Once again Faber had the checks on his desk and the noncompetition agreement to sign. Faber was sure Martin was going to sign. Then Martin asked Millard if he would give him a letter of reference. Millard refused.

Martin became agitated. Faber remembered the terse exchange this way: "Why not?" Martin demanded. "Because I don't want to," Millard said. "I don't like your attitude," Martin snapped, leaping up and leaving the office. The checks remained on Faber's desk, and the agreement was still unsigned.

September 30, 1977, the end of ComputerLand's fiscal year, was approaching. Faber wanted to complete his business with Martin before the auditors did their work, so he finally agreed to cross out the noncompetition section from the agreement. Still, Martin refused to sign or take the checks as final settlement of his compensation. Faber then asked Richard Bowman to go to Martin's house and "ask John as a favor to me to sign the agreement, and when he does, give him the checks." Bowman needed to go to Martin's home anyway. He was about to become Martin's partner in his new franchise consulting business.

Bowman quickly discovered that Martin's attitude toward the agreement had not altered. After arguing with Bowman for some time, Martin again refused to sign. But when Bowman returned to ComputerLand, he realized that he no longer had the checks. Faber gave Martin a choice. If he kept the checks, he would no longer have any claims against the company, except the stock he still had not received. If he did not accept the settlement, all he had to do was return the money within five days.

Three days after that offer, October 3, 1977, Bowman wrote Martin:

It is difficult for me to express how sorry I am that you cashed the $1,750 check which I had carefully explained was not to be cashed unless the release was signed. . . . What makes it even harder for me to take is that when I pointed out the predicament in which your actions placed me, and offered you the opportunity to undo your action, you refused. . . .

I feel our plans whereby I was to be an incorporator, stockholder and officer of the new company we were jointly to form cannot any longer be continued. I cannot place my confidence in and expend my best efforts for anyone who had treated me in this fashion.

John, this incident and your entire position vis-à-vis ComputerLand are a perfect acting out of your admitted self-destructive streak. . . .

On the other front, Loring Reed was fast discovering that to play tough with Millard was to play with fire. He had hoped his warning would have pressured Millard to buy back the note by the July 1, 1977, deadline, but well before that date he knew that his strategy had failed. Millard had a simple answer to Reed's threat to peddle the note elsewhere. The financial reports were still not being sent to Reed, but that, remembered Seymour Rubinstein, IMSAI's director of marketing, was only part of the new directive toward Reed and Marriner. "They were going to basically treat him [Loring Reed] like mushrooms. Keep them in the dark and feed them a lot of shit."

As Millard would later explain, "There was a lot of question in my mind that he [Loring Reed] had a right to have me continue with an oral agreement to provide him with financial statements after what he had done was broken his agreement to subordinate the debt . . ."

In mid-July of 1977, Reed made a date to fly out to see Millard. When he arrived, Millard was in Europe. He had not bothered to tell Reed that his trip had been extended. Loring Reed was furious: "I get out there and he isn't even there!" His foul mood wasn't helped by Marvin Walker, who would have liked to help but was bound by Millard's orders: "Loring got there, there was no Bill, and there were no numbers, and he wasn't going to get any numbers." Loring Reed was fed up with the games. He traced Millard down and got him on the phone. "I haven't gotten any financial reports!" Reed remembered saying. "What the hell is going on!"

Reed was not satisfied with Millard's answers and decided to take more concrete action against the man he had so recently loaned a quarter-million dollars. Marriner prepared to file suit against Millard and his companies in federal court. The complaint requested an injunction requiring Millard to provide financial information about all of his companies, and asked for general damages and punitive damages of $1 million. In the suit filed in May 1978, Marriner complained that Millard had been "creating new and different corporations with the assets of defendant corporations, and wasting assets of defendant corporations, all in order to avoid granting to plaintiff the interests to which it is entitled. . . ."

During the summer of 1977, Loring Reed wasn't happy with Millard and Millard certainly wasn't happy with Loring Reed. But Millard was unhappy with more than just one person. He had been traveling the world, opening new companies and markets for IMSAI right and left, and back in California they couldn't seem to follow instructions. Customers were complaining, products were defective, shipments were delayed. In late July he returned from Europe and called a meeting.

Every man and woman employed by IMSAI was assembled in the parking lot between the company's two buildings. July was not a pleasant time of year to stand out in the IMSAI parking lot. The pavement concentrated the summer's heat and the sun reflected brightly off the cars. It was uncomfortable, and people wondered what was so important that they had to stop work and stand in the blazing sun. They didn't have long to wait. The buildings had deep window ledges, cut about three feet above flower beds. Millard stepped up on one of the window ledges and in a loud voice addressed the crowd.

In the space of ten minutes Millard berated the entire company. They suffered from a lack of professionalism, a lack of incentive, a lack of just about everything except salary, as one employee remembered the talk. The speech was short, but the dead silence among the 140 or so employees, who looked at each other as though they had all just eaten some bad food, seemed to last forever.

His point was simple enough. Millard did not want to have to come back from his European triumphs and face problems with customers. That was the purpose for which his employees had been hired. They were to "handle it!" as the est phrase went. Millard had more important things to do than deal with daily operations.

The employees shuffled back into the building and quietly went back to work. There was little talk that afternoon, but the tension was in the air. Here they had worked hard to make Millard's dreams a reality and he had rounded them up like cattle and scolded them like schoolchildren. Once people recovered from the shock, they realized *they* weren't the problem, it was Millard. He had aimed and fired, but he had shot himself in the foot.

Perhaps Millard's attention was elsewhere. Not only was he busy setting up international operations in Luxembourg, but he was also trying to learn French. Millard was fascinated by the language and European culture. His diary recorded his tremendous desire to speak, read, and write French fluently, and it was full of pages where he devoted four hours or more of the day to mastering it.

Millard was so taken with the European way that he began writing dates in the European convention, with the day of the week first—7 August 1977. But the strangest thing was when a different handwriting appeared in his journal. The handwriting was only in French, and only appeared on pages where Millard was practicing his French. The handwriting, which had a distinctly feminine curve, appeared on the page where Millard practiced the phrase *Je suis contente* over and over again.

Van Natta and Killian couldn't understand the increasing frequency of Millard's trips. They wished Millard was around more. Van Natta especially missed being able to pop into Millard's office and bounce questions off his friend, the boss. They and others at IMSAI began to wonder why Millard was spending so much time in Europe when there was so much work to be done at home.

At one of their meetings at Jake's, Killian and Van Natta felt sure that Millard was going to let them in on it. "There's something I want to tell you," Van Natta and Killian remembered Millard saying. There was an expectant pause. They had known that it was only a matter of time before Bill shared this, the most intimate of secrets. But before Millard could go any further, Van Natta said that he kept no secrets from his wife. Millard promptly dropped the subject.

Upon returning from one of his trips to Luxembourg, Millard wanted to give a slide show, but his projector was broken. Fischer, the company handyman, said he'd be happy to do the repairs. As he took the machine apart, he noticed Millard had neglected to remove a couple of slides. He held one up to the light. The picture showed a young girl, perhaps in her early twenties, with dark hair and a slim figure. Fischer put two and two together.

Pat Millard had not gone to college and still could not read a financial sheet—her job was to order the food for the company lunches—but she, too, could put two and two together. It didn't take her long to discover that the business her husband was conducting abroad was not all office-related. She was a woman of action, and the day she learned the real attraction Europe had for Bill was a day some IMSAI employees would never forget. Marvin Walker was next door to Millard's office, conducting a meeting with a few employees, when he heard Pat Millard burst into the building. She didn't say a word as she strode purposefully into her husband's office and slammed the door. There was silence for a moment. The men smiled at each other as they listened in anticipation. The tremendous shattering of porcelain followed, reverberating through the wall. "There goes the eagle," they said in unison.

There was more than a little poetic justice in her bold act. In seconds, Pat Millard was down the hall and out of the building, having said everything without uttering a word.

Pat Millard would not be seen around the company for several months. Her husband would have to find somebody else to buy the lunch and cookies. But hers was not the only familiar face that would be missed. Marvin Walker was leaving. He felt he had accomplished the goals he had set out to achieve, and he was ready to tackle one of the things on his dreamlist, driving a Peterbilt truck cross-country.

Walker had always known Millard to be a gracious boss and friend and was surprised by the suddenness of Millard's question. "How about the stock?" he remembered Millard asking. Walker didn't think that he'd earned the stock, technically or otherwise. Under the two-year vesting process Millard had proposed, the full 5 percent would not be vested for several months. With his near million-dollar investments in New Mexico, the stock was not of great concern to Walker. "We had a friendly meeting and a going-away dinner, and all that, but his immediate response was 'How about the stock?'" Walker recalled. "I never forgot the question."*

But neither the breaking of his prized eagle nor the imminent departure of his dear friend Walker could slow Millard's growing fascination with Luxembourg. In August of 1977, a check was made out to the Luxembourg account in the amount of $30,000. A two-bedroom, completely furnished apartment was rented and a Renault purchased. Only days after his wife's dramatic episode, Millard returned to Luxembourg for three weeks. All told, in the next four months Millard

---

*No written record of the stock offer exists and Millard denied it was ever made. Walker had, however, received 5 percent stock in Millard's earlier company, System Dynamics.

Walker's career as a truck driver was brief. Upon arriving in Chicago with his first load of lettuce, he opened the back of the truck to discover that the refrigeration had failed and that he had hauled green, slimy mush thousands of miles.

would make at least four trips to Luxembourg. Working around the clock to set up IMSAI's international headquarters, Millard would spend more time in Europe than he did back home.

Millard's appointment of Wes Dehn to IMSAI general manager made his removal from daily operations official. "The speech" would not be heard again. It was Dehn's job to keep the flock from straying from the path.

Those who knew him best might have predicted Millard's gradual removal from IMSAI's daily operations. Millard had been successful in opening IMSAI dealerships in Tehran and Japan. He was setting up manufacturing in Singapore and working on a licensing agreement with India. Other international deals were being pursued. Some wondered whether the dream was losing its focus.

But these perceptions were at ground level. Millard soared above and saw the big picture. Few understood that Millard was battling a philosophical problem—the resolution of which would change the face of the computer industry.

Deep in his heart, Millard always knew that he would create several companies in his life. He had created one before IMSAI. ComputerLand was his third. "The one thing I didn't like about manufacturing, and it had a lot to do with a dream I had for ComputerLand, there was no committed relationship. I felt hungry, totally hungry, for a relationship that I felt was knowledgeable, and I felt was committed, and I felt was really a partnership."

Structure was important to Millard. It was essential that his companies reflect his need for order. Now that the Panama deal had gone awry, Millard was struggling to put things in their proper place again. One of the purposes of the Panama deal had been to qualify for a consolidated tax return. But time was running out. Millard couldn't file the return unless IMSAI had truly been the holding company for ComputerLand and IMS. September 1977 was the deadline to file the consolidated return.

Millard couldn't understand why the IMS stock hadn't returned from Panama. He kept hearing that it would be just another couple of weeks, and now the weeks had dragged into months. In June, Presentaciones had written to Margolis, who happened to be the company's legal counsel in the States. The company was concerned that Millard might sue. Before doing any more work, they asked that Margolis prepare an international hold-harmless indemnification agreement, protecting them from any potential claims: "... you can appreciate that certain steps have already been taken and that we at Presentaciones Musicales, S.A., are somewhat concerned as to what potential liability might obtain with any altering of the so-called original arrangement. . . ."

Putting IMS back together again was not proving easy. Millard had hired a lawyer to send his company to Panama, and now it seemed that the Panamanian company was asking Millard's former lawyer to protect them from the legal claims of his former client. No one, not even Presentaciones in Panama, seemed sure of what "certain steps" had really happened. Kojnok thought Presentaciones was concerned it might be liable for "the agreement for sale of assets, the licensing agreements, and some other agreements," but the paralegal was unsure of just where IMS and its obligations lay.

In August of 1977, with the September tax-consolidation deadline fast approaching, Millard had decided that he could wait no longer; he transferred and endorsed the Computer Shack stock to IMS and backdated it to October 29, 1976. One other critical piece of backdating was accomplished. Added to the October 12, 1976, $10,000 promissory note to IMS, one of the loans used to fund Computer Shack, was a note made in Millard's own handwriting, "paid in full 10-29-76."

The Internal Revenue Service was not told that the documents were backdated or that, in fact, at the time of both events Millard had been thousands of miles away on his "around-the-world" trip. Millard's companies would qualify for consolidated tax savings. He was only doing what his lawyers and accountants told him was appropriate. "My understanding from the accountants was that it was appropriate from the date of intention to form a holding company," Millard said later. Intention was apparently what the game was all about.

Millard couldn't have been more right. Just by changing the dates to what his true intention had been all along, he would reap enormous tax savings. By filing the consolidated return, ComputerLand's $169,000 loss saved IMSAI, and Millard, more than $86,600 in taxes. Millard didn't even make IMSAI pay ComputerLand back for the huge tax savings.

The puzzling thing was that until October 13, 1977, Kojnok was still the sole director of IMS, and the officers were his secretary, Mrs.

Felch, and Mr. Dunnett. On that autumn day the officers of the corporation submitted their written resignations. Six days later, Kojnok removed himself as sole director.

Philip Reed knew little about the elaborate backdating, or the strange corporate reorganizations emanating from the paralegal, his secretary, and an attorney. Reed had continued his occasional visits to IMSAI, but as he remembered it, Millard seldom disclosed more than the surface of operations in their infrequent meetings. They were really just keeping their friendship up to date. Reed didn't remember any formal review of IMSAI's performance. More often, Millard would proudly show Reed how much progress had been made on the company's latest exciting prototype. Management and other more pressing issues, Reed said, were rarely discussed.

Reed knew of his father's preparations to sue Millard. Where did his allegiance lie: to his father or to his friend? He struggled with the problem in his diary:

Has Bill willfully withheld [financial] statement?
Has he done it for a reason?
Reason to serve Bill? Assist Dad?
Does he expect to win?

Reed, however, was not completely alone. He had other sources of information within IMSAI besides Millard. Before Walker left IMSAI, Reed often spoke with him about Walker's concern for IMSAI's troubles. As Reed's communications with Millard drifted from the realities of the company, Walker had become his lifeline.

In late 1977, ComputerLand, as far as Reed could see, was starting to take off. After Walker had left IMSAI and given up the trucking business, Reed offered him a job at his new company in Las Cruces. In December, Loring Reed, Philip Reed, and Walker all met at the company's offices. Walker got to thinking. He knew that Loring Reed wanted out. Why not join forces with his son, take out an option to purchase the Marriner note, and then make an offer to Millard to convert the note? That way they could become more directly involved with IMSAI and save the company.

There would be no trouble getting Loring Reed's approval. "It [the note] was available," said Loring Reed. His son's proposed partnership with Walker made perfect sense to Loring Reed. Capital from Philip Reed's Auto Power had essentially paid for IMSAI's product development. Walker had worked for Millard and was instrumental in the success of the company. No two men were more deserving or better qualified to come back in and straighten the place out.

Walker knew that "Loring was really unhappy with Bill and couldn't work with him, wanted out, and offered to sell the note back to Bill." Walker had the money to buy the entire note, but he wasn't willing to take that risk, "so I proposed the idea to Phil. I would need him. He had the expertise and management and financial circles." Reed also thought Walker wanted him as a partner because they were both friends of Millard's. Together their chances of persuading Millard would be better.

Walker figured they would spend $10,000 for an option, improve the company, attract financiers interested in the 20-percent stock provision, buy the note, and then turn around and sell it to the financiers for a profit. He was optimistic about enlisting Millard's cooperation: "Bill's going to say, 'I'll work with you guys. I'll give you the financial data! Let's cooperate! We'll go find some more money and expand the company!'" Walker was looking for a plan that would benefit everybody. He did not want to own the company or control Millard. "I would be as happy as a clam to help it grow, make some money, have him buy the stock back—all twenty percent—and we'd get out with a nice profit." Walker figured his $10,000 investment would give him an opportunity to make a tenfold return.

Walker and Reed made notes about which approach might work best with Millard. One plan was to sue Millard if he declined to work with them. Walker quickly decided that was unworkable. But if it came down to it, Walker realized that a different sort of hostile takeover was possible.

Earlier in 1977, when he was still working for IMSAI, Walker had received a call one evening from Pat Millard. Destroying her husband's prized porcelain eagle had only temporarily appeased her anger. Pat Millard had come over to his San Francisco apartment, Walker said, in the hopes of getting Bill's affair off her chest and breaking out of her depression. "She was bitter and said, 'That son of a bitch!'"

Walker knew that the couple's newfound friction was an opportunity. He had even talked with Philip Reed about the possibility that

"Phil should go to Pat and try to get her to vote her 40 percent." Combined with their 20 percent, it would give a 60 percent controlling interest in the company. "At that time we knew that Pat was hostile . . . that Loring and Pat could gain control of the company." It was obvious to Walker that Pat would have been open to any kind of idea. "Bill and Pat were almost divorced in 1977," Walker recalled. Back in August, Philip Reed himself had perfunctorily written in his diary, "Pat getting a divorce. Smashed eagle."

On December 8, 1977, Loring Reed offered his son and Walker a $10,000 option to purchase the note for $500,000—double its initial price—until June 15, 1978. If they couldn't find a buyer by June, Reed also offered them a further $10,000 option good until December 1978.

Walker paid Marriner $10,000 for the option. Immediately after they received the option, Philip Reed and Walker went to talk to Millard. "There wasn't a lot of time that elapsed," Reed remembered. "Marvin Walker began to feel like something had to be done pretty quickly."

Both men seemed willing to leave Millard with ComputerLand, though the Marriner note would have entitled them to all of his companies. IMSAI was what they wanted. Reed was willing to do whatever he could to put the manufacturing company back together again. IMSAI was paying him $8,903 a month on the Auto Power deal. Walker had no such motive. In his words, ComputerLand was "small but growing rapidly," while IMSAI was "floundering but salvageable."

Before they bought the option, Philip Reed and Walker had made a pact. If Millard was not receptive to their taking a position in the company and attempting to get some outside financing to turn things around, they would not exercise the option. There may have been another reason for not exercising the option without Millard's approval. "There was a lot of discussion about whether Millard felt the note *was* convertible," Reed recalled.

That question and others would remain unanswered. Millard saw other-than-peaceful motives in Reed and Walker's secret partnership. Walker was surprised at how reserved and wary his old friend appeared. "Millard viewed it as an encroachment on his territory, a back-stabbing move," Reed remembered. "It wasn't a matter of him saying anything," Walker recalled. "He was totally impassive. He just didn't say much." It seemed as though Millard viewed his old friends as outside investors. As they had previously agreed, the two quickly retreated when Millard proved uncooperative.

Millard had an entirely different view of the true intention of Reed and Walker's proposed purchase of the note. On December 19, 1977, he wrote in his diary: "Phil Reed + M. Walker have acquired the note. They want to sell. Don't want to get involved in the company. Want to sell in 6 months. If I will help sell, then ComputerLand revert to WHM [William H. Millard]."

All in all, the Philip Reed/Marvin Walker option seemed a lot of time and energy wasted. The option was not exercised, and Walker was out $10,000. Philip Reed, however, had learned something for nothing.

11

The

Revolving

Door

It seemed that all of IMSAI's good people went to ComputerLand. It wasn't just Ed Faber, although that was bad enough. When Faber finally left IMSAI in December of 1976, many of his former employees cried. People were upset because they felt that nobody could ever replace him, and they were right.

Faber quickly hired Richard Desman, the crack purchaser who had brought tough negotiating to IMSAI's dealings with suppliers and vendors. Also hired in ComputerLand's first couple of months were top salespeople. On April Fools' Day, 1977, Abb Abley and Marian Murphy were hired away from IMSAI. The migration to Computer-Land was clear. "We figured—this is a terrible thing to say—that everybody who was really any good had gone, had deserted us [IMSAI]," recalled Dorothea Tichenor, an IMSAI employee who under different circumstances would one day also receive her paychecks from ComputerLand.

ComputerLand's first year, 1977, was rocky. Soon after John Martin departed, the company seemed to lose momentum. Perhaps Martin had been right; perhaps it had not been the time to raise prices. Inquiries for franchises dried up. But Faber was not the sort to panic. At a time when another man might have accepted anybody's money, he boldly turned away a few franchisees not up to his standards. Still, he began running ads in trade publications and even the *Wall Street Journal*. Some seemed to border on the desperate. Read one ad: "Man with an idea. Call Ed Faber." That September, ComputerLand would report a first-year loss of $169,000.

But no matter how slow things got, Faber never pressured the sales team to close a deal. It was important to Faber that potential franchisees be right for ComputerLand. Faber met every potential franchisee, and he tried to meet their wives. He wanted to make sure that the couples understood the depth of commitment they were undertaking. He always made it clear to the wives that they would not be seeing much of their husbands, and that success was not right around the corner.

One of the early franchisees hadn't warned his wife about the promising new business venture into which he had just sunk their savings. When he gleefully returned home, less several thousand dollars, his wife raised hell. Once Faber got word that there was family trouble, he would have none of it. Martin and Abley took the next flight to Arizona and gave the man his money back.*

During those early, lean times, Faber held special meetings. The whole company, fifteen people or so, squeezed into the president's office. Faber would tell them the facts, no matter how bare and dreary they might have been. He also told them that he kept close to two months' salary in reserve, just in case. People were concerned but not worried. Faber told the truth. They knew they could count on him.

But there were some things that Faber didn't tell everybody. "Occasionally there was, like, I guess, an advance from IMSAI that would keep us going a little bit longer until something else would pick up and go," remembered Laurie Marsh, another former IMSAI employee, then in charge of ComputerLand's accounts payable. Marsh remembered slow months when they had to rely on IMSAI to come through with the money to keep the doors open. Since it appeared to Marsh that IMSAI was father to ComputerLand, it all made perfect sense. "They [IMSAI] were our parent company, so as far as what they would receive; they just gave out in the beginning." IMSAI gave ComputerLand $10,000 on about half a dozen occasions, Marsh re-

---

*Martin, who had sold the franchise, protested the return of the money on the grounds that it was a simple case of "buyer's remorse."

called. Later on, the money between the two companies was handled differently. "It was more like an investment," Marsh said. "We were no longer a drain on the other company. Now we were supporting ourselves."

There was magic in ComputerLand. Started on just Millard's $10,000 personal investment, losing $169,000 in its maiden year, the fledgling company required no venture capital or bank loans to get off the ground.*

There were, of course, certain things ComputerLand had received from IMSAI: office space, personnel, administration costs, photocopying, mailing. But Millard made sure everything between the two companies was "clean and appropriate." On July 14, 1976, two months before he had even formed ComputerLand (then Computer Shack), and only a week after John Martin's first visit with Millard, there was said to have been a meeting of the directors of IMS. According to the documents, Millard passed a resolution, declaring that Computer Shack would repay twice the value of whatever services or equipment it would receive from IMS.† Later, as the debt accumulated, Computer Shack signed promissory notes, pledging to pay the sum, plus 8 percent interest, on demand, or by 1987. "Everything was clean and appropriate," Millard said.

Money was not all that ComputerLand received from IMSAI. There were benefits in having employees who had worked at IMSAI. Many former IMSAI employees still lunched with their old coworkers and often met them for drinks at the favorite watering hole, the Rare Steer.

Soon after ComputerLand was incorporated, IMSAI faced a series of emergencies. Meetings would be called, and IMSAI's top management would disappear for a few hours. Inevitably, when they surfaced, the emergency was ComputerLand. "They would say, 'We need this!' And they would hand out the paperwork for the orders and people would go and pull them, and ComputerLand would come out on top," recalled Nancy Fischer, who worked in IMSAI's purchasing department.

---

*Another $10,000 was a "loan" from Millard.
†That this unusual resolution could have been raised at such an early date, two months before the incorporation of Computer Shack, was questioned in a later trial. Strangely, the resolution requiring double payback was rescinded in 1977.

While IMSAI employees in shipping and inventory were often infuriated by these sudden requests, they found it hard to refuse a friend. They had trouble turning down a former IMSAI man like Abb Abley. Sometimes Abley would call customer service and sometimes he would call inventory, but no matter whom he called he nearly always got the equipment ComputerLand needed. "He'd call inventory," Nancy Fischer remembered. "Julie [Banuelos] would come over and she'd go, 'Hi, Nancy, I need this favor.' And I'd say, 'Okay, who do you need it for?' And she'd say, 'I need it for Abb.'"

If ComputerLand had an insurmountable problem in early 1977, it was that IMSAI computers were still one of the main products it sold. By 1977, IMSAI computers were no longer the leaders in technology. Complaints abounded in industry magazines about the machine's lack of software, and the product line became increasingly difficult to sell. Variations of the IMSAI 8080 were developed with disk drives and the latest five-inch screens, but the basic machine had changed little. It was still based on "old" technology, one step removed from hobbyists and techies.

But not far from San Francisco, change was stirring. In Silicon Valley, from Palo Alto to San Jose, newer technology and ideas were spreading the "silicon dream" beyond the techies. A few years earlier, a guy named "Woz" met a kid named Jobs. Stephen Wozniak wanted nothing more than to make computers. Steve Jobs liked computers, too, but he was also interested in money and success.

Wozniak regularly attended meetings of the Homebrew Computer Club in the garage of a man named French. Many of the members would bring Altair computers to the meetings. Wozniak was fascinated, but he couldn't afford an Altair.

When MOS Technology advertised its new 6502 microprocessor chip for $20 at the 1976 Wescon Computer Show in San Francisco, Wozniak snapped up the bargain chip. He spent the next few weeks writing a BASIC programming language for the microprocessor. Then he designed a board with the chip, complete with interfaces to connect it to a monitor and keyboard. Like a good computer hobbyist, Wozniak shared photocopies of his design with Homebrew members so they could imitate it. Wozniak called the makeshift computer an "Apple."

Jobs suggested that they start a company, but Wozniak wasn't eager to turn his hobby into work. He already had a full-time job at Hewlett-Packard. Even so, barefoot, long hair and all, Jobs could be convincing. Soon, Wozniak sold his two HP calculators, Jobs hawked his VW, and they "capitalized" their business with the money.

Jobs took the first Apple around to various manufacturers to see if they'd be willing to build more of the contraption. He arrived at IMSAI one day with the Apple in an aluminum suitcase. Killian and Van Natta were fascinated by the machine within the makeshift case. As far as they could see, the design was special and exciting. Jobs was wondering whether they would like to make a deal. After talking it over with Millard, though, they decided that they had their hands full and sent the hirsute young man on his way.

Jobs was not discouraged. By late 1976, Wozniak was well on his way to creating the second Apple, christened the Apple II. The new machine was much more self-contained. It was a complete computer on a single board, with a keyboard, power supply, the BASIC language and graphics capabilities.

Blessed by what appeared to be a commercial product, Jobs figured that all they needed was some professional advice and capital. He went to see Nolan Bushnell, the founder of Atari, who introduced him to Don Valentine, a successful Silicon Valley venture capitalist. Valentine suggested that Jobs speak to Mike Markkula, a retired Intel executive.

In October 1976, Markkula visited Jobs's garage. A few months later Markkula plunked down $91,000, which he decided was worth a one-third stock interest in the new company. He helped Jobs write a business plan, obtained a line of credit for the company at the Bank of America, and hired the company's first president, Mike Scott, a former executive who had worked for Markkula in product marketing at Fairchild. They now had product, money, credit, and management expertise. Jobs set out to grab the last spicy, secret ingredient—publicity.

Regis McKenna had little in common with the aggressive young man in cutoffs, sandals, and scraggly beard who showed up in his polished public relations office. McKenna was used to a different breed of clientele, as his marketing savvy played a large role in the success of Intel and National Semiconductor. Thus it was not surprising that his visitor's far-out proposal, like hundreds before it, was rejected. But Jobs came back anyway, eventually convincing McKenna to join forces with Apple. By attracting one of the best high-tech public-relations firms in Silicon Valley, Jobs had completed his team.

McKenna promptly ordered the design of a multicolored picture of an apple for the company logo. Then he placed an ad in *Playboy*, a tactic never before attempted by a computer maker. But the bold strike worked. National publications, not just computer magazines, began writing about the Apple and the phenomenon known as the personal computer.

The Apple II and the Commodore PET were both officially introduced at the West Coast Computer Faire in April 1977. The Apple II was unveiled in a large, well-designed booth manned by Jobs, Mike Scott, and other Apple executives. The Commodore PET sat on what looked like a fold-up card-table.

Richard Desman and Mike McConnell went to the show to find new products for ComputerLand's forty franchisees. (ComputerLand had already struck a good deal with Apple and had advertising plans that would link the two companies.) At the fair, the Commodore PET was being sold by a man named Peddle. And although he was brilliant, having designed the 6502 microprocessor and the PET, he lacked slick selling skills. Peddle and his company, like many others, were trying to finance the company with deposits. Credit was not possible. In addition, Commodore's margins were only 20 to 25 percent, compared to Apple's 40 percent. ComputerLand was not very interested that day.*

The Apple II blossomed in ComputerLand. In the late 1970s, Apple Computers and ComputerLand became virtually synonymous. The Apple II was the first computer that didn't look like a computer. With its built-in keyboard and beige coloring, the machine appeared nonthreatening and decidedly low-tech. Apple and ComputerLand were a perfect couple: the uncomputer and the uncomputer store.

But it wasn't just Apple that made ComputerLand the place to buy a computer. ComputerLand decided that the best strategy was to let

---

*Commodore computers were sold at ComputerLand stores, but they never attained the success of Apple.

the customer choose. While many customers chose Apple, they could select virtually any microcomputer made. Franchisees sold computers from IMSAI, Polymorphic, Proc Tech, Southwest Tech, Dynabyte, Hazeltine, Cromemco, Commodore, Texas Instruments, and practically any other brand a customer might request. If somebody made it, you could bet that a ComputerLand store somewhere sold it.

Other stores tried to make the decisions for the customer. Xerox sold Xerox computers. Radio Shack sold Radio Shack computers. The Computer Store sold MITS Altair. "A lot were all one-product [stores]," said Ken Waters, an early ComputerLand executive. "We got a reputation that once it [a new product] was out, we would quickly put it on the parts list."

By March of 1978, ComputerLand seemed to be making headway. Sales of the Apple II were picking up steam. Nothing could stop them now, not even the memory of John Martin. Although he had been gone almost a year, Martin's sudden departure had left many ComputerLand employees uneasy. Few considered it coincidence that, other than Millard and Faber, Martin was the only man who had stock in ComputerLand. Millard's reluctance to give equity in his companies was legend. Stories of the abandoned stock-option plan at IMSAI had filtered over to the offices of ComputerLand. To many, the reason for Martin's quick exit was patently clear.

Chris Lundberg, Sugu Aria, and Richard Desman certainly didn't consider it coincidence. On the first Monday in March of 1978, soon to be known as "Black Monday," the three men, constituting all of Faber's top executives, quit. Desman, who had been in charge of division operations, left to join Phil Reed's new company, Energy Technology. Lundberg and Sugu Aria went to the main competition, Byte Shop.

Byte Shop appeared to have every advantage over ComputerLand. They had fifty stores, better distribution, and the same products. But there was one element they lacked—Ed Faber. In a few months they faded into the background like every other erstwhile competitor.

Not once did ComputerLand stumble. In the face of beefed-up competition that March of 1978, they prepared for growth and expansion, moving from the Republic Street building into a larger facility on Catalina Street.

Soon after "Black Monday," a writer for *Fortune* magazine called on ComputerLand. His editor wanted a "who's who" story on computer manufacturers. Midway through the interview, Faber turned off the writer's tape recorder and told him what was really going on. Impressed by Faber's candid discussion of the industry, the writer scrapped his planned story. He had stumbled onto a new phenomenon.

Under the headline "The Computer Stores Have Arrived," the article in the April 24, 1978, issue of *Fortune* read in part: "Sandwiched between a liquor store and a bar at the edge of San Francisco's financial district is a new business phenomenon: a computer store. ComputerLand is one of forty stores in a fast-growing chain. . . ." The article, complete with a picture of the San Francisco store and Faber, said ComputerLand took in $875,000 in franchise fees and $500,000 in royalties in 1977, its first year.

When the article hit the magazine stands, the phones started ringing. Prior to the article, ComputerLand had averaged only three inquiries from potential franchisees a week. Now, upwards of ten a day called. Reprints of the article were made and included in franchisee materials.

A new breed of callers began contacting ComputerLand. Businessmen and salesmen read *Fortune*. Before, the only people interested in ComputerLand franchises had generally been techies and hobbyists who loved the machines more than the money they might one day reap. The new group was different. Some were just pure salesmen who knew a good thing when it came along.

Bruce Burdick had been selling worms for years in Sioux City, Iowa. He sold people worm farms along with the directions on how to raise them. Then he would buy back the worms and sell a worm farm to the next guy. He had been told that if you could raise enough worms, they could eat garbage and create worm castles or fertilizer, but somehow that never seemed to happen. Eventually, the government claimed there was no use for worms. Burdick had to find a new way to make a buck.

Flying back from a convention in Dallas, Burdick read the *Fortune* article. Maybe these microcomputers *are* the next worm farms, thought Burdick. When he showed up at ComputerLand with gold jewelry almost dripping off him and an ample belly protruding over his belt, Faber wanted to know what made him think he could sell computers. "My job is selling," Burdick said. Before worms he had sold insurance and encyclopedias, among other things. "I don't need to know the technical details. If I could sell worms, I'll be able to sell computers." Sioux City was too small to support a ComputerLand store, so Burdick was given the choice between Kansas City and Des Moines. The worm farmer moved to Kansas City. In the spring of 1979, he would boast the first $200,000 month for a franchisee and would soon own more stores than any other man in the chain.

Tom Niccoli represented the other breed of franchisee. The young IBM systems engineer was tired of the corporate labyrinth. He too had read the *Fortune* article and promptly flew from Arizona to see Faber. By the end of the day, Niccoli had Faber convinced that he had installed enough large IBM computers in Phoenix, Tucson, and Las Vegas to be able to handle all three territories for ComputerLand. What Niccoli couldn't handle was the $2,000 deposit for the first store in Phoenix. After talking to several people about the deal, he ran into Tom Beckis, an IBM salesman with an accounting and business background, something Niccoli lacked. Beckis put up the money, and the two partners opened their Phoenix store in January 1979. They would lead the network that year with $870,000 in sales. Stores in Tucson and Las Vegas followed, and Niccoli and Beckis would soon be the most powerful combination in the whole chain.

Whatever outward differences the new franchisees may have had, they all held one basic quality in common—they sold. Whether they had sold big computers or little worms was not important. The new breed was looking for something fresh, and it wasn't a nine-to-five-suit-and-tie future. They were in business for themselves, and for them the heart and soul was selling.

Millard hadn't forgotten the lesson he had learned at IMSAI. An increase in demand meant it was time to raise the ante. Millard liked formulas, and he had created one for the buy-in franchise fee. The fee, he said, would be based on 5 percent of average yearly retail sales. The fee went up to $25,000. To Faber's delight, customers kept buying franchises.

ComputerLand held on for the ride. As the pace quickened, ComputerLand employees became more efficient and effective. Time wasn't wasted because they didn't have any to waste. Communication was crisp. On the surface, ComputerLand was another IMSAI. The energy and enthusiasm were the same, for a time even the building was the same, and of course, the owner was the same. But there was a subtle difference. Little things were done differently. "When the bill comes in, pay the damn thing!" Abley remembered Faber saying. It didn't matter who it was, or how small the amount, Faber was determined that ComputerLand's reputation would be clean.

"I made sure people were paid on a timely basis," said Marsh of accounts payables. "In the beginning everything was very much cash on delivery; all of our vendors were cash on delivery." All of the vendors except, of course, one; IMSAI gave them ninety days or more to pay. Bills over ninety days often turned into promissory notes. ComputerLand's good habits paid off. Several months of promptly paid bills convinced computer makers that ComputerLand was a reliable customer. Soon companies started extending ComputerLand credit.

As the summer of 1978 drew to an end, Faber decided they had earned a celebration. September 21 would be ComputerLand's second birthday. Someone discovered that the *Guinness Book of World Records* had a listing for the most people to ever attend a birthday party. If every one of ComputerLand's fifty-two franchisees in every corner of the world held a party that day, maybe they could eclipse the magic number. Sheets were sent out to every store for customers to sign as party guests. ComputerLand telexed the stores to log the totals. Stores telexed ComputerLand. The Austin, Texas, franchise had a barbecue in the parking lot. Sorick remembered calling Bob McGuffie in New Hampshire and being told that he had sixty-seven people in his store. When she told his archrival Ken Greene of New Jersey that McGuffie was drawing a bigger crowd, Greene joked to Sorick, "Yeah, but he counted all the dogs and cats!"

The franchisees didn't break the record, but they were loose and happy and also happened to be selling a lot of computers. The whole network seemed to take a deep breath. Sales that had only reached $500,000 the first year were pushing $10 million for 1978. More than just a two-year anniversary, they were celebrating a coming of age, and they knew the wave they rode was far from its peak. Perhaps some also sensed that Apple's magic had only just begun.

Those who could see just one year into the future could picture the outline of that second revolution in microcomputing—the electronic spreadsheet, software that would bring magical manipulations of

equations and formulas down to the touch of a key. When Personal
Software introduced VisiCalc the next year, the success of Apple and
ComputerLand's marriage was guaranteed. The first, full spreadsheet
program, ideal for small businesses and a reason in itself to buy a
microcomputer, ran on only one machine, the Apple II. In the third
quarter of 1978, the first full year that the Apple II had been on the
market, ComputerLand overcame its debt and was running in the
black.

12
The
Switch

Millard brought it back with him from one of his Luxembourg trips. The large, aluminum enclosure had originally been designed to house computer terminals. But that didn't bother him. He excitedly told his staff that they were to design an *entire* computer to fit inside the aluminum box.

The engineers had a hard time keeping straight faces. Millard was proposing that they violate a basic engineering principle. How could he declare the solution without first analyzing the problem? Forcing a computer inside an existing box was like trying to cram a Formula race-car engine inside a go-cart.

Killian was the first to note the mounting posts in the box. Beyond the difficulty of getting everything to fit in the odd-shaped enclosure, he anticipated cooling problems. Killian and the other engineers suggested that they redesign the base. It wouldn't be difficult or expensive, and by doing so, Killian thought they could "get rid of some of this metal that's hanging up in the middle of the box."

But Millard's belief in the aluminum enclosure as the ideal home for his new computer was unshakable. Not even the unanimous protests of IMSAI's engineers could dampen his enthusiasm. A European friend had offered him a special deal on the boxes, and Millard was not about to pass up a bargain. It would be just the product IMSAI

needed: a professional business computer with the right "look" to justify a high price tag. In fact, Millard was partly right. In a few years
the "all-in-one computer" would be the industry standard.

The engineering department managed to ignore Millard's exhorta-
tions for a time. "That box had been sitting in the corner for two or
three months," recalled Killian, "before they [Millard and his execu-
tives] finally laid down the law and said, 'You will put our stuff in that
box.'"

Dennis Holeman was placed in charge of the newly named
VDP-80 project. Holeman was not optimistic, but his protests, like
those of Killian and the rest of engineering, went unheeded. Millard
knew they needed a hit—and fast. If they could just pop a machine
in the box in a few months, Millard thought they could stay ahead of
the competition.

Millard's managers agreed with him, but that was no surprise. Millard liked to be surrounded by agreement. And those he found particularly agreeable he promoted. Holeman had aspired to become the
manager of the engineering department, but Holeman was not very
good at "agreement." Holeman was a natural scientist who began any
project by analyzing the obstacles. When they appeared insurmountable, he was not afraid to plot another course.

But Millard considered Holeman meek and negative. In short, he
didn't have the IMSAI spirit. Millard passed over Holeman and put a
woman, Jan Vath, in charge of engineering. Vath had previously
worked in the sales department; she had no engineering knowledge or
expertise. But she had taken the training and believed. She knew
there were no problems and that miracles were always around the
corner. "Jan Vath was extremely est, right up there with Millard,"
Todd Fischer recalled. "Whatever Millard wanted, Jan Vath would
move heaven and earth to accomplish."

Vath used the same language as Millard. She often said "I got it!" to
her boss. Non-est employees understood this to mean, "I fully understand, comprehend, and will comply with what you want." Whenever
difficult situations would arise, however, Vath would employ the est
expression "Handle it!" to delegate authority. Unwanted jobs were
begrudgingly accepted with the phrase "I own it!" Generally, "ownership" came about because somebody forced you into "owning" a
problem. Ownership did not come lightly. It was not that different

from a high-interest loan—the creditor never forgot that the loan was escalating.

Vath was only one in a series of managers who fit into Millard's vision for IMSAI. Joe Parziale was another. He said "Handle it!" with particular authority. Parziale was one of the few financial officers at IMSAI who lasted more than a few months. He knew who was boss, and so he followed orders to the letter. From his bell-bottomed pants to his polyester leisure shirts, Parziale "was Italian, a chauvinist, a hard man who drove people," remembered Dorothea Tichenor, who worked under him. He was also a man who did not like to be questioned. More than most, Parziale understood that Millard did not like bad news.

John Carter Scott filled out the new management team. John had a big heart and a white cowboy hat. Scott's wife, Cherie, had been the head of Motivational Management, an est-related company. Carter was not Scott's real middle name. Cherie had previously been married to the brother of Landon Carter, who was a trusted member of the inner circle of the est organization. Not only did Cherie keep her ex-husband's last name after divorce, but her new husband adopted it as his. Cherie was one of Millard's closest friends. Perhaps that explained the shiny black Corvette that Millard cosigned for John Carter Scott when he joined IMSAI.

Scott was handsome, gregarious, and had a way with people that made them overlook his shortcomings. "One day he jumped up on my filing cabinet, spun around, and said, 'Hi! I'm John Carter Scott,'" recalled Tichenor. "It was a very charming picture. I'm not sure he had any [job] qualifications at all." Scott's flair extended to fashion. In later years, when he was still working for Millard at ComputerLand, Scott would sometimes sport a green, one-piece jumpsuit.

Van Natta thought Scott had a talent for stretching reality, and he seldom believed Scott's wild tales, but it really was true that the slender, sensitive Scott had once played for the Dallas Cowboys. Scott's surprising gentleness made him a favorite. He was not an authoritarian like Parziale or a heavy estian like Vath. Scott was sensitive to the feelings and problems of others. Those were his main qualifications, and one day he confided to his friends in production that his ambition was to be nothing short of president of the company.

After a few months, the VDP-80 project seemed stalled. Killian had been right about the mounting posts. Holeman had designed some complicated sheet-metal pieces and adapted power supplies to fit in the odd-shaped cabinet. He had done his best, but the box was just too tight. It got too hot in there, and the posts seemed to cause interference between the disk drives.

Van Natta knew the real reason why the project was going awry. No longer were he and Millard and Killian still having weekly meetings. Then Killian would have designed the computer, Van Natta would have consulted in the design, and it would have been an outrageous success.

But those days were behind him forever. After years of badgering from Millard and others at IMSAI, Van Natta had agreed to take the est training. It was not a decision taken lightly. His wife had told him that she would leave him if he became "one of them." The bimonthly company newsletter *IMSIGH* trumpeted Van Natta's graduation along with that of several other employees in an item entitled "New Esties at IMSAI."

The two weekends and two Wednesday night sessions had a visible effect on Van Natta. The skinny, frequently unshaven, not always well-washed, rather nerdy guy emerged a man. Van Natta seemed to have grown taller and put some meat on his bones. He had his hair styled and took to wearing fancy suits. Like all "graduates," he became infatuated with the language of est.

His wife was not surprised by the changes and she made good on her threat. Van Natta moved out of their home and spent the next couple of weeks sleeping on the floor at work. At first it was difficult for Van Natta's wife, but for her anything was better than having to spend a life with "one of them." For Bruce, the separation and divorce were almost welcome. He soon felt an attraction to Mary Malnerich, a perfect graduate, who worked in IMSAI's sales department. Bruce and Mary were married in November 1977. Being married, however, was not enough. Bruce discovered he wanted to be near Mary all the time. On January 1, 1978, Bruce Van Natta, one of IMSAI's founders, asked to be a salesman.

The sales department had learned from Millard that goals were what "it" was all about. There were monthly goals, weekly goals, daily goals. The mood was of a team fighting for a championship. Ingenious methods were devised to motivate the sales team.

Millard gave plenty of examples to follow. He would call marathon sales meetings to browbeat employees into surpassing their goals. Cards were written up with obscenities and passed out to the sales staff. It was all part of the training, a method designed to strip away fears and inhibitions. The cards said things like "Fuck you!" The technique was not much different from a football player bashing his teammate on the helmet to pump him up for the game. The ringing in his ears would make him that much more inclined to bash somebody else's head in. Anger was a tool to be used.

The marketing promotion for the VDP-80 was greater than anything IMSAI had ever attempted. Glossy color ads had been placed not only in *Popular Electronics* but also in an airline magazine. They were playing to a new, more sophisticated clientele, one that would be more than willing to pay several thousand dollars for a computer, and one that would propel IMSAI beyond its hobbyist roots. Tens of thousands of advertising dollars had already been spent. The computer industry was hungry for the new business machine IMSAI promised was ready to ship. The sales department was hungry, too. It was getting tough to sell obsolete machines. Sales of the IMSAI 8080 were sinking. They needed a new machine to meet their monthly goals. "You have to get a new product on the street!" Killian remembered Millard announcing.

By August of 1977, Millard ordered the VDP-80 to be included in that month's price list. Holeman, however, would not budge. The computer was not ready to go out. The VDP-80 had Persyst disk drives, the latest in high-speed storage. Temperamental as Porsches, the drives' quirks were a mystery even to the factory that made them. Killian saw other problems. The machine he examined was essentially a prototype, needing months of testing to eliminate bugs.

In late 1977 Millard called a meeting of his vice presidents and senior engineers. He began at one end of the table asking if the machine was ready to ship. The engineers said no. When the circle was complete, everyone in the room had followed engineering's recommendation for more design and testing, everyone, that is, except Millard. They were to ship the computer anyway. They knew how to manufacture. They knew how to produce. "Get to it!" Millard ordered. Joe Parziale followed with orders to ship. The engineers knew that Parziale was not really making the decision. Behind Parziale were Millard and the sales department.

Fred "Chip" Poode was one of the most professional salesmen on the staff. Despite his nickname, earned from opening the first chocolate chip cookie store in San Francisco, Poode had a solid background in computer sales. He had been a top salesman at IBM and marketing manager of a software firm. But professional success had not been enough. In 1973 he came to California, like thousands of others in the late 1960s and early 1970s, hoping to find himself.

After arriving in the Bay Area, Poode went to several human-potential discussion groups and seminars. Est was just another movement to be explored. But the San Francisco seminar turned out to be the "most significant experience" in his life. Poode "got" more insights about what made him tick and "got" clearer about his purpose. He understood what the est trainers meant when they talked about "being responsible for your life."

Poode looked forward to each day's work at IMSAI. The optimism in the sales room was contagious. Someone would walk in and say, "Let's go for a hundred-thousand-dollar day!" and though they had never before approached the mark, by five P.M. they would inch toward the number. "Miracles would happen," Poode recalled, "and happen enough so that you got to believe in it."

Poode was annoyed that the employees in production were not est graduates. Often he'd walk over to production to check on the status of one of his larger customer's orders. "Yeah, yeah, we'll get them out," the production workers would gruffly reply. But that wasn't good enough. Poode would ask them if he could have their agreement on that. "Oh, don't give me that esty stuff!" they would shout back. Poode couldn't understand their hostility. He was just trying to clarify an agreement.

Communication was so much easier with another grad; you didn't have to waste time. Graduates understood that Poode was just making sure somebody was making a commitment. Too often the people in production would say, "I'll try." Poode knew what that meant. "Try" was the word that people used *after* they'd failed, after they'd hit a long foul ball and then struck out on the next pitch. Poode wasn't asking for anything unreasonable. He could understand it when an unforeseen event made it impossible to meet an agreement. They would simply make a new agreement. But Poode hated to start a relationship with an agreement based on failure.

Production employees understood how the game really worked. They were supposed to work from six A.M. to eight P.M., "busting their butts" to meet agreements the order-takers stuffed down their throats while they merrily cheered the latest sales record. New, more unreasonable demands, however, were not all that production workers heard; there was something else they noticed about the esties. When someone in sales could not meet their half of an "agreement," they avoided the problem. "Yes, I own it!" the salesperson would stubbornly reply when questioned. Those in production learned that it was hopeless to ask again or expect results. The job was forgotten, left unfiled somewhere.

The company's forum, *IMSIGH*, tried to fill the space that was splitting the company apart. Astrology, hangover cures, and stories on breathing were not the publication's only contribution to the IMSAI consciousness. *IMSIGH* encouraged letters on the est question. One outspoken detractor angrily called est a case of the "Emperor's New Clothes." Esties, she said, "justify being suckered by suckering others." In response, one of the esties wrote a lengthy dissertation, entitled "Estianese Communication," which concluded: "It is a lie that estianese has created a communication problem here at IMSAI. Get in touch with your own negativity."

Tichenor saw what was happening. It bothered her that many orders were taken but not fulfilled. The sales department had checked them onto their quota even though the order wasn't firm until it had passed accounting checkpoints. The company was not only losing money; customers were being forgotten. "For whatever reason, many of them [orders] were canceled in 1978," Tichenor recalled, implying that Jan Vath might have been responsible. But Vath left in early 1978, and the problems did not disappear.

In 1978, Wes Dehn was the new man in charge at IMSAI. Tichenor thought that since Dehn was close to Millard, maybe he could make a change; it was an optimistic thought. Ghost orders were one of the things that you weren't supposed to talk about. Before her conversation with Dehn, Tichenor remembered what her old boss had told her: "We don't want to bring to meetings anything that is negative. We only want to bring out those positive things that are happening." Perhaps Dehn was different and would be willing to listen. But Tichenor had been wrong to hope. Dehn had taken the training and now he, too, seemed changed. Tichenor noticed that he was more into physical contact. Now he patted people on the back or gave them a congratulatory kiss. She wondered whether he was sincere.

The odd thing was that while everybody made agreements and owned problems, disagreements were common and problems were ignored. Friction was heating up like the pistons of a dry engine, and troubles other than the battle between sales and production were brewing.

Many at IMSAI thought Rob Barnaby was temperamental, but he was just a software programmer, engrossed in his work. He could spend hours staring at the dull screen, making minute, painstaking changes in a program. He didn't like to be interrupted, and his temper was as sharp and coiled as the code he meticulously designed. Like most programmers, he worked best without the distraction of daylight.

By late 1977, the first VDP-80s were being shipped, but they still had plenty of problems. Barnaby's job was to make the CP/M operating system run on the new machine. Software was his life, and he couldn't resist tinkering. One night, watching the code flicker across his screen, he thought he saw an opportunity. In 1977 there wasn't a microcomputer word processor on the market. There was only crude editing software used by programmers to juggle strings of seemingly unintelligible letters and numbers. What about taking those primitive editors a step further? If they could edit the esoteric languages of computer programming, why not English?

The intense, excited young man presented his fantastic idea to Millard. Their conversation was brief. Millard had spent all the development money IMSAI could afford creating and marketing the VDP-80. Time could not be wasted on a secondary product called a "word processor." IMSAI needed to stay on track, charging straight ahead.

But rejection only reinforced Barnaby's will. He resented the IMSAI sales philosophy that tried to relegate programming to a production task. He considered himself an artist and he knew that he had stumbled upon the labor of a lifetime. He spent his 1977 Christmas vacation tapping away at home on the keyboard. The result was NED, short for New Editor. Despite the unimaginative name, the editor was a stupendous advance. IMSAI's programmers and engineers loved the innovative program, although NED was a long way from being a full-scale word processor.

To Millard, it was still just software. You couldn't charge thousands of dollars for something almost ephemeral. Barnaby was rejected again. This time he couldn't believe Millard's arrogance. Their voices rose. It was not to be an ordinary argument. Barnaby, known for his temper, had once heaved a huge daisy-wheel printer across a room. Millard, too, was not averse to showing anger. He had once told the gentle Killian to learn to use anger as a tool.

Barnaby fumed. He was upset that Millard didn't give a damn about software. Millard didn't use words, he used only programmed responses, Barnaby thought to himself as Millard degraded him with one est phrase after another. How was it that Millard always had the last word? Now he was closing his glass door in Barnaby's face. Not this time. "Fuck you!" Barnaby yelled through the glass. "I'm gone!"

Before Barnaby's run-in with Millard, Seymour Rubinstein, another key employee, had left IMSAI.* But Rubinstein had a "flaw." He had not taken est. When Millard insisted that he take the training, Rubinstein told him that he would do so only if Millard wrote a letter stipulating it as a requirement of his employment. Rubinstein later used Millard's letter to write off the $300 seminar on his taxes as a business expense.

Though Rubinstein was excited by the stir the VDP-80 marketing promotion was creating in the industry, he was bothered by what he had seen going on in sales. Strange things were happening in production, too. He no longer wanted to be a part of what the company was becoming.

The free-lunch policy was over. The official reason given was that IMSAI could no longer afford the expense. The truth was that morale had declined to the point where employees were stuffing cold cuts in their jackets to take home at night.

---

*The savvy director of marketing was offended when Millard asked him to perform what he considered a demeaning task—writing a data processing program—for the business end of IMSAI.

Rubinstein was eager to be gone. He had his own company to start, and he was about to hire his first employee, a programmer who happened to be a former IMSAI employee.

The troubles with the VDP-80 had not gone away. The engineers tried to fix the problems as though they were minor updates to a finished product, and not fundamental design flaws. A solution of sorts had been found. When a machine didn't pass quality control, or a part was lacking, they shipped it anyway. That way they "made" their sales goal.

Three-quarters of the first VDP-80 shipments were returned because they didn't work. Oddly enough, as more shipments came back, quality control and testing were cut. They needed to meet their shipping goal. Recalled Holeman: "If they found a problem—say it wouldn't test out—people would ship anyway just to meet the monthly production goal." It made a strange kind of sense. The unit would come back to customer service under the next month's quotas. No one would miss their goals. "You haven't got some of the parts, but it's next to the end of the month and you're going to miss your goal if you don't ship them," said Killian rhetorically. "[The] answer was to ship them."

Killian, however, knew the real reason why IMSAI sometimes shipped half-empty boxes to customers who had paid thousands of dollars. "Bill [Millard] cared about having the performance of his department look good on paper. Achieving the goal was all that mattered. If that meant shipping out half-empty boxes, well, 'Gee that's too bad; we're just going to do it.'"*

By agreement, Millard was right. In May of 1978, his cute, blond daughter, Barbara, dressed in cheerleader's garb, ran through shipping and sales, shaking pom-poms and cheering, "Rah, rah, rah. You can do it!" Sales were inching toward IMSAI's first $1-million month. The whole thing had started as a lark. Bruce Van Natta had asked his wife, Mary, what she wanted for her birthday. She knew that weeks before Millard had set a goal of $1 million for the month. "I want the goal," she told her husband. As Mary had told *IMSIGH*, "We startled

---

*In court testimony, Millard did not refute that IMSAI sometimes shipped boxes with missing parts or computers that didn't work.

ourselves, I think, at our capacity for producing miracles."

Two days remained before the end of the month. They were $320,000 short. Van Natta convinced IMSAI's biggest customer to place a ninety-day order instead of a thirty-day order. Still, at ten minutes before closing time on the final day they were $9,000 short. Could they stop now? Van Natta pleaded. No, his wife chastised him. It was the goal or nothing. Van Natta had called everybody he knew. There was one possible chance. He quickly dialed ComputerLand's number. A shipping clerk answered the call; everyone else had left for the day. Van Natta told the clerk the situation. Only he could save the day. If he would just accept $9,000 more of product. . . .

"A Cool Million" read the headline in *IMSIGH*. "A million dollars, but that's becoming routine," bragged Parziale, who promised to "handle" customer service the first week in July. In addition to effusive congratulations for the $1-million month, the newsletter featured an article against the anti-homosexual Briggs Initiative "as a personal favor to all the gay friends you have"; an announcement of a "trade mission to Japan"; a special IMSAI demonstration tour of Khartoum, Damascus, and Algiers; news of an IMSAI dealer in Cairo; biographies of two new employees—one whose "primary spare-time activity is est" and another whose real religion "is a universal one"; birthday announcements; and a wedding invitation stating that "the purpose of this occasion is to participate in the expression of relationship and commitment in the context of community and family." There was also a cartoon, a poem, and a two-line notice of the resignation of Dennis Holeman.

The newsletter did not mention what for Killian and Van Natta was perhaps the most fantastic news of the month. Millard was finally going to give them the stock he had promised in 1976. In late 1977, Joe and Bruce had asked again for their stock. Bill and Pat explained to them that there was a reorganization going on. Bill was doing his best to get them the stock, but stock in what corporation?

In October of 1977 the IMS Panamanian stock finally returned to Millard. He had made himself director of IMS. ComputerLand owned all of the franchising operation's assets; IMSAI owned the manufacturing corporation's assets and was responsible for the $250,000 Marriner promissory note.

Millard was almost home. All he needed to do now was to make IMS his holding company, just the way he had intended from the beginning. What a complicated road it had been, what with the Panama deal and the mistakes! There were, however, still two problems. IMS was tarnished. Technically, it seemed, the corporation had been dissolved. Then Millard had dissolved the dissolving and brought it back to life. But after all that dissolving, no one, at least none of the lawyers Millard consulted, knew for certain whether IMS was technically alive—a valid corporation.

The second problem was the Marriner note. Millard had never forgotten the way Reed had "pulled" his agreement to subordinate the loan to IMSAI loans. If he "moved" the obligation to pay the Marriner note to IMS, the holding company, never again could IMSAI's financial future be threatened by Reed. But Millard had to be scrupulously fair. IMSAI was the company that had benefited from the Marriner note, so it would only be fair that IMSAI pay for the Marriner note.*

Millard started a fifty-five-day, three-step process to solve those two problems. There was no better way than the method Millard's lawyers decided to accomplish the feat. Since nobody knew whether IMS was a real corporation, Millard decided they had better dissolve it again. In December of 1977 Millard transferred his IMS stock for IMSAI stock. Next, IMS and IMSAI were merged, and only IMSAI survived. The purpose of that, of course, was to dissolve IMS. Once the company was dissolved, the name became available again.

So great was Millard's love for the name IMS (he thought it similar to that other greater computer company known by three letters) that he then created a second corporation, which he named IMS. He promptly transferred the IMSAI stock into the second IMS. They were working as fast as they could, but it was already January 1978, and they had lost some time because of the holidays.

IMSAI, as one of Millard's lawyers would say, "had temporarily gone away." The new IMS owned everything: the manufacturing company's assets, the ComputerLand stock, and the obligation to the $250,000 note. In January 1978 to celebrate the new year, another new corporation was born. Millard transferred all of the manufacturing corporate assets into the new company, which he named IMSAI.

Since Millard believed the Marriner note was truly an obligation of

*When Millard signed the Marriner Option & Modification Agreement in 1977, he had agreed that the note would be the responsibility of his holding company, IMS

IMSAI, he ordered the creation of a note so that the new IMSAI would reimburse the new IMS for the $250,000 by May 1, 1981.* Besides the $250,000 principal, it was only fair that IMSAI also pay IMS the monthly interest on the note. Millard had one other task to accomplish. In February of 1978, the more than $50,000 debt for equipment, supplies, office space, and cash owed by ComputerLand was paid back to IMSAI. The check did not include the thousands of dollars of interest owed. †

The path had been long, the journey hard, but Millard had finally reached the "end result." IMS was the holding company for ComputerLand and IMSAI. IMS was responsible for the Marriner note. Never again would IMSAI have to suffer from having its credit lines threatened by Loring Reed. And, by paying off ComputerLand's debt to IMSAI, Millard had insured that everything between the two companies was "clean and appropriate."

In a letter to the Bank of America, Millard's attorney Randick would provide the most succinct explanation of the incredible voyage: "Therefore, under the present structure, the new IMS Associates, Inc. (the original IMSAI Manufacturing Corp.) is the *parent corporation* and the *new IMSAI Manufacturing Corp. is the wholly owned subsidiary.*"

Millard was extremely happy in February and March of 1978. He had finally gotten his company organized so that it was right from a tax and business standpoint. Van Natta and Killian had worked long enough to vest their entire 5 percent of stock. Everything was working out as he had intended from the beginning. Millard loved things in twos. There had been two IMSs and two IMSAIs. Two others would have stock in IMSAI (Killian and Van Natta), and two others would have stock in ComputerLand (Faber and Martin). Agreements were amazing. If you focused your intention, the agreements almost became living things, capable of achieving the impossible.

There was, however, one last detail that had to be worked out before the intention of his agreement with Killian and Van Natta would be complete. Millard reminded them that they would have to pay him something for the stock to avoid being swamped with taxes.

---

*The date the principal of the original Marriner note was due.
†Neither did the $50,000 plus include the original double payback Millard had promised.

Millard decided upon $5,000 each. He knew they couldn't pay, so he suggested they sign promissory notes. Killian and Van Natta gratefully each signed the $5,000 notes, payable to IMS. In return, a few days later they received 5 percent stock certificates in what the agreement referred to as the manufacturing entity of IMS—IMSAI Manufacturing Company.

The three celebrated the moment in Millard's office with champagne. "We acknowledged we had worked together and kept the agreement," Millard later said. "We were feeling really good about it." Things were just the way Millard had intended them to be. The prophetic words Millard's sister, Kathy Matthews, had told *IMSIGH* a few months before were coming true: "I hope that IMSAI always remains a safe place for all those who play with us to be here exactly the way they are and the way they are not."

Killian and Van Natta continued the celebration at IMSAI's end-of-month party. It was a time when everyone had a beer or two or a couple of glasses of wine and let loose. Diane Hajicek, a programmer, remembered talking to Wes Dehn's wife, Pat. "I can't understand it," Hajicek recalled Pat saying between sips of her drink. "We have a million dollars in sales, but why is there a cash-flow problem? There's something very wrong here."

It was summertime. Sales were up, and Millard returned to Luxembourg. Millard was wrestling with a great dilemma. As he often did, Millard phrased the problem in the form he had learned in his est training—"what worked" and "what did not work." Millard scribbled dozens of items under each heading:

What did not work? (Last time in Lux)
sheets did not get laundered.
not doing what we said we were going to do everyday.
not getting up on time.
not completing Lux when we left it.
not having my bathing suit.
not having tool box.
having to go to store each time we decide to eat at apartment overeating.
smoking.

What worked. (Last time in Lux)
getting the furniture

talking to the kids!
having apartment clean before we got there
being in Lux with whm
taking a nap in daytime.
space between me and whm.
space that whm gave me 'that day'
to look nice every day
to have a to-do list
having dictionaries
having windows cleaned and clean
own willingness to tell the truth about sex
sex (in all its forms)

The references to *whm* were to himself, William H. Millard. The lists ran over the course of several pages and also had many references to a name that was difficult to make out. It was clear that Millard was adding up every last detail to make a fair comparison. But at the top of one of the last lists was a somewhat puzzling item that may have been the deciding element: "To be whm's wife." Was Millard referring to himself, whm, his wife, or someone else? Only he could answer the enigmatic questions he posed.

Wes Dehn had been appointed president of IMSAI. It was a blow to John Carter Scott, but perhaps Millard knew that IMSAI needed some fresh blood. Although Dehn had taken the training and even adopted the language of est, he was not shaped in the Millard mold. Dehn couldn't help but deal with problems, and he began handling the realities facing IMSAI. He tore into the accounts receivable and payable problems and the ghost orders haunting the books.

For all his efforts, the trouble was that Dehn could add. When Nancy Freitas saw Dehn approach her at the local bar with his top button loosened, tie down, and wife in tow, she guessed what had happened. Dehn had tried to reason with Millard. Dehn had done every possible calculation and knew that the situation was hopeless unless there were drastic changes. The story Dehn told would have been funny if it were not the fate of their company he was talking about.

"There are times when the sword is coming at your neck and you have to duck," Dehn had told his boss. Millard had replied matter-offactly, "Some swords are made of rubber." At that, Dehn cleaned out his desk, and John Carter Scott finally assumed the position he considered his destiny.

They were not the best of times. Millard was forced to cut his September trip to Japan short when Dehn quit. That fall, Millard had hired a Big Eight accounting firm to perform an audit on IMSAI, and the results stunned him. IMSAI had lost money during the year. How could it be? he wondered. The monthly statements that his executives supplied him had shown a healthy profit. Millard had noticed that cash was tight and that it seemed to be getting harder to pay the bills, but that had been "rationalized by communications that said, 'Well, look, you have to understand that we have got our money tied up all over the place—work in process, in inventory, and so on.'" In fact, the company had lost three times what Millard thought it had made and was in the hole $650,000. Looking back, there had been, as Millard said, "certain inadequacies in the financial control system."

The resulting layoffs were sudden and extensive. In a flash one-third of IMSAI's 180 employees were gone. "There was a group of people that all left at the same time, and it was kind of cloudy, and I had the feeling that something not very legal or kosher was going on," remembered Tichenor. Nearly all of the people laid off were hourly or low-wage employees. Other than Parziale and the resignation of Dehn, few high-salaried employees left.

It was at this time that Barbara Millard took on a critical role at IMSAI. She called the suppliers and creditors who hadn't been paid and asked for more time. She would call Philip Reed and tell him that his royalty check would be late or not coming that month. For the twenty-one-year-old woman, who like her father had dropped out of college after a couple of semesters, it was a "baptism by fire." Kathy Matthews, Bill's sister, also took on a key role at the company. Millard had been wrong to trust others, but he could trust his daughter and his sister. As IMSAI's prospects grew dimmer, Millard turned increasingly to his family.

Millard knew that IMSAI needed capital badly. Why was it that he ran out of luck when it came to financing? It seemed that he was always in the wrong place to get capital. "First of all we were always undercapitalized," recalled Millard. "Anybody who looked at our balance sheet was just [saying] 'Oh, my God.' And the biggest problem was 'How are you doing what you're doing?' Doing things that we hadn't done before."

Millard just tried to cope with the day's emergencies. "It was all-consuming, a scramble including everything—even meeting payroll. So in terms of just my own, my mental, my attention, my capacity, how much time, minutes, microseconds of the day were left over for that kind of thing, it was that there just wasn't any." Millard saw IMSAI as a champion driver racing on a course fraught with perilous cliffs; sooner or later a spinout was bound to happen.

Many at IMSAI wondered why Millard didn't raise capital by selling interest in the company. Was it just Millard's legendary reluctance to give up control? Or was it something else? Something that only a few guessed, and no one actually knew for sure?

Few at IMSAI knew of the resolution passed by the board of directors of ComputerLand on Saturday, September 30, 1978. The resolution said that it had been the intent of the incorporators of ComputerLand that IMS would provide management services to direct and advise ComputerLand. It was, of course, anticipated that "ComputerLand Corp. would enter into a management service agreement for future service at a mutually agreed upon time." The purpose of the agreement would be to "recognize the contribution that William H. Millard and IMS Associates have made in development of the corporation and to insure their continued services to the company for at least six years."

Fortunately for ComputerLand, Millard and Faber signed the management services agreement the next day, Sunday, October 1, 1978. ComputerLand would be guaranteed Millard's service for six years. Millard and IMS were to be guaranteed 10 to 25 percent of the yearly net profits of ComputerLand. *

The desperate condition of IMSAI had not stopped Millard from visiting Luxembourg. But in February of 1979 he was back in San Leandro. Morale was at an all-time low. He called a meeting. If everybody would just put out another 10 percent effort, they could save the company, Millard proclaimed. Diane Hajicek remembered thinking that it would have been impossible to work any harder. She was already spending ten to twelve hours a day at IMSAI, seven days a

---

*The management fees were also a method of paying what in effect were dividends, without personal taxes, a savings of roughly 50 percent of applicable taxes.

week. She told Millard to cut her salary 10 percent instead because she couldn't work any harder. Millard did.

Millard called another meeting. The employee stock-option plan he had promised for years had finally come through. Top employees would share in 10 percent of company stock. Millard, of course, had first explained the plan to Killian and Van Natta. It would only be fair that all stockholders contribute equally to the plan, he told them. Millard would give 9 percent and Killian and Van Natta a combined 1 percent. That way, everybody contributed equally—10 percent of their holdings. Millard would also retain 81 percent ownership, just enough to file the yearly consolidated tax return.

But stock, salary cuts, and 110 percent effort were not enough. In March of 1979, the company filed for protection under Chapter 11 of the bankruptcy code. The last-minute stock-option plan had never taken effect. Even supersalesman Van Natta was laid off in the latest trimmings.

IMSAI was down to a skeleton crew. Killian had just finished redesigning the VDP-80. He had thrown out Millard's aluminum enclosure and started from scratch. The two prototypes he created worked well. Killian, who had not taken a vacation in three years, was told that he better hurry up and take one. On the first Monday of his vacation he received a call from the office. "Get down here fast," they told him. The doors were being closed for good.

IMSAI's bankruptcy was hard on Millard. He felt as though he had brought two corporate children into the world and one of them had died: "As it was dying, I gave it the kind of thing a parent would do where you'd spend most of your time on your sick and ailing child." IMSAI's creditors thought differently. They couldn't believe what they were being told. The holdings and investments of IMS—including ComputerLand—were completely autonomous from IMSAI Manufacturing Corp. Millard was not legally obligated for a penny of the $1.5 million owed by IMSAI.

There was something else the creditors, dealers, and suppliers couldn't believe. At the IMSAI bankruptcy hearings, Millard and his wife's salary were revealed. Millard had been making $7,500 a month. Pat was being paid $10,000 a year. The year in which IMSAI went bust, Millard and his wife would report over $90,000 in earnings. Creditors could only gape in wonder. Millard had paid all his taxes, he was under no obligations. But he did have a few loose strings he needed to tie.

Killian and Van Natta weren't exactly sure what Millard was proposing, but it sounded reasonable. It seemed that their stock put them in some kind of danger from the creditors. The trustee could enforce collection of the $5,000 promissory notes. But Millard had a way out, a tactic to help them save $5,000. A corporate resolution would be passed saying that they were mistaken about the true value of IMSAI stock. Then they would return the stock. It never occurred to Killian and Van Natta that their promissory notes—unlike their stock certificates—were *not* to IMSAI Manufacturing Company (the bankrupt company), but to IMS, the holding company that owned Computer-Land and that emerged unscathed by the bankruptcy. "It was an expression of concern for them," Millard recalled later. "To produce an end result."

Millard was producing lots of end results that fall. Killian and Van Natta would not be around for the resolution prepared on October 25, 1979. Millard had been wrong about that $10,000 loan from IMS to fund Computer Shack that had been backdated in August of 1977 to show full repayment of the loan on October 29, 1979. That, Millard decided three years after the event, had never happened. He had never intended the $10,000 to be a loan (or part of the $28,000 bonus Mendelman had instructed Samuels to record). It had always been his intention that it would be a gift, and so it would be.

Next, Millard arranged for IMS to purchase the outstanding accounts receivable of IMSAI and then collect. IMSAI's largest creditor argued unsuccessfully before the United States Bankruptcy Court for Millard to produce board meeting minutes:

...All of which is necessary, not because of any fault or failing of the Objectors, but because of the devious manner in which Mr. Millard has manipulated IMSAI Manufacturing Corp., and IMS Associates, Inc., totally obscuring the identity of the debtor....

Mr. Millard *is* IMS Associates, Inc. Mr. Millard *is* IMSAI Manufacturing Corp. Mr. Millard, by this maneuver, will acquire all of the assets of the corporation he has bankrupted after incurring thousands of dollars of debts, and the creditors of the bankrupt corporation will have nothing....

The creditors' pleas fell on deaf ears. IMS bought the accounts receivable for $200,000 and Millard's sister, Kathy Matthews, began collecting on the more than $1,500,000 owed.

Millard wasn't around for perhaps the most devastating part of the bankruptcy. After Golden West Auctioneers sold everything it could, the rest was thrown out. Dumpster after Dumpster of IMSAI files, records, and the contents of desk drawers were filled each day. One Dumpster contained the remains of Millard's office. Todd Fischer had a friend sort through the refuse. He found one formal document quite puzzling. At first, Fischer wasn't sure what it was, but then it snapped into place. Millard kept an inventory list of the things that had to be stocked in his desk. Office staples such as pens and paper were not the only items: a special brand of peanut butter, a favorite cracker, a fork, a napkin—the list went on. Several copies of the document had been made on fine paper. Those who knew Werner Erhard were not surprised. Werner kept a similar list on file in case of emergency.

As IMSAI died, across the bay in Marin County a new company called MicroPro International was expanding right on schedule, having introduced a multifaceted word processor called WordStar in the summer of 1979. Some who had struggled through the last weeks at the now-bankrupt IMSAI saw a similarity to an editing program they had used before. They noticed that MicroPro's president was Seymour Rubinstein and his chief programmer was Rob Barnaby. Van Natta was another early employee. Also hired were Chip Poode, Diane Hajicek, and Killian, who made sure that those two IMSAI VDP-80 prototypes "wandered over to MicroPro."

13

The Stiff

The bankruptcy of IMSAI was the last straw. When Philip Reed discovered that he couldn't recover one dime of his investment in the defunct corporation, he sadly began counting his losses. He figured that $149,000 had been swallowed up by Millard and IMSAI. *

The intervening years had not been good for Philip Reed. Almost from the day he received his beautiful porcelain eagle from Millard in 1976 his luck had soured. It was not a good time to be in the car business. The Arab oil embargo was on, and interest rates were out of sight. Many of the solid, working-class Americans to whom Philip had sold Chevrolets had been laid off and were unable to meet their ballooning credit payments. Reed had quickly discovered that repossession was not only nasty, it was also unprofitable. He could recover the cars, but the real problem was selling them again. Philip looked elsewhere for new opportunities.

One of the many ideas shared at Jake's during those late nights had stuck in Reed's mind. They had envisioned the Widget Interface as an

---

*What Reed termed $149,000 in losses was the amount outstanding under his $500,000 Novation contract. Reed later testified that he received over $350,000 in payments from Millard for an investment he estimated at between $230,000 and $250,000.

all-purpose computer device to control appliances and turn lights on and off. What if you could take the same idea, Philip thought, and apply it to regulating energy use. With the country caught up in the so-called energy crisis, the product seemed like a sure thing. Energy was on everybody's mind and pocketbook. Reed asked for John Martin's help at Expansion Systems.

Expansion Systems was just what the name suggested. If you had a system, you could pay Martin to expand it. Martin *was* an expert in franchising and would gladly franchise just about anything. ComputerLand had a good idea of what Martin was franchising because Martin used ComputerLand as a recommendation for his prospective clients. At ComputerLand they wondered why the requests for recommendations didn't diminish as the months went by. Wasn't Martin creating a new crop of franchise companies that would serve equally well as referrals? Didn't he have any other success stories?

Reed's new twist on the Widget Interface idea was promising enough to convince Liz Corp., the family holding company, to supply start-up capital. Reed then incorporated Energy Technology and opened an office in Las Cruces. The device they were developing was essentially a sophisticated timer. A microcomputer would send signals throughout a building, turning certain electrical loads on and off to reduce peak demand, and thus the amount of the energy bill. Reed was back on the fast track. Soon, he had thirty to forty engineers, assembly workers, and salesmen. His immediate plan was to interest a network of dealers to market the product. By 1978, Energy Technology's Coby-1 energy management system was named Product of the Year at the National Electronics Convention.

During this period Reed visited Martin regularly at Expansion Systems, which by a strange twist of fate happened to be in the old offices of ComputerLand in San Leandro. Reed always enjoyed trading ideas with Martin; the two complemented one another. Martin was a clever strategist who often skimmed over details and daily operations. Reed, on the other hand, was a more deliberate planner who had his successful auto dealership experience and training to fall back on. Though Reed didn't always subscribe to Martin's methods, he considered him brilliant and helpful. For example, when Reed needed a finance man, it was Martin who came up with Mike O'Shea.

While working on Reed's plan for Energy Technology, the two stumbled upon another idea. Reed was building devices to help reduce energy use. Well, why not franchise stores that sell devices designed to reduce energy consumption in small businesses and the home? And so, Energyville U.S.A. was born. In mid-1978 Reed wrote on his calendar to "send contract and 5k [$5,000] deposit to John Martin." In August he wrote "send 2k to John Martin." The references to Martin were not unique. From 1978 to 1980, John Martin's name would be scattered throughout Reed's calendar. Nearly every week Reed phoned or met personally with Martin.

Energyville U.S.A. consisted of a business plan, a few spreadsheets, and some incorporation papers stuffed into a briefcase. From time to time Reed and Martin would "sell the company" to one another by handing over the briefcase. A favorite trading point was the airport in Tucson, Arizona, not far from Reed's home in Las Cruces. Reed remembered handing Martin the briefcase for $5,000, but neither man appears to have been too serious about the company. "I think we eventually lost the suitcase," recalled Reed. "So the company's out there someplace. . . ." Martin said, "One of us lost the key."

But Reed's calendar told another story. In early 1979 there is an unexplained entry, "John Martin 25K—15K cash." Then, several references to John Martin payments being due, references to John Martin checks, and "okays" on John Martin checks. The last reference to Energyville U.S.A. is in late 1980 and says simply, "Deadline Energyville John Martin."

Meanwhile, Reed's first energy company, Energy Technology, was struggling. The energy dealerships that Reed had hoped would help to fund the second round of financing had not materialized. There was another problem. Although Reed had one of the most prestigious laboratories in the country design the machine—the Physical Science Lab at New Mexico State—they had made the mistake of testing the energy devices in New Mexico. Once the devices began to be used in New York and other areas where brownouts and power fluctuations were common, the devices often overloaded and eventually burned up. Redesigning the product would be expensive, and Reed no longer had the option of buying answers. He had drained the last capital out of the auto dealership that he dared. He couldn't even ask Liz Corp. for more. Worse yet, the royalty payments from IMSAI had stopped.

Energy Technology had been weakened by another problem. "Phil gave O'Shea certain latitude, and within a short period of time O'Shea had embezzled a lot of money from Phil," Martin later testified in court. Martin, of course, had been the one who had recommended O'Shea to his friend. "I don't know how much it was," Martin testified, "but it sounded like a tremendous amount." Reed looked, but nobody ever found O'Shea or the money.

Despite all these setbacks, in 1979, Reed received an offer of $7 million for Energy Technology. But Reed wanted more and wouldn't sell. It was the wrong time to hold out for more. Sixty days later Energy Technology filed for bankruptcy under Chapter 11. Energy Technology was reorganized, and Reed helped negotiate the sale of the bankrupt company. But at the last second the buyer disappeared without a trace. "It was the strangest thing," said Reed. "Despite the help of the Creditors Committee, the buyer was never found."

In the next few months, Reed lost more than just a buyer. His wife divorced him and took half of their community property. The bank took his house, "took everything." Flat broke, Reed was left with a bank debt requiring payments of $2,500 per month, alimony of $1,500 per month, and the $1,000-per-month cost of putting his daughter through school.

In short, it was, as Reed remembered, a difficult time. His personal life picked up in October of 1979 when he married an airline stewardess, but his pretty new bride could not erase his debts or calm his fears. He was thirty-six, practically bankrupt, and facing years of $5,000-per-month payments.

As Reed's business endeavors soured, things were picking up for Martin. In late 1978, Millard had met someone during an est function in a hot tub in the woods. Millard suggested to his fellow tubber that he consult John Martin. The hot-tub connection paid off in a lucrative consulting contract for Martin, one that he would memorialize in a letter to Millard, expressing his appreciation and "love."

For some time Martin had been receiving correspondence from Millard's company, ComputerLand, about his 1.05 percent of stock. It seemed that ever since he had received his stock from Millard, ComputerLand had been asking for it back. The company was collecting the old Computer Shack, Inc., stock certificates and reissuing ComputerLand certificates. On April 9, 1979, ComputerLand executive Ken Waters instructed one of the company's new attorneys, Deborah Dresser, to write Martin a letter informing him of the routine change. It mentioned that Martin's stock was improperly documented. There was some legend printed on it that was wrong.

The strange thing was that Martin didn't have any such legend printed on his stock. Martin wondered if the change really was routine. Included in the papers Dresser sent were some minutes Martin was asked to approve—minutes of meetings he had never attended.

What Martin didn't know was that a week before, Waters had the new ComputerLand certificate made out with a typed restriction, changing it into a closed corporation. * "There wasn't any conspiracy to get John to secretly return the stock so we could go and put a stamp [restriction] on it," Waters remembered. "We couldn't close it [the corporation] unless John sent back the letter which we thought he had."

One day after the letter was mailed to Martin, April 10, 1979, Millard and Faber, under penalty of perjury, signed a certificate to the amendment of the Articles of Incorporation, changing ComputerLand into a closed corporation. The certificate, filed with the secretary of state that same day, also stipulated that "this amendment has been adopted with the approval of the holders and owners of records of 100 percent of the outstanding shares." Martin, however, had not approved the change.

Waters was only a ten-minute drive away from Martin. How could he know that Martin hadn't signed the document? "No, I didn't know that John—how would I know that he didn't sign?" Waters, however, did not hand-deliver the letter. And if by some chance the mail took more than one day for a round-trip from ComputerLand to Martin (between April 9 and 10) 100 percent of the shareholders *would not* have agreed to the change to a closed corporation. Martin had a 1.05 percent stock interest.

"It turned out to be false [the certificate filed with the state] because we didn't have the letter we thought we had," Waters later admitted on the witness stand. "It's under penalty of perjury and we didn't—we wouldn't have signed it had we not—had we known we didn't have it back."

Three months later, however, Waters and company were still asking for the return of Martin's stock. On July 9, Dresser again wrote to Martin under Waters's direction. In reviewing the corporate minutes for November 21, 1978, and February 20, 1979, Dresser had discovered that Martin had neglected to sign showing that he had been in attendance.

---

*Closed corporations limit the number of people who can own stock in the corporation.

She also politely reminded Martin that they were still waiting for him to exchange his Computer Shack stock for ComputerLand stock. Read the letter: "As you know, this exchange is merely because of the name change of the corporation and has no effect on your shares in ComputerLand."

The six pages of documents seemed innocent enough. There was no mention of anything about turning ComputerLand into a closed corporation, only a few waivers for Martin to sign, agreeing "that any business transacted at said meeting shall be valid and legal and have the same force and effect as though due notice was fully given." Martin might be accused of many things in his day, but never stupidity. He did not sign those documents or any others ComputerLand would send.

In October of 1979 the roles would reverse. He had some news for ComputerLand. Martin was going into competition with his old employer, preparing to launch his own computer retail chain, On-Line Micro Center. Martin was so excited about the formation of his new company that the first thing he did was tell his friend Faber. "I remember standing at the desk, and he walked over to me and put his arms around me and gave me a hug," said Martin fondly. "We had a good relationship, and he said, 'You go ahead, kid. Let me know what I can do to help you.'"

The next day, when Millard found out about Martin's new pastime, Martin was surprised to learn later that Faber had changed his tune. When Martin angrily told Faber that in a year's time he would "kick ComputerLand's ass!" Faber said simply, "Go get a marker on the board."*

In the late summer of 1980, Bill Millard invited his old friend Philip Reed to visit for a couple weeks at his new home in Piedmont. Reed saw the invitation as an excuse, an escape, and perhaps, an avenue for answers. It would be an opportunity for Reed's new wife to get to know Millard better and a chance for Reed to sort out his life.

An exclusive community nestled in the hills east of Oakland, Piedmont is known for its wealth. After all the years of struggle, Millard had finally become rich. The success of ComputerLand made it all possible.

---

*Faber denied that he ever changed his position toward Martin's announcement of competition. The arm he put around Martin, he said, was an "old Mafia blessing," as in hugging someone and giving the last kiss.

Reed was glad for Millard. "St. James," as Millard called it, was more mansion than home, and Reed remembered Millard bubbling "like a kid with a new toy" as he gave him a grand tour of the grounds. Designed by noted architect Carl Warnecke, the high front of the Tudor country-style home swept dramatically into the sky. A brick walkway curled up to the broad front entrance. When the door opened, Reed saw two chandeliers, one in the entranceway and another behind, in the dining room.

To the left was the oak-paneled office Millard would make his study; in the adjoining room Millard would put his pool table. If Reed had looked closely in the study he would have seen the slight gap down the middle of the panels. When you pressed a certain spot, the whole partition swung to the left, exposing a secret compartment.

The large living room was warmed by a marble fireplace and filled with light from three French doors opening to porticos. A fourth French door led to a brick patio, bordered by stairs cascading down to gardens on two sides. The light, airy mood carried over to the dining room where French doors were etched outside by Japanese maples that rose gently from a small rock fish pond. Farther out, in the center of the grounds, was a lawn with another small pond brimming with fish.

Later, Millard added to the opulent garden. Celebrated landscape architect Thomas Church was hired to sculpt the entire grounds with evergreen hedges. In the back of the house, hedges wafted up the side of the hill, bordering majestic oaks and redwoods. Rhododendrons, azaleas, camellias, roses, and a myriad of other flowers washed the terraces and courtyard in color. The climactic touch came later. John Watson of Dallas, Texas, installed his unique "Moon Lighting." When the whim hit Millard, he could bathe the house and grounds in magical moonlight.

Reed joined Millard on a furniture shopping spree. The cream-colored interior was decorated in orange, peach, and green. Oriental screens, prints, paintings, gentle watercolors, and sculptures—especially giant puzzle pieces—were placed throughout the house. But this was still only the first floor. A lovely staircase with an oak railing arched gracefully up to the house's biggest secrets.

Millard brought Reed into the study and asked him what was going on in his life. Philip told him the whole story—divorce, debt, alimony, and the loss of his home. It all spilled out, suddenly, uncontrollably, in a wave of emotion. Millard could see the pain in Reed's face. He knew the feeling, the frustration, of being so close, of almost reaching the top, but sliding to the bottom. Millard began to cry. Reed was the younger brother he had never had, and his brother had failed.

Reed then noticed something odd. Millard's actions didn't appear to match his feelings. Other friends to whom Reed had told his hard-luck story had quickly offered helpful advice, businesses he might be interested in, people to call, even money. Millard had no practical advice except a suggestion that Reed join the ComputerLand network as a franchisee. It seemed a shallow offering, considering all they had been through together. When Millard finished crying, Reed remembered him slowly saying, "One of the things you'll get out of this is that you will realize one day that you lived through it and having done that you can live through anything."

Reed was troubled by Millard's lack of help. Reed hadn't expected money, but after all the contributions he had made to Millard's success, he at least expected more than what was offered. "He's happy to see you where you are now," Reed's wife told him. She thought Millard viewed him as a Harvard graduate who, blessed with all the advantages, had finally stubbed his toe. His failure was an affirmation of Millard's success. Reed wasn't sure what to think. In one sense, he could almost understand Millard's actions. By not offering sympathy or practical help, Millard was showing—in the est way—how much he cared for and respected Reed. Fighters don't need help. The bruises teach them to miss the next punch. Perhaps the greatest gift, Reed reflected, *was* nothing at all.

Left with few options, Reed returned to Las Cruces. It was distressing but true; the most promising possibility seemed to be buying a ComputerLand franchise. His friend Rick Kelly would soon be opening a franchise in El Paso. The two talked about being partners. On November 4, 1980, Reed wrote a letter to Ed Faber and included deposits for two franchises.* But despite the letter and the $4,000 deposit enclosed, Reed had not really made up his mind. Computer franchising might sound exciting, but he didn't even know if he could afford a ComputerLand franchise.

During his visit with Faber that fall, Reed went through informal ComputerLand training. He received a quick tour of the company and

---

*Faber had arranged an interview for Reed with the president of Atari, but no job had materialized.

sat down to long meetings with Faber and others. Just as in September, Reed had stayed at St. James and the treatment he received wasn't ordinary. But what Reed asked of Faber was impossible. Much as he would have liked to, Faber couldn't give him money to fund his franchise. All franchisees were treated as equals, regardless of friendships. Faber wanted to help Reed, but it was against his principles. If he needed money, perhaps Bill could do something on a personal basis?

There was something Reed didn't tell Faber during his visit. Reed had also talked to John Martin a few times at Martin's competing computer franchising company, On-Line Micro Center. Reed began to feel uncomfortable about his position and called Faber. "I feel awkward going into the training because I'm talking to John Martin, and there's a possibility I may go to work for him," he said. Reed was concerned that he might complete the ComputerLand training, not be able to afford a franchise, and then end up working for Martin.

Faber was disappointed that Reed didn't see the difference between ComputerLand and On-Line Micro Center. One was based on relationships; and the other, well, Faber doubted that Reed was naive. But Faber was never one to worry over things he couldn't change. It was Reed's life, and he could live it any way he pleased.

Millard, however, took it as a personal blow. Had his friendship and guidance all been in vain? Had the commitment, the sharing, the relationship been just an illusion? Twice that summer and fall Reed had stayed at his home, and only months before he had attended his daughter Barbara's wedding. Millard couldn't fathom how Reed could ever consider working for John Martin.

14

Project

Acorn

In October of 1980 a man from IBM called on ComputerLand. Faber and his second-in-command, Mike McConnell, greeted Sparky Sparks in Faber's office. The door had barely closed when Sparks pulled out his report. "We're considering building a personal computer," he told the two men.

Faber and McConnell had always believed that IBM would not build a personal computer. That was one thing they thought they didn't have to worry about. Faber knew the Achilles heel of IBM was its inertia, and he had told McConnell again and again that the computer giant would never be lithe enough to catch the lightning-fast microcomputer market.

But Sparks was serious. Project Acorn was started and was going to happen. In the summer of 1980 several IBM groups in Boca Raton, Florida, had been working on a so-called home computer. Bill Lowe, the Boca Raton Lab director, had reported his findings to the top executives of IBM. Lowe's first proposal was to sell a home computer made overseas. It was reported later that Frank Cary, who would soon take over the position of chairman from Thomas J. Watson, Jr., told Lowe, "I want the hearts and minds of the consumer. I want an IBM personal computer." The words became a rallying cry for Lowe and his top employee, Don Estridge.

In thirty days, Lowe and Estridge came back with Project Acorn and a commitment. They promised that twelve months from that September day in 1980, IBM would announce its first personal computer.

Normally that would have been impossible. Barriers to hasty introductions were part of the checks and balances of the IBM system. Before any project could become a product, a lengthy market-requirement statement had to be filed, every component had to come from an IBM source—software and hardware—and IBM's huge internal sales force had to be consulted.

A wave of Frank Cary's hand eliminated those requirements. They would streamline the decision-making process. Estridge, the manager of Project Acorn, would report directly to Cary and IBM president John Opel at the Armonk, New York, headquarters.

Sparks wanted Faber and McConnell to write a roll-out plan for the Acorn. At their next meeting, Sparks asked them what software they would like to see on the machine—VisiCalc, Easy Writer, and MicroPro's WordStar* were at the top of the list. Negotiations with Bill Gates's Microsoft were proceeding well. IBM was contracting with Gates to provide the Acorn its operating system—the control program that would open the machine to a variety of uses. Originally called Microsoft Disk Operating System, it would later be widely known as MS-DOS.

Project Acorn was going smoothly, or was it? After a few weeks of work, Faber wondered whether IBM wasn't making a mistake. ComputerLand's greatest asset was its franchisees. Five days a week franchisees listened to customers complain about the inadequacies of current computers. Who could possibly be better equipped to assist in the design and marketing of a new microcomputer? Why don't we bring a few franchisees in on the project? Faber suggested. They knew it was a large request. IBM already felt it was taking a risk in talking to two ComputerLand employees. But to bring in a group of store owners, selected from all over the country! They would be sure to blow the lid off the project. "We didn't really want anybody outside of a select few," recalled Sparks.

"You can trust them," Faber said simply. Sparks considered his

---

*WordStar would go on to be the world's best-selling word processor, selling millions of copies.

suggestion seriously. Faber had spent more than a decade at IBM and knew how the system worked.

Mike McConnell made all the calls. "Ed wants to meet with you," he would tell each member of ComputerLand's franchisee products-evaluation committee. "We want to talk strategy." McConnell then gave them the mid-January 1981 date when they needed to be free for two days, told them tickets would be waiting at the airport, and said he wasn't sure where the meeting would be held. No one except their wives was to know that they were leaving town, and as far as their wives knew, they were going to California.

Bruce Burdick had done a lot of things in his day that other people considered odd, including selling worm farms. So he did not think it strange when he walked up to the Delta counter and asked for his ticket. "Miami" read the flight coupon. Better than Chicago, thought Burdick, who momentarily wished he had remembered to bring his swimsuit. Burdick changed planes at Dallas. Carly Philips of Austin, Texas, was on the connecting flight. Both men had been on ComputerLand's products-evaluation committee. Still, Burdick wasn't sure what it was all about when the plane touched down in Miami. Only when he was stuffed into a car with several other franchisees did he realize that they were bound for Boca Raton.

They stayed at the Bridge Hotel in Boca Raton. The franchisees signed in under their names, did not list the company they were from, and were instructed not to speak to strangers.

The next day the franchisees drove to the main Boca Raton IBM buildings. After signing in, they were escorted to a meeting room. The first day was all talk. Conversation revolved around "open" versus "closed" architecture. The franchisees talked about what had made Apple successful. It wasn't just a well-designed machine, they said. By creating an architecture that encouraged complementary products, Apple had spawned hundreds of small software and hardware companies whose success depended upon their wizardry in creating new reasons to sell Apples.

On the second day, the franchisees were assembled in the executive briefing room. In rolled a cart with a large white cloth draped over it. They had never seen anything like the dramatic unveiling that was being carried out for their pleasure. What did they think, asked the proud IBMers, as they swept back the cloth. Burdick moved in for a closer look. It was almost like déjà vu. He and his partner back in Kansas City had developed what they considered the ideal computer based on the Apple and the Vector Graphics computers. "The only real difference was that I had designed color-coordinated bezels to go on the monitor so I could put on avocado or red or yellow," Burdick joked. IBM had a different color scheme in mind.

After the franchisees had a chance to examine the computer in greater detail, they began to come up with suggestions. Why not put a couple of disk drives in? The machine before them had only 16K of outdated cassette storage. Perhaps the keyboard cable would be better on the right side? Maybe they could redesign the keyboard? The ideas flowed spontaneously. They were having fun, and soon they had a nickname for the machine: The IBM PC. "No!" said the IBMers stiffly. "The name is the IBM Personal Computer!" "But the IBM PC is so catchy!" thought the franchisees.

Except for the name, the Boca Raton IBMers really seemed to listen to their advice. McConnell noticed a difference from the other IBMers he'd talked to. The Boca Raton group didn't think they were always better or smarter, as did so many other IBMers and the countless other large companies before them that had failed in trying to capture the small-computer market. McConnell knew IBM was assisted by an army of consultants, but he sensed that they were really there to learn from the franchisees.

Don Estridge was impressed by Faber's group. ComputerLand franchisees weren't nerdy computer retailers or former hamburger franchisees. They were businessmen and salesmen with sharp insights and charming frankness. Even more surprising, they seemed to have no problem adhering to IBM's strict confidentiality requirements.

Before leaving the hotel, McConnell insisted that each franchisee search his luggage for items that might tip someone off to their Florida visit. Restaurant matches, IBM pencils, paper, and postcards were all confiscated. Suntans were not a problem: the two days had been spent entirely indoors. All of the IBM reports and notes were collected by McConnell, who carried the secret materials home in his luggage. Still, he was anxious. What if his luggage was stolen or someone saw him get off the plane at Oakland?

PART
III

15

Money

Man

In 1945, before his senior year of high school in Weed, California, Bruno Andrighetto volunteered for the Coast Guard in the hope of defending the California coast. Instead, he was assigned to a troop transport ship that ferried soldiers to the Pacific and beyond. His duties often began before dawn and were seldom finished before dusk. It was a great adventure, and those waters saw Andrighetto grow to a man.

Andrighetto was nineteen when he came back from the sea. He soon discovered that Weed didn't offer many choices when it came to jobs. Like many young men, Andrighetto went to work for the local lumber company. In just six weeks Andrighetto had one of the highest-paying jobs the company had to offer, but it wasn't much. He knew there had to be more to life than Weed.

Andrighetto decided he would go to the big city and try to become an architect. Soon after arriving in San Francisco he ran into a friend from the Coast Guard who wanted Andrighetto to become his partner in a grocery store in North Beach, the Italian part of town. It sounded good to Andrighetto, but he didn't have a dime.

His friend's father liked and trusted Bruno, however, and gladly lent him $4,000. The money gave Andrighetto an extra incentive to work hard and prove that this trust had not been a mistake. In two years Andrighetto paid back the loan. After five years in the grocery business, he spun off his own idea. Mushrooms became his specialty, and Andrighetto, soon known as The Mushroom King, began selling downtown.

In 1962 Andrighetto went "big time." He and four other produce dealers (including television's Green Grocer, Joe Carcione) built a seventeen-acre produce market south of San Francisco. Andrighetto's company, Lee Ray Tarrantino (of which he owned 50 percent), soon became the biggest at the market. By the late 1970s, Andrighetto and Tarrantino were the largest produce dealers in the Bay Area, serving hotels, restaurants, and supermarkets as far south as Monterey and as far north as Sacramento. What Andrighetto liked best about the business were all the friends he made. He could go anywhere in the San Francisco Bay Area and find a friend. In San Francisco, Andrighetto could drop in at the Fairmont, the Hyatt Regency, or just about any hotel or restaurant he liked. The best ones always bought his produce, and the food was always good when Andrighetto was dining.

By the late 1970s, Andrighetto's produce business had more than $10 million in annual sales. Growth continued, as it had for almost twenty years, at about 20 percent a year. Located near the San Francisco airport, Andrighetto also did a few million dollars of business a year in the Orient. He had friends and customers in Guam and visited them annually.

Bruno was making money and he was ready to play. During the next few years he would buy and sell in the stock market. It was a rough and tumble ride. "I lost my ass and won it back again," he said. Andrighetto even fulfilled the oldest California dream. He bought a gold mine, but all they found was dirt.

But in the late 1970s a new mineral was helping northern Californians strike it rich—silicon. Andrighetto bought Commodore Computer stock in 1978 and sold it in 1980 for a cool profit of $1 million. These computer companies are okay, Andrighetto thought. Fresh from his success with Commodore, Andrighetto wanted more. If microcomputers were selling well, Andrighetto wisely reasoned, the stores selling them would also one day boom.

Andrighetto dealt with three different brokers at three separate companies. He gave Bob Ciappone a call and told him that he wanted to buy stock in a store that sold computers. Ciappone knew of only one large computer store chain, ComputerLand. Andrighetto made a few more calls and heard that ComputerLand had quite a few stores. All the brokers said the same thing, "ComputerLand is the biggest." Ciappone then told Andrighetto that he knew only one person who had stock in ComputerLand. But Ciappone didn't know how many shares John Martin-Musumeci had and whether he was willing to sell. That was for Andrighetto to discover.

In the fall of 1980, Andrighetto visited Martin-Musumeci at his home. The two diminutive Italians hit it off from the start. "He's a happy little Italian boy, and I'm Italian, right?" explained Andrighetto. In a couple of hours they pounded out the basics of a deal. But before Andrighetto signed, Martin-Musumeci suggested that he talk to some officers at ComputerLand.

Bruno met Ken Waters and Bob McMillan for lunch at a seafood restaurant in Hayward. Andrighetto listened while the men told him what a great and good person Millard was, how the company was growing tremendously, and how if they had the money, they'd buy the stock in a minute. Then, as Andrighetto remembered, they told him that an offer of $32 million had recently been made for the entire company. Andrighetto calculated what 1 percent of $32 million was worth—$320,000. On that basis, he figured that the $350,000 or so Martin-Musumeci was willing to sell his 1 percent of stock for was a good buy. If somebody was willing to buy the whole company for $32 million and they wouldn't sell, it had to be worth even more, Andrighetto reasoned.

Waters doesn't remember telling Andrighetto of any sales offers. He said, with a smile, that the $32-million offer was the kind of story that Andrighetto would like to believe, especially since there was something that Waters and McMillan *didn't* tell Andrighetto at that lunch.

One year before, in late 1979, after Martin's announcement of starting On-Line Micro Center, Waters had paid a visit to his old pal. He brought Mike McConnell and Bob McMillan along for the friendly visit. McConnell remembered browsing through Martin's promotional materials and seeing that John Martin claimed to be the founder of ComputerLand. It was just the sort of thing he expected from Martin, and he laughed to himself.

The three were surprised that Martin was going to become a competitor. Waters told Martin he considered it "unethical" for a prior consultant to open a rival chain. Martin disagreed. Waters and his fellow ComputerLand executives then discussed the second problem.

They felt that it was a "conflict of interest" to have one of their three shareholders start a competitive chain. "I'll handle that," Martin said. "I'll sell you guys the stock."

Waters and company reported back to Faber, who in turn reported to Millard. Waters then learned that ComputerLand wasn't interested in buying the stock back from Martin. The three officers, of course, were free to buy the stock.

McMillan and Waters bought lunch for Martin's finance man at Denny's. Over hamburgers, they settled on $65,000 for the stock, a price that calculated to roughly eight times the company's earnings. Then Waters, McMillan, and McConnell, for varying reasons, decided not to buy the stock. Even when Martin offered to let them each pay monthly installments of $400, the three declined.

Andrighetto knew none of this, and the three men sitting before him didn't consider it their place to tell him. Besides, they were in no hurry to talk Andrighetto out of buying Martin's stock. Maybe there was more to the story than Waters and McConnell let on? They knew Millard was uncomfortable with Martin as a shareholder, no matter how small, and if they wouldn't buy the stock, well then, why not Andrighetto?

Andrighetto was happy to have met the young men. They seemed like good, honest, hardworking guys, and he liked the idea of investing in their company. Now he had only to close the deal with Martin. From the way Martin was talking, Andrighetto got the feeling that he needed the money. Martin started at $350,000; Andrighetto started at $150,000. For two days they haggled. Finally, on December 19, 1980, they settled at $225,000. After they fixed the price, Martin got Andrighetto to agree that he would pay him a $25,000 kicker if the stock earned a certain amount.

But before Bruno actually received the stock, a few technical details had to be worked out. Andrighetto's attorney visited the offices of ComputerLand, where Waters gave him corporate minutes and some other papers to review. Everything seemed to be in order. Andrighetto's attorney then typed an agreement stating that there were no restrictions on the stock.

Waters invited Bruno over to ComputerLand. Andrighetto came with Martin's attorney, Charles Dell'Ario. Martin wanted a representative to make sure that when the stock was handed over, he would get his $225,000.

Waters wasn't part of the meeting. An assistant gave Andrighetto the new certificate with the ComputerLand name. Someone had typed the following words and added them to the back of the stock certificate: "And those restrictions applicable to closed corporations as defined under corporate code section 158." Dell'Ario knew from his conversations with Martin that the stock was not closed. But they had what they came for—the certificates—and he wasn't interested in "getting in a pissing match."

Waters knew that Martin had never signed the certificate changing ComputerLand to a closed corporation, and that the papers they had filed with the secretary of state certifying that they had the approval of 100 percent of the shareholders were false.* But he also felt that none of that mattered. "I could have closed the corporation another way," he recalled. In 1977, before Martin had received his shares, Millard and Faber held 100 percent of the stock. Waters had chosen to go through the formal legal process of asking for Martin's approval in 1979 because he was sure Martin would sign. "But potentially," he said, "you could argue we were a closed corporation back in 1977." In 1977, there were no minutes or resolutions. Waters knew that ComputerLand was really being closed way back then. It had been Millard's intention from the beginning; it was just that they didn't get around to typing up the resolutions. Waters was only fulfilling what was real and true.

Waters was excited. By bringing Andrighetto aboard, "who looked to be fine," he had solved the 1 percent "conflict of interest," and they no longer had to worry about Martin. Waters was so focused on getting the stock from Martin to Andrighetto that he or his assistant neglected to make one more change. "It just did not occur to me at all to put the right of first refusal on Andrighetto's stock," Waters later said.

Of course, there was no right of first refusal on ComputerLand stock, and never had been. But Waters would realize later the seriousness of his mistake—that he should have completed Millard's intention and added the right of first refusal. "If I had to do it over again, yes."

There was one other thing Waters overlooked. Andrighetto may have "looked to be fine," but he soon seemed to have a lot in com-

*Waters testified to this effect in court.

mon with Martin. Andrighetto liked Martin so much that by the late spring of 1981 he would invest hundreds of thousands of dollars in Martin's On-Line Micro Center. Martin was aggressive, and Andrighetto respected him. "You know, you like to see a person like that get ahead because he's a little short shit," Andrighetto said about his friend. "He looks up to everybody." Andrighetto enjoyed at least an inch or two over his short friend.

One of Martin's best weapons was what Andrighetto called his great tongue. In spite of never having gone to college, and only having finished his junior year of high school, Martin seemed knowledgeable. Andrighetto was continually surprised by his "great memory" and "imagination in franchising." The other thing that amazed Andrighetto was how Martin achieved so much with so little. "He does all this with no money, which is amazing."

Every month, Andrighetto received the ComputerLand shareholder's report. Andrighetto also received comparisons against previous years. "I could just see they were growing like a son of a bitch."

A little while later, in January of 1981, Martin asked Andrighetto if he'd like to buy part of a note that would entitle him to not just 1 percent but 20 percent of ComputerLand stock. "Jeez, you gotta be kidding," Andrighetto said. "Send me a copy of the note."

When Andrighetto got a copy of the Marriner note, he took it to his friends. First he took it to Mr. Moretti, a retired banker who had worked at the Bank of America. "It looks to me like it's a good note," Bruno recalled Moretti saying. Then he took it to his friend, a retired judge. "Well, Bruno, there could be some minor problems, but over the long haul the note is good," Andrighetto remembered the judge saying. Still Andrighetto wasn't satisfied. He took it to a downtown San Francisco law firm and got their advice. The firm concluded that based on the information available, the note would be good.

Andrighetto may have been a speculator, but he seldom gambled without first checking the odds. He had consulted three experts—a banker, a judge, and a lawyer. All said the note was good. On either the twelfth or the fifteenth of January, he can't remember which, Andrighetto gave Martin the first payment for a piece of the Marriner note—$50,000. Later, Andrighetto would pay another $200,000.

In return for Andrighetto's $250,000 Martin would give him a 28.6 percent share of the note. (Others besides Andrighetto would later receive shares in the note.) To Andrighetto it seemed a good deal. He figured the whole note would be worth more than $5 million, making his $250,000 investment eventually worth more than $1 million in ComputerLand equity.

Andrighetto understood his role. He was the money man. He didn't know much about Marriner, and he didn't need to know. The only important fact was that Martin needed him. "He was losing money right along. That company [On-Line Micro Center] never made a dime; it kept draining his cash," Andrighetto recalled. "That's why he needed me to buy the note."

16

The

Connection

In the late fall of 1980, Philip Reed moved into the Motel 6 on Whipple Avenue in San Jose next to the Nimitz Freeway. Martin lent him a car, and each morning Reed would drive across the Dunbarton Bridge to Martin's office at On-Line Micro Center. One gray morning, the engine blew up just as he reached the other side of the bridge. Smoke billowing from his hood, Philip managed to coast into a liquor store parking lot jammed with large men passing money and small packages back and forth. Reed felt their eyes consider what fun it would be to tear open his three-piece suit, clearly the guise of a clumsy undercover cop. He asked the store owner if he could use the phone. "Use it and get out of here!" the man barked.

On those evenings when he had a working car, Reed would pull into the McDonald's next to his motel, order his customary Quarter-Pounder With Cheese, and return to his "fleabag room" and watch TV. Sleep, not to mention digestion, was difficult. Only a beer can's throw away, the freeway seemed to run through his room. One night he woke to a sudden crashing sound. It was no longer a dream, it had finally happened, he thought, as he frantically jumped out of bed. A truck had hit the motel! But the truck was nowhere to be seen, and in the morning Reed read about the largest earthquake in years.

On-Line Micro Center was struggling. It had been in operation nearly a year when Reed began consulting for the company that fall. Although Reed thought Martin had a good concept, he soon discovered that Martin was running the company with "virtually no financial controls." Reed had another concern. Martin seemed to be trying to reinvent ComputerLand, and Reed wondered if it was too late. Reed examined the company's books to discover where they stood. Martin had told him that On-Line had lost about $200,000. After Reed added the numbers up, he estimated that the figure was closer to $1 million. Reed worked on a realistic business plan. The first thing they had to do was raise money.

On the day that Philip Reed was scheduled to begin the Computer-Land franchisee training, he was not to be found. Subsequently, Faber discovered that Reed had gone to work for Martin. "I was very disturbed," Faber recalled. "He [Reed] had an opportunity to gain a great deal of inside information." Faber knew that other Computer-Land competitors had paid deposits to learn the chain's secrets. He wondered whether Reed had done the same.

Pat Millard was also stunned by the news. She had rented furniture for Reed so that he would be more comfortable during his stay. How could Phil do such a thing? Pat wondered. She remembered the visit she and her husband had made to Philip's Las Cruces home earlier that year. "We had a long conversation about John Martin, and he had said that Martin had owed him money at the time and he was having trouble getting money back from him. And what he said was if he got his money back from John, he didn't intend to ever work with John Martin again."

Pat Millard was angry. She knew Philip had received privileged information about ComputerLand, and now she believed he was taking that information over to Martin, the competition. "So I felt that Phil Reed had certainly had to sell something out of himself in order to go to work for John Martin." From that day forward, Pat Millard no longer trusted Philip. Her husband would not change so easily. He could only hope that the strength of his belief would pull Philip back, mend their friendship, and rekindle their love.

• • •

Marriner and Co.'s annual meeting of the board of directors was held the afternoon of June 25, 1980, at Powers & Hall. Marriner's 1978 federal lawsuit against IMS and Millard had been a success. Millard's attorneys had argued in vain that since there had been no written agreement to provide financial statements—just an oral promise— Millard was under no obligation to provide Marriner with information about their $250,000 investment.* Under court order Millard was finally sending financial statements, but Marriner's legal fees on that matter alone had totaled over $25,000.

"My directors thought I was crazy," remembered Loring Reed. In addition to the worries Millard had caused him over the years, there was considerable embarrassment. In all his years Loring Reed had never been taken for such a ride. While his lifelong friends had built multimillion-dollar empires, Loring had wasted time and money on a comparatively trivial investment. Other than the IMS note, Marriner had few assets. His directors were eager to liquidate the few hundred thousand dollars' worth of investments remaining.

Before the summer of 1980 ended, Loring Reed called Millard once more. Price was no longer important. Loring Reed would be happy to sell the note for $300,000, although the $50,000 premium didn't approach the expenses and aggravation Millard had caused. Millard said he would have to consider the offer and would get back to him. A little later Loring Reed received Millard's answer from his son Philip. During one of his visits to Millard's home, Millard had rather suddenly begun talking about Loring Reed's offer to sell him back the note. "That's *not* convertible into ComputerLand," Philip remembered Millard asserting. "I think I'll just wait for that [note] to come due."

In Millard's mind, paying more than 12 percent interest on a five-year loan would be dishonest, unfair, and nothing short of usury. The prime rate of interest in 1980 was 21 percent. He knew Marriner had not been taking any great risk when they loaned him the quarter-million dollars in 1976. Marriner had already received more than $120,000 in interest. Rewarding Loring Reed any more would be against his beliefs.

Millard congratulated himself on sticking to his principles. By not

*In Millard's two succeeding lawsuits, the question of an oral agreement would again prove pivotal.

buying back the note early he would save not just his integrity, but interest. The interest payments on the $300,000 loan he would need to pay off the Marriner note would be 21 percent—$63,000 annually. The sensible thing, Millard realized, would be to continue the monthly 12-percent interest payments on the note and send the $250,000 next spring when the note came due. Counting those unspent prime-rate interest payments he would avoid, and the $50,000 less he anticipated paying for the note, Millard figured he would save nearly $70,000. Loring Reed would have to wait.

Considering Millard's response, it would have made sense for Reed to have just sold the note, as he had threatened before. In 1980 one would have thought there would have been little trouble selling a 20-percent note in ComputerLand, the largest computer franchising chain in the world. Loring Reed drummed up numerous good prospects, but there was one seemingly unavoidable catch that soured any potential sale. Prospective buyers quite naturally wanted to meet Millard. "You knew what that was going to be," Loring Reed said. "He [Millard] was going to give them a song and dance that they weren't entitled to ComputerLand." If only Millard would quit insisting that the note was not convertible to ComputerLand, Loring Reed thought, then the damn thing would sell itself. But the chances of Millard changing his position on the note were about equal to the chance of the sun not rising in the morning. There was only one way to sell the note, thought Loring Reed. Find somebody who knows the industry, knows ComputerLand's value, and more importantly, knows Millard. Find someone not only willing, but eager, to take the risk.

On December 11, 1980, a special meeting of the board of directors of Marriner was called at the offices of Powers & Hall; Frank Gerrity, Albert Creighton, Andrew Bailey, and Loring Reed were in attendance. Reed brought up the subject again—"that damned Millard note" they called it. Reed filled them in on the latest developments. The most recent prospective purchasers had backed out. Sell the note for whatever you can get over $250,000, the directors told Reed.

Loring Reed had talked to John Martin-Musumeci several times since they first met in 1976, when Martin-Musumeci was working for ComputerLand and was simply called Martin. Loring Reed never bothered with the longer appellation. Theirs was a business relationship, not a social one. Martin first heard about the note during a meeting while working at ComputerLand and had been trying to buy

it from Loring Reed virtually from the day he left the company. Philip
Reed's calendar recorded a trip John Martin had taken to Boston two
years before in 1978.

Martin had made Loring Reed plenty of offers over the years, but
Reed had never taken the deals seriously. With Martin, Reed said, the
cash was always going to come later. "He was one of those guys [who
say] a dollar down, a dollar when I can catch you." The only way
Reed would deal with Martin was "cash money" up front.

Perhaps things had changed. Philip Reed, anyway, seemed to think
Martin had something good going. He was out there in California,
consulting for Martin's new computer company. Perhaps Martin had
finally come up with some money after all. Loring Reed spoke with
his son often. In one of their conversations he dropped the line, "Ask
John if he has got any interest in it for cash money."

Lawyers and lawsuits were a part of business for John Martin-Musumeci. The day was not far off when he would drive a red Italian
convertible with a bumper sticker proclaiming "My lawyer can beat
your lawyer" and brag that twenty attorneys represented him. In 1980,
Martin employed the Oakland law firm of Wendel, Lawlor, Rosen &
Black to represent him in various pending actions. As he had before,
Martin convinced the firm to take much of the work on contingency.

When Martin first spoke to Loring Reed about the note, he didn't
have any money. Reed made it very clear that the only way Marriner
would sell was if it got all of its "bait back and then some." Miraculously, a few weeks later, Martin said he had the cash. Reed didn't
trouble himself as to the money's source. All that mattered was that
Martin had "rustled it up."

On March 3, 1981, one of Wendel, Lawlor's lawyers, Charles
Dell'Ario, took a United flight to Boston. That evening he met with
Loring Reed and Marriner's attorney, Andrew Bailey. Dell'Ario and
Bailey were friendly and exchanged drafts of a tentative agreement.

Martin arrived the follow morning. Loring Reed met them in Bailey's corner office at Powers & Hall. Dell'Ario was impressed by the
large, New England office with wainscoting and tasteful finishings.
He wasn't surprised, however, when Martin tried to change the
$300,000 deal. Before the meeting, Martin had "talked strategy" and

devised a clever plan to improve the arrangement that he and Loring Reed had previously agreed upon. His tactics were colorful but simple. Several times Martin left for California. "Hell, he'd go out and come right back in," Loring Reed recalled. "If you'd had a videotape of it, he'd have won an actor's prize. It's the kind of guy he is. Hell, I think he walked out three times!" Dell'Ario thought Reed was bemused by Martin's histrionics, but he and his lawyer wouldn't bend on the deal.

Finally, after two hours of dramatic bargaining, Martin consented to sign the agreement. Then Martin wanted the note. "You're not even going to get your hands around that note until I have the $250,000, and then I'll trust you for the last $50,000," Reed told Martin. The down payment, a $50,000 check, was drawn on Martin's money-market account. Weeks would pass before the second payment of $200,000 would be received. Neither Dell'Ario nor Martin explained why the agreement was being signed by a company called Micro/Vest Corporation, and Reed never bothered to ask.*

On Saturday, March 21, a meeting was called to draft the conversion letter. Loring Reed flew out to join his son Philip, John Martin, Charles Dell'Ario, and other lawyers at Wendel, Lawlor's Oakland offices. But before the letter was written, Loring Reed brought them up to date. As Philip Reed described it, his father discussed the history of the note, including all of the difficulties he had suffered with Millard. Dell'Ario remembered it more colorfully: "Bailey and Loring did some tale-swapping about Millard's stunts."

Although there "was never any written agreement, even with Bruno," Dell'Ario assumed that the shares of the Marriner note purchased by Micro/Vest were simply split into thirds by Andrighetto, John Martin, and Philip Reed. As far as he could see "it was Bruno's money, and Phil brought the opportunity." Why else would Loring Reed be playing such a helpful role in helping them convert the note? "I would be surprised if Loring Reed didn't know [of Philip Reed's share in Micro/Vest]," Dell'Ario speculated. "It might have influenced him to make the deal, a filial gain."

*Martin later claimed in court that the deal was not complete until they were dropped off at the airport. "I think we consummated it in the men's room," he said without further explanation.

It was true that On-Line Micro Center wasn't turning out the way Philip Reed had hoped. A lot of the things Martin had projected were not coming true, and Reed winced as he watched Martin make one enemy after another in the industry. "Well, he had this huge fight with some of the uppers at Apple and told them he was going to sue their asses off, so they never wanted to do business with the guy," said Reed. "A bunch of things like that had happened."

Reed had come out to Silicon Valley to reimmerse himself in the industry, but also to get some equity in Martin's company. The way the funding was going it didn't look as if a lot of equity was going to be available. Reed deduced that since Martin knew On-Line wasn't working out well, Martin would transfer Reed's stock interest to Micro/Vest.

At their March meeting in Oakland, Martin began to disclose his strategy. He had decided that Micro/Vest should remain completely anonymous and surprise Millard with a notice of conversion. "I wanted this to be an issue strictly on the basis of the documents and the contracts, and hopefully by smoking out Millard, it may have come to that. . . ." Martin remembered. But Martin had another, more personal reason why he wanted to mask their identity with a shell corporation. "I considered [that] he [Millard] personally may come after me or be upset because of me, and I was frightened of him, and I thought that by being insulated from it that I would have protection in the situation."

Philip Reed wondered whether that was the right idea. "If you wanted to design it to get Bill's cooperation, you would not have done it that way. All of a sudden Millard—when he was not even aware that the note had been sold—gets a notice of conversion from a company that he's never heard of." But at the same time, Reed could not help but remember what had happened in 1978, when he and Marvin Walker (also a friend and former employee of Millard) had approached Millard with an option to purchase the Marriner note. Millard had responded to their openness with suspicion about their true motives. In the face of Millard's anger, they had declined to act on the option.

Andrighetto wondered what the big deal was. He was already a ComputerLand shareholder, having bought John Martin's original share. Obviously ComputerLand wouldn't object to his holding the note. John Martin started ComputerLand, so Millard must love him. And Philip Reed was an old friend of Millard's. What was all the fuss about?

Philip Reed said he wanted to be "up front with Bill" and "tell it like it is." Martin had asked for and received his advice; he did not have to take it. Martin and Andrighetto had purchased the note. Reed said that he "was on the outside, looking in, and wasn't going to second-guess the decision."

Dell'Ario said he simply listened to the advice of his client. "Micro/Vest was a front to avoid the idea that John and Phil were part of Micro-Vest for as long as possible," he recalled. "Martin took the position that it would make it easier for them to convert."

While Loring Reed had met all of the principals in Micro/Vest, he said he "knew nothing, but I didn't care a hell of a lot. I had the money. I could have sold it to the Ethiopian government as long as I got the money."

Loring Reed did, however, know that ComputerLand was potentially valuable. He had examined the September 30, 1980, financial reports, which showed sales at $61 million and profits approaching $1 million. Reed also knew that Martin was ready to go to any and all legal lengths to convert the note. "When we made that agreement with Micro/Vest, you could see damn well we knew there was going to be a lawsuit," Reed remembered. "We were *selling* a lawsuit." Central to Reed's deal with Martin was his agreement to help Micro/Vest "obtain the stock of conversion." In return, Micro/Vest would pay all of Marriner's legal fees and expenses. But Reed was not just doing Martin a favor. Should Micro/Vest convert the stock or receive a specified settlement from ComputerLand, Micro/Vest was obligated to pay Marriner an extra $100,000 on top of the $300,000 buyout price of the note.

On the Micro/Vest side, it was clear who was paying some of the company's bills. A March 2, 1981, invoice for Martin-Musumeci's and Dell'Ario's airfare to Boston totaling $1,738 was charged to On-Line Micro Center, Inc. Who actually made up the Micro/Vest group was less clear. The entry in *Dun & Bradstreet* would list only an address and the name of the president. On March 15, 1981, Robert Mussman, the official president of Micro/Vest and a lawyer, was given 2 percent of the note, and Martin's old friend and former Computer-

Land attorney, Richard Bowman, also received 2 percent. But those percentages were paltry compared to Andrighetto's and Martin's shares. Another friend of Martin's would receive 26.6 percent of the note. But the papers establishing that fact would not be signed for nearly a year.

17

Wild Card

It was a letter that Loring Reed had dreamed of writing for nearly five years. The albatross around his neck named Millard would soon be gone. But in his March 28, 1981, letter to Millard, Loring Reed was careful to omit one fact. Technically, Micro/Vest did not yet own the note. Martin had tried to give Reed a personal check for $200,000, the second payment of their deal. Reed did not want a personal check from Martin—only a cashier's check would be sufficient to release the note. And so it happened that Marriner did not receive the $200,000 and mail the note to Micro/Vest until April Fools' Day, 1981.

Mr. William H. Millard, President   March 28, 1981
IMS Associates, Inc.
P.O. Box 10408
Oakland, CA 94610

Dear Mr. Millard:

Please be advised that Marriner & Co. has sold to Micro/Vest Corporation all its right, title and interest in the May 1, 1976 note from IMS Associates, Inc. to Marriner in the face amount of $250,000.00 as amended by the Option and Modification Agreement of May 16, 1977, together

189

with Marriner's rights under the January 24, 1979 Settlement Agreement between IMS, its subsidiaries and Marriner.

As you know, the Option and Modification Agreement provides:

"At any time prior to maturity . . . the holder hereof shall have the right . . . to convert this note into that number of shares . . . of the maker, and also of all other corporations . . . owned directly or indirectly by the Millard's . . . (specifically including but not limited to IMSAI Manufacturing Corporation and Computer Shack, Inc. (now ComputerLand), Hayward Computer Shack Co. (now Hayward ComputerLand), IMSAI Singapore and Republic Advertising Corporation) equal to twenty percent (20%) of the issued and outstanding number thereof determined as of the date of conversion. Upon receipt of the holder's written notice to convert, the maker and other affiliated corporations as indicated herein shall forthwith issue and deliver to holder . . . certificates . . . upon conversion."

Micro/Vest Corporation has expressed its intent to exercise these full conversion privileges of the note to acquire twenty percent of the voting, participating stock of each of IMS Associates, Inc.; ComputerLand Corp.; ComputerLand DISC, Inc.; ComputerLand Europe, Inc.; Republic Advertising Corp.; ComputerLand Franchising Corp.; V.L.F. Corporation (Hayward ComputerLand); IMSAI Manufacturing Corp.; IMSAI Europe; IMSAI Singapore; and Transworld Eximports; and of any other corporations owned or controlled by you.

As you know, the conversion is effective upon the date of the notice thereof. Please forward all accrued interest and all future financial information to Micro/Vest Corporation, Robert C. Mussman, President, 1056 Sanders Drive, Moraga, CA 94556.

Very truly yours,

MARRINER & CO.
P. Loring Reed, President

Loring Reed would state in his 1982 deposition that he didn't know Millard would be upset by the sale of the note to Micro/Vest, a group essentially controlled by his competitor Martin. "I had no idea. If he didn't want it to happen, he could have picked up the telephone and called me." Neither Loring Reed nor his son, however, informed Millard prior to March 28, 1981, that Marriner was selling the note to Martin. Years later, after the Micro/Vest trial, Loring Reed would provide a different perspective on his motivation. "Probably he [Millard] was upset. I couldn't care less. Jesus, he upset me enough, God sakes, for five years."

It was easy for Loring Reed to imagine what went through Millard's mind: Millard thought he could stop Reed from selling the note to anyone else, because as soon as prospective buyers would get to see him, he'd tell them that they weren't entitled to ComputerLand stock, and that if they tried to get the stock, he'd take them to court. To Loring Reed, Millard's motive was clear. "He thought we wouldn't convert because we wanted to liquidate our company and he'd get the damn thing for $250,000 whenever the note became due in May."

But that all changed when Millard received Reed's letter and another letter also sent on March 28, 1981. Millard was in for a big surprise: The other letter was from Micro/Vest. The sender of the letter made certain that each and every Millard company received a copy:

March 28, 1981

Mr. William H. Millard
Ms. Patricia H. Millard
IMS Associates, Inc.

ComputerLand Corp.
ComputerLand Disc, Inc.
ComputerLand Europe
ComputerLand Franchising Corp.
Republic Advertising Corp.
IMSAI Manufacturing Corp.
IMSAI Europe
IMSAI Singapore
Transworld Eximports
V.L.F. Corporation (Hayward ComputerLand)
P.O. Box 10495
Oakland, CA 94610

NOTICE OF CONVERSION

Ladies and Gentlemen:
    Please be advised that Micro/Vest Corporation has acquired from Marriner & Co., Inc. all of Marriner's right, title and interest in the May 1,

1976 note from IMS Associates, Inc. to Marriner in the face amount of $250,000.00 as amended by the Option and Modification Agreement of May 16, 1977, together with Marriner's rights under that certain Settlement Agreement dated January 24, 1979 between IMS, its Subsidiaries (as used in that agreement) and Marriner.

Pursuant to the terms and conditions of said note and Option and Modification Agreement, we hereby notify you of our election to convert the note into that number of shares of any class or classes of voting stock of IMS, and also of all other corporations and business entities owned directly or indirectly by Mr. and Mrs. Millard including, without limitation, ComputerLand Corp.; Republic Advertising Corp.; ComputerLand Franchising Corp.; V.L.V. Corporation (Hayward ComputerLand); IMSAI Manufacturing Corp.; IMSAI Europe; IMSAI Singapore; and Transworld Eximports, equal to twenty percent (20%) of the issued and outstanding number thereof determined as of the date hereof.

The conversion is effective upon the date hereof. Please forward all accrued interest and dividends to the undersigned henceforth. We expect that you will issue the certificates for the shares forthwith as provided in the note and the Option and Modification Agreement. You will be contacted by our attorneys to accept delivery of the share certificates. They will also wish to arrange to examine all the books and records of the various corporations, as provided in the January 24, 1979 Settlement Agreement.

Your anticipated cooperation is appreciated. Micro/Vest looks forward to your continued success and that of our corporations.

Very truly yours,

Micro/Vest Corporation
Robert C. Mussman, Sr.
President

Millard didn't know what to make of the two letters. He consulted his attorney Ondrej Kojnok.* Who the hell was Micro/Vest? They decided the best policy was to act as though Micro/Vest didn't exist.

Law Offices
Kojnok & Schiavenza

Ondrej Kojnok, APC

*Kojnok had passed the bar in late 1977.

Mark D. Schiavenza, APC
Of Counsel
Richard Gladstein
Harry Margolis

April 3, 1981

Marriner & Co., Inc.
Suite 201
167 Worcester Street (Rte. 9)
Wellesley Hills, Massachusetts 02181

Attn: Mr. Loring Reed, President

Dear Mr. Reed:

On behalf of my client, Mr. William Millard, and IMS Associates, Inc., I thank you for your letter of March 28, 1981, addressed to Mr. Millard with respect to the disposition of your rights and interest in the May 1, 1976, Note from IMS Associates, Inc. in the amount of $250,000, as amended.

We took the matter under consideration and shall respond to you in due course.

Cordially yours,

Ondrej Kojnok

OK/js

cc: James Brosnahan, Esq.
Mr. William Millard

Nearly five years of shenanigans had hardened Loring Reed. Kojnok's signature and Margolis's name on the letterhead brought back not-so-fond memories. Nothing Millard did anymore was a surprise. If Millard wanted to wave his legal guns one last time, that was just fine. Reed sent the letter and some other information to Martin. It was important to document Millard's every move.

It took more than a month after the letters from Loring Reed and Micro/Vest for Millard to formulate his response. In his March 28 letter, Loring Reed had clearly stated that all rights in the Marriner note had been transferred to Micro/Vest. On the same day, Micro/Vest had written that it elected to convert. In one sense Millard's letter would not differ from his attorney's previous correspondence to Loring Reed. The existence of Micro/Vest would not be acknowledged. But Millard's letter would go deeper than that tacit denial. Every other letter that Millard had sent to Loring Reed had been personally addressed. This one was to be different. It read:

29 April, 1981

Marriner & Co., Inc.
167 Worcester Street
Suite 201
Wellesley Hills, Mass. 02181

Dear Sirs:

Pursuant to our agreement and promissory note, enclosed is a cashier's check in the amount of $250,000.000 (two hundred fifty thousand dollars).

With this payment, we consider our obligation to you to be fully discharged.

Thank you for you cooperation.

Very truly yours,

IMS ASSOCIATES, INC.

William H. Millard
President

WHM:eam

Loring Reed calmly took the check and mailed it to the owner of the note, Micro/Vest, who in turn returned the check to Millard. Finally, Loring Reed thought, he was out of the mess. "I had nothing to do with it. We had got our money, and as far as I was concerned that problem was settled."

On April 30, 1981, Micro/Vest filed a complaint in the Alameda Superior Court of California, demanding 20 percent of the voting stock of all the Millard companies, the cost of the suit, damages equal to 20 percent of all dividends paid by the defendant corporation since March 28, 1981, and to top it off, that date's interest payment of $2,258.06.

18

PC Magic

In the spring of 1981 the basics of the contract had already been agreed upon. Price, the most important feature of the deal, remained to be discussed. Don Estridge was a confident man, and he had a $30-billion company to back up his confidence. He began detailing the pricing that IBM had created for the Acorn. He showed the price for the printer, the monitor, and the system unit. After about twenty minutes, his presentation approached its climax. The world's largest computer company was willing to offer a 35-percent margin. "How many would you like to buy at that price?" Estridge asked Ed Faber hopefully.

"One," Faber said without cracking a smile. (Faber would buy one of just about any machine to give it a look.) Although understated humor had always been one of his best weapons, Faber was also quite serious. At the margin IBM was offering, 5 percent less than any other manufacturer, ComputerLand was unlikely to buy many of IBM's new personal computers.

A grimace cracked across Mike Shabazian's face. He had just given up his position as IBM Palo Alto branch manager to manage the ComputerLand account for IBM. He was now hearing that his account did not exist.

The meetings between IBM and ComputerLand continued, but it

was essential that nobody other than Faber and McConnell know of IBM's visits. Shabazian had to go undercover, develop an image that would disguise his true identity. IBMers usually drove fancy cars; Shabazian always drove to ComputerLand in his Volkswagen. IBMers never sported mustaches; Shabazian began to grow a dark, thick mustache. When Shabazian arrived at ComputerLand, he would announce only his name and no affiliation. Quickly he would be shuttled into Faber's or McConnell's office. The blinds were drawn. ComputerLand people kept track of any other IBM visitors in the building that day. Even people from other divisions of IBM (selling terminals and other secondary products) couldn't know that Shabazian was on the premises.

It wasn't easy for Shabazian. All he could tell his friends in nearby San Mateo was that he had a new job. His friends' wives wondered what kind of job a man could have and be at the grocery store at ten A.M. in his shorts. Shabazian's family was also in the dark. His wife understood. She was an IBM employee, too, and knew that there were some things you just didn't talk about. Mama Shabaz was different. She loved to talk. She couldn't understand why her boy wouldn't tell her everything.

For security purposes Shabazian's home became his office. One day he forgot to leave his phone attached to the answering service. The phone rang and rang, until Mama Shabaz just couldn't let it ring any longer. She picked up the receiver. A man with a heavy British accent asked, "Is Mr. Shabazian there?"

"No," said Mama Shabaz in her thick Armenian accent.

"Tell him that Derick of the GGBI is interested in the Acorn in the Oak channel."

"Who you with?" Mama Shabaz said. There was a pause, and then she heard the receiver click.

With her arms crossed and her dark eyes centered, little Mama Shabaz could look pretty mean. She was waiting for him at the front door. She had grown up in Russia and was nobody's fool.

"Somebody called from the KGB," she said to her son. "Tell your mama what you done!"

For several months, Mike Shabazian had more than just his mama to worry about. He already had his hands full at ComputerLand. There was no problem with Faber. Shabazian got the feeling that Faber liked playing with the big boys again. It was as if Faber had been given another chance to make the major leagues. Both enjoyed the game—the negotiating dance that was at the heart of IBM. The two of them would talk for hours, and at the end it would be hard to tell who was selling and who was buying.

But the others. Oh, Christ! Shabazian had spent a decade, half of his professional life, at IBM. At his IBM branch office in Palo Alto, he had been proud to bring the IBM code to life. In Shabazian's office you didn't have to look over your shoulder after a job had been assigned. People in every position were capable. The smallest details were meticulously observed. Memos or documents marred by even the most inconsequential error—a typo or a heading slightly off center—weren't sent out, even to colleagues. You wrote it again. That's right, all over again! Dress was also carefully controlled. Shabazian preached responsibility to his employees. A sloppy tie was an indication of a sloppy man, and a sloppy man was an indication of a sloppy mind.

How could he say this to ComputerLand's executives? Other than Faber, they had all grown up at IMSAI or ComputerLand, grown out of the 1960s, out of a cottage industry, and now, finally, into something resembling a company. Shabazian liked Mike McConnell. He was bright, but what had he done before ComputerLand—he had run a counterculture day-care center! Before that he had been an est trainer. He just *hadn't* done the right roadwork. In meetings with IBM he was "lunch meat." Marian Murphy used to wear peace buttons and ride boats in anti-nuke protests. And Don McConnell, Mike's brother, was an ex-hippie whose last job had been as a writer for a militant publication for the blind. They were all smart enough —the McConnells were Yale graduates, and Murphy went to UC Berkeley—but Shabazian pictured them more easily on that neighboring California campus stirring up protest, not running a corporation.

From what Shabazian could see, there were no controls, no information systems department, no forecasting. "They were people-dependent. The only solution they had was to work longer hours. They didn't have the tools."

Shabazian's job was to turn this marketing organization "with no concept of computers, a franchisor that happened to be selling computers" into a company that IBM could trust. ComputerLand, Shabazian recalled, "had to learn how to dance with the elephant."

Shabazian watched Faber take his morning walk to look at invoices and get a physical idea of where the business was going. Those days would soon be gone, Shabazian thought. It was time for a little IBM-like structure.

It had been a year of rising expectations for ComputerLand. Don McConnell, in charge of ComputerLand's marketing, had watched one billion-dollar company after another sweep through Computer-Land, proudly displaying its newfangled microcomputer and enormous advertising plans. ComputerLand was the largest computer retailer in the world. Who else would sell their wonderful products? Nondisclosure forms were signed, and ComputerLand was let in on secrets that would transform society.

Few of the companies seemed to have a sense of humor. Texas Instruments came to visit on Halloween in 1979. Faber dressed as a cowboy and Murphy as a witch. Faber made Murphy keep her pointed black hat on during the meeting. He put one studded boot on the conference table and clicked the gun's chamber as the Texas Instruments executives spoke.

Don McConnell got a kick out of the way the big corporations couldn't seem to operate in groups of fewer than six. Xerox was perhaps the most vexing of all. They always sent a different six. That way, McConnell figured, you spent most of your time with pleasantries, getting acquainted with someone who in all likelihood you'd never see again. On the day of a group's arrival, McConnell would scurry around the company to find someone to help him endure the inevitable half-day presentation and make his department seem larger.

IBM's Madison Ave. advertising firm also seemed to like working in groups of six. Why couldn't they just send him their ideas? McConnell wondered. From what he could see, IBM was throwing money at problems, spending more dollars than he could imagine.

Every detail of the Acorn had been analyzed. A consulting firm had been hired to discover the proper colors for the machine, manuals, and other secondary materials. "In the 1970s, bright primary colors were popular," McConnell remembered them telling him. After detailed analysis, the firm had unearthed the colors of the 1980s—gray and rose. Because of this unquestionable truth, the manuals would be gray and rose, the machine would be beige with gray highlights and black disk drives. And carefully placed in the calm backdrop of the planned Chaplinesque advertisements would be a single rose.

While McConnell thought IBM was solving problems with money, Shabazian knew better. To Shabazian, every effort of IBM was planned as carefully as a football play. And Shabazian knew that behind each effort was the imprint of one man: Estridge, the perfect boss, the quintessential IBM executive—cordial and charismatic but also equipped with the technical knowledge to spar with anyone. His clear vision of the marketplace separated him from the pack. Intuitively, he seemed to know every detail of what the Acorn would need to be a success—from the type of software to the touch of the keyboard and the style of the documentation.

Estridge also happened to be a personal friend of IBM's president, John Opel. That, along with Chairman Frank Cary's personal interest in the success of the project, didn't hurt. Frequently, Shabazian and Sparky Sparks would meet with Estridge in West Palm Beach and take an Eastern or Delta flight to New York City. An hour's drive later, they would wind up at IBM's corporate headquarters in Armonk, New York. Approval for the things they needed could come only from the top. Estridge would meet with Opel or IBM's Corporate Management Committee.

After several sparring matches between Faber and Estridge, the price had finally been settled. The two men were developing a friendship based on mutual respect. Faber had told Estridge the three things retailers were interested in: "number one margin, number two margin, number three margin," and so it was not surprising that the margin Faber and Estridge agreed upon was about 5 percent better than IBM's original proposal and in line with the rest of the industry —40 percent.

But one thing was holding up the Acorn's official introduction. Another division of IBM was planning to introduce a microcomputer designed exclusively for word processing. The product had evolved out of an earlier machine called the 5110 and was now called the DataMaster. But the IBMers in Boca Raton didn't see much evolution and wondered whether it might more aptly have been named Dinosaur. DataMaster was big and ugly, ran slowly, and cost twice the projected price of the Acorn. And it was only a word processor and could perform no other tasks. There were a lot of New York IBMers behind the machine, however, and they were not going to let it disappear. A decision was made that the DataMaster would be announced in late July, at least a week before the Acorn.

At first Faber was unconcerned. The DataMaster was such a weak product that he figured it would only highlight the advanced features of the Acorn. But then the DataMaster's shipping date slipped. Faber looked at the calendar. Their cushion was disappearing; only a few weeks remained before ComputerLand's International Conference in Canada. IBM *had* to introduce the Acorn before the conference. Faber was damned if he was going to fly to Toronto, stand up before two hundred franchisees who had lived on rumors all summer, and not tell them what they were dying to hear.

One more hurdle remained for IBM to leap. A group of ComputerLand franchisees needed to be trained prior to the announcement. IBM worried that they would leak details of the product. "We'll take care of that," Faber said. Murphy was in charge of organizing the Acorn training. She loved the mystery of it. When a franchisee would ask where and why she was going to send him away for a week, she always said the same thing: "You've been chosen. Do you want to go or not?" They all did. Twenty franchisees had been selected.

Shabazian was waiting at the Bridge Hotel with nondisclosure forms for the franchisees to sign. Elliott Greene (not to be confused with New Jersey's Ken Greene) somehow had convinced Murphy to let him bring his wife along. There was one condition, however. She, too, had to sign the nondisclosure forms, and since the Bridge Hotel was an "IBM hotel" full of people from other IBM divisions, she was not to talk to anyone. Mrs. Greene sat by the swimming pool all day and read fashion magazines. Many women would have been envious of her position. So many men were asking so many questions. They all led up to the same final question. But she would casually reply, "We're in the clothing business."

For three days the franchisees received a crash lesson in the Acorn. Hardware, software, and sales techniques were all part of the course qualifying them as IBM's first authorized dealers for the Acorn. Shabazian was the main trainer, but Sparks was there, too. Even Estridge showed up on Saturday in a plain shirt and cords. The "students" spent one day taking Acorns apart and putting them back together again. They were getting pretty good at it, but it seemed they always ended up with an extra screw or two.

For months Sparks and Estridge had stared at the poster board. Written at the top were those three magical letters—*IBM*— and then underneath a blank with a question mark, and finally at the bottom, the words *Personal Computer*. All they needed to do was fill in the blank. Unlike every other IBM computer before it, this one would have a real name, not just a numerical identity. "We didn't want to stick another number on it," remembered Sparks. Everybody in the Boca Raton group submitted a suggestion, and out of dozens of names six were chosen. Still, nothing seemed to fit. Perhaps that eight-bar, three-letter logo and the words *Personal Computer* were all that needed to be said. With any other company, the title would have been missing something, but with IBM it seemed to strike the right tone of understated elegance.

Noted designer Massimo Vignelli selected the relaxed Garamond Bold script for the title. The logo would be a small silver square on the left of the machine. The words would be black, and that same space (where the blank had been on the poster board) would remain under the large, dominant, eight-bar *IBM*, seeming to give the reader an opportunity to pause on the significance of the letters. And then, in Massimo's wisely selected Garamond Bold, tucked unobtrusively in the left of the square, those two simple words that would define an industry—*Personal Computer*.

They had the name. They had the computer. They had the price. They had the franchisees. Everything was on schedule, or so Shabazian thought. The announcement was planned for the second week of August 1981, right before ComputerLand's International Conference. There was a new hitch, however. Armonk wasn't sure they could announce availability for the Acorn in Canada.

"Christ, that will go over well," Shabazian thought. "You announce the hottest new computer product in Toronto, Canada, and then tell them, 'Oh by the way, you can't buy that—that's just for Americans.' Come on guys, Think again!" But IBM had rules about these things and had to consider how the rest of the world would react. IBM had already acquired FCC and UL approval for the computer, but was still working on Canadian Standards Association (CSA) approval. The day before Shabazian and the trained franchisees were scheduled to fly to Toronto, no change in policy had been heard from Armonk.

Shabazian kept on the phone all afternoon, pestering lawyers and Armonk executives. Finally they gave in, and a "seat of the pants" deal was telexed to Shabazian with what he called "quick pricing." There was only one catch. Lew Berkovitz, the first Canadian ComputerLand franchisee, was celebrating the end of the franchisee training class. Shabazian left messages all around the hotel. It was no use. Berkovitz was not to be found.

At three in the morning, the banging on the door rang like Christmas bells to Shabazian's ears. He pulled the merry Berkovitz into his room and told him, "You gotta sign." Berkovitz hadn't drunk *that* much; he had to have his lawyer look at the document. But lawyers meant days and Shabazian had only hours. "You gotta sign!" Shabazian repeated. "There's no time!" But the most persuasive argument was, "If you can't trust IBM, who can you trust?"

By about four-thirty A.M. Shabazian was taking the Acorn international. After a couple of hours sleep, Berkovitz made his way to Sparky's office. Pictures were taken as Berkovitz wrote his signature on the historic document. The first ComputerLand franchisee had signed on to sell the Acorn. In a few hours they would be flying to Toronto.

Rumors of IBM's new microcomputer had been stoked by trade magazines for months. The world knew it was coming; it was just a question of when.* On August 12, 1981, International Business Machines Corporation introduced the IBM Personal Computer simultaneously at the Waldorf Astoria Hotel in New York and at Boca Raton, Florida. Estridge handled the New York press conference, and Sparks took care of the Boca Raton preview.

"The International Business Machines Corporation, once slow to recognize that computers were getting smaller, is apparently determined not to make the same mistake in the emerging personal com-

---

*One of those other companies that had consulted with ComputerLand couldn't wait. On July 21, hoping to steal IBM's thunder, Xerox announced its 820 microcomputer. Besides the high price tag and limited capabilities, the 820 had another glaring deficiency—its name. But Faber had warned the huge corporation, "For God sakes, call it something. Call it Sam. Don't call it a number."

puter," said the *New York Times*. Leading the newspaper's business section, an article titled "Big IBM's Little Computer" spoke of how the Personal Computer's "combination of good features," including the 16-bit microprocessor, more than twice as fast as the 8-bit chip Apple and other microcomputer companies had relied on, posed "the stiffest challenge yet to Apple and Tandy."

The price wasn't as low as hoped, and the machine was not a technological breakthrough, but even so, those three letters in Garamond Bold "sent reverberations through the industry." As Mike McConnell told the *New York Times*, "People will know that personal computers are not a fad or a flash in the pan." But for McConnell and others at ComputerLand, the most important fact reported was that only two retailers would be carrying the new line: ComputerLand and Sears. Even that announcement understated the dominant role ordained for ComputerLand, for Sears had only five stores ready to sell the machines.

There was one man at ComputerLand's Toronto conference who received a standing ovation. Mike Shabazian didn't need a speech. He knew how to get the crowd's attention. "Hello, I'm Mike Shabazian," he said, looking over the more than two hundred franchisees. "I'm here to sell the IBM PC, and I'm damn proud of it!" he said to thunderous applause. Watching that day was a man who Shabazian would soon know well. He didn't give a speech, but for the first time Bill Millard was formally introduced to the franchisees. Millard and his wife stood up in the auditorium, smiled, and waved to the crowd.

Once the celebrations had died down, the franchisees were asked to commit to an initial order and project how many IBM Personal Computers they would sell in the coming months. Forecasting was as familiar to most of the franchisees as magic. The industry was too young to bother much with projections. Sure, they had high expectations for IBM's Personal Computer, but even profitable Computer-Land stores didn't sell many more than a couple of hundred computers a month. Remembered Elliot Greene, "We kind of looked at each other and scratched our heads and put a number down. We weren't sure which way it was going to go. How high is high?"

Elliott Greene ordered twenty-five. Chuck Faso of Chicago ordered ten. Tom Niccoli of Phoenix ordered ten for each of his four outlets. Bruce Burdick made a gutsy order of about seventy units for his group of stores.

Back at the ComputerLand stores the phones wouldn't stop ringing. Before the conference was even finished, orders were rushing in. "We demanded deposits on every one of them," Elliott Greene recalled. "There was no pressure about price." But after each store got its demonstration machine, they could do little but take orders and wait. "We didn't get any machines for three months," Niccoli recalled. "We gave a lot of demos—a ton of them." Many stores had waiting lists of one hundred people or more. All they could do was take deposits, write down names, and pray for machines.

Where had all the PCs gone? There wasn't much ComputerLand could tell the frustrated franchisees. IBM was trying to get the bugs out of their shipping was the most often heard reply. Meanwhile, Shabazian was trying to locate a warehouse. Twelve engineers were flown out from Boca Raton. It seemed there *was* a small problem with the first 750 machines—the wrong type of screw had been used in the wrong place. IBM was concerned that there was a potential for shock. The engineers worked around the clock to replace the screws. Faber supplied them with ComputerLand warm-up jackets to keep them toasty in the unheated warehouse.

IBM had never shipped anything like a personal computer before. There were so many different parts—system unit, monitor, keyboard, software. Keyboards came from Raleigh; the monitors, software, and system units from Boca Raton. IBM would load the different parts into the trucks. Three to four days days later, they expected the PCs to arrive at corporate ComputerLand, but eight, nine, and ten days later, the trucks came straggling in. Some of the PCs were missing parts and were damaged. What was going on? Shabazian wondered.

Shabazian flew back to Boca Raton and took some pictures of the packed PCs in the truck just before they began their journey. When the trucks arrived in Hayward, he took new pictures. They didn't match. After some more checking Shabazian discovered that the routes many of the truckers were taking to California were unorthodox—Boca Raton, Memphis, Chicago, Denver, Oakland. He deduced that the clever truckers were squeezing in extra fares to make a little money on the side.

Sealing the backs of the trucks solved that problem. But still, when the computers arrived at ComputerLand, there often was no place to put everything. Inventory wasn't computerized. No one really knew how many machines they had. Back in Boca Raton and Raleigh,

IBM manufacturing was having its share of problems, too. Like the rest of the world, it had greatly underestimated the response to the IBM PC. Already their 10,000-machine production schedule for the last quarter of 1981 was slipping. Only about 6,500 machines would be shipped.

Though shipments would increase in 1982, ComputerLand franchises would pine away, wishing for more PCs, knowing that the miraculous machines sold themselves. But despite the problem of the screw, the snafus in shipping and receiving, and the allocations, everyone knew that IBM would eventually find the answers.

Not long after the IBM press conference, there was another big piece of news at ComputerLand. They had finally been told who owned Micro/Vest. Mike McConnell hadn't been concerned when he first heard about the suit. "Someone sued us, someone sued Bill, big deal." McConnell assumed the suit was without substance. In December of 1981, when he discovered that his old friend John Martin was part of Micro/Vest, he became even less worried. McConnell knew that Martin was a litigious sort. "The story was that MITS Altair had sued him, [and] that Dick Brown up in New Hampshire had sued him." ComputerLand's executives laughed over the absurdity of the situation. "We laughed because we were the first ones who hadn't sued him, and he sued us."

19
Loose
Ends

On April 23, 1981, Charles Dell'Ario met with David Mills, an employee of On-Line Micro Center. Dell'Ario was informed that fees for four lawsuits he was handling for Martin were incorrectly being charged to On-Line Micro Center. Revised billings were sent, crediting On-Line Micro Center with the fees charged to it for cases from January to April. Recalled Dell'Ario, "At a certain time they began charging the fees to Micro/Vest."

David Wendel, the managing partner in the firm, was beginning to wonder whether Dell'Ario had done the right thing in taking on Martin's voluminous legal problems. On May 21, 1981, nearly a month after Micro/Vest's suit had been filed against ComputerLand, Wendel wrote Martin asking for payment by specific dates for services rendered. Without such payment, Wendel stated, ". . . We will be forced to suspend work at that point and seek to withdraw from representation . . ."

At least three lawyers at Wendel, Lawlor were working on one Martin suit or another. Dell'Ario had done much more than simply file the original complaint in the Micro/Vest case. He also went to the secretary of state's office and the Department of Corporations. There he obtained information about the structure of Millard's numerous corporations, when stock was issued, and to whom. At the same time, Martin collected copies of shareholder notices and odds and ends of financial statements. Richard Bowman had unearthed other documents. With Martin's and Reed's help, Dell'Ario assembled a diagram illustrating the events that led to the inevitable lawsuit.

The secretary of state keeps a record of corporations by numbers. Although a corporation's name may change, its number remains the same. Dell'Ario traced all of Millard's corporations and created a chart illustrating their evolution. Then he added a time line.

What had once been a confusing jumble of names became strikingly clear. Millard, as far as Dell'Ario could see, had "flimflammed the two engineers." They had been promised stock in IMS and then given stock in the soon-to-be-bankrupt IMSAI. "The [corporation] numbers don't change," Dell'Ario said.

No longer, it seemed, was Micro/Vest the only one with a complaint against Millard. Killian and Van Natta's stock represented another potential 10-percent claim against ComputerLand. Dell'Ario discussed with his clients the possibility of "buying or acquiring Killian and Van Natta's shares." In June or July of 1981, Dell'Ario said, "Phil went to Killian and wanted to buy the shares." It was, he recalled, an "attempt to shake the thumb in [Millard's] eye." Word came back that the engineers wouldn't sell.

Philip Reed, however, said he didn't meet with Killian until a year later, in the spring or summer of 1982, after he had begun work with a company called Businessland.* "I was back out here and running into old friendships. I think we were looking for some engineering talent at Businessland, and I had a great deal of admiration for Joe, so I called him and we got to talking about one thing or another and had lunch. And I found out that he and Bruce had a claim against Bill." John Martin also said that at about the same time he met Killian at a restaurant and drew a diagram on his placemat, showing the intricate web of reorganizations.

None of these meetings, which Dell'Ario was convinced occurred by the summer of 1981, concerned Dell'Ario greatly. Even without the added threat of Killian and Van Natta's extra 10-percent claim, Dell'Ario was warming up for what he expected to be a "slam-dunk"

---

*The name was not the only similarity to ComputerLand. Businessland, too, was a chain of computer stores. But Businessland would own, not franchise, its stores.

suit. The convertibility of the note was laid out in plain English. The only possible fight would be how much of Millard's riches they would collect—20 percent, or more?

Since the note stated that the bearer was entitled to 20 percent of all of Millard's corporations, Dell'Ario believed that Millard's labyrinth of companies and subsidiaries would have a pyramiding effect equal to 20 percent of each corporation. "By the time you got to the lower tiers it was more than fifty percent," Dell'Ario recalled. "Twenty percent all the way down the line is the intention of the language." Dell'Ario was also convinced that the 1977 Option and Modification Agreement was intended to extend the agreement beyond 20 percent. "The modification extended the agreement because they didn't trust Millard. He had tried to screw them all along the way."

Dell'Ario was also hopeful of a quick settlement because he knew one of Millard's attorneys, Margot Wenger, from his days at Hastings Law School.

ComputerLand's response to the suit didn't surprise Dell'Ario. Their August 4, 1981, answer to the Micro/Vest suit said the note was not "negotiable, assignable or otherwise transferable by the maker," that Marriner's sale of the note "was not an arm's-length, good faith transaction," and was made for the "purpose of injuring and interfering with the business of the defendants." Finally, the answer asserted that IMS Associates, Inc., paid Marriner $250,000 "as timely payment in full of its obligations under the Note. . . . As a consequence of said payment, the conversion rights of Marriner and of plaintiff, if any, were extinguished."

With the case only a few months old, Dell'Ario considered the tersely worded reply a matter of tactics. He was surprised when the tactics remained unchanged. "Later on," he said, "lawyers usually cut the crap." But in a conversation with Wenger he discovered that they were serious. "Millard had convinced them of a fiction—that it was only because of the friendship between Millard and Phil [Reed] that he agreed to sign the note."

That theory was contrary to the facts as Loring and Philip Reed had told Dell'Ario. Dell'Ario could see for himself that Loring Reed's 1978 suit against Millard did not smack of affection, and Millard's discharging of Philip's debt in IMSAI's bankruptcy hardly seemed friendly.

The case seemed a cinch. If Dell'Ario had a problem, it was Martin. "Martin was not paying for other work," he recalled. "He was technically in default of his contingency expenses."

In early September of 1981, Dell'Ario told Martin he could no longer represent him unless he paid his bills. Then in October, Martin's legman, Richard Bowman, met with Dell'Ario asking him to continue representing his boss, and to assure him that Martin had no problem with the amount of his firm's fees. When the bills remained unpaid, Dell'Ario made a final proposal. He told Martin that he was willing to continue to represent Micro/Vest, even though his firm could no longer afford to defend him in the other pending actions. "He refused, and said, 'Screw you!'" remembered Dell'Ario of Martin's angry response. "If you can't do both, forget it!"

Martin's action was not as bold as it seemed. Bowman had been making the rounds, working up new prospects for Martin. A gifted trombone and tuba player, Bowman had once played in a Dixieland band. He called one of his old fellow musicians from Berkeley High School, a successful Marin County attorney by the name of Harold Nachtrieb.

Bowman visited Nachtrieb in the late summer of 1981, accompanied by his friend John Martin. They put the whole deal on Nachtrieb's blackboard. Later on, Nachtrieb met "the rest of the people, Bruno, Mussman. . . ." He couldn't remember whether Philip Reed was present.

Martin and Bowman told Nachtrieb that "Wendel, Lawlor [Dell'Ario's firm] had gotten into a beef over other matters and withdrew from all matters, including Micro/Vest." Such disagreements between lawyers and clients were common and didn't concern Nachtrieb. The case appeared open and shut, and the 10-percent contingency fee was appealing. He took the case.

Nachtrieb began by shifting Micro/Vest's strategy. Up to that point Micro/Vest had concentrated on how much money Millard's companies might be worth. Little attention had been given to what defenses Millard might present. Nachtrieb decided to file a motion for Summary Judgment to force Millard's lawyers to "lay their case out, so we could know where they stood." Nachtrieb expected a documentation of conversations between Loring and Millard, including the time and place. But Millard's lawyers responded with a simple assertion that Millard had an oral agreement with Marriner, granting him a right of first refusal, among other things. Why were no details provided? Nachtrieb wondered. The place, the time?

At one of the court hearings, Nachtrieb saw that his old law partner, Joe Rodgers, was on Millard's legal team. "God damn I'm glad you're on this case because this is going to take some creative lawyering!" Nachtrieb enthusiastically told Rodgers. His old partner had just started his own firm. Millard was one of his first and most promising clients. Rodgers was friendly and seemed willing to negotiate.

Nachtrieb had good reason for expecting Rodgers to want to settle the case. Over the years, Millard had accounted for ComputerLand as an 80-percent subsidiary. If it hadn't been an 80-percent subsidiary (and if Micro/Vest's 20-percent note was good, it couldn't be), Millard might owe huge corporate and personal back taxes. But the next time they met, Rodgers seemed indifferent and cold. Settlement or negotiations no longer appeared possible. "I'm sure he reported that to Millard, and Millard saw it as an expression of weakness," explained Nachtrieb. "I tried to open the lines of communication, and there was no response."

Meanwhile, Philip Reed was still having money troubles. He needed his share of the Micro/Vest stock to pay off family debts, and Martin wasn't helping. True, Martin had finally come through with his share of the Micro/Vest note, but what good was a piece of paper? Reed needed cash, not another investment, and Martin was holding him up.

Martin was not the sort to give something for nothing. In February of 1982, when Martin gave Reed a "beneficial interest" of 26.6 percent in Micro/Vest, he quite naturally had given himself a right of first refusal. If Reed wanted to sell his 26.6 percent share, Martin retained the first right to buy.

Reed thought Martin had until March 23, 1982, to exercise his right of refusal. That was before he received Martin's two-page letter complete with extensive quotations from the "documents" in question. Read Martin's letter in part:

By our discussion when you handed me those papers, I thought it was only for my input and opinion and they were subject to change; hence they did not constitute an actual offer being made to anyone. Therefore, according to my interpretation, I have 21 days from March 10 to exercise my right of first refusal, which 21 days would expire March 31, not March 23.

It was an oddly legalistic letter to be receiving from a partner and friend of several years, especially since Martin noted that "it is unfortunate that your family needs make these transactions necessary."

But despite Martin's posturing, on March 12, 1982, Reed received a two-and-a-half-year, $250,000 interest-free loan from Bruno Andrighetto. As collateral, Reed put up half of his 26.6-percent interest in the Micro/Vest note. Two days later, Andrighetto purchased outright the other half of Reed's share in the note for $250,000. Reed was suddenly half a million dollars richer. He had received more than what Martin and Andrighetto had paid for the original note.*

A couple of weeks later, Martin offered Andrighetto 10 percent of the note for $600,000—more than double the price Andrighetto had paid for Reed's 13.3 percent. On-Line Micro Center was failing, and Martin wanted to capitalize a new company, Software Guild. Andrighetto refused the deal.

As the Micro/Vest principals bought and bargained shares of the note among themselves, preparation for the case that might make their shares worth something was moving into a second stage. Depositions were beginning to be taken. On April 19, 1982, Martin Quinn (Rodgers's partner and associate) took the deposition of Philip Reed. The first week of depositions was held in Rodgers's office in San Francisco. A conference table occupied the center of the room. When Philip Reed entered the office that Monday morning, Bill Millard, Pat Millard, and Barbara Millard were sitting at the other end of the table. They would remain there during the first four days of Reed's deposition.

No one could ignore Millard's presence. It was as though he had sucked all the oxygen out of the room. He seemed larger than ever and closer than the ten feet he sat from Philip Reed. There were no greetings. Reed nodded and thought he saw Pat Millard nod back. Reed was nervous; the attorneys were nervous. Reed knew only too well why Millard had come. He had come to see how Phil had changed and how he could have done this terrible thing to him. Reed

---

*Over the next few years Reed made payments to Liz Corp. that totaled over $150,000.

thought Pat Millard's reasons for being there may have been different. She had never been afraid of learning things. "Pat was probably there to find out," said Reed. "I mean, Pat knows Bill. She's lived with him a long time and she loves him. And I'm sure she's dedicated to him. They've had their problems, but Pat and I were friends, separate from Bill and I being friends." Apparently Pat Millard was there to find out for herself whether Reed had really done something terrible.

Once he grew accustomed to the tension, the presence of Millard and his family ceased to bother Reed. He wanted them to hear what he thought and believed. Reed told the truth because he had always found it easier to tell the truth. "I tried to be brutally honest, and where there was a question in my mind, I answered it in favor of Bill." His lawyer had given him a standard instruction not to expound in his answers to questions. Later the lawyer would criticize Reed and tell him that he was giving Millard the benefit of the doubt. Reed was not sure he had made a mistake. At least Pat Millard seemed to have learned something.

Millard's deposition began the following week. Although the deposition would be taken over the course of years, consume weeks, and run more than a thousand transcribed pages, Nachtrieb saw what he was up against in the first few seconds. He began the deposition in required fashion, by asking Millard's name. Millard looked out the window. Those in the room wondered whether there was something they didn't see. More than two minutes passed. He pursed his lips.

"William," he said, not that differently from the way a proud conqueror from another age might have said it upon being taken prisoner. The next pause was shorter, thirty seconds. "Millard."

It was like dealing with a kid, Nachtrieb thought. When is this guy going to realize that the courts aren't his playpen? Nachtrieb tried to be civil. He offered coffee to Pat Millard and was encouraged when she accepted. The next day the same cordial gesture was rejected, and she seemed to look right through him. "After Millard talked to her, she wouldn't accept any more offers." By now, Nachtrieb thought, Millard's childish behavior was no surprise. In February, Quinn had taken Loring Reed's deposition at Powers & Hall in Boston. Millard was present for that one, too. After Quinn asked a series of questions, everyone went on a break. Through the richly paneled wall Nachtrieb could hear Millard screaming at Quinn.

Besides the Reeds, Millard, and perhaps Martin, there was really only one other deposition of consequence. Frank Gerrity had been ready for his turn. He knew that Marriner stood to gain $100,000 if Micro/Vest was successful in its suit. Gerrity would answer questions honestly, but he was not naive; he was not about to volunteer information.

After the first hour or so, Gerrity began to wonder about the ComputerLand attorneys. They didn't seem to be asking the right things. Detailed questions were asked about the note and Marriner. Gerrity wondered, why they didn't ask about Philip Reed's involvement?

"I thought they [the depositions] were badly done," Gerrity recalled. "They didn't ask me questions that it seemed to me they should have." Gerrity had answered all the questions honestly, but ComputerLand's attorneys "didn't dig." Afterward, when he talked to Albert Creighton, the other director on the Marriner board, his friend said the same thing.

Gerrity had mixed feelings during his deposition. While preparing for his deposition, he had read of Philip Reed's involvement with Micro/Vest. Loring Reed's deposition said that he had received financial statements on ComputerLand for the year ending September 30, 1980. Gerrity and Creighton didn't remember ever being shown those statements, charting ComputerLand's 1980 sales at $61 million and profit at almost $1 million.

On April 30, 1982, the case took a new turn. ComputerLand had "discovered" that Nachtrieb and Alameda Superior Court Judge Kroninger were members of the same men's club, the prestigious Bohemian Club. The two had also visited one another at their homes and played music together. Worse yet, Nachtrieb had a "direct financial interest" (his 10-percent contingency interest in the note) in the litigation. The day began with Rodgers suggesting that Judge Kroninger "withdraw from the case" since his "impartiality might reasonably be questioned."

Nachtrieb looked at his shoe and wondered how they could be so stupid. Sure he was friendly with Judge Kroninger. He was friends with a half-dozen judges! But Kroninger was harder on him *because* of their friendship. Rodgers would have to be pretty naive not to realize that he was taking a hell of a chance.

Kroninger proclaimed his total ignorance of any "financial interest" Nachtrieb might have in the case. He then recited how many clubs he belonged to, calculated their combined membership at five thousand, and estimated that a quarter of their members were lawyers. "For you to suggest that I could not and should not preside in a case in which those thousand or so lawyers might appear seems to me ludicrous at best," said Kroninger. Then, the following exchange took place:

"I rather suspect that your invitation to me to voluntarily disqualify myself is simply a way of accomplishing judge-shopping without having to exhaust your peremptory challenge, and if that is your purpose, I think it's a pretty shabby act as well," said Kroninger.

"You say you think it's a shabby act as well. Apparently Your Honor considers that there is more than one shabby act?" asked Rodgers.

"Yes, the other one I think is to suggest to me that I have from the inception of my presiding in this case known that there were reasons I should have withdrawn from this case."

ComputerLand's request that Judge Kroninger disqualify himself was denied. Not long after, Kroninger granted partial summary judgment for Micro/Vest. He determined that there were no oral agreements restricting the note. The contract was enforceable. He decided that the amount the note would convert to—20 percent or more of Millard's companies—should be settled by trial.

On July 12, 1982, Kroninger disqualified himself from the case.

Perhaps it was coincidence, but just as Micro/Vest seemed to be meeting with success in court, their former attorney was growing tired of Martin's broken promises. Six months had passed and still Martin hadn't paid his bills. In December, Dell'Ario had been told to relax, that Martin had "no problem" with the fees and would pay him promptly. In April, Dell'Ario prepared to file a claim against his former client. Martin found out about the impending action and called Jacob Levitan, a senior partner in Dell'Ario's firm. Levitan was told that Martin was about to receive a lucrative consulting contract arising out of a $2-million refinancing of On-Line Micro Center. He would soon have plenty of money to pay his bills. The firm withheld legal action. Martin received the financing, but Dell'Ario and his firm were still unpaid.

On June 21, Dell'Ario filed his second declaration in his firm's lawsuit against Martin and his numerous companies. On the same day, Martin sold 6.665 percent of the note to Bruno for another $125,000 to help start his new company. Dell'Ario's declaration was simple and clear. His firm wanted to be paid for the more than ten lawsuits in which they had represented Martin. Dell'Ario knew what was going on:

> ... there is additional probable cause to find alter ego and personal guarantee liability as Defendant Martin's modus operandi. As the lawsuits recited above so aptly demonstrate, a large percentage if not the majority of the numerous lawsuits and pending actions against Defendants... quite often arose out of the corporate Defendants' inability to pay their bills.
>
> Defendant Martin has used assets of his various corporations for his personal benefit. Defendant Martin caused ESI (Expansion Systems Inc.) to pay this firm an initial $10,000 retainer to represent not only ESI, but also Martin's other companies, himself, and in certain instances his wife. . . .

20

As the

Eagle Flies

In 1982, Millard declared that he would visit every ComputerLand franchise outside the United States. The international franchisees were ecstatic. Most had never met Millard and saw this as a unique opportunity to get a moment of the owner's ear. Home at the new Hayward offices, there was a feeling of relief. "As long as he was visiting these guys, he was out of our hair," said Mike McConnell, who remembered Faber telling him, "Mike, this is good for us; this is important."

Soaring in his newly purchased Learjet at altitudes of 30,000 feet and speeds of over 500 mph, Millard put his mark on the globe. Australia, Europe, Japan, Canada, Indonesia, and South America were all stops on his exhausting world tour.

Selling computers beyond America's borders was not easy. In 1982 the IBM PC was not yet available outside the U.S. (excluding Canada), and many countries still had trouble even getting Apple computers. Office automation and the personal computer revolution were concepts that simply didn't yet translate into many languages. And so the arrival of Millard was greeted in each far-off land with celebration and hope. If he was willing to visit their country, then certainly he must be willing to help their businesses.

Limousines picked Millard up at airports; banquets were prepared

216

for his pleasure; and dignitaries were produced to cast an offical air over his visits.

Millard made an excellent first impression, and many of the international franchisees were optimistic. He seemed to listen to their woes. He heard how they were always last to receive products, of shipments few and far between, and how they seldom saw many of the services that stores in the United States enjoyed. Millard was appalled. Looking them straight in the eye with his characteristic intensity, he told them that *he* would solve their problems.

But it was a two-way street. Some of the international franchisees were not playing by his rules. In Chile, in lieu of a royalty, Francisco Rojas paid a markup on the products he received from Computer-Land. Large foreign royalties were against the law in Chile. These and other facts were not important to Millard. After long nights of careful calculations, he had determined that the royalty of 8 percent was perfect. If the franchisee in Iowa paid 8 percent, then the franchisee in Santiago, Chile, would pay 8 percent. It did not matter that Francisco Rojas received services inferior to his American counterpart; it did not matter that the franchisee's government would not permit the payment of royalties. Everyone had to play by the same rules.* Soon, some of the foreign franchisees would regret the special attention that ComputerLand's owner bestowed upon them. Meetings with Millard could end up costing their businesses money.

At ComputerLand's Hayward offices, many wished that Millard's travels would never end. Like the international franchisees, they came to view his visits with apprehension. Troubled by the international franchisees' complaints about product availability, Millard would return to the U.S., call a meeting, and say, "What's this about product? What's this about?" McConnell recalled. "Everything became a crisis. Whatever was in front of him was the only thing that existed in the whole world, and that was the unfunny part about it."

While Millard was circling the globe, ComputerLand was starting to become a household name. What Midas was to mufflers and McDonald's was to hamburgers, ComputerLand became to personal computers. In 1982, ComputerLand opened more than 100 new stores to reach an international total of 318. Worldwide sales topped

*Millard ordered the creation of a ComputerLand company in Santiago for the sole purpose of collecting royalties that could not leave the country.

$300 million, yielding $10,768,000 in profit! A healthy chunk of what remained after taxes was distributed to the stockholders in the form of dividends—$2,834,000. Millard felt it was only appropriate that the dividends be large. He owned 95 percent of the stock.

ComputerLand's success, however, was really just a reflection of the power of IBM. Once the giant company got its manufacturing under control, the trickle of sales in those last months of 1981 took off in earnest. One hundred and sixty thousand IBM PCs were shipped in 1982—64,000 in the last quarter. The market was exploding.

All of those people who had waited for computers to become safe, reliable, and socially acceptable were pulling out their plastic and charging the tool of the future. If IBM, a company that employed hundreds of thousands and made more than the gross national product of many nations, had deemed the little boxes useful, then the time must be right.

In 1982, ComputerLand grew up. Faber's job that year was to be the spokesperson, to be out in the world, to be in the media, remembered Abb Abley, who one year before had become Faber's executive assistant. Faber was in the limelight. He was the man. He took on the role and the responsibility of president of the world's largest network of computer retail stores. Manufacturers, retailers—in fact the whole personal computer industry—looked to him for direction. Articles poured forth from the *Wall Street Journal* and *New York Times*.

IBM PCs were finally beginning to arrive with some regularity. Shabazian had struggled through the shipping, scheduling, and inventory nightmares, but working with Faber had made it all worthwhile. It wasn't only that they were both IBM vets. They were also ex-jocks who wouldn't take any crap. "Ed and I got along fabulously well," Shabazian recalled. "He knew IBM. He wouldn't take any shit from me, and I wouldn't take any shit from him."

Only months before, Faber had phoned Shabazian after discovering that Shabazian had talked Mike McConnell into accepting a large order of PCs. "He thought I'd muscled McConnell into placing too large an order," Shabazian recalled. "What do you think—I'm some kind of whore that would screw my major customer?" Shabazian shot back. The frankness was appreciated by Faber. Shabazian began to understand his own special role. "Faber was the father figure," he said. "I was the only one who would talk back to him."

But those challenging, exciting days were threatening to end for

Shabazian. Project Acorn was drawing to a close. Estridge wanted him back in Boca Raton. Shabazian knew what that meant—more money, less responsibility, more boredom. He told Faber that IBM was getting dull.

Faber could understand that thinking, having left IBM himself, and so he quickly offered Shabazian a job as vice president of finance. Shabazian, who said he "couldn't balance his checkbook," accepted the job on one condition. He never wanted to go duck hunting and he never wanted to take the est training. Shabazian became, in his words, the first "non-est trained" ComputerLand executive.

In the fall of 1982, the fateful calls began. Abley was answering Faber's phone in those days and was surprised when Millard began calling. He had hardly ever spoken to Millard before. All of a sudden Millard's office was calling, wanting to know Faber's schedule and sales results.

Then there were the meetings. Millard and Faber would disappear on Wednesdays. At first there were only morning meetings, but it wasn't long before the meetings stretched into the afternoon and swallowed whole days. They would meet in Faber's office. Millard had an office but it was empty. Soon, that too changed. One day Pat Millard arrived with a decorator, and in no time Millard's barren office was furnished in grand style. They would meet in his office from then on, and it was clear who held the upper hand. Faber may have been the president of the company, but Millard owned it. Millard had inserted a buy-back clause in Faber's stock agreement, and eventually Faber's holdings were down to about 4 percent. Combined with Andrighetto's 1 percent, that gave Millard the dominating 95 percent.

As Millard's visits grew more frequent, Abley felt the hopelessness return. Some acted as though nothing was happening, but he could feel a threat approaching silently, covering him like a shadow. When Abley saw Millard, he saw IMSAI, frustration, and failure. He knew that Faber was upset by Millard's more frequent visits, but he also knew that Faber was not the type to talk about his problems. Others watched the pressure build. "It was a struggle for him to come in and deal with Bill," recalled Murphy. "Anyone who knew him [Faber] knew that he was really unhappy about Bill's getting more and more aggressive and that Ed wasn't going to put up with it," McConnell remembered.

Millard focused his time and energy on corporate policy. The franchise agreement needed revision. Faber thought the franchise agreement was just fine the way it was. But Millard knew better. Policy was not being properly followed.

Ken Waters was assigned to begin drafting a new document. Millard wanted a lot of new provisions. From May until August of 1983, Waters worked on an agreement that he said "management thought we could support, that was balanced." He struggled to please not just ComputerLand's owner, Millard, but also the man he considered to be his real boss, Faber.

Over the course of several months, thousands of executive man-hours were spent meticulously revising the franchise agreement. The franchisees were asked for their input. "We spent days going through every line of the franchise agreement, going through where we thought it needed to be changed," recalled Tom Niccoli, who by 1983 owned seven stores in Phoenix, Tucson, and Las Vegas.

In many ways the effort was a success. The new document was tighter and spelled out more clearly many of ComputerLand's responsibilities to the franchisees. A videotape was made of Millard explaining the new agreement. Managers from ComputerLand's overseas companies were flown in from around the world to view the seemingly endless reels of tape. "He doesn't do anything short," recalled one ComputerLand executive in amazement. "This is a two-day videotape of Bill going through it line by line."

But the franchisee agreement was only the beginning. The more digging Millard did, the more he discovered that his policies were being ignored. One of Millard's principles had been that the price of a franchise should be 5 percent of retail sales for the average store in the chain. By 1983 sales were rising. "Our franchisee fee was moving up. . . . Everyone was saying this is ridiculous," Mike McConnell recalled. "McDonald's franchisee fee was $12,000, ours is $50,000. That's fine, but don't take it to $75,000."

Every six months they had to show Millard the average sales, calculate the figure that 5 percent represented, and give their recommendation. In the spring of 1983, no one wanted to give the franchisee fee presentation. Everyone knew what Millard would say, regardless of any recommendation. Faber asked McConnell to type up a presentation. McConnell met with Faber and Millard in the new ComputerLand building on Santana Street. Millard examined the report, which proposed that they hold the franchisee fee at $50,000.

Millard seemed to agree with the report's recommendation. "But then he remembered that he had a principle about this thing," McConnell said. "He had a principle about this, and he had almost been tricked by these businesspeople into violating one of his principles."

"What I need are the pros and the cons," McConnell remembered Millard demanding. "There are no cons. This is just a sales job. You're just trying to convince me to do something. You're not telling me the negatives!"

Millard would not stand for someone who purposely disobeyed his orders. Millard threw the paper on the floor and started grinding it into the rug with his shoe. The meeting had ended. Later, Ken Waters asked McConnell how it went. "I knew we were in trouble when he started grinding the paper into the floor with his foot," McConnell told Waters with a smile.

The issue was no longer whether Millard was going to freeze the franchisee fee. The issue was whether McConnell was a traitor for having proposed the seditious act. The franchisee fee was raised to $75,000. It took an extra effort for many of ComputerLand's senior officials to stomach Millard's actions.

Faber was ready for the blow. He had expected the change and felt it earlier than any of them. Soon after the IBM PC press conferences in 1981, Millard had begun to emerge from the self-imposed exile that he and Faber had decided would be "politic" in light of IMSAI's 1979 bankruptcy.

But it was now 1983, and the time IMSAI's bankruptcy had bought Faber was running out. No longer could Faber argue that IMSAI's ugly failure required Millard to stay in the background. And a lifetime in business was not enough to prepare Faber for the personal battle that lay ahead.

The problem was simple. Blessed as he was with tremendous patience, even Faber had his breaking point. The meetings with Millard were lectures, and it was clear who was giving the talk. After a time, Faber devised a plan to help endure the rambling monologues. He brought Mike Shabazian into the meetings, and the two would play together. While their eyes seemed to follow Millard's incantations, each drifted off to a favorite place. Faber was in his hunting gear, tucked behind a blind in a western Mexico swamp, bagging ducks. Across the way, Shabazian pushed off a windswept Colorado cornice and skied through sugary powder.

"What do you think?" Millard suddenly asked Faber, who at the time had been counting his ducks.

"That's a good question, Bill," answered the still mud-splattered Faber. "What do you think of that, Mike?"

Like a hot potato, back and forth the question would be tossed, until it finally cooled down and Faber could return to his swamp and Shabazian to his snow.

Soon the vacation would be cut short. Suddenly, unpredictably, Millard would wander into a real issue—not just a trivial corporate policy that wasn't being followed. It was then that Faber would throw down his boots and shotgun and put up a fight. They argued endlessly, like two walruses battling for territory. Shabazian would brush off the snow and imagine the walls bellowing out with the sheer intensity of Millard's proclamations. He listened as Faber argued with Millard about the huge dividends and fees that found their way to Millard's management company, IMS, and into Millard's pockets. He listened as Faber argued about needless expenses like corporate aircraft. Any fool could see what was happening. Millard wanted to run the whole ship, and this time the battle was for the helm.

For all of Faber's arguing, he was not naive. Millard owned 95 percent of the stock; he could do whatever he wanted. And as the swamp and the ducks grew more distant in his imagination, Faber knew what to do. He was a practical man.

In his seven years at ComputerLand, Faber had worked hard, enjoyed himself, and made a lot of money. He owned a small piece of ComputerLand, received a generous salary, and was paid healthy dividends.* Before joining ComputerLand, Faber had made excellent investments and had been financially self-sufficient for many years.

It was time to get on and do some other things in his life. He and his wife had talked about a winter home in a warmer climate. He had always wanted to learn golf, and of course, he loved to travel, hunt,

*Under Millard's buy-back plan, Faber had sold about 1 percent of his stock back to Millard. Faber would not disclose his salary in interviews, but Shabazian stated that his own salary, as second-in-command, was $250,000 annually.

and fish. Faber was not worried. Since the day he hired Mike Shabazian, he had been preparing and grooming him for the time when he himself would leave. The two ex-IBMers worked closely together, and Faber had tried to teach Shabazian everything he knew.

Other IBMers had been hired, too. They were a different breed from the average ComputerLand employee. Many of the company's senior employees had been hired because they had worked at IMSAI, taken the est training, or been willing to work hard for little money. The IBMers were professional managers. They taught ComputerLand managers how to manage and how to motivate. They brought with them rules and organization, and Faber hoped they would keep the company solidly on course.

In May of 1983, in one of their meetings, Faber told Millard of his plans. Millard was surprised and shocked. He wanted to know all of Faber's reasons for leaving. "I want to do something else with my life," Faber told Millard. "You want to spend more time in the company, and I don't need to be here. I've had a lot of spotlight and all of that. Now you go ahead and run it."

"Why don't you take the week off and we'll come back in next week and talk about it?" Faber recalled a stunned Millard saying.

Millard didn't want to make Faber go away. At the same time, Faber thought that Millard sensed the opportunity. He was comforted that Faber wasn't going to run off and start a competing company, as Martin had. Faber wanted to remain a member of the board and would be happy to continue as a full-time advisor and consultant to the company. He offered to play any role Millard desired—other than the day-to-day manager of the business.

"He jumped at that. He said, 'Oh, that's terrific!'" Faber recalled. When the week passed and Faber's mind remained unchanged, Millard suggested that he take the summer off.

Millard understood Faber's reason for wanting some time to think: "We had worked together for a number of years, and what he told me was that he wanted to, just literally for personal reasons absolutely having nothing to do with anything else, explicitly what he said but I understood him to mean what he repeatedly and enthusiastically and vigorously encouraged me to do, be and understand, was that he really wanted the opportunity to do some things in his life he had never done before and he had been waiting for all of his life."

Millard was willing to support that: "So I supported him doing what he needed to do no matter what that was, whatever that was, and I'm not the person to ask what that was, but whatever that was, that's what it had to be."

The official word was that Ed was on vacation. But as the weeks passed it was clear that this was no ordinary vacation. Faber let the company's officers know that he wasn't coming to the office and that if they wanted to talk to him, they would have to go to his house. Bill didn't seem to know why Ed was gone. Shabazian got the impression that Bill thought Ed was sick or something. "Oh, no, he's coming back. I promise you he's coming back," McConnell recalled Millard insisting. "He just needs some time to get his head together."

As far as Faber was concerned, his head was just fine. He had fished and hunted all summer. Golf was more difficult than he had imagined, but then he had always loved a challenge. Faber was perfectly happy doing nothing. Doing absolutely nothing at all.

That summer the 1983 International ComputerLand Conference was held across the bay in San Francisco. It began as all the other International Conferences had begun, with an opening address from president Ed Faber:

"Each year I look forward to this conference. It is the one time when our network is not spread across five hundred store locations but gathered in one. . . . This year there is much to consider. . . . We have never had weightier issues to discuss. But first let's put the issues in context. ComputerLand has made it. We have arrived. . . .

"In June we held the first meeting of the Network Advisory Council, where we sat down with store owners from across the U.S. and Canada for two days of open talks. . . . Here are some of the things that emerged from that meeting, as well as from earlier regional meetings. They are things that at least some of you feel. Corporate's whole attitude has changed. Store owners are no longer friends; they are pawns to be controlled by rigid contracts. Ed Faber has gone away. Corporate policy is being determined by some shadowy force. Some think it's IBM; some think it's the legal department; some think it's the chairman of the board. . . . Many of the rumors grew out of the general feeling that corporate had changed directions. Some saw the changes as negative. They felt there had to be a new, negative influence at the helm. Some pointed at Mike Shabazian and the other

Bill Millard, chairman and founder of ComputerLand, circa 1983. (*Photo courtesy of ComputerLand*)

Philip Reed, friend and business partner of Millard, went on to help found BusinessLand and eventually became part of the Micro/Vest group headed by John Martin. (*Photo courtesy of Philip Reed*)

INSET: As president of Marriner & Co., Loring Reed loaned Bill Millard $250,000 and received the promissory note that was eventually purchased from Marriner by Micro/Vest. (*Photo by Harding-Glidden; courtesy of Loring Reed*)

Joseph Killian (*left*) and Bruce Van Natta (*right*) helped establish IMSAI. Eventually both went on to work at MicroPro, maker of the best-selling word-processing program, WordStar. They too would sue Millard. (*Photo by Judith Calson; courtesy of the* San Francisco Chronicle)

INSET: Bill Millard and his wife Pat conferring with counsel at the Killian/Van Natta trial. (*Photo courtesy of the* Oakland Tribune)

Ed Faber, chairman and CEO of ComputerLand, in his office in 1986. (*Photo by California Photo Service; courtesy of ComputerLand*)

John Martin-Musumeci, the franchise man behind the ComputerLand concept, relaxes in his Hayward office—ironically in the original ComputerLand building. (*Photo by Paul Glines; courtesy of the* San Francisco Examiner)

The three principals of Micro/Vest—Philip Reed (*left*), John Martin-Musumeci (*center*) and Bruno Andrighetto (*right*)—celebrate in the Alameda Court House after winning an estimated $341 million judgment against Bill Millard in 1985. (*Photo by Reginald Pearman*)

INSET: Werner Erhard, founder of the multimillion-dollar est empire that teaches self-awareness. (*Photo by AP/Worldwide*)

Herbert Hafif, the attorney for Micro/Vest, and Barbara Millard discuss settlement terms at a December 1985 meeting between Micro/Vest and the Millards. (*Photo courtesy of the* Oakland Tribune)

INSET: Flamboyant criminal attorney Terry Giles represented Bill Millard after the Micro/Vest trial and successfully defended him against fraud charges instituted by Joe Killian and Bruce Van Natta. (*Photo by Roy H. Williams; courtesy of the* Oakland Tribune)

Bill Millard in a rare photo session not long after losing the 1985 Micro/Vest trial. (*Photo by Ed Kashi*)

new people we brought in. Some decided it was Mike Walter and his lawyers. But some old-timers suspected it was Bill Millard who was 'moving in' and that ComputerLand would go the way of IMSAI. I'd like to address that last fear. No one inside the company would believe it for a minute. From the very first day of ComputerLand, Bill Millard has been the source of every major decision. . . .

"One of the worst side-effects is the idea that any policy in ComputerLand is set in concrete. I want to emphasize the point as strongly as possible. No one has ever been smart enough to make a rule that works in every case. No rule or policy in this corporation is so rigid that it's beyond discussion. None. . . ."

Faber received his customary standing ovation. Some, however, took mental notes of his candid speech. They wondered whether Faber would be in a position to keep the promises he had made.

ComputerLand franchisees had a great year in 1983—215 new stores were opened, bringing the total to 548. The franchisee network had more than $777 million in sales. Although ComputerLand no longer had an exclusive on selling the IBM PC, business was better than ever before. A few stores had recorded $1-million months. Things weren't bad for corporate ComputerLand, either. The company doubled its revenue to over $60 million. Net income jumped dramatically to $31 million. Dividends had doubled to $5,329,000.

The slick, 18-projector slide show accompanied by music kicked off the conference and summed up the new image. They were breaking into the big time and not afraid to flaunt it. Attendees liked the new ad campaign: "Make Friends With the Future."

Sure, there were problems in the network, but they didn't appear to be anything they couldn't handle. Many were concerned about the new franchisee agreement, and others didn't like the hard line corporate was starting to play. And they had heard all the rumors about Millard. How he had presided over the bankrupt IMSAI, how he was a friend of Werner Erhard's, and how he was wrapped up in Erhard's California cult, est.

Millard's first introduction to the franchisees had been two years before, at the 1981 International Conference, when he and Pat Millard had only stood up in the crowd and waved. Two years after that introduction, even those who worked for him at ComputerLand's corporate headquarters didn't know what to expect. "Bill Millard to most of us was kind of a mystery guy," recalled Marian Murphy. "He was sort of this chairman of the board that nobody really saw."

"As the game became larger," Millard told the *San Jose Mercury News*, "the franchisees got concerned. The more reclusive I was, they just went crazy to know who's behind this."

Not even his own staff knew what Millard would say at the 1983 San Francisco conference. A space of several hours was left open on Saturday, the final day of the conference. Millard had notes, but had not prepared a speech. As he walked to the podium, Faber said, "Give it to them, Dad!" shook his hand, and patted him on the back.*

Millard seemed to need the encouragement. He spoke slowly, punctuating phrases with pauses that stretched on as long as half a minute. It was difficult to know what Millard was saying; he seemed confused and distracted. Est terms dominated his language. After a while some thought they could understand what he was talking about —he was charting his vision for ComputerLand. The trouble was that Millard spoke abstractly, and many of his creative examples drifted by the audience like hazy smoke rings. ComputerLand will be a bridge to knowledge for all people and all countries in all types of lifestyles and all businesses, many thought they heard Millard predict.

Employees Sheri Sorick and Abb Abley sat in the back and watched the franchisees fidget. An hour had passed. They were embarrassed for Millard and the audience. "Get to the point and get the hell off the stage," Abley remembered thinking. "I really thought a lot of franchisees were going to leave," Sorick recalled. "I really wasn't sure that they were going to stay there much longer."

But no one left, and Millard continued, halting now and then to catch a thought or image just out of reach. Many sitting in the audience that day would remember it as the worst speech they had ever heard. But that was their problem. Millard was journeying in a land where the limits of time and language did not exist. Sorick thought she understood: "Millard was like Alice in Wonderland when Alice falls down the rabbit hole and enters into a world of imaginary characters. He had a brilliant mind but it was all in his head, and it was hard for him to communicate what he saw in the future because it was so different from the rest of the world."

There was no question about Millard's sincerity. He said things

---

*Faber gave Millard that nickname because the chairman was one year his senior.

like, "You can count on me." And, "Sometimes I won't always get it the first time; you may have to keep beating me on the head." Finally, he almost broke down, overwhelmed by emotion. "I would die before I would fail you," he told the audience in a halting, wavering voice.

Somehow, Millard had pulled himself together and finished his ordeal. Beads of sweat glistened on his brow. He watched the franchisees rise and clap. They were giving him a standing ovation! Few had understood what he had said, but they respected his courage and knew his intentions were good. Millard was a visionary who thought in terms of the whole world. If the franchisee from Cedar Rapids wasn't exactly sure how Millard's global view would help his sales, he still had pride in being part of a greater cause.

Millard would take the podium once more to present Faber with ComputerLand's First Founder Award, the first and only award given to anyone other than a franchisee. The award honored Faber's crucial contribution as ComputerLand's president over the past seven years. It marked his elevation under Millard's new corporate structure to the post of vice-chairman.

Mike McConnell watched with mixed feelings as Faber carried off the Steuben crystal eagle in triumph. Millard was trying to pretend that this was a natural transition for Faber, who had done his job and was now moving on.

McConnell knew how the official story would go: The company was in such good hands. Bill was a great leader and had always been behind things anyway. From where McConnell stood, with his view of both men's true contributions to ComputerLand, it was all a farce. The man who built the company was being forced out by the man who owned the company.

21
Office
of the
Chairman

Abley had a good idea why Millard had called him over to ComputerLand's newly purchased headquarters in Oakland. As he
took the elevator up to the top floor of the plush new office, Abley
wondered how he would respond.

The Japanese prints on the wall made Abley feel as if he were in a
museum. He had expected what Millard had to say, but the words
sounded dull and hollow, as if spoken at the end of a tunnel. "Will
you do for me what you did for Faber, be my executive assistant?"
Abley heard Millard say.

"Sure. Absolutely," Abley said.

"Can I trust you?" Millard said.

Abley winced inside. Later, he would wish that he had found the
courage to say what he really felt.

"Of course you can."

The minute he had said the words Abley knew that he was lying.
Trust began with faith not suspicion. If Millard had to ask, then he
obviously didn't trust him.

"I want you to tell me every single thing you hear from the franchi-
sess," Millard said.

"Why don't you just talk to them yourself?" Abley thought. There was no way he could tell Millard all the awful things franchisees said about him. Millard was setting him up to be a stool pigeon and a liar.

By the end of the second week Abley had had enough.

Millard would give him all sorts of orders without telling him why. Working for Faber, he had always felt a part of things. With Millard he felt jerked around like a puppet on a string. Millard constantly wanted to know the whereabouts of his top executive, Mike Shabazian.

"Find Mike Shabazian for me," Abley remembered Millard asking during the first two weeks.

"He's on a plane flying back from Dallas," Abley said.

"Well, I want you to get ahold of Mike and let me know in thirty minutes where he is."

"The guy's on a goddamned plane!" Abley wanted to say. Even though loyalty had never been one of his problems, he was tired of being at Millard's beck and call. But as frustrated as he was, Abley was persistent, and somehow he got hold of Shabazian. He called the Dallas terminal and just as Shabazian's plane landed, had him paged.

Abley asked Millard if he could tell Shabazian what he wanted to see him about.

"Tell him I want to see him in my office the minute he gets back in town," Millard told Abley.

Abley felt sorry for Shabazian. He may have been the second in command, but he, too, was being jerked around. Faber never would have treated Shabazian so poorly. It drove Abley nuts.

Shabazian thought back over the last week's work, wondering what Millard's request was about as ComputerLand's Learjet flew him halfway across the country. When he arrived at the Hayward airport, he gave Millard a quick call. "What's this all about, Bill?" he asked.

As Shabazian waited for Millard's response, the silence seemed to grow. "I don't know whether I want you to work for me anymore," Millard said.

On the drive up to Millard's office Shabazian worried. He had never been fired before, and it was too late to go back to IBM. But suddenly, just as he pulled into his numbered parking lot, he knew what to do. He swung open the door to Millard's office. Millard had barely gotten out of his chair.

"Bill, I've never been fired before. Fire away!"

Millard sank back into his chair and smiled. "Let's talk."

Two weeks later, Abley mustered up the courage to tell Millard that he would have to find somebody else for the job. Once he had made the decision, however, Abley then had to make an appointment to see him. Millard had one person devoted solely to managing his calendar. "He had five damn people, and [yet] one person could do everything for him," recalled Abley. Millard had his calendar aide set aside three hours for their meeting.

Abley could have said everything in fifteen minutes, but he managed to stretch it into three-quarters of an hour. He told Millard that their styles were not matching, and that the best way he could support him was *not* to be his assistant. Abley prepared for the worst. Now was when Millard would tell him how he had failed him and was fired.

"That's fine," Millard said, staring intently at him from across his desk. Abley had never felt so awkward and uncomfortable. He had run out of things to say. Despite the twenty-foot conference table, maroon couches, love seat, and gold coffee table, Abley realized there was nowhere to hide.

"Look, Bill, we're done. You've got a couple hours here, you could get some more work done," Abley said.

"No, no," Millard said gently.

For the remaining two hours of their scheduled three-hour appointment, Millard sat staring at Abley.

"There was no abrupt change at all of any kind," Millard said of his taking over the management of ComputerLand in 1983. "The policy was where I put my focus: Policy and International. I focused my attention to seeing to it that brick by brick we jealously guarded the design of the relationship that we would have, and again, the ethics and morality that would drive the company and the ideal."

Millard created four divisions: International, U.S., Corporate Affairs, and Corporate Policy. Barbara, Millard's daughter, who had never worked for ComputerLand before, was made vice president of corporate affairs. Soon, she became vice president of corporate policy.

Millard explained that he had created the new divisions in his image. Each division represented a different aspect of himself. "We have to Millardize this company," he told his divisional executives, one of whom was already a Millard.

What employees disliked most about the new organization was Corporate Policy. Under Faber there had been no such thing. Faber knew what was going on in the company. His daily walks brought him down to the heartbeat of operations. When he saw or heard of something that he didn't like, people knew about it fast. The problem was cleared up. He didn't need a policy department to keep people in line.

Millard did not walk around the company. Excluding social occasions, few employees other than top executives ever saw Millard. He worked at the new executive offices in Oakland. Soon he would have thirteen assistants to manage his calendar, phone, travel, and office. Millard thought of the Office of the Chairman (OC) as his eyes and ears. But first he needed a mouth.

Millard was about to send out his first major communication to the franchisees. He was worried. The franchisees were forming what he viewed as a militant group, the International Association of ComputerLand Dealers (IACD).

The Association didn't think they were militant. They just didn't like the changes they saw taking place at corporate headquarters. Ever since Millard had made his presence known, the old-boy system Faber ruled so fairly had disappeared. Now, legal technicalities were all they heard about. Before Millard, ComputerLand barely had any lawyers at all. Now there was Walter and "The Legal Department."

Millard needed to write to the franchisees to tell them what he felt and believed. First off, they couldn't use the word *ComputerLand* in their association's name. That would be a lie, Millard knew. ComputerLand was not party to their wayward ways. In the letter, to emphasize key points, Millard underlined words three times and followed them by numerous exclamation points. Grammar and punctuation were missing. There were just the principles, highlighted in dramatic fashion.

Millard took the letter to Don McConnell. Over the years, McConnell had written Faber's speeches for conferences and other major events. At first, McConnell wondered whether it was possible to turn the words into something resembling standard English. But with a little work, he replaced Millard's "raw emotion" with normal rhetorical devices. Millard was amazed that his personal beliefs could be expressed in everyday English. He saw the power of McConnell's skill. In the letter Millard threatened action against the group unless it changed its name. They eventually changed the name to the International Association of Computer Dealers (IACD). And McConnell became Millard's written voice, producing all his key memos, letters, articles, and speeches.

The Office of the Chairman was the essence of Millard, the part of the company that most closely followed his principles. It was critical that there be a strategic buildup of the Office, executed by a professional. Henry Fiur, a public relations wizard from Hill & Knowlton, was hired as vice president of corporate affairs.

Fiur looked to be the man for the job. Intense and confident, he wore large gold rings and watches. A New Yorker, he considered ComputerLand employees amateurs. "Where's the executive lunchroom?" he would yell. Fiur promised to make the OC as efficient as the White House war room.

Fiur and Don McConnell helped Millard pick his assistants. It was a delicate, demanding task. Few professionals got along with Bill. But when Glen Udine, who had volunteered at the est organization Breakthrough, wrote a letter full of "high ethics," McConnell knew he was right for the job. Udine was typical of many of the young OC recruits: he had taken the est training and had volunteered for the est-sponsored organizations. Although tired of working for little or nothing, Udine didn't want to give up the excitement of being part of a high-integrity cause. Karen Zurlinden was also an ideal candidate for the Office of the Chairman. She had worked on Werner's staff.

Hiring disciples of est was not enough. Millard wanted to insure that all of his top management understood the principles by which he lived. A South American linguistics professor was hired to teach them the basics. Fernando Flores's company, Hermenet, happened to be in a partnership with Werner Erhard. * Hermenet gave seminars and sold software.

Two weeks before Christmas 1983, Millard ordered all of his officers and directors—about forty people—to attend a weekend Hermenet seminar. The previous week all of the U.S. officers and

*The word *hermenet* derives from *hermeneutics,* the study of methodological principles of interpretation, as of the Bible.

managers had met for a weekend strategy session. Millard was asking them to give up yet more of their free time before the holidays. The timing could not have been worse.

Millard's Office of the Chairman, however, could not have wished for more. They pleaded with Millard to let them attend. Nothing would please them more than to spend a weekend without pay in a closed room. In est circles, Flores was said to be a certified genius, and if that wasn't inspiration enough, he was a personal friend of Werner's.

Communication was what Flores was all about. Est seminars were about keeping agreements, but Flores emphasized promises.

The Chilean Flores, however, had a rather strong Spanish accent. At the end of every sentence he would say "clear." For most of the people in the room, it was the only word they understood. Between Flores's est jargon and poor English, nearly everyone was lost. Flores didn't usually give the seminars himself, but because Millard was also a friend of Werner's, he was doing it as a special favor. Millard knew that $450 a person was a small price to pay for the knowledge offered.

In the back row a pot was growing. Marian Murphy was accepting bets on the proceedings. The gamble was on how many times Flores would say "clear" before the weekend was out. Nearly everybody was willing to throw in a dollar.

To the OC, the seminar was less serious than est. You could go to the bathroom or eat food if you wanted to, and each day was a non-strenuous ten hours. Chad Hill, ComputerLand's new public relations director, however, had never experienced anything like it. Hill had taught communications at the University of Louisville. From the little he could decipher of what the Chilean was saying, this was the strangest communication theory he had ever heard. Hill raised his hand and said he didn't understand. Flores told him to come up front. Hill should have known better; you were never supposed to question, never supposed to ask why. Hill was an example of the bad. And when Hill would not agree with Flores's theory, he was sent back to his seat like a disrespectful student. "They tried to break me," Hill remembered.

Meanwhile, Murphy was getting out of control. In general protest of the seminar, Murphy wore one of her Berkeley buttons that said, "I don't love you anymore since you ate my dog." Survival and sanity for Murphy depended on trying to see the humorous side of

ComputerLand. The trouble for her was that Flores was worse than est. "I don't know what his trip was," said Murphy. "I can't believe you could find anybody there who liked it besides, potentially, Bill Millard. It was goddamned awful. We all had to do it; we all had to try to be polite."

Many threatened to quit rather than endure the whole twenty hours of unintelligible jargon. Murphy was ordered to apologize for her show of disrespect, and for a time her job hung in Millard's hands. "Here were all of the managers of the company for two of the three weekends in December when they could be with their families. They were all at weekend crap with the company," recalled one of Millard's staff. "They didn't want to have an est seminar pressed on them and were really angry when they couldn't understand the guy who was giving it." But when it was all over and done, Deborah Kinch was the lucky girl, having guessed that through the course of the interminable weekend the South American linguistics professor would say "clear" 13,000 times.

Millard would later apologize for the fiasco. Never again would he dare force est down the unwilling throats of his officers and directors. But there were other ways to bring the ethics of est within the organization. The OC was encouraged to buy Hermenet "Communication" software, and it was an offer they were hard-pressed to refuse.

"I always had the feeling in dealing with Werner's staff that they felt they outranked me in my organization," recalled Don McConnell, Millard's chief of staff. "They would call and request something with the unspoken, but tacit, 'Oh, you're giving me a little resistance on this one. Do I need to have Werner call Bill?'" It was often easier to buy the software or accede to their other wishes.

The ethics and integrity of est were not enough, however. The OC also needed security. An unauthorized magazine article proved that. In October of 1983, *Forbes* published "The Instant Billionaire," an article detailing the incredible wealth that Millard enjoyed. The magazine estimated ComputerLand's value at $1.2 billion. Millard, "this tremendously rich man," it said, owns 98 percent (it was actually 95 percent) of ComputerLand. Never again would the money or power be so enjoyable. Henry Fiur was furious. It was the last thing they needed. Within weeks, President Ford's ex–Secret Service man, Ernie Luzania, was hired along with ex–FBI man Walt Boyle.

A few ex-policemen were hired, but sometimes they had to be

restrained. They were nothing like Luzania and Boyle, who wore nice suits and were perfect gentlemen but for their service revolvers, bulletproof vests, and uncanny ability to work a crowd or do an advance.

Advancing is the heart of security. It was up to Luzania and Boyle to inspect any hotel or restaurant where Millard would be traveling. Without attracting the least attention, they checked for bombs, bugs, snipers, and of course, potential kidnappers. Once, when Millard was scheduled to go to the Virgin Islands, they discovered that his hotel was across from a place frequented by the Rastafarians. Just to be safe, they changed hotels. To complete the security team, Millard's driver was sent to the Sears Point Raceway for evasive driving training.

But the real heart of the Office of the Chairman was something you couldn't touch, taste, or feel. Those thirteen or so handpicked assistants, among the privileged few whom Millard saw daily, were entrusted with the greatest responsibility of all. It was up to them to overhear conversations, to find the secrets few would tell, to root out "unalignedness" whenever and wherever it was to be found.

"Unalignedness" meant you weren't on the same track as Millard. It meant you weren't running straight. It meant you were, quite simply, fighting the principles. What the violators didn't understand was that there was a reason behind every principle. Millard knew they were becoming a giant organization and needed to take on the structure of a $1-billion company.

Millard didn't just separate the company's functions into divisions; he also separated them by buildings. Accounting was in Oakland now instead of Hayward. If manufacturers wanted to check on their account, they would have to talk to purchasing in Hayward, obtain the information, then call a different phone number in Oakland to find out how the purchase order affected their latest invoice.

It didn't matter that before it had seemed easier; that before when someone had a question in accounting they could walk down the hall to purchasing and sort it out. It didn't matter that employees now felt separated and that divisions seemed to conflict rather than compromise.

The distance and the divisions were all part of Millard's master plan for ComputerLand's expansion. Millard knew if only he could discover the principles behind all things, then order would be universal and growth would be unlimited.

Policies began to be created. Most were written by the Corporate Policy division, but some were written by the Corporate Affairs division. The executives had long discussions about how the policies would work.

Shabazian and the other IBMers he brought with him understood the role of policies; IBM had reams of policies. But ComputerLand was still in the 1960s as far as Shabazian could see. Suits were as rare as business degrees. Management and decision-making were at primitive levels. Policy wasn't everything, but at least it was a start.

Shabazian, the company's first "gray hair," began the painful process. Wage and salary administration were instituted. So were performance planning and objective setting. It was a shock for many of the old-time ComputerLand employees. Some thought it was happening too fast; some thought it was stereotypical IBM; and some recognized its value. But Shabazian knew it had to be done or the company would never survive.

Corporate Management Committee meetings would discuss policy endlessly. "This is how we do it at IBM," was a frequent refrain. Some executives began to wonder whether those people really worked for ComputerLand. It was clear that their corporate hearts still beat for IBM.

To many the policies seemed like little things, but Millard knew them to be the foundation of something great. He was serious when he talked about the Millardization of ComputerLand. For example, Millard liked his desk clean, and so everyone was expected to have bare desks by five P.M. That was one of the first policies.

Millard also decided that the officers should have company cars based on their rank. A fleet of BMWs, Audis, and Jaguars was purchased. Millard chose a Mercedes and gave Barbara a Jaguar. Some officers were happy with their own cars and didn't want the company cars. "You will have a company car, and it will be this one," Millard told each reluctant executive.* Officers were given numbered parking places at each ComputerLand building. They had to park in their assigned spot.

It came to Millard's attention that some employees were neglecting

*One executive already had a car on the approved list. The color, however, was not on the approved list and he was ordered to keep his BMW off the premises.

to report small gifts that manufacturers or franchisees gave them. A policy was written requiring that all gifts be reported and turned in to the Gift Department.

It was discovered that employees had also been logging the miles they flew for the company on bonus mileage programs. The Policy Division declared that the company owned those miles and forbade individuals to accumulate them for their personal use. Soon after, however, the airlines stated that bonus mileage certificates could be issued only in a person's name, not a corporation's. Employees stopped recording the miles.

These were only a few of the hundreds of internal policies that poured out of the Corporate Policy division. Thick, expensive policy manuals were printed on fine paper. Everyone was required to have the latest edition.

Most policies went down about as easily as cod liver oil. Don McConnell didn't particularly like enforcing them, but he could understand the OC's role. They were a little like the White House staff. That nobody liked them didn't mean they weren't necessary. He imagined that what they were doing was not that different from what happened at any other large company. And he had to admit there was a special satisfaction when he would see or hear of something or someone particularly unaligned. "Why would anyone do something so wrongheaded?" Millard would exclaim in wonder, then thank McConnell for the good work.

Millard was just making sure that nothing was going on that he didn't know about. Some in the company, however, had another name for the staff of the Office of the Chairman—the "Thought Police." Perpetrators of "unalignedness" and other crimes against the OC were, of course, "Thought Criminals."

ComputerLand's U.S. division was one of the greatest perpetrators. "We had a bunch of cowboys who were always looking to find ways Shabazian was not listening to the chairman," remembered Shabazian. "There was always this continuous witch-hunt going on—'What are you doing that Bill doesn't know about?'"

Internal policies, however, were only the beginning of the new era of control. One of the biggest responsibilities of the Corporate Policy division was to regulate the relationship between the corporate office and the franchisees. Judgment calls were no longer allowed. A list of rules was enacted. Penalties were enforced when the rules were broken. Exceptions were seldom allowed, and exceptions could come only from Millard.

It was shock to the franchisees. They had grown accustomed to ComputerLand helping them with their problems. Before Millard, if they had a check that bounced, they would call up, explain the situation, and tell the company that a new check was on the way. Generally the problem was solved quickly, without rancor.

"We could work with them that way," Tichenor recalled. "But it got so that if a franchisee bounced a check, he was going to be punished, put in a different kind of box."

People like Tichenor were rare. New, enthusiastic, unquestioning employees were hired every day and they followed the box system like the Bible. The franchisee would call and the new employees would read off their little list, "Well, I can't do that; I can't do that; I can't do that. . . ."

"There was an attitude that these are the rules by which you run your franchise. You break the rules, we yell at you," Murphy remembered. "I'm [the] parent and you're the child."

More than most parents, Millard liked to catch his children with their hands in the cookie jar. Marian Murphy was in charge of franchise relations, and from the day Millard came on, franchisee relations weren't very good. Lots of franchisees didn't fit in the boxes that were created for them, and Millard sometimes wanted to call a franchisee to find out whether it was time for him to leave the organization. Murphy believed that Millard often taped those conversations. That was where Murphy drew the line. She would phone the franchisee and secretly warn him before Millard made the conference call.

What the franchisees couldn't understand was that Millard was only trying to be fair. He wanted to be cared for and respected, but he also wanted to make it right for everybody. That's why he had to treat everyone the same. Millard was always honorable. His actions, as he would say, always came from the heart, from straightforward, honest caring. That is why he had to tape their conversations, to insure that the hand of justice was uniform and perfect. Anything else would be a lie.

Senior ComputerLand employees began to wonder when they would be given the responsibility to make a decision. Whereas Faber would give an assignment and let his executives figure out how to accomplish it, Millard wanted to talk about how it was going to happen; Millard wanted to have input about how a project would change things or how it would take place. It was an adjustment for the executives. They weren't accustomed to having to sit through several hours of meetings to explain how they were going to do something that was really still just an idea.

Millard, however, knew that every decision was important, no matter how small. It was the principle that mattered to him. Millard chose the menu for conferences and the color of the tablecloths. No decision, no matter how seemingly insignificant, was beyond his reach.

Millard's Office of the Chairman had to read every publication, see every videotape, and clear every piece of information the company produced. Millard was a perfectionist, and he was worried that someone might misuse his name or that unalignedness might surface. The process was not unique to ComputerLand. At IBM it could take days just to approve a letter.

Millard also knew that it was his duty to carefully maintain documents, record phone calls, and store hundreds of hours of videotape. Society would not forgive them if they failed to chronicle the process. By the end of the century, ComputerLand would be the next General Motors, the new model company the world would seek to imitate. Millard knew that nations from around the globe would study his formula for the franchise fee, his rule for royalties, his rules for how stores should look, his rules for how fast stores would open, his rules for *everything*.

If a rule didn't seem to work, it wasn't replaced or adjusted. Millard would instead order programs to rationalize the rule. To justify the high 8-percent royalty fees he charged franchisees, Millard created new programs for the franchisees or hired more people. It didn't matter that the programs or people weren't needed, or even wanted.

"It was as though you went out and hired everybody here and said come in with a plan tomorrow to tell me why I've got you," said Burdick, who like most franchisees would have rather had the money than the programs.

"I don't really remember any programs because I don't remember anything working," said ComputerLand's first franchisee, Ken Greene.

To Millard, the franchisees were being ungrateful. He felt that a lot of things had not been done right because they had been stingy and sloppy and didn't have enough employees, lawyers, or policies. "To be fair he really did hire people in every area in the company," Mike McConnell recalled. "They'd say, 'Oh, Bill, you know we could do this for the franchisees.' And he'd say, 'Oh, okay, good. Hire those people.'"

Many of the people Millard hired were supposed to watch other people. That was for their own good, of course. The hardest group to keep an eye on were the international franchisees. Millard hired someone full-time to watch the foreign part of the ComputerLand empire.

Some of the policies his lieutenants enforced covered little things. Millard required that there be on file a photograph of every franchisee and a copy of the franchisee's agreement. Millard wanted to be able to see whether each store was up to policy.

Design specifications were created for the stores. Doors had to be a certain height; walls had to be at certain angles. Overseas, these requirements could cost franchisees enormous sums of money. And then there was the expense of policing the requirements.

"Bill, that's going to cost a lot of money. We're going to have to hire people to do that," protested Mike McConnell, then president of International. "Not only that, but you have people in Policy studying what I'm doing. I have to hire people just to talk to them about what I'm doing. For every job in the policy division we're creating another job in the operational division." "I know, Mike, that's fine," an astounded McConnell remembered Millard telling him. In the spring of 1983, McConnell had five people working for him in International. Two years later he had eighty.

But the money wasn't spent only on programs for the franchisees. Millard needed company planes to serve and visit his worldwide network more efficiently. He ordered two planes in 1981. The first was a King Air, $2-million, two-engine, turboprop plane that seated eight. The second was a $5.5-million Learjet. Next came the Falcon 50, a $10-million jet that seated eleven. With the planes came the ComputerLand flight department: a chief pilot, copilot, mechanic, and of course, hangar space. The romantic Millard ordered that his wedding date, 3/4/56, be the number on all his planes.

The journey they were taking, however, would require more than just wings. They needed land to spread their roots. A dude ranch near Grants Pass in southern Oregon was purchased. Millard hired the previous owners of the ranch to run the operation, and with an infusion of capital the aging ranch was turned into an elegant Computer-Land retreat called Paradise Ranch. Three ponds stocked with fish, a swimming pool, hiking trails, and tennis courts surrounded the cabins. The sparkling white, simple rooms of the cabins housed fifty. There was horseback riding, bicycling, a nearby golf course, a restaurant, a recreation barn with pool and Ping-Pong tables, television, a bar, and sofas around the crackling fire.

Millard liked to send his executives up to Paradise Ranch for weekend retreats. There was a small airstrip nearby just long enough for the Falcon 50. Millard was a gracious, marvelous host. A little surrey would take visitors to the cabins. Each guest's every need was taken care of. Millard even kept a stock of Shabazian's favorite cigarettes. Millard bought a place for his parents nearby the ranch, and he often made the trip to Oregon just to see his folks.

The ranch was only part of Millard's expanding empire. A vineyard was purchased near Pleasanton, a viniculturist hired, and the old roots pulled out of the earth to make room for new vines. Some of the neighboring wineries worried that Millard's new vineyard would become a ComputerLand campus.

Millard's house, of course, had also been purchased by the growing empire. But ComputerLand hadn't actually purchased the property. The ranch, the vineyards, a fish farm, the house, and the planes would all be owned by subsidiaries of IMS. That way the nearly $2.4 million in losses they would sustain in 1983 and 1984 could be written off against ComputerLand's booming sales.

22
Family

F ranchisees around the world noticed ComputerLand's new corporate attitude. In Copenhagen, Gunnar Ass was looking forward to the opening of his store. He was excited when he was told on
a Thursday in November of 1983 that Millard had arrived in Luxembourg and had called a special meeting for Saturday. All the major
European ComputerLand store owners would gather at Computer-
Land International's offices for the meeting.

Millard began the meeting with a talk that older franchisees had
heard before. ComputerLand was a family, Millard said. It was important to him that all of his family—down to the smallest member
—was well fed, housed, and cared for. Gunnar liked this approach.
Millard seemed to care about the European stores at least as much as
the American ones. Gunnar knew that many American companies
cut corners with their European divisions. He was pleased that Millard was different.

Then quite suddenly, as though someone else had begun speaking,
Millard's tone changed. He had talked to a Swiss banker and been
told that business practices in Europe were different from those in the
U.S. The banker had told him that European businesses often did not
report their full income.

The room grew quiet. Many had never been so insulted in their

242

lives. How dare this rich American come over, butter them up with talk about his caring, and then accuse them of cheating! But they were Europeans and were brought up in style. They would not respond in kind. One by one, they calmly told Millard that the Swiss banker was wrong. Reporting laws in Europe were actually stricter in many ways than those in America.

Millard did not believe them at first. After a while he began to get the point. If the meeting was not a success for Millard, it did accomplish something for the European franchisees. Those who had questions about Millard before the meeting no longer wondered what he was like.

Perhaps the strangest thing was that the confrontation could easily have been avoided. Millard had picked up the idea about cheating from an Austrian he had met at a cocktail party in California. The Austrian had told Millard he was a consul, but Mike McConnell discovered that he was only an honorary consul and hadn't lived in his native country since World War II. After the cocktail tip, Millard organized a dinner meeting with all the top Computer-Land International people and told them he didn't really think they could franchise anymore in Europe. McConnell asked whether he could look into the matter. "Sure, you look into it, but I don't see any way around it," McConnell recalled Millard saying. "Then he [Millard] started remembering other things he knew. 'Taxes in Sweden are ninety percent. Everyone knows the Italians keep double books. . . .'"

McConnell personally interviewed the German consul and the American trade delegation in Paris. They interviewed people all over the world, franchisers, franchisees, heads of trade delegations, assembling a massive volume that basically said, "There was not one shred of evidence to support this idea." Millard still didn't believe McConnell, even though the study shot holes in his arguments: Personal income taxes were high in Sweden, *not* business taxes. And as to the allegations about Italy—they had no Italian franchisees!

But Millard's personal conviction remained unshaken. He prepared to end all business in Europe. What if the franchisees told you in person that they weren't cheating? McConnell asked as a last resort. "Yes, maybe that would convince me," Millard stubbornly replied.

• • •

Franchisees in the United States had felt the changes from head-quarters much earlier. At first, it seemed to make sense that Millard was running things. ComputerLand was no longer a small company, and though Faber had been the right person to bring the company through its first seven years, maybe now that the company was approaching maturity, a new approach was needed.

Or so some believed until they came to know the work of Millard's new general counsel, Mike Walter. Ken Waters had given the new version of the franchise agreement to Walter for review. Walter, who had franchise experience from working at Meineke Mufflers in Houston, found the document verbose and imprecise. He told Millard that by changing the document's form he could create a better, smaller agreement to replace the old franchise contract.

In principle Ken Waters agreed with the lawyer's suggestion. At least, that is, until he discovered Walter's real intention was to cut from the agreement everything that ComputerLand had previously promised to do for franchisees and leave only the litany of things that franchisees were to do for ComputerLand.

Amazingly, the thousands of man-hours already spent in creating a comprehensive document were forgotten. Millard was impressed with Walter's brilliant insight. By promising nothing, ComputerLand could remain flexible, free to adapt to a changing market. If a franchisee didn't trust an agreement that promised nothing, then he shouldn't sign on in the first place. The agreement, as proposed by Walter, came to be known as "The Blank Page."

Ken Waters was astonished. Not only was The Blank Page totally one-sided, but Millard acknowledged its one-sidedness. Under the new agreement, ComputerLand was not even under any obligation to sell computers to the franchisees. And there were no fewer than thirty different reasons for which a franchisee could be terminated.

The new form contained a deposit arrangement with strict deadlines and penalties. Once you signed the agreement, you had 120 days to open the doors. Bad weather, construction delays, even illness or a death in the family were not sufficient to grant an extension. "Bill had provisions that if you missed the one hundred and twenty days, you paid a penalty," Waters recalls of the unforgiving document. "We could terminate, keep all the franchisee fee, and find a new buyer."

There was one catch with Millard's new agreement. In a later article to franchisees, printed in the in-house magazine *InLand* and entitled "The Concept of The Blank Page," Millard acknowledged that some franchisees resented the agreement:

> It was the point when some franchisees thought that "Corporate stopped caring about the stores." It was when, for some, the deal became "everything for Corporate, nothing for the stores" or as some said, "Corporate has 500 excuses for terminating the franchisee. The franchisee has nothing."

They did not understand. Millard knew that The Blank Page supported the economic and relational physics of the ComputerLand system. The Blank Page was the result of careful analysis. Millard realized that most American businesses didn't function in that manner, but ComputerLand wasn't like most businesses. They were not trying to produce an ordinary result. They were trying to create an outrageous result, and nothing could stand in their way.

When the franchisees got hold of The Blank Page, however, they did their best to fill in the blanks. "We had a Network Advisory Council meeting and the members represented to Bill that they had a lot of problems," Ken Waters remembered. "Bill claimed that he had not read the [Blank Page] agreement that was sent out by Mike Walter, but had relied on his representation that the agreement was substantially the same under the terms he wanted." Ken Waters, however, believed that as with almost every key legal contract at ComputerLand, Millard had gone over the document with a fine-tooth comb.

When some franchisees started raising points at a meeting with Millard, Waters recalled that Millard said, "I don't see a problem with that; why can't we change that?" Waters shook his head in disbelief. They were back where they were a year ago. Millard was opening up every single provision to debate. Waters began working on Walter's revision of Water's revision. Waters began filling in The Blank Page.

Committees were the path that would lead them to the answers they sought. Millard set up several committees. The committees researched, performed analyses, and compiled reports. Millard never made a commitment to any of their suggestions, however. "I understand what you're doing now," Tom Niccoli remembered Millard saying over and over again. "Now let me look at it and get back to you."

Committees, however, could not solve the problems Millard and his lawyer seemed to create. Walter was one of the reasons the International Association of Computer Dealers (IACD) was formed in the first place. When Walter began making threats about franchise terminations, the franchisees grouped together in defense and started the IACD. When Faber saw that Millard viewed the IACD as a militant organization, he helped form the smaller NAC (Network Advisory Council, composed of seventeen franchisees representing the whole country) in the hopes that Millard would listen to the smaller group.

Franchisees readily admitted that they feared and disliked Walter. They knew Walter was behind the new, hostile Blank Page agreement. "His attitude was, 'You don't like it. I'm going to sue you and run you out of business,'" said Ken Greene, who liked Walter and remembered him as an "all right guy." But Greene also recognized that behind Walter's friendly façade was a tough attorney from the Bronx.

Walter was out to get the cheaters. He thought that franchisees were cutting corners, holding back royalties, and breaking the franchisee agreement. Walter was going to do his damnedest to catch them.

"I think Millard liked him because he was really pro-Millard and anti-franchisee. He was like Millard's hit man," remembered Niccoli.

"Yeah, Mike came out of the Midas Muffler world.* Mike was a franchisee killer and that's what he did," said Ken Greene.

In January of 1984, ComputerLand finally came up with an idea the franchisees liked. Waters, Millard, and Walter had noticed that public offerings of computer companies were making the headlines. Why not take ComputerLand public? Millard met with several investment banking firms—Salomon Brothers, Merrill Lynch, and First Boston.

Out of discussions with the leading investment banking firms in the country, Millard crafted a plan all his own. He called Ken Waters into his office. They would *not* take the company public, he told him excitedly. Instead, they would form a new corporation called CSI (ComputerLand Stores Incorporated), half-owned by the franchisees and half-owned by ComputerLand. For that privilege, Millard decided that franchisees would hand over to him 25 percent stock in

*Walter actually had worked for Meineke Mufflers

their stores. To earn its 50 percent, Millard decided that Computer-Land would contribute its "marketing value."

Franchisees would then pay a 2.4 percent (of sales) dividend to CSI. That would be the sole revenue stream for CSI—the only source of funds for the public company. ComputerLand would pay nothing. Millard, of course, would have all the voting rights to the CSI stock. Public shareholders, including the franchisees, would have no voting rights. You can't do that on the New York Stock Exchange, so Millard got an exemption on the American Stock Exchange. That was when he started talking about taking the stock offer to every country in the world.

Why did Millard want the franchisees to pay dividends into CSI? "It was strictly for tax purposes," said Waters. "Because then the publicly held company could have excluded 85 percent of that tax."

But since the dividend was not deductible, the franchisees would effectively be paying 4.8 percent into the shell company, said Waters. And that 4.8 percent would be on top of their 8-percent royalty fee and 1-percent advertising fund. In total, franchisees would have to pay nearly 14 percent per month in royalties, advertising, and CSI dividends and taxes. To the franchisees, the terms and conditions were nothing short of ludicrous.

There was another minor detail. If by chance a franchisee couldn't pay his dividend, ComputerLand would have a fiduciary duty to fire the franchisee and take over management.

A committee was formed. For the next several months the first order of business for many franchisees was CSI. Franchisees figured they could convince Millard to tone down some of his wilder demands. The majority of the owners spent $1,500 or more per store for Price Waterhouse inventory audits. Mysteriously, sales seemed to rise at the same time.

"They ran the numbers," Waters said. "They began selling more because they could see that they'd get more stock because they thought it [the public offering] was based on sales."

In NAC and regional meetings Millard would display his CSI projections that he had doe on an IBM PC. If they took CSI public, the company would get a price-to-earnings ratio of seventy, he enthusiastically proclaimed. Waters figured they might get a ratio of twelve or fifteen. An extraordinary success would have been a value of twenty.

Ken Greene listened to all the talk and watched Millard produce projections on computer spreadsheets. He never believed the stock offering was a real possibility. "The numbers that were being conveyed as potential would have made it the biggest public offering the world had ever seen." Still, Waters didn't give up hope. He still wanted to convince Millard to make a few changes.

The plan seemed to overlook a few realities. How were franchisees going to pay out 14 percent of their gross sales when some were beginning to have difficulties paying 9 percent? Running sales up to look good for the stock offering had overstretched a lot of franchisees' capital. Businessland and other new retailers were offering stiff competition. ComputerLand franchisees looked to corporate headquarters for help.

They would have had better luck looking up to the sky. Millard would not bend on royalties. "It was chipped in stone," Burdick recalled. And the worst part of the 8-percent royalty fee was that Millard himself admitted it was totally arbitrary. "It was a flat deal," Millard remembered. "That's the number we play."

Millard's intentions were good. Deep in his heart he wanted ComputerLand to be different from his previous experiences: "From my soul I wanted something more; I wanted a committed relationship." Millard threw himself into his work, searching for the universal truth. "If God were doing it, this is the way he'd do it," Burdick recalled Millard saying at NAC meetings.

Few doubted that Millard was trying his best to be as complete and fair as God. His calendar assistant laid out a daily computerized schedule that started at six A.M. and ran past midnight. Millard began the day with yoga. The morning was spent meticulously adhering to his systems. Millard's personal assistants thought the routine a lot like what they had seen while working for Werner. Millard also loved to keep records. Up on the fourth floor of the Oakland headquarters, Millard kept monstrous, detailed records.

Millard made it a policy to respond to every letter. If it wasn't appropriate for Millard to respond personally, he would send the letter to Shabazian. When the OC received a response from Shabazian, a follow-up letter would be sent to insure that the problem had been handled.

Since Millard wrote few of his own letters or memos—and he sent out lots of those—what with the reading and approval, just going through the mail and keeping up with the backlog consumed his mornings. The rest of the day was filled with meetings and appointments.

In addition to his work with ComputerLand, Millard was active in the community, sat on several local boards, was a friend of Cornel Maier of Kaiser, and even met occasionally with Oakland's Mayor Lionel Wilson.

The nights were as busy as the days. Millard knew that a man of his position and wealth had to appreciate the fine arts. And so he had season tickets to the San Francisco Opera, the symphony, the American Conservatory Theater, and the Berkeley Repertory Theater. There were few nights when Bill and Pat Millard weren't seen at one show or another. Millard often didn't enjoy these events, but he knew that he was doing the right and appropriate thing by going.

When Millard wasn't on the town, he was often hosting a delegation from Luxembourg. No expense was spared. He gave sumptuous luncheons with local mayors and executives of high-tech firms in attendance. Often the night was highlighted by a San Francisco Bay dinner cruise on a luxurious yacht—all, of course, at the invitation of Millard and his family.

With what little time remained in his busy day, Millard met with the officers of ComputerLand. One night a week he invited his presidents to dinner at St. James. Another night he invited individual presidents and their vice presidents. With the nights that were left, he invited executives of the top personal-computer companies. Weeks went by without a free evening with the family.

Bruce Burdick knew Millard was doing this not for himself, but for ComputerLand and the dream. Burdick may have come closer to understanding Millard than any other franchisee. He could go on Millard's plane and understand what he was trying to accomplish. Unlike the other franchisees, Burdick tried to share Millard's dream when he could understand him. But Millard wasn't always willing or able to share his dream, even with Burdick. There were no words to describe his vision.

"He wanted this worldwide, godlike thing," Burdick recalled. "I always likened him to Patton. He was in his fifth or sixth reincarnation. He was seeking this final perfection."

Indeed, as the months passed, the franchisees saw a military style evolve. One day a stranger showed up at an NAC meeting. He was dressed in a suit and sat next to Millard and followed him everywhere he went. Millard has a bodyguard! the franchisees laughed. Millard was developing an entourage. Sometimes there was more than one bodyguard. At his side Barbara, his attorney Walter, and two stenographers were taking notes of the meeting, as if some great trial were unfolding.

What the franchisees didn't know was that Millard had also devised a special seating chart. Hours were spent figuring out the arrangement that would empower them to higher communication.

The room had to be comfortable but not too large, or they would lose their focus. The precise distance between seats was critical. The seating had to form a U, not a circle. The relative positions of Shabazian and Barbara were critical. Millard knew that they were "transmitting" things just by where they sat. "Everything was trivial," recalled Shabazian. "We would take longer to figure out the seating arrangement at the NAC [meeting] than we would putting in a ten-million-dollar order to IBM."

The franchisees did see, however, at least one purpose behind the elaborate organization, the bodyguards, and the stenographers. When Millard felt a franchise was vacillating on a point, he would stop the meeting and tell the stenographer to read back the person's previous remarks. After publicly humiliating the person, Millard would move on. No one was ever permitted to read back Millard's remarks.

Each NAC meeting's proceedings were supposed to have been typed up by the stenographers and sent out to the franchisees. But the meetings, often several days long, translated into hundreds of pages and several pounds of verbiage. Somehow, Millard's office never quite got around to sending out the transcripts.

During the meetings, Millard particularly enjoyed humiliating Shabazian. Millard would tell him off or simply tell him to shut up. "He nailed Shabazian two or three times in front of people. Just really knocked him down to his knees," said Niccoli. The franchisees, who often received similar treatment, sympathized with Shabazian after meetings. Burdick, however, reached a point when he would listen no more. After one exceptionally cruel exchange, Burdick told Millard that he had to tell him something in private. Millard told him to go ahead, although one of his aides stood by. "Well, I'd like to talk to you alone," Burdick said. "No, go ahead," Burdick remembered Millard insisting.

"You can't cut your people down in a meeting in front of me! That's something you do in a back room or your office," Burdick told Millard. "If you do that in front of me again, I won't be in your meetings!" Millard nodded. He didn't tell Burdick to leave, and he didn't do it again. Burdick had discovered something only a few dared.

23

Around

the World

By the spring of 1984, Millard was moving fast to fulfill his worldwide objective. In the April issue of the ComputerLand in-house magazine, *InLand*, in an article entitled "The International ComputerLand Network," he wrote:

> For the last three weeks (this was written in the second week of April) I have been traveling around the world. I mean that literally. Flying Oakland to London, then to Luxembourg then to Bombay and Singapore and Sidney and home via Fiji. . . . In the past two months I've been in touch with ComputerLand in almost every part of the world, and ComputerLand is in almost every part of the world. Several aspects of this experience were immensely exciting to me. There were signs that the vision I have had of ComputerLand from its very first day is now becoming a reality. It is a vision of the International ComputerLand Network. . . . The second phase is a building of a network of corporate facilities stretching around the world. These are not simply regional support offices: they are duplications in almost every way of our world headquarters operation in California. . . .

ComputerLand did not have any stores in Bombay. But Millard had a purpose bigger than business in visiting one of the most overpopulated cities on earth. Before Bill made big decisions, he liked to journey close to the center of a new project. What better place to see hunger than India?

Millard's friend Werner Erhard had come up with the next best thing to est. It was called the Hunger Project. Werner's goal was to end world hunger by the end of the century. According to est, all that would be necessary for such a great result would be consciousness raising. And Werner had lots of experience in raising consciousness. He had raised more than a half-million consciousnesses to the tune of $300 or more per head.

Huge seminars in coliseums were organized across the nation. The seminars raised a lot of consciousness. They also raised a lot of money. With the money raised by raising consciousness, the Hunger Project gave more seminars to raise more money. Some thought the effect miraculous. Maybe they *would* solve world hunger before the end of the century.

Millard talked to some Indian industrialists about the Hunger Project on his visit to Bombay. He wanted to get a practical feel for how ComputerLand could help solve world hunger. Millard's daughters Barbara and Ann also visited Bombay, and Ann could barely tolerate the pain and suffering. Barbara, however, was taken by the idea, and when she threw herself into a new project, her enthusiasm knew no bounds. She was not like her father, who approached new ventures cautiously. "Barbara could be jacked up into believing in unlimited reality for a month at a time," said one of the OC staff.

But Barbara was not alone in her enthusiasm for this great humanitarian cause. ComputerLand employees had sent Millard letters encouraging him to take more of a stand for est and against hunger. They wrote of how the most inspiring thing about working at ComputerLand was Millard's "appreciation of Werner." Millard respected their intention, but wrote back saying that it was inappropriate that there be any outward link between the two organizations.* You couldn't ask people who worked at ComputerLand to praise est. Having said all that, Millard still wanted to be part of Werner's high-integrity cause. He began investigating how ComputerLand could help end world hunger.

Hunger was not the only great task Millard faced that year. In

---

*Millard sat on the boards of Erhard-related companies and donated huge sums to Erhard-sponsored organizations.

1984, Millard broke through the Great Wall of China. A passion for the Far East, begun during his first visits for IMSAI in the 1970s, was coming into full bloom. Japan was already on board. The new goal was Communist China. But when Millard first met officials of the People's Republic of China in 1983, he saw no way he could bring ComputerLand to China. Then, in early 1984, Millard was invited by San Francisco mayor Dianne Feinstein to a reception for the Chinese premier. Of the guests, only Millard (through the help of his advisor on China) was able to engage the Premier in conversation. Afterward, Millard reconsidered what the Chinese had said to him a few months before. It had struck a chord in Millard; it was the same attitude with which he lived every second, every minute of every day: "More is possible than you think."

In the spring, Millard invited Werner to join him on another trip to the Far East to discover those new possibilities. It was a spring of possibilities. In April, ComputerLand hosted its first tennis tournament, the ComputerLand/U.S. Women's Indoor Tennis Championship. The ComputerLand logo was tacked on everything from the scoreboard to the ball boys' shirts to courtside banners. ComputerLand commercials were aired throughout the nationally televised event. Millard himself presented the champion's trophy—he named it Excalibur—to winner Martina Navratilova. Fashioned of silver and gold, and embedded in a solid block of cut crystal, the trophy was designed by James Houston and like the award Millard had given Faber, created by Steuben Glass.

Tennis was only part of Millard's new program of lavish promotions. ComputerLand had sponsored a special musical event commemorating the 250th anniversary of London's Royal Opera House. Starring two of America's most prestigious opera singers, the concert was broadcast during Easter week over the Public Broadcasting System.

But the Far East trip would be a different sort of promotion. They would travel in the Falcon 50 and Werner would carry the title of "advisor." It was to be an exchange. Millard arranged for Werner to visit with his Chinese masters and Werner would take Millard to see some Zen masters in Japan. The Office of the Chairman was ordered to keep Werner's presence on the trip a secret. The press would never know of the trip, and other than the company's top executives, ComputerLand was ignorant of the new, temporary member of Millard's staff.

How much things had changed. Only a year before, Millard had given the company a special gift—Werner had visited Computer-Land. To the company's many devoted followers of est, it was like a visit of the Pope to South America. Even Faber spent half an hour in his office with Werner. Not everyone was impressed, however. Officers who weren't est graduates seemed embarrassed. They didn't know what to say or how to act. Werner would make profound proclamations such as, "You are about more than computers," and the officers would stiffly reply, "Yes, we sell software and books."

For the workers, the highlight was Werner's walk through the company. There was no doubt about Werner's handsomely chiseled features and his mystical blue eyes. Women who had taken the training found him irresistible.

The trip to Japan began with the visit to Zen masters. The heads of the Japanese ComputerLand franchisees were invited on the journey. How different was their chairman from other American executives, with his appreciation of their culture and way of life. And in the same courtly manner in which Millard lived, when he dined at the finest Japanese restaurants, everything was silently taken care of. Millard and the rest of the party would enter the restaurant and order dinner. Across the street, behind a car or a pillar, Ernie Luzania would be watching. Millard never had to touch money or even pay a bill. "If you were Bill's guest, it looked as if you were just walking into the restaurant, eating a meal, and walking out," remembered one of his staff. "No bill being presented, no money being shown whatever. It was all being handled by Ernie."

From Japan they traveled to China. There, Werner assisted Millard on all the negotiations. Millard's aides noticed an interesting side effect. Millard seemed more effective in Werner's presence. When Millard began to drift off into one of his monologues, Werner would shake him back to reality with a cutting word or phrase. It was clear that Millard wanted to impress his friend. Millard's aides later called it the most successful trip he ever took.

On May 15, 1984, in Beijing, the capital of the People's Republic of China, Millard and officials of the PRC's ministry of the electronics industry signed a letter of intent for a joint venture to create a network for microcomputer systems in China. Declared Millard on the historic occasion, "We're talking in terms of the first hundred years."

With the foundation of his international empire in place, Millard returned to reinforce the home front. He decided that the problem with the U.S. franchisees was that they had strayed from the basics. They needed a few lessons in fundamentals. And so in the June 1984 issue of *InLand* appeared the first of a series of articles that Millard wrote under the heading "The Fundamentals of ComputerLand." The first article was titled "The Franchise System, Avoiding an Adversarial Relationship":

. . . Franchising is not for everyone. It's not the only road to success. It is for people who want to be their own bosses but also want to be part of a committed relationship.

You must want both. If all you want is independence, then you don't want to be a franchisee. . . . I want people to do one of two things. I want them either to be enthusiastically committed to the ComputerLand system and relationship as it is both designed and intended. Or I want them to flee as fast as they can. . . . It's fine with me if people flee. . . .

Part II of the "Fundamentals of ComputerLand," headlined "Sharing Revenue from Trade-ins and Warranty Reimbursements," explained why stores should pay royalties on trade-ins and reimbursements from manufacturers for warranty repairs. Wrote Millard:

It might look as if a franchisee has a choice of ways in which to maximize profits. One way would be to seek ways to avoid royalties and concentrate on maximizing unshared revenue. The other way would be to wholeheartedly support the revenue sharing agreement between franchiser and franchisee and work together to seek to maximize the revenue to be shared. It might look at first as if the first way, avoiding royalties, would be the most profitable if it were possible to get away with it. My message from these two articles is that it is not more profitable to avoid sharing the income.

. . . It is not as if the 8% royalty were payment for certain specific services. It is the revenue sharing mechanism that supports the entire Computer-

Land system. . . . The owners of ComputerLand corporation, of which I am the principal one, have set the profit as a percentage of corporate's income, so that while increased network revenue increases the owner's profit, that percentage does not increase. . . . Let's take this cycle further: more revenue to corporate = more services to stores. More services to stores = more services to attract and convey to customers. More services to attract and convey to customers = more customers. More customers = more revenue to the store. More revenue to the store = more revenue to corporate. More revenue to corporate = more services = more customers = more revenue, etc. . . . I am simply describing economic physics. . . . The system is worth supporting.

The final "Fundamentals of ComputerLand" article, "The Concept of the Blank Page," appeared in the August issue. Under the heading, "The Risk of the Blank Page Contract," Millard wrote:

Theoretically the blank page seems to open the possibility for horrendous abuse. It looks as if we could collect royalties, put them in the bank and forget about providing any services at all. We could probably make the stores do virtually anything. It seems as if corporate could make them do things that would be stupid, that would be uneconomic and drive them out of business and any franchisees who refused to do those stupid things they'd lose their franchises. . . . If corporate put an order out to the network to do something stupid and wrong and maybe even unethical the franchisee agreement wouldn't mean a thing. Franchisees wouldn't follow the order and eventually the courts would stop us. It is a great myth that people can be forced to do things they don't want to do. I have no illusion about that. The truth is that there is no way for corporate to be irresponsible for very long.

Final preparations were being made on the Learjet. This time there was no doubt in Shabazian's mind. Failure and humiliation had weighed on him nearly the whole year. Unwilling to sign The Blank Page, virtually no U.S. franchisees had opened new stores for the first six months of 1984. In Europe, store openings stopped completely, as owners waited for The Blank Page to be filled in. Finally, in June, after six months' work on the third revision, Ken Waters had patched the document back together.*

*By then The Blank Page's author, Mike Walter, had left to work for Entré, a competing computer retail chain.

It was funny, thought Waters. The document finally drafted was almost the same as the one he had revised nearly a year before. Millard would chart out radical courses, and the wind—or the franchisees—would blow him back to Faber. Perhaps Millard was right; things really weren't changing. Certainly, there was no good news. At the beginning of an NAC meeting in June of 1984, Millard announced perfunctorily that CSI was finished; ComputerLand's public stock offering was history.

Facing the franchisees was getting tougher for Shabazian. He had always been a team player, and he would be the last guy to cross his boss in a meeting with the franchisees, no matter how difficult his boss might have become. Shabazian felt that he and Millard had the same goals; they just wrestled on how to get there. He kept trying to convince himself that things would get better, that he could steer Millard back on course.

But in meeting after meeting, Millard would scold him and treat him like a child: "Shabaz that's wrong! Shabaz that's not right!" Shabazian learned that there were only two possible responses to Millard's treatment. He could parrot exactly what Millard wanted, or he could remain silent. And if he was silent, as he was so often these days, what was the sense in going to the meetings?

At the airport, Shabazian pulled Millard aside and asked if they could talk for a moment. They retired to an executive waiting room.

"I quit; I resign," Shabazian told Millard.

"Why?"

"Because I hate you, Bill. I hate you and I don't respect you."

Melancholy crept over Millard's face. Silently, he reached over and gently placed his hand over Shabazian's thick fist.

"I love you," Millard said.*

Millard looked a long time into Shabazian's deep, mud-brown Armenian eyes. In that moment, in that look, hopeless almost, afraid like a motherless animal, Shabazian saw that Millard had utterly lost the gift of trust. Shabazian's pure hatred was a raindrop of truth. Someone, at last, was telling Millard what he believed.

"I need you there, Mike," Millard pleaded. "What would it look like if you didn't come?"

---

*Shabazian was not aware that part of the teaching of est is to return aggression with the appearance of love.

He felt sorry for Millard, not because of what he might face without him, but because of what Millard faced every day and would face the rest of his life. Then, suddenly, Shabazian broke the gaze and heard the roar of jet engines. "Oh, Christ," he thought, the weight of Millard's palm still upon his fist, "the guy *does* pay me a quarter of a million bucks a year!"

Shabazian had never doubted Millard's generosity and good intentions. Outside of the office, at the ranch, or at St. James, Millard was a. kind, gracious host and friend. There were times when he was magnanimous beyond belief. "I thought it was the most marvelous thing. When he went bankrupt at IMSAI, the people that were out money, he was going to pay them all back—with interest!" recalled Shabazian. "Now that he had all this money he was going to pay them back!"

Millard's plan to reimburse IMSAI's creditors had all the makings of Dickens's A *Christmas Carol*. There was no doubt that the chairman's heart was in the right place. Millard knew intentions were what was important. It was enough to *talk about* paying back the dealers and suppliers dragged down with IMSAI. That in itself was a marvelous gesture, and if Millard's attention drifted away to the latest, greatest crisis before he actually paid anyone a dime, that minor oversight would be forgiven.

Millard held the letter aloft as he strode into the Denver Hotel meeting room. He had just received the message from IACD telling him that they were tired of his broken promises. They wanted results and were going to kick into gear. Only two franchisees were members of both the IACD and the NAC—Elliott Greene and Tom Niccoli.

Millard sat down and calmly read the letter. "There are two Association members in this room," Niccoli recalled Millard saying. "I will not sit down and go over my strategic planning with the enemy." Shabazian was not there to help, nor did he join the meeting later.

Niccoli responded, "Bill, you know that Elliott Greene and I are sitting here in the room, and we're on the Association. And I'll tell you right now I think it's in the best interest to everybody in this room and ComputerLand as a whole to have this strategic planning session. If that means that Elliott and I get up and walk out of this room and don't come back, that's just fine. For the good of the Network this meeting has to go on." The whole room was silent. Greene voiced his agreement. One by one franchisees began standing up for Niccoli and Greene. Finally, the meeting began.

Millard kept Niccoli and Greene after the meeting for two and a half hours. Niccoli felt as if he were being scolded for being a bad boy. He had had enough. Niccoli had worked his tail off for ComputerLand, and this was the thanks he got. Life was too short for that kind of treatment.

In the morning Niccoli's bags were packed. But before he could check out, three or four franchisees talked him into staying for the start of the next meeting. The franchisees told Millard that it was all or nothing—either Niccoli and Greene stayed or all thirty of them would walk. Millard gave in. At the end of the day Niccoli even apologized a bit and told Millard that he was not the enemy, and that he was not going to take all the information they were discussing and hand it over to the Association.

Everybody was excited that Millard finally saw it their way. The franchisees walked into the next day's meeting eager to see Millard's strategic plan unwrapped before their eyes.

"Let's get started," Millard said. "Where should we begin?" The franchisees were confused. Don't you have an outline, or anything; something of where you think we're going? "No," said ComputerLand's owner, CEO, and chairman.

Millard suggested that they define the business they were in. It was a sentence he was searching for, a statement of the business. The franchisees looked at each other and wondered how they would get anywhere at that pace. And they were right. For the next day and a half sentences were put up on the board describing where they wanted to go. Many franchisees wanted to go home.

"It was another way of stalling us. What in God's name could we have taken away from that meeting and given to the Association even if we would have wanted to," Niccoli recalled. "The bottom line was [that] he had no plan and was looking for us to give him a plan."

Niccoli simply didn't understand. Millard was trying to be fair to everyone, fair to ComputerLand, fair to the Association, and fair to himself. Anyone who knew him well could tell that. Perhaps the best example ever of his fairness was the 1984 ComputerLand International Conference later that summer.

Marian Murphy had spent months preparing for the elaborate affair in Boston. All the blueprints were drawn for the stage. Millard's speech was written. He would give the main address, reminding the franchisees of all the things he had done for them. The night before the opening of the conference, most of the soundstage was built and everything appeared on schedule. Then Millard arrived. It wasn't fair or appropriate, the chairman decided, that he give the main address. He ordered that his words be shared among his presidents. Each of his presidents would give a piece of his talk.

Murphy had about twelve hours to transform the stage. They worked furiously. Four music stands replaced the podium. At about four A.M. the stage was as ready as it ever would be, but the four presidents hadn't even had a chance to rehearse. The four of them stood up behind little music stands with their notes. "It was just like a third-grade play," remembered Murphy. "I mean we had a camera on Ken Waters blowing his nose while Barbara would be talking. It was just horrible."

Part of the problem was that Waters and Shabazian were not aligned. "He gave us all these little music stands and we all sat there like little Miss Muffets, and I fought that and fought that and fought that," said Shabazian. But no matter how hard Shabazian fought the idea, he knew that behind the incredible embarrassment he faced was Millard's sense of trying to be fair, of insuring that everyone was *playing*. And so it was that Shabazian got on the stage and read his part with the rest of the Muffets.

It wasn't quite fair to describe the performance as a third-grade play. There was plenty of comedy, too. Shabazian and Waters kept missing their cues and letting the franchisees know that somebody else was pulling the strings. "Shabazian would say stuff and roll his eyes. Ken and Shabazian were just terrible, they were obviously suffering through it," recalled Murphy.

Beyond the embarrassing production was the issue of the words the presidents were reading. Franchisees didn't want to hear about all the great things ComputerLand had done for them. They felt, as one ComputerLand executive put it, that they were "getting the shaft." Millard was pressuring them to open more stores than they could afford, forcing them to follow needless, costly policies. ComputerLand was developing into a different sort of company, a one-way street going the wrong way.

It wasn't just that sales were slumping; profit was diving, too. Sales had shifted from the street to the office. No more was the fellow who walked into your store your regular customer. The best stores had realized long ago that the biggest, most stable market was high in the towers of corporate America. The major ComputerLand stores hired huge sales staffs, whose only job was to call on the banks, insurance companies, and other great consumers of computers. Opening more stores made no sense. The store was like the name, a symbol, and no longer the reason for success, or even survival.

But Millard didn't have the time to listen or put them back on track. In the fall of 1984 he boarded the Falcon 50 for another visit to China. The traveling party consisted of his wife, Mike McConnell, pilots George Shattuck and Bob Miller, and Luzania of the security department. They flew direct to Shanghai. Fourteen hours later, Shattuck began shouting from the cockpit. Directly beneath them flew a V-formation of MiG fighter jets. As they approached Shanghai, their fears increased. Lining the runway were soldiers.

But the military response turned out to be merely formal greetings. Millard and company were invited to the first of many banquets at Beijing in the Summer Palace of the Emperors. By day a tourist attraction, the palace had been transformed that evening for a banquet in their honor. Dusk was falling just as Millard's red-flagged limousines arrived at the gates in a driving rain. As if by magic, the gates opened and they spent the next fifteen minutes winding through a maze of gardens and pavilions. When they visited the palace the next day, they understood why they had lost their way. The palace encompassed several hundred buildings spread over grounds nearly the size of Hayward. Minister Jiang welcomed them as "old friends" in the elegant palace. They sat down to eat thousand-year-old eggs. More eggs and banquets followed. Millard was further honored by an invitation to join in the celebration for Chinese National Day.*

After the festivities, Millard returned to Hayward to make a management change. In November, he appointed his daughter Barbara president and chief operating officer of ComputerLand. Mike Shabazian, Mike McConnell, Ken Waters, and Vincent O'Reiley would all report to the twenty-six-year-old who had not finished one full year of

*Only diplomats and the most favored guests of the Communist party receive this honor.

college. Although promotion materials would say that Barbara had worked for IMSAI, IMS, and ComputerLand all her life, she had worked for ComputerLand barely a year. Her boss would be the one she had had all her life, her father.

Millard didn't seem to want the party to end. In November, Millard and San Jose's mayor hosted a reception and lunch in San Jose for the Grand Duke and Duchess of Luxembourg. Later, Millard gave a private dinner for the royal party at St. James.

The royal visit was only the beginning of the festivities. That year the ComputerLand Christmas party would be held at the elegant Galleria in San Francisco. More than two thousand ComputerLand employees, spouses, and friends would attend. Preparations were elaborate. At the last minute, only a week before the party, Millard decided he wanted to give everybody a gift. It was too late to have something specially engraved. But Millard was unbending in his wish that every last person leave the celebration with a token of his gratitude.

Snow-sprayed Christmas trees and a multitude of lights decorated the extravagant fashion showpalace. The Fifth Dimension was performing, and besides tearing up the huge dance floor, the merry revelers could watch the popular group from four different levels as they sipped drinks from one of the many bars.

A three-course, sit-down dinner was served with red and white wines. Rock Cornish game hen was the main course. Millard gave a speech, but he was speaking softly and not everyone seemed to hear. His exact words were not important. There was a real feeling of pride and celebration that rang through the air. Not just any company could give a $200,000 party in a slumping market and hire The Fifth Dimension. They were working for a winner, and the employees felt more unified than they had in months.

Sales had soared to $1.4 billion in 1984. They knew the company had been spending too much money and their chairman was a bit eccentric, but there was also something special, something magical in ComputerLand. Millard was able to reach out and touch each of the thousands that made up the ComputerLand family. On every table, little gift boxes had been placed. Inside the soft tissue wrap were teddy bears, sea gulls, birds, and penguins—little glass ornaments for everyone to take home to hang on the Christmas tree.

The glass ornaments were lovely, but they were nothing compared to what Millard planned to give to the world. Chad Hill, formerly vice president of public relations, was being promoted to vice president of social responsibility. The first social responsibility Hill was entrusted with was the elimination of hunger by the year 2000. Millard promised Hill a million dollars of ComputerLand's advertising budget. Hill prepared an elaborate, expensive brochure and started developing a Hunger Kit for the chain's 600-plus U.S. franchisees. Those efforts were only the beginning, however. By late spring, the print ads would hit.

But the present Millard asked for was even more than ending world hunger. Intuition told him that he needed a new lawyer for the upcoming battle with Micro/Vest. Millard decided that Raymond Berman, his Washington, D.C., Williams & Connolly attorney, wasn't up to the new challenge. Millard ordered Ken Waters to bring him Irving Younger within forty-eight hours. Younger had worked on the case before. His smooth argument had been responsible for charming an earlier judge into granting a motion for Millard. But the glory of that triumphant day in court had been brief. The motion Younger argued had been reversed. And Younger himself had left the prestigious firm of Williams & Connolly to teach.

Waters soon discovered that Younger was even farther removed than they had imagined. When he called the University of Minnesota, where Younger had gone to teach, Waters was told that Younger was to be found in warmer territory. He was giving a seminar in Hawaii.

No distance was too great for Millard. Waters dutifully loaded the Learjet with several boxes of trial briefs and transcripts and flew to the islands. He found Younger packed and ready to go. After refueling they headed back to Hayward, where Millard would have another chance to charm the silver-tongued orator back into his camp.

PART
IV

24
The
Advocate

It was the summer of 1984 and despite the cool morning fog of San Francisco Bay, Harold Nachtrieb was feeling the heat. Each day Nachtrieb could feel the pressure squeeze tighter. He had never had a client quite like Martin. Every word and every pause had a purpose. Martin wanted Nachtrieb to explode, to tell him off once and for all. But Nachtrieb was too intelligent and sophisticated to take the bait. He would not give Martin the satisfaction.

Martin was looking to raise the stakes, to find a new quarterback, a new lawyer with a major reputation. Nachtrieb knew the request was not unusual, but he also knew that he had earned his 10-percent contingency fee with almost three years of hard work. If it weren't for his two friends, who knows what would have happened to him? "I would have been fired if not for Bruno and Phil," remembered Nachtrieb.

Philip Reed played mediator. He had known Martin longer than any of them and knew how to deal with his temper. Martin was right; they did need to find a trial lawyer of national caliber. But they didn't have to toss Nachtrieb out like a used-up car after years of faithful service. Reed hadn't forgotten how fast Martin had burned through Dell'Ario.

Martin had another reason for wanting to up the ante. There was

267

talk that Irving Younger might try the case for Millard. Before Younger came along, Millard's case looked hopeless. Only Younger appeared capable of putting new fire in Millard's battle.

Martin had heard of a man who might just be Younger's match. His brother-in-law worked in the Claremont, California, office of the flamboyant personal-injury lawyer Herbert Hafif. Two other lawyers were being considered—Joseph Alioto and Joe Cochett—but Martin's brother-in-law kept saying that Hafif was the one to choose.

Hafif's achievements were impressive. At one point in his career he had won more million-dollar punitive-damages cases than any other lawyer in the country, and by the mid-1970s his small firm had won 13 percent of the existing million-dollar-plus victories. Hafif was named "National Consumer Advocate of the Year," voted "the greatest President in the history of the State Trial Bar," and was the featured civil trial lawyer in the CBS-TV documentary "Justice in America."

Hafif won huge punitive damages on intellect, a chameleonlike personality, and an uncanny ability to charm juries. He seemed able to adopt the colors of the day with an ease that could only be instinct. It was no coincidence that Hafif was not an Ivy League graduate and had not begun life with money. Growing up in a tough section of Newark, New Jersey, Hafif hadn't even had the good fortune to belong to the right ethnic group. All young Hafif cared about was getting home from school in one piece. When he was just six years old, his father died, and his English mother remarried not long after. "I was called a dirty Arab *and* a kike," remembered Hafif, who just wanted to be "a member of the human race."

Young Hafif moved to Los Angeles with his mother and stepfather and soon ran away from his new home. The fourteen-year-old's hairy barrel chest, trunk legs, and dark eyes made him seem years older. He went to school during the day and lied about his age to get a night job in a restaurant. Hafif returned to his family before graduating from high school, and soon after bought a piece of property in the Claremont hills and built himself a one-room house.

After high school, Hafif dug ditches and then joined the Army. No longer wanting to be afraid, he took up boxing and became regional Army champion. The fear didn't completely leave him, though, until he became a paratrooper. Jumping out of airplanes made him face death.

The Army, college, and law school were only the prelude to the growth of Hafif's business empire. He opened the Royal Tahitian, a popular local restaurant and club that featured name entertainment like Richard Pryor and Louis Armstrong. Hafif's expanding enterprises included thirteen corporations, among them successful painting and contracting businesses.

But no matter what Hafif did, and he did a lot, he did it with verve and a fighter's instinct. When he couldn't afford proper publicity for the Royal Tahitian, he mapped out a clear marketing strategy. Free tickets were given to every gas station in the vicinity. The station attendants told their local customers of the great show, and out-of-towners looking for excitement were steered in the right direction.

After his unusual business experiences, Hafif found the hallowed profession of the law a breeze. "Trial work is duck soup compared to a lot of that stuff," Hafif said, remembering the nights when he had to be the master of ceremonies for his own club. Hafif also had political aspirations. He ran for governor of California and put in a stint working on Jimmy Carter's presidential campaign. But some would remember Hafif more for his eccentric individualism than for his talent with words. Unhappy with Carter two weeks before the 1976 presidential election, Hafif took out full-page ads in the *Los Angeles Times* denouncing his former boss as "a mean and vindictive man." That was the end of Hafif's political career.

When John Martin showed up at his Claremont office in the summer of 1984, Hafif was nearing his second decade as one of the most successful trial lawyers in America. Hafif had enjoyed wealth and fame for many years. "God's been playing dirty tricks on me, dumping money on me," Hafif said. "Maybe He figures I'll know what to do with it." Another front-page trial with gilded lawyers' fees would not be enough to whet his appetite.

And so it was that Hafif's first impression of Martin was not good. Hafif was not sure what to make of the excited little man who paced about his office. "He's a peripatetic gerbil," Hafif said. "His metabolism runs at a fifty-million rate."

Martin was taking the wrong approach with Hafif. "He was asking me to audition, where I'm used to, 'God would you?'" Hafif thought that he'd be "more comfortable *suing* him than representing him." After several of Martin's unsuccessful overtures, Hafif told Martin what he thought of his offers:

"Fuck you!" Hafif said.

"We want you!" Martin pleaded.

"You've got to convince me I want *you*," Hafif said.

"You want more [money]."*

"Then hire them."

Martin then left Hafif's office, leaving him with a bunch of contracts to sign "so he [Martin] could tell me what to do with the case." Hafif told the "pushy little bastard" he could "shove it up his ass."

Fortunately for Martin, Philip Reed and Bruno Andrighetto met with Hafif before matters got out of hand. "They wanted me because I didn't give a damn," said Hafif of Reed and Andrighetto. But still, Martin kept boring ahead, telling Hafif how much money he was going to make. Why should he give a damn!

Then, at the last moment, Martin found the right button. He started telling Hafif how the "ruthless" Millard had "used him up." Martin convinced Hafif that Martin really had been responsible for the concept of ComputerLand. Hafif could see how painful it was to Martin that he had received no credit, no recognition for his work. "It touched me. Here he was bleeding in the stomach, scared to death of air travel, and he [Millard] throws him away like an old shoe."

Hafif also wondered why it was taking so long to bring Millard to justice. At first he thought Micro/Vest's lawyers must have been to blame, but then he saw that wasn't the trouble. It was Millard. "He was forcing hundreds of depositions, and suing them for punitive damages for having the audacity of asking him to fulfill his contract." Micro/Vest had already spent more than $1 million in their attempt to bring Millard to court.

Hafif was starting to get interested. Money wasn't what had attracted him to the law. After running numerous businesses, Hafif had settled on the law for the simplest and purest of reasons: American justice.

It wasn't mountains or friendly people that made America great. Hafif knew that Russia also had great mountains and friendly people. And Hafif was damn sure that legislators, those "gutless wonders," weren't what made America great. One thing made this land of liberty great—the law. "Bullshit the Constitution! The Constitution put

---

*Hafif demanded a higher fee than the other lawyers Martin interviewed.

to vote loses every time!" bellowed Hafif. "Russia has a great constitution; it's just not followed."

The freedom to say "Goddamnit, I'll sue!" Hafif fervently believed, was what made America the greatest nation on earth. In America, the powerful cannot brush aside the law. And it is not judges or lawyers who made the law mighty enough to challenge the rich. Hafif knew that the strength and courage of the law came from those twelve men and women—the jury. "Anonymous, they come into existence, and then they fade back into anonymity. They give us security to feel we can talk to people like us. The sense that we can get to the people."

The only trouble with Hafif's magnificent legal system was that it was theoretical. He knew the cost of reaching the common, fair ears of the jury was tens, or even hundreds, of thousands of dollars in legal fees. The rich and the powerful throw paper in the way of justice. Demands to produce reams of evidence and the filing of numerous cross-complaints put victims on the defense. The rich and powerful honed the tricks. Corporations know all too well that they can write off the cost of defense, and what is a few hundred thousand dollars paid to lawyers to weave a labyrinth of paper, twisted enough so that few can reach the light of justice?

At fifty-five, Hafif knew that he only had so many top trial years left. If he was lucky, perhaps fifteen. But he also knew that trial lawyers seldom pursue difficult cases in their sixties. He had to choose carefully if he was going to make a lasting contribution. Even so, he knew that you didn't have to "redo the seascape" to rejuvenate the law. You could also lead by example. Hafif wanted to send a message to millionaires and corporations: "Do this and you may pay through the nose. Some son of a bitch who is clever and creative and deadly in court is going to bring you to task and hit you where it hurts."

Hafif didn't take on the Micro/Vest case "to represent a bunch of businessmen (all of whom had enough money already) who were trying to get more money." Fame was also not enough to make him devote months of his life to the case. Unlike other famous trial lawyers, he was not interested in dragging his "ass in front of every microphone." It was the chance to *make a difference* that caused Hafif to take a case from a man who "at times amused me and other times distressed me."

But before Hafif signed on, Martin wanted money. "Before I even started to represent him, he told me he was bankrupt—that he had put his software company in bankruptcy." Martin wanted Hafif to give him $50,000 in cash and sign an elaborate contract determining how and when the money would be returned. "Martin says I have to sign a goddamned agreement—like I *wanted* to lend the money." But despite his protests Hafif eventually did lend Martin the money.

Hafif began work on the Micro/Vest case, but the matter of Nachtrieb remained. While Nachtrieb was vacationing in Los Angeles, Philip Reed called him and asked whether he would meet Hafif. "No problem," said Nachtrieb, who then let Reed know in a gentlemanly way that if he was replaced without his consent, he "would sue them; kick up a fuss about it." It was a bravado move because California law states that a client can remove his lawyer for any reason.

Five minutes with Hafif convinced Nachtrieb that there would indeed be no problem. "I knew he was the man it would take to deal with Millard," said Nachtrieb, who had spent three frustrating years discovering that reason and logic were insufficient with Millard.

As the minutes ran into hours, Nachtrieb realized that if Hafif was not a genius, he was as close to one as Nachtrieb could hope to meet. Hafif's mind just seemed to have more circuits than other people's. Nachtrieb told Reed that he'd be delighted to work with Hafif, and Hafif was willing to share the case with Nachtrieb. "He [Hafif] told Micro/Vest that he'd be happy [to take on the case] but only if Micro/ Vest made peace with me," Nachtrieb recalled. "That way he'd not have to deal with another lawsuit when it was over with Millard."

Nachtrieb was impressed. Not too many lawyers had personal feelings for other lawyers. Nachtrieb gladly split his 10-percent share in the Micro/Vest note with Hafif. Five percent with Hafif was worth a lot more than 10 percent without him. But Hafif stood to gain far more than Nachtrieb. He would also collect a percentage of whatever punitive damages he was able to squeeze out of Millard.

Considering all the shares of Micro/Vest that Martin had been selling, it was surprising that Martin needed a loan from Hafif. Since 1982, Martin had sold pieces of his share in the note. The initial price had been about $19,000 for 1 percent, but Martin hadn't sold much at that price. Not until 1984, when prices started to soar, was Martin interested in selling.

Italian-American businessmen, starting with owners of a San Francisco garbage company recommended by Andrighetto, were some of Martin's favorite customers. Golden Gate Disposal bargained with Martin until they came to the price of $600,000 for 2 percent. At $300,000 a "point," as Martin called it, that represented a fifteenfold increase over the 1982 price, and one hundred times what Martin paid for the whole note in 1981. At the price Martin was selling shares, the Micro/Vest note would have to have a $30-million value just to offer an investor the return of his investment.

After selling to the garbage men, Martin found a different sort of customer. Bill Agee and Mary Cunningham, famous for their love-crossed careers at Bendix, joined the crowd. Martin upped the price for his new friends—$375,000 was the new, magic number for one point. Martin had made nearly $1.5 million. And what had Martin paid to earn those riches? Bruno had put up the $250,000 to buy the note.

But $1.5 million was not enough. Martin raised the price to $400,000 a point. Friends, however, were given a break. Occasionally, Martin went as low as $300,000 a point. For his new lawyer, Herbert Hafif, he sold 2.5 percent for $500,000. Martin then sold some more. He was nearing $2.5 million in sales of his Micro/Vest stock. "We weren't syndicated," Andrighetto explained. "Every time he'd [Martin] lose his ass, he'd sell another piece."

While Martin sold, Andrighetto bought. But Andrighetto was smart. He bought most of his shares when the price was low, just $19,000 a point. Andrighetto had bought 13.3 percent from Philip Reed in 1982 for only $250,000. But Andrighetto wasn't only buying for himself. He bought shares for his family, his friends, and even people who worked for him. These different groups came to be known as Andrighetto Group No. 1 and Andrighetto Group No. 2. (The first group was the garbage men.) By late 1984, Andrighetto and his friends controlled nearly half of the Micro/Vest note.

Philip Reed, like Martin, profited by the garbage connection. By the eve of the trial he would have earned more than $1 million selling shares.

Sales of Micro/Vest shares had been buoyed by an amazing concurrence of events. First, the 1983 *Forbes* "Instant Billionaire" article publicized the success of ComputerLand. Second, except for one earlier, reversed ruling, the court had consistently sided with Micro/Vest.

Twenty percent, or more, of ComputerLand appeared to be Micro/ Vest's. It was for the trial court to decide how much, and the trial date grew near.

Larger than all of those influences, however, may have been Martin's enthusiasm. It was Martin who believed; Martin who talked of the Micro/Vest note being worth hundreds of millions of dollars. There were some who wondered whether the price Martin put on the note—nearing $500,000 a point—was inflated. According to one of Martin's newest lawyers, Tom Camp, the price was a steal or outrageous "depending on whether you listened to Martin or somebody else."

Perhaps there were other reasons for optimism. Killian and Van Natta had filed suit in 1983, asking for another 10 percent of the ComputerLand empire. But their case appeared more difficult to prove. They had to show that Millard had somehow defrauded them of ComputerLand stock when he had first offered them stock in IMS, and then—two years later—given them stock in the soon-to-be-bankrupt IMSAI. Even if the court eventually accepted that they had been defrauded of stock, they still had to prove that being defrauded of IMS stock (the holding company that eventually owned ComputerLand) had defrauded them of ComputerLand stock.

Time might be their greatest enemy. Ten years had passed since Killian first came to work for Millard, and five years had passed since the two engineers had received their stock in 1978. Many documents had been destroyed in IMSAI's bankruptcy, and the years had faded memories. And while the statute of limitations only starts running when a victim first realizes that he has been defrauded, some might question why Killian and Van Natta took so long to make their claim.

But for Micro/Vest these questions were irrelevant. Another lawsuit was another brushfire that ComputerLand had to put out. Killian and Van Natta's lawyer, John MacGregor, was spending thousands of dollars on discovery. He was finding new documents, new witnesses. MacGregor worked in the same Marin County office as his friend Nachtrieb. The two shared documents, depositions, and strategy. Without spending another penny, the Micro/Vest team of lawyers had grown stronger.

With enthusiasm riding high, the Micro/Vest legal team suggested to Hafif that he take Millard's deposition. Despite the weeks of questioning, Nachtrieb and the other lawyers hadn't gotten much out of

ComputerLand's owner. Millard hadn't changed from that first deposition with Nachtrieb. When asked a question, he still would purse his lips, turn slowly, look at the ceiling, and swing back with a semivacant look of contempt, asking, "What was the question?"

Nachtrieb's frustration had peaked earlier in the summer when he had filed a motion to complete Millard's deposition on videotape. Protested Nachtrieb to the court, "His nonverbal demeanor in answering the questions was artificial, contrived, and wholly unlike that of a responsible witness appearing before a trier of fact."

But the court refused Nachtrieb's request to put Millard on the tube, and Millard continued as he had begun. And why not? In the confines of deposition Millard could use the tactics of intimidation he had learned from his friend Werner and est. Hafif, however, knew the jury would be another matter. He was in no hurry to meet Millard. Why should he give Millard an opportunity to get comfortable? "Why do I want to educate the son of a bitch?"

Not taking Millard's deposition was Hafif's way of "putting Millard off." One day while Philip Reed's attorney, Neil Falconer, took Millard's deposition in his San Francisco office, Hafif walked by the glass-doored room. Everyone saw him go by, including Millard. But after talking briefly to another of the Micro/Vest attorneys in a nearby office, Hafif left.

Later in the week Hafif returned to watch Millard "do his act." Millard's lawyers were friendly to Hafif.* Millard was not so polite; he never looked in Hafif's direction. "If I'd been a chalkboard or a fly on the wall, he'd [have] looked at me," Hafif recalled. "It was too much non-turning." Hafif decided to lay the bait. He walked to the end of the room where Millard was vacantly looking out the window. Hafif also looked out the window. Then, slowly, gently, Hafif turned. As Hafif turned, Millard turned. It was like a circus routine performed by clowns.

Amused, Hafif returned to his seat and listened. Falconer proceeded to ask Millard whether ComputerLand was ever a closed corporation. Then, Hafif said, Millard gave one of his "patented fifteen-minute" answers: "I was a closed corporation. . . . I was closed. All I ever wanted to be . . . was a closed corporation. . . ."† It could

---

*Later, they would be chewed out by Millard.
†Hafif's capsulated version of Millard's deposition.

have gone on forever, but Hafif stopped the staccato declarations short.

"I can relate to that," he said with a sly smile. "I always wanted to be John Wayne." The room broke into laughter, except of course for Millard, who kept his expression intact.

"Well, Herb, but then you'd be dead," said Falconer.

"That all depends on whether we're talking about reality or the appearance of reality," Hafif said, smiling again and taking leave of the group.

Hafif was not surprised when Millard's attorney, Raymond Berman, came to talk about settling the case. "Millard has an excellent chance of being destroyed," Hafif told the attorney. But the settlement discussions didn't go very far. "When Berman brought it up, Millard was furious," Hafif said. "To Millard this was a game. Settlement indicated weakness."

There was nothing gentle about the way Hafif took the depositions of Faber and Waters. "I ripped them up," said Hafif. "First I was friendly, then I jabbed them real good." During the deposition of Ed Faber, Hafif prompted ComputerLand's vice-chairman and former president to admit that he had never seen or read the promissory note now owned by Micro/Vest. His company had spent several million dollars defending a lawsuit about which he knew nothing.

But Hafif knew that simply winning the case would not be enough. If they played the game the way the rest of the world did, they would play into Millard's hands. Hafif would have to win big. "If we won twenty percent of IMS's stock—even ComputerLand—he [Millard] could just stop paying dividends. He could pay [himself] in salary, management fees, [or] divide the company up."

Hafif needed a mechanism for "getting money." He did some research and then had an idea. Why couldn't they sue for conversion of the stock?* They had sent the notice to exercise the stock option in 1981. "It was our stock from that day. He [Millard] is withholding stock just like someone withholds a [borrowed] lawnmower."

The problem with Hafif's amazing reasoning was that if they sued only for the stock, they would only receive the value of the stock at the date of conversion—which in 1981 wasn't more than a few mil-

*A legal concept defined as the wrongful exercise of dominion over the personal property of another.

lion dollars. It was then that Hafif decided on a two-pronged attack. They would sue to have the stock issued to Micro/Vest, as well as their percentage of dividends. Hafif thought it would do the trick. The dividends would be millions of dollars, and "enough money to hurt [Millard] so he has to deal with you."

The rest of the Micro/Vest team was stunned. Hafif was basically proposing that they add an intentional tort claim to their case. It was a novel, if not unique, approach to a contract suit. At first, Nachtrieb thought the idea was crazy. There had been a simple breach of contract. Millard had agreed to give the holder of the note 20 percent of his stock and had reneged on the deal. But Hafif argued convincingly otherwise. In the almost four years since Micro/Vest sent Millard its notice to exercise the stock option, Micro/Vest's 20 percent of dividends had been filling Millard's pockets. That, Hafif reasoned, was conversion—a civil form of tort—similar in some respects to theft.

Nachtrieb knew the theory was attractive. Long before, he, too, had realized that it would not be enough merely to win 20 percent of the stock. Millard would still be the majority shareholder. "Had we won twenty percent of ComputerLand it would have been no control, no public market, no dividends, twenty percent of another lawsuit, and the right to keep filing stockholders' suits forever," said Nachtrieb.

Without great debate Hafif's tort amendment was approved by the court. ComputerLand's attorneys didn't appear to realize what was happening. "They thought [I was] some personal-injury lawyer. 'What is this conversion?'" said Hafif, recalling their confusion. He figured their first impression of him was not of an intellectual but a shoe salesman. "They underrated me because I swear a lot." But behind his rough appearance and language Hafif had a stinging tongue armed with intellect. And behind the brains and talent was a man who couldn't be outworked. Hafif didn't sleep much, and when he tried a case, he hardly slept at all.

Mexico was where Hafif went to begin his heavy trial preparation. In October of 1984 he took eleven years of Millard's business financials to the sprawling white estate he had designed near Ensenada, just an hour south of the border. "They wanted me to hire CPAs. I had thirty-nine accountants in thirteen corporations. I could tell if the chef was taking home the meat."

His preparation would be tedious, but unlike many lawyers, Hafif never worked without design. He knew that one of Millard's lawyer's arguments would be that ComputerLand had been started out of the profits of IMS—not the $250,000 Marriner note. Perched on a Pacific bluff, by his curved pool under the brilliant Mexican sun, Hafif searched for points that would pop Millard's balloon.

Meanwhile, at the other end of the continent, by the bitter-cold Atlantic, the Marriner & Co. board met at the offices of Gerrity Lumber. They told Loring Reed that the circumstances of the sale of the note, coupled with the discovery of the identity of its purchasers, didn't look good. At the very least there was the appearance of impropriety. "You can't prove a thing," said an indignant Loring Reed. Gerrity's son, who worked with his father at the lumber company, was bothered by Loring Reed's choice of words. An innocent man wouldn't talk about proof, he reflected. He believed that an innocent man would say, "I didn't do it."

Frank Gerrity was troubled by the implications of Loring Reed's story. Reed claimed he hadn't known of his son's involvement in Micro/Vest until months after he sold the note to Martin. But wasn't it Philip Reed who had put the two men in contact? Gerrity pondered. Philip Reed had tried to buy the note once before in 1978, and Philip Reed was working for Martin when he had put Martin in contact with Loring Reed. It was hard to believe that Reed had no inkling that his son stood to profit by the deal. The only possible way that could be true, Gerrity thought, would be if young Reed had kept his arrangement with Martin a secret from his father. That, Gerrity reasoned, would amount to deceit, and Gerrity could not believe that Philip Reed would deceive his father. He knew how close they were. "They [Philip and Loring] saw each other constantly," Gerrity recalled. "Hell, [it wouldn't surprise me if] he'd tell [his father] how many times he made love to his wife."

Frank Gerrity was also puzzled when Reed's attorney, Bailey, told him that Micro/Vest was now willing to pay several hundred thousand dollars more for the note. If Micro/Vest hadn't done anything wrong, why did it want to pay more? From the way Loring Reed had described Martin, he did not sound like the type who gave money away. "I mean if I sold you my house for $2 million, and then you found that you could sell it for $3 million, I don't think you'd come back to me and say, 'By the way, since I can sell this for $3 million, here's another $200,000,'" Gerrity reasoned. Did Micro/Vest sense their vulnerability? To Gerrity, the offer was evidence of a "guilty conscience."*

Why hadn't Marriner just converted the note and given Micro/Vest the option of buying stock in the converted note at an agreed upon price? Gerrity reflected. Micro/Vest could have agreed to pay any potential legal fees, as it already had. And since Marriner was the maker of the note, there would have been no question of transferability or rights of first refusal. "It would have taken the teeth out of Millard in the lawsuit," speculated Gerrity.

Gerrity wondered why Loring Reed hadn't shown Creighton and him all the current ComputerLand sales figures and discussed the whole issue: how Millard might fight conversion of the note, and how Loring Reed's son was involved with Micro/Vest. "If he had just done all that, and then said, 'All right, now what price do you want for this note?' we would have agreed on a price and that would have been all she wrote," Gerrity reflected. "It would have been a happy deal."

It would have been the straightforward, honorable way to proceed, and Gerrity had never known Loring Reed to be different. Was his opinion of Loring Reed changing? On the eve of the trial, in December of 1984, "Hafif made some tentative agreement [with Marriner]," claimed Frank Gerrity's nephew, Daniel. "Micro/Vest didn't want it to come out that Loring Reed was [to be] paid extra."†

Things weren't going the way Hafif had planned: "I find out he [Martin] was back there negotiating [with Marriner] unauthorized. I got pissed. John wanted to pay something. My opinion was that that was dangerous. After it got to that stage, I probably wrote a letter

*Gerrity didn't know that just weeks before Martin bought the Marriner note in 1981, he had sold his 1 percent stock in ComputerLand for $250,000, seeming to place a minimum $5-million value on the 20-percent Marriner note. Martin (through Andrighetto), however, paid only $250,000 for the 20-percent Marriner note. Ken Waters claimed that the company's 1980 $61-million gross earnings gave the note a minimum value of $800,000.

†In 1984 Hafif's offer of several hundred thousand dollars had still not been accepted by Gerrity and Creighton for Marriner.

back, something to this effect: 'You don't have anything coming. These guys bought it square, but apparently John [Martin] and Bruno [Andrighetto] are willing to pay [Marriner] $650,000 if they [John and Bruno] come out fine.'"

25

Heaven's
Gates

The jury could watch them pull up in their Mercedes-Benz SL. Behind the tinted bulletproof glass, in the comfort of the leather seats, sat Bill, Pat and Barbara Millard and their two bodyguards. Permission was asked for Millard's bodyguards to carry their guns into the small courtroom on the fourth floor. When John Martin found out about that, he complained. Why couldn't *his* bodyguards bring in *their* guns, too?

A mesh of concrete and steel, the Alameda Superior Court is only a few miles from where Millard delivered newspapers as a boy. Not more than twenty miles down the freeway is San Leandro, and a little farther, Hayward. Beneath the building, in the basement, is the data processing department Millard managed more than two decades ago.

Judge McCullum's court, like all the other courtrooms in the Alameda Superior Court, is simple and unpretentious. The jury sat in plain chairs, with only a long, thick railing separating them from the rest of the court. The witness's chair was no different from those of the jury, except that it stood alone and above the jury box, accompanied by a microphone.

Among those sitting in the audience that brisk January day were the three Millards (plus two bodyguards), Bruno, his wife and daughters, Phil Reed and his pretty new wife Jill, John Martin and his wife (and bodyguards), about fifteen lawyers, plenty of reporters, a couple of photographers, and an artist sketching the scene.

ComputerLand had already committed its first blunder. Because Millard had countersued Micro/Vest for fraud and other unpleasantries, each key member of Micro/Vest and Loring Reed were allowed to be represented by a different attorney. Hafif was pleased; it gave them an opportunity to appear as victims. At Neil Falconer's law office in San Francisco they had practiced their roles carefully. Hafif would start with a sweeping prelude, and then each of the four lawyers would emphasize a particular theme, elaborating on each major failing of Millard's. "You have to orchestrate the case, and Herb did it beautifully," remembered Nachtrieb. Hafif set the tone and pace. Everything else was just background to his performance. He began by putting things in historical focus.

"This fellow Millard just a few short years ago in 1973, and you will think back to that—Patty Hearst is somewhere, and Nixon is having his share of problems and there is everybody from Joe Alioto to Jerry Brown running for primary. . . ."

As Hafif continued his historical drama, he wanted to make sure the jury knew the players. At each new turn in the story he would have his clients stand in the courtroom so the jury could get a good look. Philip Reed and his wife would stand. Loring Reed would stand. John Martin, too. But Bruno was not willing to wait for his introduction. He corrected Hafif from the audience.

Hafif was not dull. Like a modern painter, he boldly used bright colors. Realism wasn't his style. Sometimes the colors ran and the lines crossed, but nobody really minded because the picture was grand. Hafif leaped into the heart of his opening argument: "That twenty percent they put in writing. They put it in writing and they spelled out what it meant, and they took three and a half months or whatever before they actually signed the writing. So there is no question [about] what they said in the writing. They said, 'You get twenty percent. You get twenty percent when you want it and you send us a notice of what is called conversion when you say you want your twenty percent, but you can't get it for free. You've got to cancel your two hundred and fifty thousand bucks. . . .'"

Hafif seemed a basic, likeable guy, the type you could imagine chugging a few beers with while watching the game at a local bar. Millard had a different sort of attorney; his attempt to woo Younger back into his camp had failed. Money had not been sufficient incentive. The fate of his empire would rest on Raymond Berman's shoulders.

Like Hafif, Berman began by introducing his clients. But the Washington, D.C., lawyer gave a different impression to the working-class jury. "We represent IMS Associates, Inc. That is the holding company through which Mr. Millard and his wife seated in the front row on the left-hand side of the courtroom, owns all or most of all his companies. We represent several subsidiaries of IMS Associates, Incorporated which are also associated in this case. . . ."

Companies and lawyers it seemed, not people, were what Berman introduced to the audience. Unlike Hafif, he invited no one to stand. After his less-than-scintillating introduction, Berman eloquently argued Millard's oral agreement and the incredible tale of Micro/Vest's conspiracy: how Loring Reed, Philip Reed, and John Martin all turned on Millard. The prologue was complete. The curtain went up.

Loring Reed walked heavily to the stand, raised his hand to take the oath, and sat down. The once-handsome gentleman had aged considerably since Martin's February 1981 visit to Boston four years earlier. Extra weight hung about him and there was a thickness in his face. Hafif asked Loring to tell the court about his education and early business background. They heard of his Harvard degree in economics and his three years in the Navy. Reed then began an elaborate description of Marriner's business. The court heard a half-hour description of wool combing and the wool trade. Occasionally, Reed would lose his concentration and ask Hafif to give the question again. He seemed a nice old man.

Hafif began a pattern that would remain unchanged throughout the trial. At every available opportunity, his eyes were on the jury. It was as though he were inviting them to join him on a journey. Hafif was not an unpleasant man to look at. He had a hewed appearance, as though he'd been carved from redwood or granite. His hands were big and thick, and they often came to rest on the jury railing as he listened to the story unfold with the twelve men and women.

Then, as though he were trying to make it more interesting for all of them, Hafif began to pick up the pace. The leisurely beginning was forgotten in a barrage of questions. In minutes, Hafif established that Loring hardly knew Millard when he made a $250,000 investment in his struggling company. In a rush, Hafif covered the written agreements, the wild Panama scheme, Millard's refusal to provide financial statements, the subsequent federal lawsuit, and finally, the sale to Micro/Vest. The drama built to a breathless crescendo.

Throughout his examination of Loring Reed, Hafif continually made reference to "that fellow over there." Hafif had just the thing to disarm the smile that Millard beamed like a spotlight. When he asked Reed what he thought of Millard's 1976 attempt not to allow Marriner to participate in ComputerLand, Hafif pointed at Millard. The jury followed his finger and looked at the smiling man.

"What do you call that?" asked Hafif.

"We call it stealing where I come from," said Reed.

All eyes were on Millard. Reed was calling him a thief and all Millard could do was grin. He had chosen his expression, and like a poker player, he had to wear it to the end. "You can't keep a smile," remembered Hafif later. "A smile starts to look like a death mask."

Berman was an even bigger man than Hafif, but the weight seemed less focused. He began his cross-examination of Loring Reed on a different note. Berman spoke more elevated English and apologized when he phrased a question awkwardly. He wanted to go a little slower than Mr. Hafif; he wanted to ponder a few of those details that had been brushed over in the preceding performance.

The jury listened as Berman revealed that Loring Reed did know Millard before the Marriner note after all, had actually met him twice and attended an early planning meeting of IMS Associates with his son. And after the note was signed, Reed gave Millard dinner at his home, lent him a car, set him up with a potential customer, put him up for the night, and gave him breakfast.

Berman then casually picked up another line of questioning: "Incidentally, did you ever tell Mr. Creighton or Mr. Gerrity or even Mr. Bailey that your son had become a participant in the Micro/Vest group?"

"Yes, when I found out about it," Loring Reed said.

"If Mr. Gerrity testified in his deposition that he was never told about that, would you say he was in error?"

"I know he is in error," Reed said.

"And if Mr. Creighton testified he didn't find out about it until the fall of 1983, would you say he's in error?" Berman asked.

"I know he's in error, and I'd like to tell you why," Loring Reed said.

"Go ahead," Berman encouraged.

"Because Mr. Gerrity called it to my attention that he had seen there was a Philip Reed involved in this Micro/Vest investment and he said to me, 'Is that you?' and I said, 'No, it's not me.' And it was Philip, and I told them both so," Loring Reed said.

There was another casual question Berman wanted to ask: "Incidentally, was it your practice to share with the other members of the board any of the financial information which you received about companies in which Marriner had an investment?"

"Yes," Reed said.

"And if Mr. Gerrity and Mr. Creighton testified that they had not been given the most recent ComputerLand statements which were available to Marriner, would you say they were in error?" Berman asked.

"I . . . I can't recall. I can tell you what they did have. They did have the seven months' statements which I had given them [through April 30, 1980] . . . ," Reed said.

"If they testified that those were the most recent statements which they had received, and if in November of that year you had more current statements through the end of September 1980, which you had not shared with them, would they be in error?" Berman asked.

"If they say so, I'll agree with them."

Pierce O'Donnell, the attorney in charge of representing ComputerLand, continued Loring Reed's cross-examination. Like Berman, he, too, was a big man, but soft, not thick and powerful like Hafif. Under his questioning, Reed testified as to when he found out the actual percentage of his son's interest in Micro/Vest.

"I told you I just found out about three weeks ago," Loring Reed repeated.

"And you never asked him [Philip Reed]?" O'Donnell asked.

"Why should I?" Loring Reed responded, returning the question.

"What is his interest? What did he tell you finally, or what did you learn?" O'Donnell asked.

"What?" Reed said.

"What did you learn his interest was?"

"I think it's thirteen percent, and I congratulate him for getting it for nothing. He probably didn't dare. If he'd have paid for it, I would have shot him!" said Loring Reed.

"Why would you shoot him if he had paid for it?" asked O'Donnell.

"What?" Reed said.

"Why would you have shot him if he had paid for it?" repeated O'Donnell.

"Because he is paying for a big lawsuit," Reed said.

"So you're proud of your son to get something for nothing," O'Donnell asked.

"You bet I am," Loring Reed said.

"And did you encourage your son to get something for nothing?" O'Donnell asked.

"You bet I do!" Loring Reed said.

"You think that's ethical?" O'Donnell asked.

"I know it's ethical!" Loring Reed said.

"Getting something for nothing; you'd like that?" O'Donnell asked.

"Yes, I do," Loring Reed said.

Over at ComputerLand's table, Berman's partner Steve Umin was surprised by Reed's combativeness and what he interpreted to be wavering admissions. Reed seemed to be saying that he had encouraged his son to get a share in Micro/Vest for nothing. When Umin first took Loring Reed's deposition, he thought him a straightforward New England businessman. Surely, thought Umin, Micro/Vest was favored by every betting observer of the court. Few doubted the outcome. What was really at trial was the amount of the victory. There was no reason at all to falsify a single thing on the stand. Umin leaned forward in his seat, thinking to himself, "This guy's going to lie about every question."

When Philip Reed took the witness stand, the ladies in the courtroom strained for a closer look. Nearing his midforties, Reed was still lean and blessed with fresh, boyish, all-American good looks. There was a strong resemblance to his father. But Philip Reed wasn't only younger and healthier than his father—his whole manner breathed a lighter tone. Friendliness came easily to Philip Reed, and it seemed the most natural thing in the world when he addressed Hafif as Herb and later, when Berman took up cross-examination, he called him Ray.

Hafif didn't fool around. He got to his main point quickly. "Now there's been a claim made that in addition to all those things, he

[Millard] wanted that this deal would never be assignable or have any right of first refusal on it?" Hafif asked.

"Not definitely, not part of the package that I went back to Marriner with, and Herb, if it had been, I don't think I would have bothered to go back because we really wouldn't have been able to offer them [Marriner] anything for their investment," Reed said.

"Okay. In other words, well, let's just take it, why couldn't you make this nonassignable? I mean, you know, the guy doesn't want to give you board seats; the guy wants to keep eighty percent; the guy wants to only give up twenty percent. The guy is three hundred thousand [dollars] in the hole, losing thirty thousand [dollars] a month and he says, 'By the way, I don't ever want you to assign this note.' What would be wrong with that?" Hafif asked playfully.

"Aside from the fact there is a limit on what you can propose to an investor when your company is in that kind of a position, it virtually makes the investment valueless," Reed said.

Once Hafif had gotten that point out of the way, he had fun with the juicy stuff: How Millard kept changing the deal on Philip Reed, first cutting his royalty agreement, then asking him to sign a special subordination agreement, and finally threatening him (through his lawyers) when he complained over the Panama deal. Philip Reed's response to this sudden change of heart, Hafif showed in colorful testimony, was nothing short of warm, trusting friendship. There wasn't a nicer witness who would take the stand.

But on cross-examination, Berman brought out another aspect to Philip Reed and Millard's close relationship: "In your business dealings with Mr. Millard during that period of time, did you have a feeling that you trusted him and he trusted you?" he asked.

"Yes," Reed said.

"You made a lot of handshake deals with him?" Berman suggested.

"We agreed on the fly as to the way we were doing things and sooner or later tried to get that down into some form that we could remember later."

O'Donnell's cross-examination cut deeper into the opening Berman had created. It seemed to contradict the testimony Hafif had elicited from Philip Reed on the Marriner agreement. Oral agreements between the two men were common. He read the court a section of Reed's deposition where he admitted that he had discussed rights of first refusal with Millard at various times.

O'Donnell then read a section where Philip Reed was asked about a letter he sent on April 26, 1976, to Loring Reed's attorney, Andrew Bailey.

QUESTION: One of the corporate records that your secretary forwarded to Andrew Bailey was the bylaws of IMS Associates, Inc., was it not?

ANSWER: Yes.

QUESTION: And those bylaws in April of 1976 contained a provision on a right of first refusal, did it not?

ANSWER: I guess I mean to accept your characterization, if that's what this is, is a right of first refusal.

QUESTION: In essence, it says before a shareholder of IMS can sell his or her stock they have to offer it for sale on the same terms and conditions to IMS.

ANSWER: Okay.

The court then heard that Philip Reed never had any written employment agreement with IMS. Once again, O'Donnell looked to Reed's deposition for the answer:

QUESTION: Was the relationship between you and Mr. Millard such during the years 1974 and 1975 that you had confidence in him that changes to the agreements that existed between your two companies could be made orally without being reduced to writing?

ANSWER: Yes.

Philip Reed also didn't have a written employment agreement with Martin. It seemed that oral understandings were a common way of business for Reed.

Bruno Andrighetto took the stand. He talked about the produce business and how he had written scripts for Joe Carcione's well-known television show. In between, he blurted out a story about his losses in the gold mine. The crowd laughed.

Andrighetto talked fast and his eyes sparkled with the attention. His friends were watching, and for many of them it was the first time they had heard him speak without swearing. ComputerLand's attorneys did their best to endure. They knew that Andrighetto was irrelevant to the issues in the case, and that Micro/Vest's purpose in putting him on the stand was defensive. "You have to show with names like Musumeci and Andrighetto that it's not a dark Mafia plot to take over Silicon Valley," said Umin. But the defensive move was a success. The jury enjoyed the bubbling, vibrant man, and Andrighetto seemed to be a charming grandfather.

The second half of Umin's "dark Mafia plot," John Martin-Musumeci, took the stand. Hafif had to do something about that name, so he asked his client to tell the jury why he had that dash between the "Martin" and the "Musumeci." After a few minutes of that, Martin told how he started ComputerLand, how Millard worked him to the bone, wouldn't pay what he promised, and finally dumped him when he was no longer needed. He sacrificed so much for Millard that he was bleeding from the stomach and spent a year in intensive medical care, visiting his doctor daily.

Umin and Berman listened with disbelief. They knew that Martin was a clever man who had planned carefully for this day. They thought Martin's motive for giving a 26.6-percent share in the note to Philip Reed was obvious. Martin knew he needed Philip Reed's testimony to make the deal fly. "You want to get the best testimony possible, buy the witness. You want to buy the witness, you give him a piece of the note," speculated Umin. "You can be sure that he [Martin] didn't do it out of the goodness of his heart."

26

Judgment

Day

It was one of those days in court when nothing seemed to happen. The testimony was dull, and the day dragged on with the introduction of evidence and other technical details. Hafif timed it just that way: "They were stalling along, trying to run out the clock." The trouble was that Hafif was the master of the two-minute drill.

Hafif went into his act in the afternoon. He'd eye the clock, throw up his hands, look embarrassed, and plead with the judge to speed things up. "I made the jury think they [ComputerLand's lawyers] were so wasteful of time," said Hafif.

At a few minutes before four P.M. Berman finally had no more paper to shuffle. Nearly everyone in court thought the judge was going to recess and send them home for the day. Nearly everyone that is except Hafif. The judge asked Hafif what witness he'd like to call. Hafif paused and then pointed to the man protected by bodyguards. "I'd like to call Mr. Millard to the stand."

All the careful preparation, all the coaching, all the mock trials in which Millard had been victorious were left behind like notes for a high-school test. Like a magician, Hafif opened his colorful bag of tricks. You could feel it in the air—the rabbit could pop out of any hat. He started with the issue of Marriner's federal lawsuit, which

Hafif said came about because Marriner was asking for financial statements.

"You had given them financial documents in the past, hadn't you?" Hafif asked.

"Yes, I had," Millard said.

"You recognized that the right of conversion didn't mean a thing in terms of having any particular value if they didn't know what they were going to convert into, right?" Hafif said.

"No, I did not recognize that," Millard said.

"Well, sir, if you have a right to convert into a company, in fact if you have a right to convert into a series of companies and you can't figure out whether they are making or losing money or what they're doing with their assets, and you can't figure out whether they are worth converting into and giving up your note, you have certainly diminished the value of the conversion rights, haven't you?" Hafif said.

"Yes, you have, and that is a different question than [what] you asked me. You asked me if it reduced it to no value. That's not true," Millard said.

It mattered little that Millard was technically right. Hafif had tricked him, led him out into the open and toward the first trap. Hafif went on with the peripheral issue. In little more than a minute he had gotten under Millard's skin.

"Give me the question again," Millard said, gripping the arms on his chair.

Millard eventually brought up what for him was the real issue: "There was a lot of question in my mind that he had a right to have me continue with an oral agreement to provide him with financial statements after what he had done was broken his agreement to subordinate the debt to any and every bank to whatever extent necessary for the company to obtain credit from that institution."

"Well, now, that isn't really true either, is it, Mr. Millard?" responded Hafif.

Millard's eyes were blazing. He had forgotten the jury. There were only two people in the courtroom as far as Millard was concerned— himself and Hafif. The crowd watched his knuckles go white as his hands clenched the chair tighter. "He glowered at me like a crazy guy," said Hafif, who playfully moved back and forward, sticking his neck out and peering at Millard as if he were some odd animal in a cage.

The fact that Loring Reed did not get financial statements was not true for the man sitting on the witness stand. "There was no with-holding at all on my part . . . that was in any way a withholding from Loring Reed or Marriner," Millard insisted.

"Well, he didn't get them," Hafif said deadpan.

"Well, you say that. I don't know whether he got them. He had complete access to the company—the truth is Loring Reed, Phil Reed, Marriner, had complete access to anything that I had access to during that period and that's the truth!" The veins on Millard's fore-head showed.

"Well, we'll explore the truth here," Hafif said.

"Yes, we will, Mr. Hafif, that's why we're here," Millard chal-lenged.

"That's one of the reasons," said Hafif, too swift to allow Millard to have the last word.

Hafif then explored the real reason why the financials stopped ar-riving: "What I'm saying [is that] you have no recollection nor any document nor any letter in your files anywhere that says you sent him any financial statements since September of 1976, the date that you started this corporation called Computer Shack. That's the month you started it, isn't it?"

"I believe it was September twenty-first, and it was completely known to Loring Reed. There was no secret about that. He knew it before it was even going to be formed. There was nothing withheld. There were no secrets at all about that, so what are you making out of that?" Millard said angrily, staring at his questioner.

Hafif's answer was gentlemanly. He could be playful now; he had Millard on the run.

"Well, you see, it's not up to *me* to make anything out of it, Mr. Millard. I am just going to ask you some questions and then these people are going to make up their minds about it," Hafif said, looking as he always did, not at Millard, but at the men and women of the jury.

It was then that Millard began talking out of turn. A simple yes or no was not sufficient. There was more he wanted, and needed, to say.

"Excuse me, Mr. Millard," Hafif said in his most polite tone.

"You don't want the rest of the answer?" Millard said, seeming surprised.

"Well, you see, you've got all these lawyers over here. They're real good, and they're going to give you a shot. I'm not."

The hands gripped the chair tighter, but Millard would have done better to have loosened his hold. It was after four-thirty. The day was finished. In just a few minutes the damage had been done.

The next morning there seemed hope. The jury saw a changed Millard. A night's rest had relaxed ComputerLand's owner. Now his hands rested on his lap, and he even ventured a smile.

Millard may have looked ready for anything, but he was not ready for Herbert Hafif. After the previous afternoon's beating, the jury was ready for some heavy hitting. But Hafif would not, as some of his own clients demanded, take Millard's "ass apart." Just as the courtroom seemed to anticipate action, Hafif changed the pace and began a more insidious unraveling.

"I knew we'd see a marvelous, diplomatic Millard," said Hafif later. "The next day he was so sweet." What no one expected, however, was that Hafif would also seem sweet, beginning his day's examination slowly, politely, in a gentle, light voice. But his intent was clear.

First, he told Millard that while he understood that he had a lot to say, he'd appreciate it if he answered the question he was asking, and not something he'd asked before. Having let Millard know who was in control, Hafif looked him in the eye and gave him a preview. "And I'm going to show, Mr. Millard, that you are not worthy of belief. So no matter how nice I say it, those are the nasty things I'm going to do."

"Counsel has made another opening statement. Do we have a question?" Berman asked disdainfully. The objection was too late. The tension had returned to Millard's face. Hafif started from the top with the by-now-familiar story. He invited the court to return to January of 1976, when Millard had been turned down by the Bank of America for the final, final time.

The story built slowly. With Millard's reluctant memory it would take some time for Hafif to build the evidence for his conclusion—

that Millard's company was heading down the drain when Philip Reed secured the Marriner loan.

Several minutes later, Millard was mixed up on the dates again. He looked confused as he struggled to answer. "I thought you were asking me to compare '78 to '76 at this time—oh, God!"

Perhaps Millard knew what an easy target he was, sitting there alone on the stand. The shot came suddenly, without warning. At first many thought it was just a toy gunshot. But some knew the booming sound was real. Philip Reed watched Martin, sitting in front of him, dive under his seat. Others were ducking for cover. "Christ, it's happening," thought Nachtrieb. "They're going at it with guns!"

"Please close the door and lock the door, please!" ordered the judge. The bailiff quickly pulled the blinds and locked the door, sealing them in. "Ladies and gentlemen, we will stand easy until we can ascertain what is going on."

Outside, they heard a struggle, yelling and screaming. Minutes after being sentenced, a defendant had bolted. The female bailiff had wrestled him to the ground. In the struggle, the criminal had grabbed her gun and blasted a hole in the woman's restroom. They were still fighting for the gun.

In the meantime, the judge slipped out through his chambers to see what was going on. Millard's initial fear had passed. He stepped down from his chair, and in front of the jury, began talking to his questioner. Hafif listened, as Millard told an anecdote related to the shooting. Hafif was polite as Millard spoke freely in front of the men and women of the jury. The sudden friendly gesture, against a backdrop of glowering and intimidating stares, came as no surprise to Hafif. "I had his number. His life depended on me."

Outside the courtroom, the sentenced criminal was winning his desperate battle. The gun was beginning to turn toward the outmatched bailiff. But suddenly a middle-aged man with a big belly and a bad heart dove into the fight, and wrestled the gun away from the desperate criminal.

After the commotion ended, the lawyers, jury, and judge decided that was enough excitement for one day and they recessed until the next morning. Millard's second appearance on the stand had lasted just fifty-five minutes—thirty minutes more than his first. Now it seemed Millard had to fear not only the piercing questions of Hafif, but for the safety of his own life.

• • •

The third day didn't improve for Millard. Hafif asked him about the first agreement, the short temporary note, written up when the Marriner money was first wired to California in early 1976.

"You never told Loring Reed in writing that his was an incomplete agreement, did you? Hear my questions: in writing?" Hafif asked.

"No," Millard said.

"You never made a note in your diary, which includes such things as where you ate dinner with Loring Reed that night. You never included a note that said it was an incomplete agreement, did you?" Hafif asked.

"No," Millard said.

"And you can't recall a specific conversation when you called Loring Reed and said, 'This is an incomplete agreement, Loring.' You can't recall any specific comment to that effect as to when, where, and how it took place, can you?" Hafif asked.

"No," Millard said.

Hafif then moved to step two, the second Marriner agreement.

"The second one was longer than the first one?" Hafif asked.

"Yes," Millard said.

"But now what you want these people to believe is that that document, the second written document, was incorrect in terms of explaining your agreement. Is that what you want them to believe?" Hafif asked incredulously.

It was almost as though he were addressing a child, and by now the jury could almost mouth the answer.

"It was not complete," Millard said.

Hafif read the terms of the agreement, emphasizing the section about stock conversion. Then he read Millard's diary, which documented the agreement but said nothing about the part Millard claimed was absent.

The rest was a romp. Hafif brought in some of the more colorful details: Millard's Cadillac, the corporate backdating, the twice-indicted attorney, the Panamanian tax deal. He then described how it was Millard's contention that the note only convert into IMS—not ComputerLand—which consisted of the company-owned vineyard, ranch, planes, and of course, Millard's home.

Millard wouldn't budge, however: "What counts for me is the agreement!"

Hafif, as always, had an apt, ad-lib response: "You see, I have a very difficult time, Mr. Millard, because I just keep reading the agreement. That's what got me confused."

Millard was the last witness Micro/Vest called to prove their case. After he stepped down, they could only cross-examine the defendant's witnesses, and as a last resort, call a witness to rebut some damaging testimony. Before putting his case to bed, Hafif tried to tell the story one more time in the form of a question.

But Hafif never got to finish. Berman objected to the 207-word question, and Hafif didn't really mind. "I might as well go out on that one," Hafif said, knowing that the question would be answered not by Millard, but by the twelve men and women of the jury.

The defense called itself, the Millards. The jury got to hear the story according to Millard. It was the chance Millard had been waiting for. He told how the first Marriner note was presented to him as "something temporary," and how "the relationship between Philip Reed and I [sic] and his father at this point in time was blind, absolute trust, friendship and even love."

When Millard returned from his first marketing trip, after the money had already been in IMS's bank account for nearly a month, "I had this document to sign, and it wasn't the document I was expecting, and he [Loring Reed] told me that was going to take longer to develop than he had expected and this was to simply be in the file until the other document got developed."

But because he did not want to cause trouble or further expense, Millard signed the agreement without further discussion. "It was just costing money, and I agreed to sign the document as it was. I agreed that that was all true." And that, more or less, was the story which Millard had spent four years and millions of tax-deductible dollars defending.

But behind every great man is a great woman, so perhaps it would be Pat Millard who would really offer the greatest defense of her beleaguered husband of nearly thirty years. Umin wasted no time in having Pat Millard demonstrate that Philip Reed had been the closest friend Millard had ever known. "He had never had a brother and he had always wanted to have a brother, and if he had, he certainly hoped that the relationship with his brother would have been exactly what he had with Phil Reed," said Pat Millard.

"Did there come a time, Mrs. Millard, when your husband finally lost trust, confidence, or love for Phil Reed?" Umin asked.

"Yes," Pat Millard said.

"Can you tell me when that was?" Umin asked.

"It's when he sat across the table from Phil Reed when his deposition was being taken for this case."

"What happened after Phil Reed's testimony concluded?" Umin asked.

"My husband left the room and he broke down and he cried, and he said, 'I thought Phil Reed would tell the truth.'"

"I have no further questions, Mrs. Millard."

Hafif began his questioning gently. It was odd, but for some reason that day Millard was not in the courtroom. The woman jurors couldn't help but notice his absence. Hafif made it easier, however. Each time he mentioned Millard's name, he pointed to his empty seat. It would take only a couple of minutes for Hafif to arrive at the critical question.

"Is your husband inclined to overstate, misrepresent things?" Hafif asked.

"What things?" Pat Millard asked.

"Anything; everything?" Hafif asked.

"I'd have to say sometimes he does," Pat Millard said.

"Okay. Thank you," Hafif said graciously. "Now, let's take Phil Reed. You've never known him to misrepresent anything, of your own personal knowledge, have you? Not one thing in your whole entire life did you ever know Phil Reed to misrepresent to you?" Hafif asked.

Hafif was taking a chance. Smart lawyers seldom ask questions to which they don't already know the answer.

"No, that's true," Pat Millard said without hesitation.

Those three words meant more than hundreds of exhibits and days of testimony. They were the words of a wife who admitted it was her husband—and not the "enemy"—who could not always be trusted.

Hafif moved fast: "So the only basis that you suddenly feel betrayed by Phil Reed is based on what somebody's been telling you, and other people have been telling you. Nothing that Phil Reed ever told you, no lie, no misrepresentation, nothing you ever heard Phil Reed say, right?"

"Right," Pat Millard said.

"Okay," Hafif said.

And then, as Hafif looked at the jury for his next question, Pat Millard volunteered the confession he sought.

"Anything that I, basically, that I would have heard that I have said here today would come from either Ed [Faber] or Bill," she said.

The rest was almost too easy. Hafif showed that the (effective) co-owner of the ComputerLand empire couldn't read a financial statement and knew virtually none of the facts critical to the trial. But Hafif was careful not to be rough. When Pat Millard stepped down from the stand, everyone knew her to be a pleasant, not very well educated woman, who, despite her apparent naivete and lack of polish, was unwilling—no matter the price—to lie.

Concrete images were what Hafif gave the jury. When he was finished with a witness, you felt that you knew him or her, for better or worse. And each time Hafif stood up, the entire courtroom knew who he was. He had made sure of that from the first day. He was as much a part of the scene as the jury railing he ran his hand over, the witness stand he walked toward, and the clock he checked to know when to speed or slow his tale.

Some of the ComputerLand attorneys seemed to have just gotten off the plane. They were strangers to the jury, and they vainly tried to make sure the jurors hadn't forgotten who they were. "My name is Pierce O'Donnell, and I represent ComputerLand," he said with an almost merry lilt in his voice. Once or twice was enough—but five times?

There were other witnesses, but they were no match for Hafif. Even Ed Faber fell before Hafif's quick tongue, blasted for defending a lawsuit of which he knew nothing, and for signing the closed corporation resolution (under Millard's direction, Hafif claimed) he knew to be false.

Ken Waters fared worse. ComputerLand's general counsel seemed to sink in a sea of forgotten memories and circular answers that appeared more damaging than outright admissions. It was "not one of my better days," Waters told an industry publication, acknowledging that his answers "got a little bit fuzzy."

And Randick, the lawyer who helped Millard draft the Option and

Modification Agreement, and admitted to being paid at least a thousand dollars by Millard to testify, claimed he had not read the documents, even though Hafif gave them to him before he testified. These were easy openings for Hafif, and the boxer in him isolated each man's weakness and delivered the blow.

Nearly two months had passed and still no evidence had been filed on the cross-complaints. The Reeds, Martin, and Andrighetto had spent nearly a million dollars defending themselves against Millard's accusations of fraud. So much the better for Micro/Vest. They would be given five closing arguments, five chances to show Millard's character in greater detail. The Micro/Vest attorneys searched for fresh new ways to expose Millard's flaws.

Hafif's closing argument, like every movement of his eyes, hands, and body during the trial, like every word or sentence he spoke, had but one objective, one listener: "This is a simple, simple fact situation. It's an agreement; it's in writing. It was done not once; it was done three times. . . . Now you get to decide it. You don't have to submit your decision to a congressman. You don't have to lobby for it. You are the most powerful people in Alameda County right now. You decide. . . . But now let's give justice, and I think we're all going to feel a lot better about that."

Although a fine attorney and a talented tuba player, at heart Harold Nachtrieb was a frustrated writer. So perhaps he realized it was his big chance when he began scribbling a few verses of poetry. The first draft turned out better than he had imagined. He proudly showed it to Hafif. The boss was worried. Most of the jury had probably never heard a poem like it before. It was a risky maneuver. They might think it queer, pretentious, and worse—complicated. But when Hafif read the final draft, he began to like the idea. The rhymes brought out the ridiculous, storybook tragedy of the case. Hafif gave Nachtrieb the okay to read his 21-stanza poem as the finale to the "show," the closing, closing argument of a four-year legal battle.

And so it was time to decide. The twelve men and women walked out into the hallway, past the bullet hole, and into the room with the long laminated table down the center. While deliberating, juries customarily ask for key exhibits to draw out the major points of the case before rendering their judgment. But they had hardly begun when their foreman banged on the door. The bailiff looked in to see what they wanted. "Please bring us a copy of Mr. Nachtrieb's poem."

27
Heaven

Daniel Gerrity had an office in the Lincoln Building on East 42nd Street in New York City. He had gone to law school and passed the bar but had not practiced in years. Real estate was his business, and he profited handsomely on developments speckled throughout the eastern United States.

On the morning of March 13, 1985, Daniel Gerrity drank his coffee and read the *Wall Street Journal*. The story jumped out at him: "An Alameda County jury has ordered ComputerLand Corp.'s founder to honor a nine-year-old note that may cost him as much as $400 million in company stock. . . ."

Gerrity dialed the Massachusetts number frantically. "What's going on here!" he demanded of his uncle. Frank Gerrity had not read the paper yet and wasn't quite sure. As he listened to his excited nephew recite the incredible news, he wondered how he could have been so wrong. There was a time when he had considered Loring Reed one of his closest friends. Frank Gerrity was only half-listening as his nephew told him that they had to do something, anything, call Bill Conway, arrange a meeting of the board.

The next day the jury recommended punishment—$141 million in punitive damages. That enormous award—thought to be the largest in California history—was added to the 20 percent of Computer-

Land stock Millard had to hand over. Newspapers predicted the total judgment might be worth half a billion dollars. Micro/Vest gave a more colorful account of how far the billionaire had fallen. Hafif boasted to the press, "I may be able to force Millard into personal bankruptcy." Martin vowed to take the company public and run it under "different rules than those of Millard."

Frank Gerrity knew what he had to do. He had to tell Loring Reed what he thought of what he had done. He remembered his father's favorite saying: "You can work your whole life earning a reputation and lose it with one mistake." In the lumber business, Frank Gerrity had many opportunities to bend the rules. Companies would offer him sweetheart deals and cash. But his father's picture still hung in his spare New England office, and he never forgot that durable piece of advice. Precisely what he told Loring Reed—face-to-face—the rest of the world would never know. It was the way Frank Gerrity did things, and he wasn't about to change now.

Dan Gerrity arranged for a meeting with Bailey. His brother joined him at Bailey's office at Powers & Hall. Gerrity remembers Bailey "admitting in so many words that it seemed fishy," but Bailey "swore up and down" that Loring Reed had sold his stock without knowing that his son was involved. Reed senior didn't have anything to do with Micro/Vest, protested the lawyer.

The next meeting was held the night before Marriner's May 7 stockholders' meeting, the first held since 1980. Dan Gerrity pondered the possible explanation for the five-year gap in meetings: "Reed probably didn't want us to know what was going on."

Dan Gerrity listened as Bailey again spoke in Loring Reed's behalf. Bailey said that Reed's 40-percent stock in Marriner proved that no wrongdoing had taken place. Why would Loring sell to a group in which his son owned only 26 percent? If Loring Reed was interested in making money, he would have held on to the note, Bailey argued. Gerrity did not like the pitch. It was too pat, too contrived. And it seemed to Gerrity that Bailey acted strange and was unnecessarily nervous.

Dan Gerrity grew more suspicious when Bailey made his next pitch. The settlement offer Martin and Hafif had made before the trial was still good, Bailey told them enthusiastically. Now the price was $600,000. "Bailey thought it was a great offer," recalled Bill Conway, Gerrity Lumber Company's attorney, who also attended the meeting. "We listened and we talked to them. We didn't know if it was a great offer."

Conway was not encouraged that Micro/Vest would still not put their offer in writing. "Micro/Vest didn't want it in writing," Dan Gerrity recalled. "They feared ComputerLand could use it against them to impeach the credibility of what Loring Reed said [in the Micro/Vest trial]."

Although no final decision was made on Hafif's offer, one thing was decided. The Gerritys and Creighton agreed that Loring Reed should not be in control, and that they would propose the change the next day at the May 7 stockholders' meeting. Loring Reed appeared to be bothered by that suggestion, Dan Gerrity noticed. He seemed to take it as a personal affront, and as the meeting continued, Dan Gerrity and Conway watched him become increasingly agitated.

Up to that point Loring Reed had let Bailey do most of the talking. It was then that Loring Reed asked them to let him at least stay on the board of the company he had presided over for almost two decades. "It was an appeal," Dan Gerrity recalled. "He wanted to stay on the board even though a different group was in control." Loring Reed apparently knew he was neither appreciated nor wanted, but he was not completely alone. Bailey, despite his open friendliness with Micro/Vest, also did not offer to resign. By that time, however, the Gerritys and Creighton considered Loring Reed and Bailey as "the other side." They viewed Loring Reed's and Bailey's unwillingness to resign as evidence that they were part of Micro/Vest.

Dick Gerrity was voted Marriner's new president, and the Gerrity family company bought the Reeds' stock, including the Liz Corp. shares and the 811 shares Philip Reed personally held. The Gerritys, however, paid a premium. The Reeds demanded that the $600,000 Hafif offer be added to the value of the company—at that time valued at only a few hundred thousand dollars.

The Reeds were out, but the trouble was not forgotten. Bill Conway, Marriner's new attorney, was ready to file suit against the Reeds and Micro/Vest. Herbert Hafif then repeated the previous offer of $600,000. Oddly enough, the offer was made in a letter, first sent to Bailey, who in turn sent it on to Conway. "It was a very iffy offer, not crystallized or anything," Conway recalled. "The letter didn't say when we would be paid." And when Conway began to look into Micro/Vest and the offer, "there was wet and mold under every rock we turned." The letter was written after the May 7 stockholders' meeting. Marriner had until June 1 to respond. Dan Gerrity got the impression that Micro/Vest wasn't interested in negotiating: "They told us to take a leap."

Herbert Hafif received another sort of response to his offer. On July 3, 1985, Marriner filed suit against Micro/Vest, the Reeds, John Martin, Bruno Andrighetto, Andrew Bailey, and Powers & Hall in the Massachusetts District Court, asking for damages of $1.2 billion.

28

A New Look

Bill Millard carefully viewed his lunch guest on the security monitor. He had a rather ordinary face. In the middle was a peaked, snub nose, and if you looked closely, a few broken blood vessels. He was not tall, and his thinning hair was a dull brown color.

Little stood out about the overweight man in the blue suit ringing the bell at the house on St. James Street. On his cuffs, just beneath his engraved initials, glowed gold cuff links. Below, on his wrist, hung a thick, sculptured gold watch. On his finger, a gold ring. And in his hand, a sleek, black, alligator-skin briefcase. You could see his hypnotic, pale-blue eyes only when he took off the dark sunglasses.

Few guests had been received at St. James since the Micro/Vest trial. Millard had been optimistic about his chances in court and had even left the country before the punitive damages were in. He had scheduled a four-week trip to Europe and other outposts of the ComputerLand empire.

But after spending less than a day in Luxembourg, Millard heard the news of the massive punitive damages. The Falcon 50 was refueled and headed back home. Except for a couple of visits to gather his things, Millard would never again be seen at the Oakland ComputerLand office. "He came once because we had arranged for him to walk through and say hello to everyone because nobody had seen him and everybody was wondering where Bill was," recalled one of his staff.

The final stage of construction at St. James was nearing completion. Over the years, Millard had transformed the country home into a modern technological palace. First, earth was scooped out of the side of the hill to enlarge the garage to fit six cars. Then, to protect Millard from having to walk outside, a tunnel was dug from the garage to a spot directly under the middle of the house. Sixty feet of white hallway, lined by paintings and prints, led to a gold elevator, tastefully angled to the left. Opposite the elevator were two plush red chairs and a full-length, gold-framed mirror. Behind the mirror, a walk-in safe was protected by its own separate alarm.

A golden dial over the elevator pointed to G (for garage), the first of five floors. Directly above, the basement had also been completely redone—the rich, wood-paneled elevator opened to the exercise room, carpeted in electric red. Pink gardenias on gray papered the walls, but even that jumble of color was overshadowed by the shiny concentration of machines. In the corner was a large, white tanning bed, complete with digital counter. There was a computerized walking machine, a computerized rowing machine, a glistening Universal weight machine, and a bicycle machine. Millard, who had once completed a 100-mile bicycle race, loved to play a laser disk and pedal furiously into the color images that unfolded before him on the giant screen.

Mirrors at the other end of the room amplified the jangled mix of colors and machines. Off to the side was a spacious bathroom, a large sauna, and a Jacuzzi. Millard liked to finish his Jacuzzi or sauna with a blast of cold water. A special shower head was installed with a refrigerated tank that instantly shot 40-degree water. Next to the Jacuzzi and shower was a conference phone.

In the basement were two massive furnaces and a huge central air-conditioning system that heated and cooled the large house. Two full rooms were crowded with the maze of ducts, wires, and motors. Security and safety had also been incorporated into the older residence. Controls to set off fire and burglary alarms had been placed next to the elevators and in other key locations. And of course, there were security monitors throughout the house. But the biggest change loomed far above. You had to press A on the elevator, and rise beyond the first and second floors, to reach the Aerie, the new Office of the Chairman.*

The elevator opened onto a roundtable of couches, light streaming in through a long, broad skylight. Ahead was the eight-chair board-room table where ComputerLand's top executives would meet. At the end of the room hung a picture of Millard at Paradise Ranch, stand-ing in front of family and staff, excitedly holding up a live eagle perched on his hand.

Beyond the board table, two steps led to a narrow room whose ceiling angled to a point. A small desk looked out a window and toward San Francisco. The spare, almost monastic room became Millard's office, although he still used the downstairs study occasion-ally. He would spend hours upstairs, working relentlessly, sipping Ca-listoga mineral water.

On the other side of the Aerie was an alcove with two corner desks and a window looking back onto the courtyard. Two young female assistants would work there, answering the phone for Millard and managing the office. Don McConnell and several other aides from the Office of the Chairman drove daily to St. James. The rest of Millard's staff, including Barbara and the presidents, had to shuttle to the Aerie whenever Millard's participation or signature was required.

A billion-dollar corporation had moved its headquarters to an attic. It all made sense. Millard was more comfortable at home where his every need was taken care of. At St. James he enjoyed a full staff. A woman had even been hired full-time to take care of Millard's ward-robe. Encompassing an entire room, the chairman's clothes were me-ticulously sealed in plastic garment bags. Each bag bore Millard's initials, WHM, and a description of the contents, though the plastic was clear. For example, every one of the more than thirty pairs of shoes included a description. Shirts were arranged in large bags num-bered 1 through 16. Dozens of suits filled a ten-foot rack. Organiza-tion was exquisite. Each morning, his dresser would have that day's attire freshly pressed and ready, though Millard often never left the house.

---

*Millard's aides hypothesized that he named the room Aerie (Webster's Dictionary: "the nest of a bird on a cliff or a mountaintop") because of his love, shared by other est followers, for the eagle, their symbol of power and excellence.

Food and cleaning, of course, were never a concern. There was a full-time cook and a full-time maid. A handyman took care of repairs, and a gardener groomed the grounds. But the most important people were not employees. Pat Millard provided the emotional support her husband needed. And Millard's youngest daughter, Elizabeth, who ran the Millard Foundation, a charitable organization devoted to Erhard-sponsored organizations, would also soon work at St. James.

Family was where Millard sought comfort and support. And ever since he had been a little boy, family had meant women. First there had been his five sisters, and now there were his three daughters and wife. It was not surprising that other than the handyman and the gardener, no men worked or lived at the house. Feminine charm and warmth seemed to calm Millard.

He needed the rest. The trial had shaken him visibly, and friends and ComputerLand employees were concerned. Few, however, knew the real reason why Millard seemed so defeated. It was not the money or the humiliation. At the heart of it was something much more essential. The principle with which Millard had fashioned his glorious, billion-dollar castle had washed out to sea. Child of the Depression, the son of a railroad clerk, Millard had been raised on stories of the evil, lying, and cheating rich. Brighter than his desire to become rich burned his vision of becoming rich with integrity. Many at ComputerLand had heard him preach of how it was not necessary to lie, cheat, and steal to be an enormous, outrageous, unlimited success. It was the period on every sentence of Millard's life.

So it was that Millard did not know the ugly reflection he saw in the newspapers. He was not familiar with this greedy man who Micro/Vest claimed had reneged on his deals. That William H. Millard was an image, not a person; a caricature, not a man. But Millard had seen the evil that had created the "other," a coughing, sputtering judicial system gone amuck, strangling Corporate America. It was a mortal threat, he thought, a mortal threat to everybody! Nobody was safe anymore. It was open season on rape, robbery, and pillage through the courts!

As a boy Millard had looked up to the courts as one of the highest institutions of Truth. Now that the twelve men and women had let him down, maybe the world had, too. Maybe he was wrong and had been foolish, even a little naive, to believe that you could make it without lying, cheating, and stealing.

Millard was clear that Micro/Vest hadn't won through integrity. They didn't deserve a penny, and staring the huge $141-million punitive judgment straight in the eye, he knew the courts could not be blind forever. He had never had anything but a total commitment and desire and longing for the truth, the whole truth, and nothing but the truth to be known and declared. And if, and when, that magical day arrived, Millard knew he wouldn't have to say a word.*

Thus it was no accident that brought the man with the pale-blue eyes to Millard that day, although Terry Giles would later consider it fate. Giles, like Ken Waters and Ron Helms of ComputerLand, had also attended the Pepperdine Law School in southern California. Giles was one of the most successful graduates of Pepperdine and returned often for commencement speeches. Waters and Helms had heard Giles speak, and his reputation was well-known. After the Micro/Vest disaster, the two lawyers looked him up. Berman's services were no longer desired.

In his heart, Millard believed that he would be allowed a second chance against Micro/Vest. After a successful appeal, the case would be retried. But on the horizon, Millard was anticipating another battle. Killian and Van Natta's case was heating up, and their suit presented a claim for 10 percent more of his fortune. Millard charged Waters and Helms with the job of finding a new lawyer who would not just try the Killian/Van Natta case, but be prepared for a retrial of Micro/Vest.

In the late 1970s and early 1980s, Terry Giles was one of the top criminal lawyers in southern California. For eight and a half years he defended clients who he wasn't sure were innocent and won verdicts that he didn't think were correct. Giles learned that the system rewarded the best lawyer in the ring, not necessarily the innocent party. Along the way, Giles made a nice living for himself. He bought a Toyota dealership, owned part of a broadcasting company, part of a

---

*Not personally, that is. Millard hired Bob Gray & Associates in San Francisco to orchestrate a public relations campaign centering on the "crisis in the courts" that had caused the injustice he had suffered.

bank, as well as part of a nightclub that specialized in magic and sleight of hand.

And then, one bright southern California day he got someone off. At first, it seemed nothing special. Giles was always getting people off. But this time would soon prove different. A couple of years later, his former client killed two girls in cold blood. Giles didn't feel responsible, but he found no comfort in his technical innocence. Yes, he had followed the solemn code of legal ethics and given his client the best defense possible. But was that enough anymore? He wondered whether he was becoming part of the system, this strange machine that went by the name of Justice, but seemed more concerned with rules and technicalities. Where was Justice in the lives denied those two dead girls? he wondered.

Giles' law partners couldn't believe what he was saying when in 1983, despite one of the most lucrative criminal-law practices in southern California, he called it quits.

But that afternoon at St. James, he was listening and thinking like a lawyer again. He was good at it, and he got plenty of opportunity to listen. Millard told him what had really happened with Micro/Vest. The two men's eyes, equal in intensity and focus, seemed to pull together. As the meeting stretched past lunch, Giles realized that Millard was much more than just another client. Millard was the man he had been destined to meet. Giles understood "where Bill was coming from on the Micro/Vest suit." In the following weeks and months, Giles would examine court documents and uncover yet more evidence that seemed to justify Millard's truth.

Giles knew Millard's biggest mistake. The softhearted Millard ended up getting attached. Pat Millard put it the best when she said that her husband "collected strays." Millard's great failing was his compassion for the weak. For every moment of brilliance, Millard had allowed himself to be surrounded by an incompetent.

That afternoon at St. James would be the beginning of a new life for Giles. He would come to view the forces that brought him and Millard together as magical. He would come to see Millard as a great thinker, a visionary, and count him as one of his best friends. So complete would be his dedication that Giles would alter his appearance for the sake of Millard and the trial that he vowed to win. Giles would install a full gym in his house and hire a masseuse to rub away the unsightly pounds.

Millard liked Giles' business background, his entrepreneurial ventures into the car business, banks, and other companies. Most of all, though, Millard liked Giles' disillusionment with the law. Giles could not erase the memory of those two girls, and from that day on, it seemed as if his whole life had been a preparation for working with Bill Millard.

For Millard, too, it was the beginning of a new life. Cosmetic surgery was scheduled for May. There were some risks involved; the results of such operations were generally more favorable with women. Since the operation essentially pulled back the skin on your face, an operation on a man could potentially stretch your sideburns behind your ears. And there was no guarantee against the most awful accident of all. What if the surgeon's sense of proportion was wrong and you peeled off the bandages only to find that the two sides of your face did not match? One side, light and youthful, lines swept back beyond sight. And the other unchanged, with everything you had hoped to have forgotten, the heavy bags under the sad eyes, the deep wrinkles, and most of all, the unmistakable imprint of your own past.

PART

V

29
Fool's
Gold

Barbara Millard was doing everything that could be expected of a twenty-eight-year-old president of a billion-dollar corporation. It was just that what they were asking was impossible, crazy, and unbelievable! How could the court be so unfeeling?

But the California appeals procedure has little to do with feelings, and on one point, at least, it is quite unforgiving. To appeal a case you must post a bond of twice the amount of the pending punitive damages. In the Micro/Vest case damages were assessed at $141.5 million. To appeal the case, ComputerLand would have to post a bond of $283 million.

They had done impossible things before. A quarter-billion-dollar bond sounded beyond their reach, but so had many other goals. Barbara and her staff contacted all the companies that might be able to issue a bond. But there was a problem. Lloyd's of London and the other bonding giants consulted wanted collateral, something ComputerLand and the Millards didn't have.

To protect the judgment for Micro/Vest, the court had put the assets of ComputerLand into the hands of a court trustee. So it happened that when Barbara Millard began looking for a bond, she had nothing—not even St. James—to offer as collateral.

She expressed her frustration in a taped interview with one of her assistants, later to be transcribed, edited, and sent in a communication to the franchisees. She said, ". . . Everything was going very nicely with that [the bonding] until all of a sudden we hit the worldwide underwriting and bonding capacity. And then it's like, 'Oh, shit!'"

Her father, however, was not panicking. After the verdict came in, Millard's aides noticed that he held a series of meetings with a Slavic-looking man few had seen before. "He was talking with Kojnok behind closed doors," remembered one aide. "Nobody knew why." Hardly anyone knew that Ondrej Kojnok had been Harry Margolis's assistant in Millard's aborted 1976 Panama deal and had once been a director of IMS. But in one sense, Kojnok's presence was not surprising. The Czech tended to turn up when the pressure was on. When Micro/Vest sent the conversion notice in 1981, Millard used Kojnok to fire off threatening letters.

In June of 1985, Millard felt confident enough to take his trial-aborted European trip. There was something irresistible about sinking into the cream leather seats of the Falcon 50. And Millard's chef always prepared some marvelous meal they could heat up in the plane's microwave oven and enjoy after takeoff.

The nine-country, four-week trip was highlighted by a special reception in London by the Chamber of Commerce. The doorman, dressed officially in the requisite red jacket, announced, "Bill Millard, chairman of ComputerLand!" In Europe, Millard was still treated like royalty. Prime Minister Margaret Thatcher even engaged him in a five-minute conversation.

But the thousands of miles had not ended Millard's obsession with the Micro/Vest trial disaster. Sitting with his top assistant at an exclusive Geneva restaurant overlooking the sparkling Swiss lake, Millard talked on and on about the trial. "I don't understand why it's happening to me!" he complained to the woman who had accompanied him on the marathon trip. Encouraged by a few glasses of wine, his assistant joked, "Bill, it probably has nothing to do with this lifetime."

Millard, however, was not about to give up on his current lifetime or reputation. On May 28, ComputerLand began running a series of full-page ads in the *Wall Street Journal,* to spur corporations to "commit" to end world hunger. The first ad read, "Why ComputerLand Decided Not to Send Money to Ethiopia." The second read,

"Hunger. Disease. Death. And Some Other Topics to Bring Up at Your Next Board Meeting."

In a prepared remark, Millard said that ComputerLand chose *not* to contribute money directly to Ethiopia in favor of using "our time and energy to begin an ongoing *forum.*"

The franchisees had already received their Hunger Kits. Designed to help franchisees promote the campaign locally, each kit included a sample speech, sample press release for local newspaper editors, information on ComputerLand's stance on hunger, and a ten-minute film on famine.

Noble as Millard's intentions appeared, franchisees wondered what their chairman was getting into. Summing up the view of most of the profit-squeezed retailers, one franchisee said, "It won't help us sell computers."

Millard's other campaign was swinging into force. ComputerLand's attorneys called the judgment "un-American" and warned that the award could lead to the liquidation of ComputerLand. "It's one thing to punish; it's another thing to kill," said Pierce O'Donnell.

Next was the European campaign. Millard had recently hired the public relations firm of Bob Gray & Associates to schedule interviews in Paris and other major European cities. Nine reporters showed up at a press conference in Paris. As an aide who attended the conferences remembered, "We were painting it [the huge punitive damages Millard suffered] as a trend." But Millard began to wonder whether such publicity was the right route to take. Said the aide, "I think he [Millard] worried that Bob Gray might affect the appeal. Not enhance it." Soon, the public relations firm's services were no longer requested.

Back in the United States, settlement discussions were blowing up. Millard had offered Hafif 10 percent of the stock in return for waiving the $283-million bond. Hafif wrote Millard's attorney, unimpressed: "I have to feel that he [Millard] is trying to embarrass me in front of my client. . . . I really feel that he is insulting my intelligence."

A few days later, Hafif's mood worsened. Millard had told the press that he had received a bond commitment. Stories had followed in major newspapers. Hafif wrote again to Millard's lawyer because he knew that while Millard didn't have a bond, he did have money. It was just a question of priorities: "He has the corporate money to put up for 'binding' bonds that don't exist, and for fixing up his house at a cost of $500,000 *since* the judgment, but he has no money to pay the costs? He's abusing my agreement to stay execution, and is rubbing it in my face."

Hafif had a point. Despite the headlines and the company statements, ComputerLand could not, or would not, raise the money for the huge bond. After several hearings, the court agreed to reduce the bond to $25 million. Barbara Millard had figured out the next step. If they could find the $2.1 million they needed to get approved for the bond, she wouldn't want to pay for the bond. "Our intention all along was to go back to the court and say, 'Okay, we've got it now, but let me tell you why you don't want it.'"

But the "instant billionaire" could not even raise the $2.1 million needed for the $25-million bond. Still, his daughter wasn't worried. The court had asked them how much they could post, and when they had not known how much money they could raise, the court had proposed the $25-million bond figure.

Everything seemed negotiable. "At that point it was more of a conversation with the court than it was an edict, if you will," Barbara Millard said. "It was all based on what we thought we could do." She knew that if they went back to the court there was no reason to think that "fundamentally they don't still believe that we should have the opportunity to appeal without having to post the $283-million bond. Rather they will allow us to appeal posting whatever it is we can post." It did not seem to matter to her that Micro/Vest won the case, that ComputerLand owed it $141.5 million and 20 percent of company stock. Apparently, Barbara Millard and her father's lawyers would decide whether they needed to post a bond to appeal the case.

How could the court possibly intend anything else? Barbara Millard was not concerned about that. What bothered and troubled her was a more dangerous trend. Negotiations with Lloyd's of London continued after the premature announcement of a deal. It was not true they had been turned down, Barbara insisted, as press accounts had suggested. She sent a warning to the franchisees: "At this point I am much more concerned about the very real problems we may face by virtue of this kind of press. Very much more concerned about that than I am about the reality. The reality is as I've laid it out, and is not cause for a lot of concern."

Barbara Millard had taken care of reality. It was just as she and her father had intended. All they had to do was stay aligned, forge ahead, and fight the enemy: "I suggest and exhort you to do the same and batten down the hatches to weather the storm that the press chooses —the press and Micro/Vest are inflicting on us. . . ."

Reality, however, just wouldn't go away. The court had meant what it said when it had issued the $25-million bond order. Barbara Millard's intentions, it seemed, were not aligned with the court. Things were looking bleak. The lawyers huddled with Millard and came up with a new plan. It was to be used only in case of emergency. Filing for bankruptcy might stop the court from executing the judgment. "If we were unable to get a bond, the judgment became executable," Ken Waters said. "Micro/Vest could have gone down to the bank [ComputerLand's] in San Leandro and attached the stock." Waters never really believed Micro/Vest would want to jeopardize Computer-Land. But IMS, Millard's personal holding company, was another matter. "If you were Bill Millard and Pat Millard, it was not crazy at all. He was preparing to defend himself," Waters said.

Barbara Millard's mood was not helped any by the franchisees at the 1985 International Conference. The franchisees were complaining again, clamoring about the royalties, Micro/Vest, and Millard. As Barbara faced the masses of angry faces, she remembered what her father had told her. The system was good; the system was strong; the system would survive. The franchisees' problem was perspective. They were looking for external defects, when the bad was within. The problem was in the Ferraris and the second homes they had bought when things were good and easy. There was nothing wrong with the system.

Ken Greene had heard it all before. It was only that the face was female and she rambled a little less. But the source from which the words emanated was no different, and the longer she continued in her monotone, the more furious he became. "People were looking for ropes and trees," he recalled metaphorically.

But the best of the speech was yet to come from Barbara. While franchisees bought new cars, took vacations, and ignored their businesses, thousands of people had been dying of hunger—twenty-four of them every minute. And while the franchisees were complaining about money, they could have been saving lives. Barbara had seen them in India. Barbara understood. ComputerLand had spent hundreds of thousands of dollars to make the franchisees understand.

The hunger packet had been prepared and sent to each franchisee, complete with sample press releases for them to fill in and distribute in their city. They should be ashamed! What was the matter with them?

Dave McDonough and Norm Dinnsen of San Diego never knew. The two powerful, popular franchisees always got a suite at these events and this time they hardly moved from their room. There weren't many reasons to go downstairs and hear what went in one ear and out the other.

Drinks and jokes mixed easily in the raucous party atmosphere. Some franchisees learned that the best way to "handle" what Barbara Millard was saying was simply to ignore it. But McDonough and Dinnsen were also working. Their hotel suite was headquarters for the IACD. Franchisees would wander up, have a couple of drinks, and listen to some colorful jokes, and by the time they left they were one of the fraternity. At the beginning of the conference, the group had about 125 members. After a few days of the McDonough and Dinnsen voting drive, they had doubled to 250, nearly half of the U.S. franchisees. Chad Hill, ComputerLand's former director of social responsibility in charge of the Hunger Project, signed on as their public relations man.

But Barbara had greater troubles. An intruder had entered their midst. "Barbara freaked out," recalled one of Millard's aides. "Killian was at the conference." In one sense, there was nothing extraordinary about Killian's presence. He was a senior employee of MicroPro (the maker of WordStar), which like numerous other software companies had an exhibit at the conference. But the Millards knew that the office of Killian's lawyer was located in the same building as Nachtrieb's, the Micro/Vest lawyer. No chances were taken. "Security talked to him," one of Millard's aides said. "He was hustled out."

If only rumors could so easily have been squelched. They were all over the conference. The top franchisees had been the first to notice something strange happening. Product shipments—especially IBM PC shipments—were slowing. Franchisees' checks for products were being cashed by the corporation, but many of the goods for which they paid were not arriving. What many franchisees didn't know at the time was that a fund was being created in case ComputerLand decided to go bankrupt. To some within ComputerLand it was a perfectly logical plan. Build up a surplus, go Chapter 11, use the surplus to run the company, and then start paying the creditors. To franchisee Chuck Faso, "That was real serious, out-and-out fraud." Added Tom Niccoli, "They were building a fund to go Chapter 11 with . . . get Chapter 11 protection and have cash there."

Shabazian, the president of the U.S. division, knew that ComputerLand had "slowed payments to IBM," and he had seen the resulting "product interruption of two to three weeks." Shabazian also noted the sudden attention to corporate expenses. Travel and other expenses were paid for in advance with cashier's checks (Millard and his wife also made sure there was no debt on their credit cards). On at least two separate occasions, Shabazian said, the bankruptcy plan was ready to kick into action. Cashier's checks were made out to employees twice.

According to Waters, "Bill planned to take ComputerLand bankrupt." It was Shabazian who made the phone calls broaching it to major suppliers. First, he spoke to Vic Goldberg at IBM, then to John Sculley at Apple, and finally to Rod Canion at Compaq. The message was the same for each executive: "ComputerLand may go bankrupt."

Barbara Millard knew whom to blame. It was only the latest machination of a plot that she and her father had fought for years. She had not forgotten John Martin's promise to run ComputerLand under new management. "It was devastating. Herb Hafif, the day he put the word 'bankruptcy' in the same sentence with the word 'Computer-Land' . . . that hit the *Wall Street Journal* and within literally thirty-six, forty-eight, seventy-two hours our stores lost bank lines. Unbelievable! Customers canceled orders like a direct cause and effect, and the stores went nuts. I mean you could imagine, my God!"

The franchisees didn't have to do any imagining. Most lost their credit in days. And they had no doubt as to the cause of their troubles. "Millard used that to counter the execution of the judgment. . . . It's just something that his lawyers came up with as a chess move, and we were the ones getting screwed," recalled Burdick, the only franchisee who stood and clapped for Millard at the 1985 International ComputerLand Conference. "Really at that time I lost a lot of respect for Millard. When my bank sees shit like that, they say, 'What's going to happen when they go bankrupt? How are you going to get a product? How are you going to pay us?'"

Burdick and the major store owners in Dallas, Phoenix, San

Diego, Seattle, and other large metropolitan markets had an answer for the man who threatened to drag their businesses down into the black hole of bankruptcy. "I had the deals lined up," said Burdick. "We all had our IBM contracts on our desks filled out ready to be mailed in. Some [of the franchisees] had mailed them in and just didn't want to execute them until they got mad or something."

IBM had never dealt directly with individual franchisees before. Suddenly, the computer giant was offering its deepest discounts to ComputerLand franchisees and groups of franchisees that could muster the necessary volume. Was IBM's allegiance shifting from corporate ComputerLand to the franchisees—the men who actually controlled the major PC markets in America?

Barbara Millard knew that there was a reason behind IBM's change of heart. ComputerLand had 400 percent of the volume required for the pricing they received from IBM. Nobody else was even close. Barbara Millard was doing everything she could to win lower costs for the franchisees, but IBM wouldn't budge. "We did not receive the discount appropriate to our volume," recalled Barbara Millard. "And it did very nicely for IBM to make sure that ComputerLand did not grow beyond X percent of their [IBM's] volume." If only IBM would give them the discount they deserved, she thought. Then the franchisees would have a reason to stay.

30

The Fall

Even with a full rubber fishing suit and heavy pants underneath, Ed Faber could feel the cold of the river rush against him. The sun hadn't risen over the pine-covered mountains, and the world seemed to pause in that silky awakening between night and morning. He snapped the long rod back into the darkness and out into the river. The line whistled, curving lazily through the gray sky.

The best part about fishing was the silence. You became a part of the river, a part of the scene, and the occasional flick of your wrist and fly of your line was no more a disruption than the bugs dancing on the water or a squirrel scurrying up a tree.

In that silence Faber cleared his mind. Two years away from the corporate world had brought him an inner calm. He had followed the duck season wherever it took him—from California to southern Arizona to Mexico. In the summer, when he wasn't hunting or fishing, he was out playing golf. Learning that peculiar game had taken time, of course. The old baseball player had to forget habits picked up on the diamond, swinging the wood. But soon he grew to love the rhythm of golf—the sweeping stroke, the release as the ball jumped off the clubface, and the simple pleasure of watching the white sphere sail toward a flag waving in the wind.

Only a few days remained in September. At noon, as the river turned blue, they would release twenty-five shining fish—weighing more than 160 pounds—back into the icy water, and Faber and his friend would drive to Redding, California. They wouldn't stay long. Saturday was the opening of the pigeon season. Pigeons were the next best thing to ducks.

Barbara had her executive meetings on Wednesday. Attendance was down. Shabazian and Waters were no longer with them. After a loud, heated argument with Barbara, Shabazian had gone on a vacation, from which he had yet to return. Waters had not really left ComputerLand's employ. He had just moved his desk south to the office of Terry Giles, where he was helping his fellow alumnus prepare for the Killian/Van Natta case, and the hoped-for day when the Micro/Vest case would be retried.

The meeting opened with discussion about some of the new franchisee programs recently instituted. Then Barbara Millard brought up the main subject. The Association (IACD) had called a special meeting for the following week in Chicago. Everyone knew what that meant. The more than 350 franchisee members were going to debate seceding from the network.

Barbara Millard had always met other crises with calm. They had talked about the franchisees' concerns and devised programs to help them. Solutions were available if only they looked hard enough. Today, she sensed a difference. She could see it in the eyes of her officers. Fear was what she saw, and she realized she had never before seen them so disempowered.

Barbara was ready to fight for the things she believed. Not fight literally, but just act, and act callously. Act in a way that would produce a result. But her executives were not prepared to fight. Around the table she went, asking each to communicate their fears about the concerns of the franchisees. Although many of the problems they talked about would never be handled, just voicing them utterly altered the situation. One by one the officers spoke their fears about what might happen in Chicago. For Barbara, "It was a very interesting place to get to." They no longer needed to discuss whether the franchisees' plan was good or bad. ComputerLand now had to deal with the fact that revolution was happening, and that "it must be arrested, or it must be stopped or solved," or the empire would collapse.

Decisive action was needed—something, anything that would convince the franchisees to stay together. But what could that possibly be? They talked and talked, and Barbara finally decided that what they really needed was "input."

Early the next morning Barbara called her executives back into her office. A conference call was placed to the Network Advisory Council. Lasting more than two hours and eight minutes, the call was really about one person. Bill Millard had to go, the NAC said in not very gentle terms. "Okay," Barbara said, having expected that blow. "I have to ask you the next question, and I'll ask you to be frank with me, as if you were speaking to someone else, and I need to ask you, 'What about me?'" There was a pause on the line. The network advisors debated among themselves.

The NAC replied, 'If you have a shot, it would be to bring Ed in and to give him absolute authority as the chief executive officer." And then they paused for emphasis: "The authority appropriate and commensurate with being the chief executive officer."

Finally it was clear where they were coming from. "It was like, 'Okay, great, I got it!'" remembered Barbara, who hung up the phone, had a short "chat" with her executives, and then drove over to St. James. Her talk with her parents was short, not more than ten minutes. They agreed with their daughter's plan. They also agreed that they couldn't afford to let anything "pierce the perception of what really was true." If anyone with the last name of Millard worked anywhere in ComputerLand's management, there would always be some doubt in the franchisees' minds as to whether Faber was really the boss.

The Office of the Chairman had felt the pressure growing all summer. Statements to the press had become more and more defensive, and there seemed to be no issues other than franchisee dissent and Micro/Vest. Don McConnell and Glen Udine were in charge of the statements, but there were so many lawyers to consult with that when the work was done, there was always another press release needing to go out.

When he wasn't pushing out another release, Don McConnell was reading *Inside the Third Reich* by Albert Speer. He found himself

324   ONCE UPON A TIME IN COMPUTERLAND

drawn toward the book, although he had read it before. McConnell was amazed by the parallels he saw between what he called Millard's "strongman bureaucracy" and Hitler's Third Reich. Out of Millard's presence, he would make comparisons between the two groups. "It would just drive people crazy to have me compare their situation [with the Third Reich]," remembered McConnell.

The rest of the OC simply didn't want to hear. They had believed that there was no way the courts could be as unfair as it seemed. No punitive damages in any other case had ever stood for more than a few million dollars. Even the celebrated Ford Pinto award had been reduced to $5 million. Since nobody had been physically damaged in the Micro/Vest case—not so much as a singed hair—they all agreed that the punitive damages were an enormous mistake. "It seemed so wrong that we were pretty clear that there was no way they would allow the company to be transferred to these assholes just because you couldn't post the bond to appeal. We couldn't believe that," recalled McConnell.

But as the months had passed, it became clear to McConnell that the courts "were that unfair and that the [ComputerLand] lawyers were admitting that, 'Yes, it might well be.'" McConnell, Millard's voice to the troops, knew the end was near. "It was clear to us that even if the company was probably going to be okay, this wonderful thing that we put together with Bill—Bill is the modern hero leading the company of the future—that was doomed."

"Yes, I understand the problem," Faber said to Barbara Millard on the long-distance phone call. It was Friday. Two days remained before the meeting in Chicago. The drive home from Redding was surprisingly fast. Once home, Faber got cleaned up and changed. He arrived at St. James about four-thirty P.M.

Faber talked with Bill and Barbara Millard and then listened to the tape of Barbara and the NAC's conference call. The complaints were not new, but the anger was greater than he had expected. For two hours and eight minutes he listened to the NAC members damn Millard. Was it too late? he wondered. Had it gone too far?

In the confines of Millard's home they talked terms. Faber told them he was willing to return, but only as chief executive officer with full authority to run the company. Millard had asked him to come back as early as June, but had never been willing to give him the full reins. This time it seemed they knew the terms of the bargain. "Yes, that's it," Barbara said confidently. But there was more, Faber said. Barbara would have to go. The animosities ran too deep.

Faber also wanted to be chairman of the board. Millard, however, would not give up that final degree of control. He assured Faber that he would be given full authority to run the company, without any interference. Faber took his word. He did not ask for a raise, and Millard did not give him one. Faber was paid the same salary he had received since 1982. The only difference was that unlike the past two years, he now had to work for his money.

Barbara had never felt as competent, as clearheaded, and as in command of herself in her whole life. It was an exhilarating time because she had realized what needed to be done and had acted: "It got done literally within hours, and it absolutely handled the problem." Barbara considered it an enormously positive experience; she was proud of herself. The future of the network had depended on prompt action, and she had come through. She had boldly undertaken the enormous task of persuading her father to resign, and when her own resignation was required, she, too, had done it. In terms of her commitment it was probably her greatest contribution to ComputerLand. There was some truth in what she was thinking. In a few hours, she had accomplished what her father had been unable to achieve in over twenty years of business. She had let go.

The jet lifted sharply off the runway and banked steeply into the sky. The ComputerLand Falcon 50 was flying light that Sunday. Only Faber, his wife Nancy, daughter Bonnie, Abb Abley, and the pilots were on board. In a few hours they would land at O'Hare airport in Chicago.

The day before, on Saturday morning, Faber had called an emergency meeting of ComputerLand's officers. Five minutes before the meeting Faber had told Vin O'Reiley, president of the policy division, that as far as he was concerned, O'Reiley was a president "without a portfolio." Everything in O'Reiley's job and the group underneath him was going to be abolished or broken up. When the meeting was finished, Faber had eliminated the jobs of all the division presidents. Only Mike McConnell was left, and he was no longer a president.

That morning, as Faber spoke to the remaining officers, he did away with some of Millard's more extreme policies and cut the advertising fund in half. He did some quick financial projections, but there wasn't time for much else. Explained Faber: "I had one day to get to Chicago to get to this meeting where they were going to blow up."

Many franchisees at the O'Hare Holiday Inn were surprised to see Faber, but not everyone was excited about his arrival. After he had a chance to settle in, Faber prepared to meet a select group of the IACD membership at the bar. As he rode down in the elevator, Faber looked forward to a warm welcome. These were the same men he had helped bring into the business several years before.

But demands, not welcomes, composed the greeting. The IACD members wanted the royalty rate slashed. They wanted hard announcements and changes that would put some lift in their sagging bottom lines. "We didn't get off to a very good start with Ed," remembered Elliott Greene. "Ed would not commit to anything."

"The warm welcome I think Ed was anticipating didn't happen," recalled Dale Sissney, president of several Dallas stores. Faber seemed hurt by the group's coolness. He knew the authority Millard had given him. He understood the pressure the company was under from Micro/Vest. Why didn't the franchisees trust him as they had before?

Some in the IACD were worried. They imagined Faber, in his debonair way, striding in the next day and melting the concerns of the hundreds of IACD members without having promised any real change. Before they would agree to let him talk to the membership, they wanted to know precisely what he planned to do.

They were closer to the end than Faber had imagined. What could he tell them? He understood the problems they faced. A few changes he could make immediately; the rest would take time. He sure as hell hadn't come back to rule over the demise of ComputerLand! If that was their intention, then he would climb back on the Falcon 50 and go fishing. He couldn't make the pigeon-season opener anymore, but the salmon were still jumping back in the Klamath River.

Hardly thirty minutes had passed when the meeting ended abruptly. "It was almost like there was nothing he could do," recalled Sissney. "Whatever he could do was too little, too late."

After Faber left them, a few of the members stayed to talk. Perhaps they had been a little rough with their old friend? Maybe they were asking too much? They called his room and convinced him to come back. The second time around Faber seemed to calm down, but Greene remembered that he was still adamant about one issue: "Ed said, 'Hey if you guys bring suit, that's the end! I walk away!" It was late when the men finished talking. In a few hours Faber would give the most important speech of his life.

The standing ovation was no surprise. However dire the situation, he was still Ed Faber and they hadn't forgotten. He looked over the sea of faces and saw friends. "For those of you who may not have met me or for those who have forgotten what I look like, I'm Ed Faber," he said with characteristic aplomb. And then to another wave of applause he added, "There is a real live IACD; you're acknowledged as being here." To Millard, the IACD group had never officially existed.

Faber told them the conditions under which he had returned. The 1 percent advertising fee would be removed until the first of the year, and he announced an improved royalty plan. But most of all, Faber made some promises and commitments and asked for thirty days to show some progress. Then he opened the meeting to questions.

"How much authority do you really have?" asked one franchisee. "Do you really have complete authority?" asked another.

That was one question that Faber couldn't answer. Millard still owned 96 percent of ComputerLand stock and was chairman of the board. Even Faber had to wonder about that.

31

Down

and Out

After the Chicago meeting, Faber boarded the Falcon 50 and began the journey to California. Somewhere over the Rockies, at about thirty thousand feet, Faber leaned over to Abbey. "You know, this is the last voyage this plane's going to make." In the next few weeks, the Falcon 50, the Learjet, and the King Air would all be for sale.

A lot of things were readied for sale that week at ComputerLand. Soon the fleet of executive cars would be auctioned off. A schedule was set for moving employees out of the Oakland buildings and preparing the huge facilities for sale. Faber didn't have to worry about where to fit the transferred people. In the next couple of months about three hundred people, more than a quarter of the company, were given their walking papers. Counting Millard and his daughter, a dozen officers would be gone. There was something else that would go. Faber made clear that he never wanted to see one of Millard's policy manuals again.

ComputerLand was being reinvented. After eliminating entire divisions, Faber made drastic cuts in what remained. In a couple of months, Faber would accomplish what Millard swore he would never do—reduce the royalty fee from 8 to 7 percent. By dismantling the advertising fund, stores were receiving close to a 2 percent break on their gross sales. Faber had begun to reverse the equation. Corporate was in business to help the franchisees make a profit—not the other way around.

The new, healthy, spartan atmosphere could be seen in the plans for the company's Christmas celebration. This would not be a repeat of the $200,000 affair Millard hosted the year before at San Francisco's elegant Galleria. An empty ComputerLand warehouse was chosen for the party. Cool concrete would be decorated with four Christmas trees and crepe paper. A disc jockey would be hired, and they would dance away the afternoon under the influence of wine and beer. Fried chicken and potato salad would make up the main course. The projected cost was about $7,000, or roughly seven bucks a head.

But there were some things even Faber could not change. He and Millard were not getting along. Faber might be CEO, but Millard was still the chairman, and Millard could not shrug his duty, his commitment to be involved. Though Faber didn't feel any "heavy animosity" from Millard, it was clear that the press had targeted Millard as the troublemaker and Faber as the savior.

Terry Giles knew the friction between the two men was growing, but he didn't consider it any of his business. There were other, equally serious problems that seemed to demand his attention. Millard had invited Giles to sit in on all the attorney meetings. What Giles saw was disturbing. The lawyers would decide upon a certain course of action and then Millard would send the discussion spinning out of focus. "By the time the meeting was over, the information that Bill was relying upon, and the information he was receiving, was different than what I knew everybody intended to communicate to him," said Giles. At first Giles thought maybe it was just his imagination. But as time went on, Millard began to open up, and they'd talk about business. "Things were getting more and more discouraging and more and more difficult," remembered Giles. "It looked like bankruptcy was a distinct probability."

Giles was also concerned that "Avakian, the trustee for the Micro/Vest trust, seemed to be much closer to Ed [Faber], Ken [Waters], and Herb Hafif than any of Bill's people." Giles was afraid that perhaps the Honorable Spurgeon Avakian, a retired Superior Court judge, was starting to get a tarnished view of Millard. Few had overlooked the way Faber and Waters had stopped returning Millard's phone calls.

When they stopped returning *his* calls as well, Giles knew it was getting serious: "Actually what they were doing was they had stopped returning calls altogether to anybody related to Bill in any way whatsoever."

To many, however, Giles was still considered to be relatively neutral, merely Millard's attorney for the Killian/Van Natta case, and not directly interested in Micro/Vest. "I became sort of a garbage pail of tidbits of information," said the lawyer. When someone didn't have anybody else to talk to, they called Giles. What Giles caught wind of, however, was more than a tidbit. On the Thursday before Thanksgiving, he heard of a meeting scheduled to be held the following Tuesday, November 26, 1985, in which Hafif, Faber, and Waters would be present. It sounded ominous. "I felt that probably Herb [Hafif] was going to put together some kind of very hard hitting approach to go in and have the company seized from Bill in court—have him forcibly removed as chairman."

By coincidence, Millard called Giles that morning at his southern California office. Giles' office was the size of a large, elegant French home, though it housed only Giles, two assistant lawyers, a paralegal, and a couple of secretaries. Visitors were impressed by the European stone parking lot, the carefully manicured hedges, the French doors, and the elaborate, ever-present security system, including digital locks on each office.

Millard was not his usual cheery self. Remembered Giles, "He was just down and a little blue and wanted to talk . . . he didn't know what it was, but he was sensing some impending doom." Giles looked up at his shiny, custom brass ceiling and then at the time on his thick gold watch. "I can talk right now," he told Millard. But Giles had barely gotten back to work when Barbara Millard called—she, too, was sensing something ominous. Giles was unsure whether he should tell them of the meeting he had been warned of in confidence. Yet he felt he could not hold back. His first duty was to his client. He called Barbara and told her the news. Her reaction was immediate. "You've got to talk to Bill!" he said.

"Bill, I have a way out for you," Giles told Millard on the phone. "I have an idea. It's unique. It's different. And I don't know if I can sell it to everyone, but I think I can. If you are open to my coming up and talking to you about it—even though this isn't really my business or anything—I'd be glad to do that."

"Come up right now," Millard said.

"No, I'm not going to do that. I want you and Pat and Barbara to get some good sleep tonight. Go to bed early, get some good sleep. I'll come up tomorrow morning, and we'll all be fresh because I'm going to tell you a lot of things you won't want to hear."

"Okay. I got you," Millard said.

Giles took a morning flight. It was just the four of them—Bill, Pat, Barbara, and him. They sat in Millard's study, on the left wing of St. James. There was no fire in the fireplace, although the weather was turning cold. Millard's copy of *Wealth and Poverty* sat on his large oak desk. In the corner, on the bookcase, a little black conversation piece read, "My mind's made up. Don't confuse me with the facts."

But that was precisely what Giles had in mind. The time for facts had arrived. Giles ran through everything he felt about the Micro/Vest case, the mistakes that he thought were being made, and why so many people had turned on Millard. The way Giles saw it, Micro/Vest was really a case of a relationship gone sour, and the two parties, not that different from old lovers, blamed each other for their pain. "The point I was making with Bill is that if things are happening that you don't like, you can't place all the fault on other people—but they also can't put all the fault of that on you either." Once Giles had got "all that garbage" out of their minds, they could deal with the real issue. "I told them about the impending meeting and why I thought the ball game was almost over for Bill."

Then Giles presented the first half of his plan. Millard would step down as chairman. He and Barbara would step off the board and give the chairmanship and the voting rights to Millard's stock to Faber. Although Giles had never even met Hafif, he thought that he could strike a deal with him to eliminate the threat of bankruptcy. But Giles needed absolute authority to make decisions. He wasn't going to play the messenger. If Millard trusted him, great! If he didn't, then it wasn't going to work.

It was an interesting thing to discover, thought Millard. Even if it wasn't so in terms of who was causing the problem, or what the source of the problems was, it had developed to the point where it was clear that it no longer mattered. Said Millard, "Okay. So it's kind of like I realized: 'Oh, okay, one way to address that is if that's what's perceived is to operate on that basis.'" You could also solve the problem by perception.

Friday morning was almost gone. Giles had until Monday to head off the suspected Hafif/Faber meeting. He called Ken Waters's secretary: "Becky, let me just tell you I have some important information for Ken and Ed—the most important information they could ever hear. I have to get hold of them. If Ken knew what it was I had to tell him, he would want you to tell me where he was. . . ."

Sequoyah Country Club has plenty of trees and a little water as well. Faber was battling both that crisp November day, but Waters's game was pretty good. Even better, they were playing with two bankers who were interested in some business. As he walked down the fairway, Faber thought back on how little things had changed. Only a few weeks ago, Millard had promised him that he would have total control. But the only place Faber had found control was on the golf course, and even that was tentative.

At least Faber didn't have to worry about Martin anymore. Martin had been asking him to be the president of some computer chain he was going to buy in Minneapolis. Martin wouldn't say why he wanted Faber to preside over a chain that was currently bankrupt. "John [Martin] thought the [ComputerLand] franchises would break," said Waters. "The [bankrupt] company would be a vehicle [for uniting the mutinous franchisees under one roof]. John could own the entire thing."

There was one catch in the Minneapolis connection. Martin needed Faber to make it fly. Waters recalled Faber's characteristic blunt response: "He had asked Ed [Faber] to work for him, and Ed said, 'You don't have a company.'"

Soon after, Faber had called Hafif. "Tell him [Martin] to stop calling me," Faber told the Micro/Vest lawyer.

But even with Martin removed from negotiations ComputerLand still could not meet the reduced $25-million bond to appeal the judgment, and temporarily, at least, stave off the huge Micro/Vest judgment. The final deadline neared. The company he had nursed into the world was teetering toward bankruptcy.

Waters saw him first. They were on the 13th green when he puttered up on the golf cart. It was Terry Giles, dressed in a suit, waving from the cart. He had something to talk to them about. Barbara was waiting in the clubhouse. Giles said they would wait for them to finish their round. Waters and Faber both got triple bogies on the 14th hole, tossed their clubs in their bags, and headed in.

Faber could not believe what he heard. "They [the Millards] were really disconnecting themselves totally from the business," he recalled. "Apparently it was Terry Giles talking with Barbara, and Barbara agreeing, and the two of them talking to Bill." Faber was astounded. He had considered such a change impossible.

On Monday afternoon Giles and Waters flew to Claremont. Giles had a surprise for Hafif, given to him by a friend who had worked in Hafif's campaign for governor. Giles walked into the lawyer's office, and after a brief introduction, Hafif started to "rag on Bill Millard, talk down Bill, and say how stupid my client was."

"Now wait a second. I'll tell you what. I'll make you a promise," Giles said. "I won't talk about your clients if you don't talk about mine." Giles needed to tell Hafif what his position was. "You've got to understand something right off the bat. I really respect Bill Millard. I think he's one of the best thinkers I've ever met in my life. I admire the man and consider him one of my friends. And we won't get very far at all if we're just going to badmouth each other's clients.

"Besides," Giles continued, "a guy like you who has done all the things you have, run for governor and everything, a man I really admire, I just wouldn't think you would be involved in that kind of conversation."

And at that Giles said, "Let me just show you how much I like you . . . ," and pulled open his lapel to reveal a Herb Hafif for Governor button. Hafif leaned back in his chair and said, "Whatever you want, you got it."

The next meeting was held in the ComputerLand conference room. Hafif, Andrighetto, retired Judge Avakian, Barbara Millard, Faber, Waters, and a number of ComputerLand lawyers were gathered. Giles outlined the new (sans Millard) management structure for ComputerLand (two franchisees now sat on the board with Faber), and the new agreement with Micro/Vest. The deal extricated ComputerLand from the lawsuit. IMS would pay whatever damages necessary, with a limit of 27 percent of IMS's stock in ComputerLand. But if IMS and ComputerLand won the appeal, Micro/Vest would still receive 3 percent of the company. Faber was overjoyed. "The business was out of Millard's hands. Our [Faber and Waters's] stewardship could not be affected before 1994." That was the date Millard could return to run his company. To make the whole thing work, an agreement was reached to take ComputerLand public within the next two years.

But the deal was not quite done. Hafif needed the support of the entire Micro/Vest group. Later that day, exhausted, he met with the Micro/Vest investors. He had just finished "the greatest negotiating effort I know of in the law." He cautioned Micro/Vest that Millard could back out any moment. "What more could you ask for?" Hafif recalled. "Millard was out and we had given up nothing."

But for some in Micro/Vest it was not enough. "Martin and Agee were badmouthing me. It hits you out of the blue," said Hafif. "I'd just completed a full-blown miracle." But miracle or not, Hafif and Nachtrieb were asked to leave the room.

Some members of Micro/Vest wanted to read every last bit of the settlement. "I told them we didn't have all the time in the world," Hafif said. "Don't count on Millard signing it tomorrow," he warned. "He could change his mind tomorrow." But John Martin wanted his lawyers to look at the settlement. Martin had sold shares to many of the Micro/Vest investors, so they listened to his advice. Martin wanted the full amount of the judgment, not a compromise, and his idea of a deal included the $141.5 million punitive damage. Explained Waters of the man he considered a friend, "John would have gone for the jugular."

One day went by. Just as Hafif had anticipated, Millard had changed his mind. He claimed there was a part of the agreement he had not read. He wanted dividends—lots of them. Faber was angry. The company couldn't afford dividends, let alone the millions Millard demanded. About midnight, Faber received a phone call.

"Reach down and tell me what you got there," Hafif said.

"What do you mean!" said Faber.

"I want to know if you'll ride shotgun with me in front of thirty-five others [Andrighetto, Avakian, Giles . . .]," Hafif said, adding, "We have a deal. It's done, signed!" Millard, of course, had not signed the settlement.

"Tomorrow you appoint the board," Hafif said. "We have a deal, tell him [Millard]! Let him sue you."

• • •

Christmas at St. James that year was more extravagant than ever. A snowmaking machine, the type used at ski resorts, was brought onto the lawn. Tons of snow were manufactured and shoveled around the grounds. There in the hills of Oakland, twenty miles from the Pacific Ocean, glistened a winter wonderland for all to see. At night the special "moon lights" cast a milky, magical glow about St. James. As usual, Millard played beautiful music on his grand piano, and those not averse to defeat watched him skillfully sink one pool ball after another. But beneath his ever-present cheer and smile, Millard was calculating, planning his next move as meticulously as he lined up the multicolored balls on the smooth green felt.

For almost five years Millard had fought Micro/Vest on principle. Control was essential, and even majority ownership had been unacceptable to the 27th richest man in America. Now, after a compromise on the dividends (Millard got less than half his previous stipend—$3 to $5 million) Millard was letting go of the ledge, leaping off into the unknown. Pieces of one of the most private, closely owned family companies in America would soon be available on the stock market to anyone with a few hundred dollars rumbling around in his bank account. Millard was moving on, thinking of tomorrow, and the American pioneer spirit that burned within him was looking west.

32
Paradise

Millard, the "Global Citizen," as he called himself, was spinning the bottle and waiting to see which way it would point. Over the last few months he had become philosophical about the wrenching conflict that had thrown him out of his own company: "Maybe at the cosmic level this is all working perfectly. . . . I don't pretend to know who is in control of this thing called the World and Life and the Cosmos, but if you look at it, hey, it looks quite normal and natural and about right, and through history there's nothing that novel either."

For fifteen years, Millard had nursed the perception that the point, not the middle, but the point, of human, sociological, and industrial progress had moved west. Projecting a hundred years into the future, Millard believed that the voice of history would declare—without any ambivalence at all—that what was most valuable and most important would have happened in the Pacific Rim. One hundred years ago, Millard figured, men in comparable circumstances lifted up stakes in New York and moved to California. Two hundred years ago, they left London and Europe and moved to Boston, New York, or Philadelphia. Of course, that might have looked stupid if you were part of a successful London industrial or financial institution, but let them laugh, Millard thought.

No matter how wild and outrageous it seemed, Millard knew his plan was right. It became clearer and clearer in his mind. His reasons had not been logical but sensory: "It has to do with putting myself in that part of the world. . . . It's kind of like when I don't know all there is to know about what's next, I will put myself in the place where it is most likely to show up."

Where Millard showed up was "the farthest point west under the American flag." Saipan was like a dream. Millard had lived practically his whole life in California and had always thought it would be great to live on a tropical island. Now, he owned several acres of a South Pacific island.

Because of the time difference, the flight to Saipan took two days. After a stop in Honolulu, the plane swept over a few thousand more miles of blue water and touched down in Guam. After changing planes, it was only a short hop to Saipan.

From his window, Millard could see the forest-topped slopes of Mount Tapochau. Looking toward the west shore, he marveled at the pristine strip of white coral-sand beach. The rest of the shoreline was lined with steep, perilous cliffs, broken only by an occasional sandy cove.

Millard arrived in the spring of 1986, although Saipan seemed always in spring, blessed by an average temperature of 78 degrees that varied but a few degrees yearly. The rainy and typhoon seasons were several months away.

Millard had not come alone. In addition to Pat, Barbara and her boyfriend came along for the ride, as well as Millard's daughter Elizabeth and her husband. Not counting mates, the only nonfamily member in the group was Millard's secretary, Lynn Knight, who happened to be a high-school friend of Barbara's. She also brought her husband. Millard would supply jobs for everyone.

Millard and his wife bought a small home overlooking Laulau Bay in the village of San Vincente. His wife and daughters were overcome by the possibilities. The only thing that seemed to trouble Barbara was that she had to leave her black Corvette back home. The speed limit on the island was a tepid 30 mph.

Millard quickly discovered other shortcomings to paradise. The electrical voltage varied, and he had trouble making his computers run smoothly. As always there was an answer to the problem. Although the Saipan utility system was run by the government of the

Marianas Islands, Millard planned to start a utility company. Soon, he would form the Commonwealth Utilities Corporation, and if all went as scheduled, take over the Commonwealth's water, power, and sewage operations.

By late May 1986, the Millards had been in Saipan nearly three months. Except for a society piece in the *Oakland Tribune* entitled "For Millards, It's Like Starting Over," no one seemed to have noticed their sudden departure. It is one thing to be forgotten, but there is nothing worse than being forgotten on your birthday. On Monday, June 2, Millard was fifty-four years old. The celebration was a small, private affair.

But the next day Millard held a more public celebration. The silence he had maintained for almost nine months would end. Millard held a press conference. None of the major wire services or big U.S. newspapers sent a correspondent to cover the event. Despite the sparse attendance, it was a happy day for Millard. He was announcing his intention to sell his 96-percent share in ComputerLand.

Saipan was one of the last U.S. territories offering a near complete rebate of capital gains taxes. By selling ComputerLand while he lived in Saipan, Millard figured to save roughly 20 percent in capital gains taxes. With the price tag rumored as high as $500 million, Millard could avoid $100 million in U.S. taxes.

The June 4 *Los Angeles Times* read in part:

Millard might have reasons other than the tropical weather for his move to Saipan. As part of the Northern Marianas Islands, the island is a U.S. possession of the type that was recently upheld as a tax shelter for U.S. citizens, according to Richard G. Heller, a partner in the Los Angeles office of Peat, Marwick, Mitchell & Co.

In a case involving the U.S. Virgin Islands earlier this year, a federal judge ruled that a U.S. businessman who became a resident of the islands satisfied his U.S. tax liability—which happened to be considerably smaller than the U.S. burden.

Heller said the U.S. Senate's version of tax reform, now being debated in Washington, specifically closes that loophole and cites, among other regions, the Northern Marianas by name. If the bill is enacted as now written, the loophole would be closed as of next Jan. 1—the date by which Millard would apparently have to sell his holdings to avoid paying U.S. taxes. "It's very clever," said Heller.

Six thousand miles Millard had come and still they didn't understand! Why did the press always look for the trivial, the inconsequential, the banal? "No decision is based on that kind of criteria," Millard angrily told the *San Francisco Examiner*. Millard felt that his reasons for having chosen Saipan for his island paradise were quite profound.

Three hours and fifteen minutes from Tokyo, and four and a half from Hong Kong, Millard could hardly be more centrally located. Millard thought Saipan was right about where Hawaii was in 1940. He calculated that in the next twenty years, the little island would make as much progress as Hawaii had in the past forty-five. The local Japanese tourist industry seemed ready to explode. Millard was excited about the prospects for his new utility company and had spent over $5 million on one hundred acres of choice property overlooking lovely Laulau Bay, in which he planned $50 million of development. Most of all, Millard was impressed by the pro-business climate that seemed to welcome him as much as the sweeping beaches and the flowery air. For the first time in years, it seemed, he could breathe deeply. Far behind he had left that parasite known as American greed.

But Millard had not gone as far as he imagined. Bruno Andrighetto shipped fruits and vegetables to Guam, and he had friends in nearby Saipan. Why, Andrighetto even knew the man from whom Millard had bought some property! Weeks before, Andrighetto had received a letter from his friend, the governor of Saipan. The governor was a big property owner, some said the biggest on the island. The governor wanted to know about Millard. Andrighetto's response was long and colorful. He didn't leave anything out.

Millard, of course, knew nothing of the letters, and if he had, he probably would have been unconcerned. He knew the sale of ComputerLand was a gift, not only to the potential buyer, but ultimately to himself. Who could possibly be against such a marvelous end result?

Said Millard, "That whole opportunity for the next ten years has got to be for somebody in the world, the most thrilling, the most exciting, the most beneficial for them; the place for them to focus their resources and energy and attention to facilitate that; for somebody in the world that is the optimal, ultimate thing for them to do. Not for me, okay." But the miracle of the offering was that it empowered Millard "to do the same thing."

Millard meant that literally. "I needed to move my resources. My financial resources are where my heart is, where my body is, where my mind is, and to marshal them, to organize them, to align them, to focus them in a concerted, coordinated structure to address what is the biggest, the most exciting, the most nurturing and valuable thing for me to focus on for the next ten years."

Global was the only limit Millard would place on his plans. High technology was close to his heart. World trade was at the center of his spinning universe. He could see the entire structure of international trade rocketing through incredible change, opening opportunities that hadn't been available for centuries. Millard wanted to be a part of that New World.

Over in Hayward, Faber was fuming. Millard goes to the other end of the world, and then what does he do—pull a surprise news conference! The phone rang endlessly. The press delighted in catching ComputerLand with its pants down:

"The announcement by Mr. Millard . . . caught the company by surprise." *Wall Street Journal.*

"Millard's plans a surprise to executives at ComputerLand . . ." *Los Angeles Times.*

"ComputerLand executives were caught off guard because they were given no forewarning of Millard's announcements." *San Jose Mercury News.*

Millard was like the eccentric uncle who, wherever he went, left a whirlwind of trouble. "He created problems by himself," Faber recalled. "When you do something like he did, you get all kinds of—oh, I don't want to call them strange people, but—opportunistic people—who want to put together deals and so on. You have to at least answer their phone calls." ComputerLand franchisees were one of the biggest callers. They too had uncles or friends or people who just might be the buyer Millard was looking for. For more than a week, Faber and Waters spent most of their time answering odd phone calls and bizarre letters.

Micro/Vest seemed equally caught off guard, but the group quickly regained its composure. One Micro/Vest principal—there were only three: Andrighetto, Martin, and Reed—took advantage of the opportunity to hurl a cruel challenge to Millard. The man, who talked to the *Wall Street Journal* regularly, spoke on the condition that his name not be mentioned, but the reporter left what seemed a thin veil for those who cared to know the source: "At least one Micro/Vest principal expressed surprise at Mr. Millard's announcement, though he didn't rule out Micro/Vest as a potential buyer. . . ." The next sentence mentioned John Martin-Musumeci, the only Micro/Vest principal named in the entire article.

Bill Millard's wanderings had not only confounded Faber and Hafif, but also confused the world's most prestigious financial newspaper. The rest of the *Wall Street Journal* article was noteworthy for its misunderstanding of the basic facts. The article attempted to capsulize the history behind Micro/Vest: "Mr. Millard eventually offered to settle with Marriner, but by then the note had been sold to Micro/Vest, which included several former Marriner officials."

If the reporter had called the United States District Court in Massachusetts, he would have discovered that eight months earlier Marriner had filed a $1.2-billion suit against Micro/Vest and was rushing to file an additional affidavit to prohibit Micro/Vest from collecting its winnings in the Micro/Vest trial.

Perhaps there were some who considered these unnecessary details. ComputerLand knew all about Marriner's lawsuit. Barbara herself had visited Marriner's attorney, Bill Conway, at his Albany, New York, law office in February. And of course, Micro/Vest knew all about Marriner's Massachusetts lawsuit. In January of 1986, Hafif had sent a letter accusing Marriner of bad faith and malicious prosecution, among other things. Things were confusing enough. Why complicate matters? The truth was that a sale of ComputerLand would benefit just about everybody. ComputerLand would get rid of Millard; Micro/Vest would get some cash; and Millard would save tens of millions of tax dollars needed to fund his global activities.

Few had ever accused Millard of undue concern for the feelings and sensibilities of others. The creditors and dealers he had left behind in the wreckage of IMSAI's bankruptcy certainly didn't accuse him of that emotion. Nor did International ComputerLand franchisees faced with his charges of cheating. The truth was that Millard didn't really mean to upset, or even hurt, people. He was only following his personal beliefs, and to break with those beliefs would be to commit the greatest of all lies.

Millard really believed that the world would see brilliance in his move to Saipan. They would applaud his brave entrepreneurial spirit and print grand stories of how, like the pioneers of another age, he was going west to tame new, wonderful lands. And in his adopted home, the Saipanese would welcome him as the benevolent entrepreneur and cheer his efforts to put their tiny island on the map.

But a lot of locals liked Saipan just the way it was—small, quiet, virtually unknown, and the last and greatest tax dodge under the red, white, and blue. When Millard started announcing his bold plans to the world, the local Marianas Legislature, the U.S. Congress, and the Internal Revenue Service pricked up their ears.

Three weeks after Millard's birthday announcement, a few minor tax changes were enacted by the Commonwealth of the Northern Marianas Islands. Before that, the Saipanese—many of whom happened to be temporarily transplanted Americans who had come into money—enjoyed a 95-percent rebate of U.S. taxes. The new law cut that rebate to 50 percent of income over $7.5 million, and to 25 percent for income of $20 million and more. Millard was specifically named in the abrupt overhaul of the tax code that the *Los Angeles Times* reported as "tailored to rake in some of the ComputerLand loot from Millard, or 'any other millionaire who comes out here [Saipan] and plans to use the Commonwealth as a tax haven.'"

What kind of a government could do such an irrational thing? Millard wondered. Millard promptly canceled his $50 million in planned real estate investments for the island, resigned from his barely warm chairmanship of Commonwealth Utilities Corp., and demanded that his directors do the same.

"Millard finds Trouble in Paradise," was the headline in the *San Francisco Chronicle*, which like the rest of the U.S. press made light of Millard's newfound misfortune. The Millards may have been down but they were far from out. Millard had dealt with this sort of thing before. A principle was at stake, and he was not about to flinch in the line of fire. "Bill would very much like to stay on the island," Millard's assistant Lynn Knight said in the *Chronicle* article. But she added, "He is keeping his options open."

Apparently the U.S. Congress was also keeping its options open. Reported the *Los Angeles Times:* "In an obscure provision apparently inserted by a Joint Taxation Committee staffer who was bothered by news of Millard's move, the tax reform bill now awaiting final approval in Washington contains tax 'anti-abuse provisions' aimed at anyone who moved to the Northern Marianas, Guam or American Samoa, retroactive to Jan. 1, 'without regard to motive.'"

Millard told the Saipan Chamber of Commerce that he could structure the ComputerLand sale to avoid the clutches of the new local tax. One legal tax dodge would entail stretching out the payments from the sale so that the capital gains each year would fall below $7.5 million—assuring Millard of the maximum 95-percent tax rebate.

At the very moment Millard planned to circumvent the island's new tax law, his attorney said that the hastily passed amendment proved that avoiding taxes had nothing to do with Millard's 6,000-mile relocation. "I've been telling everybody all along that Bill's [move] had nothing to do with taxes. Nobody believed us. Now maybe they'll believe us. It doesn't matter what happens in Saipan taxes," said Giles.

Why did Millard tell the world about his planned legal tax dodges if he didn't care about taxes? There were no answers to the contradictions that seemed to twist their way across the great blue expanse of the Pacific. Questions were all the press seemed to pose. Would Millard figure out a way to outsmart the local legislature? Would he be able to avoid the new law by selling his stock to a foreign investor? What the press didn't know was that Millard was again calling on his old counselor Kojnok. It was on Kojnok's advice that Millard had come to Saipan in the first place. Millard flew the attorney to the island for a couple of weeks in August to figure out a way to straighten out the deal.

Perhaps his tax situation could be improved. It was reported that Millard was trying to arrange a meeting with the president of Palau, another South Pacific island. Perhaps when Palau ended its United Nations trusteeship, it could accommodate all of Millard's needs.

But Millard had even more immediate concerns. The Killian/Van Natta trial was only a few weeks away; $300,000 had been raised by investors who had bought shares in the suit for 10 percent of Millard's empire. And although St. James was officially for sale for $2.4 million, Bill, Pat, and Barbara would return to their former head-quarters. Millard would bring several books with him, including L. Ron Hubbard's *Dianetics*. But another, much larger volume would consume much of his free time. Down in the study, on his desk, next to his copy of *Wealth and Poverty,* two volumes of the *1954 Internal Revenue Service Code* would soon be littered with yellow markers.

33
The Truth

Each day, Millard was the first in the courtroom. Pat Millard would follow him through the heavy doors, down the aisle, and over to the defendant's table on the right. For much of the next two months in the fall of 1986, Millard sat there, hands crossed, wearing a kind, tranquil gaze.

Less than two years had passed since the Micro/Vest trial and Millard was practically back where he had started. Little had changed. To his left sat two former employees who claimed he had cheated them out of ComputerLand stock.

Only Millard seemed to have changed. Gone were the bodyguards and the herd of lawyers that had surrounded him in the Micro/Vest case. One lawyer, Terry Giles, sat at the defendant's table. Millard, dressed in subdued brown and gray suits, sat at the corner of the table directly facing the jury, with his wife at his side.

Everyone rose as Judge McCullum entered the courtroom. The day before, the handsome, silver-haired black man had instructed the jury for an hour on the intricacies of fraud. Throughout McCullum's monologue, Millard wore that same half-grin, his head lifted slightly like a model student listening to a lecture. Not once during the entire hour did he take his eyes off the judge. No one in the courtroom could match his concentration as he sharpened his focus on the man who had presided over his greatest defeat.

Killian and Van Natta's lawyer gave his opening statement first. A tall, mature man, John MacGregor moved slowly and the words drawled from his long, kind, wrinkled face. He had talked only a few minutes when he seemed to have lost his place. His voice grew even quieter as he remembered what he had wanted to say and faced the jury. "This is a case of fraud. But it's also a case of friendship that developed into love and trust, and it gradually evolved into manipulation and betrayal."

"Would you repeat that last phrase," called out one of the jurors.

The judge asked the court reporter to read back the phrase and told MacGregor to speak up. MacGregor cleared his throat, took a long, deep drink of water from the plastic cup on his table, nervously looked over his notes and continued.

He told the story haltingly, forgetting names and places, and often paused to check his notes. Though Millard had heard it all before, something had happened to his concentration. Millard only glanced occasionally at MacGregor, appearing more bored than bothered by his words. Millard was busy making notes on tiny yellow pads.

MacGregor was winding to the close of his opening statement. ". . . What ended up in the final conclusion of the manipulations that occurred, he [Millard] ended up putting the rich company on one side and the poor company on the other side. Because in fact, they should have all been together. . . . Finally we believe the evidence will support a finding by you, and we will prove that Bill started—Mr. Millard—ComputerLand with the assets of the company that was owned in part by Joe and Bruce, the plaintiffs, and that he concealed all of that from them. Thank you."

It was an awkward ending, lacking polish and snap. Only half an hour remained until the day's final recess. Giles grabbed the opportunity and stood up. Grueling workouts and pounding massage had eliminated most of Giles' unsightly fat. He thrust his shoulders back. "Your Honor, we elect to give our opening statement at this time." Giles strode athletically to the corner where the plaintiffs' large charts were placed and began handing them to MacGregor. Then he asked his client to bring over their charts. Wearing that same grin, Millard brought the large placards over to Giles. "Thanks, Bill!" Giles said, loud enough so that everyone could hear.

He pointed to one of the placards Millard had brought up and read a newspaper story describing Millard as a "boy wonder" at the age of twenty-three. Giles' voice rose, charged with reverence: "Mr. Millard truly was someone at the cutting edge of the computer industry. The evidence will demonstrate that is not happenstance. That the Silicon Valley, the computer industry, just happened to be in and around the city of Oakland and the East Bay. It happened because of men like Mr. Millard who just happened to grow up, be born and grow up in this area.* If he had grown up in New Jersey, then maybe the industry would have been located on the East Coast instead."

For the next few minutes, Giles contrasted Millard's career with Killian's and Van Natta's: "Well, in 1955 when he was the boy wonder of Pacific Finance, Mr. Killian was in the fourth grade; Mr. Van Natta was in the fifth grade. . . ." By 1973, Killian and Van Natta were no longer in grammar school: ". . . what were Mr. Killian and Mr. Van Natta doing at that time? Neither had had a job yet in the computer industry. Mr. Van Natta—and this will be from his own words —had been spending quite a few years of his life up to that time engaged in poetry, friends, and bohemian life. That's what the evidence will be!"

Giles' pale blue eyes seemed larger now, and as he stared at the jury, shaking his hand for emphasis, below his cuff links the bulky gold watch shone. ". . . As Pat Millard will say about Bill, one of the things he does is he collects strays to work for him in his companies. And the truth of the matter is, as she will describe Bruce back in those days, I think it [sic] was probably perfect words, he was weird and odd-acting. Might wear shoes to work, might not. Very unkempt. Might sleep in the corner of the office that night. Might go home." And then Giles paused for the dramatic line: "There were a lot of weird and odd-acting people that collected in and around the Berkeley area in the early seventies. Bruce Van Natta was one of them." Millard was no longer making notes on his tiny pads. His head was high, his smile loose, and his eyes seemed to twinkle.

Millard, Giles continued, kept his oral agreement with Killian and Van Natta to give them stock. "He gave them the right to buy five percent of the company—an option. There is a difference between

*Millard was born in Denver, Colorado, and Silicon Valley is on the opposite side of the bay.

the right to buy and giving someone the stock. And that's the first major dispute in the case."

Giles couldn't have been more right. The case was about keeping your agreements, a subject close to Bill Millard's heart. For the next two months, Giles would argue that Millard had not given Killian and Van Natta stock in exchange for their valuable 1-percent agreements—he had merely given them an option.

Millard's diary never mentioned an option. But that didn't stop Giles from reading from the March 1, 1976, entry and emphasizing the phrase "I cause them to procure." To Giles the words meant "option to buy."

Giles had one last thought to leave the jury with before he finished for the day: "Ladies and gentlemen, throughout this entire case you've got to watch the evidence so very carefully, because we contend that there will be a lot of mudslinging, and we are going to try to clean that up. . . ."

The next morning Giles began innocently enough. His voice was calmer and his hands waved less, but soon the course Giles plotted was clear. He claimed that the oral agreement was only an option to buy the stock, and thus "Mr. Killian and Mr. Van Natta never owned any stock in the corporation until June of 1978. And if they never owned any stock in the corporation until June of 1978, then you know . . . all of that stuff about the various changes in corporate structure and all of that, it doesn't matter. It doesn't matter because at that time Mr. Millard still owned one hundred percent of his company.* The option hadn't been worked, and by God as an American citizen he has a right to do anything he wants with a corporation he owns!"

Money wasn't important to Millard. "The evidence will be that Mr. Millard never built his companies for the money. He built his company for the company, for what it could do for the world. . . ." Millard was different from the people who began to crowd around him. "Yeah, he made a lot of money. Yeah, he's a rich man," Giles said. "But the money isn't what it was about for Bill Millard. But as the evidence will show, [for] all the people around him, it was for the money."

The "Greed Factor" was surfacing, Giles said. ". . . If you went in to see Mr. Millard and sat down and you said, 'I got a great idea. We

---

*At the very least Marriner owned 20 percent and Faber and Martin a few percent.

are going to make a lot of money off of this. We are going to do this and do that and make a ton of money,' Bill would say, 'Pass. Not interested,'" Giles said, shaking his head. "[It] wasn't what turned him on."

When Philip Reed and Marvin Walker tried to buy the Marriner note in 1978, they told Millard they were "all going to make a killing. Ah, we are going to make some fast bucks!" Giles said, waving his hands as he walked in front of the jury. "As soon as Phil Reed talked about, 'I am going to buy into your company, and I'm going to help you resell it, and we are going to make some fast money,' Bill turned off like that!" Giles snapped his fingers twice as he paced back. "It was like walking over to the TV set and turning it off. The picture went out and the volume went off."

But Reed and Walker weren't the only bad people in Millard's world. "John [Martin] would charge what the traffic would bear, cut a different deal with everybody. It created problems, lawsuits. Millard sat down and talked to him and John Martin's attitude, as the evidence will be, was, 'Hey, look, this is fantastic. We can sell these things like crazy. Bill, we can make such a fast buck off this thing you can't believe it!'"

Giles shook his head and stared into the eyes of the jury. "Do you remember the evidence I told you about Bill Millard's personality? When John Martin said that, it wasn't just like turning the TV off. It was like kicking the tube, like the TV would never go on again. That was it. John Martin wasn't going to be around anymore."

But Martin was a different man, a type with whom Millard had never tangled. "As John Martin walked out the door of Computer-Land, he told Bill Millard and Ed Faber and everybody else who could hear him, 'I'm going to bury you!' Now, there will be testimony that . . . some people who heard that [comment] thought he might actually try to kill somebody. . . ."

Giles saved the thickest, dirtiest mud for last: ". . . I am going to present some evidence to you which I think will disturb you. And that is that Killian and Van Natta, during the same period of time that Mr. Millard was keeping his promise, giving them five percent of the company, they were engaged in conduct to deceive William Millard, and to steal. Strong words, huh?"

A few of the jurors glared over in Killian and Van Natta's direction. Van Natta had slumped down in his chair and clenched his hands, covering his mouth. Killian's jaw was locked in tension. Giles was just hitting stride. "I have evidence that they were involved in a conspiracy to steal one of the most important assets of the company they worked for, IMSAI manufacturing company." It was no accident, Giles said, that Rob Barnaby and Seymour Rubinstein were off at MicroPro selling a word processor called Word Master (an early version of WordStar). And its resemblance to the program Barnaby had designed at IMSAI—NED—was no coincidence.

Giles' voice dropped as he completed the final piece of his alleged conspiracy. "Sometime either at the end of 1979 or early 1980, Diane Hajicek, in a state of serious depression, depression so serious that after she made her phone call to Bill she entered a hospital a few days later, in a state of depression, calls Bill Millard and apologizes to him for being involved in the stealing of the software that she was involved with working on at IMSAI."*

Millard lifted his head higher and smiled as Giles proudly uttered the final words of his opening statement: "I don't get to tell you what the truth is. You get to tell us what the truth is. . . . Because the truth is what we are more than happy to deliver."

The courtroom was nearly empty. Five minutes remained until the jury would be called in. "Should I go up there now?" Millard nervously asked Giles. "Sure!" said his lawyer confidently. Hands in his pockets, Millard walked up the two steps to the witness chair, sat down, and began to wait. He looked even younger and more handsome today. His muted gray tie, striped red, complemented his blue suit, and his slim gold wedding band symbolized his simple, understated elegance.

"You can't sit up there yet!" joked the court clerk. "I get to swear you in and try to make you laugh." Millard smiled, walked down from the stand, and talked to the court reporter, who was the same woman who had transcribed the Micro/Vest trial. "I guess you won't have any trouble spelling my name this time," Millard joked.

Millard was trying awfully hard to do it right. Talking about his up-and-down career, he had recently told the *Oakland Tribune*, "The

---

*Giles asked and received permission from the judge to prohibit Hajicek from entering the courtroom. Giles promised that he would call her as a witness.

story of this is, you get to do it over until you do it right." There was no doubt that Millard was focused on doing it right this time, the second time around.

Millard seemed well prepared for the role. He addressed his answers to the jury, a few of whom smiled back at his enthusiastic responses.

Millard had to correct MacGregor. The lawyer had constantly been making reference to the "journal" Millard kept. "It doesn't look like a journal. I have a little trouble when we use the word 'journal.' I mean, you know, I wrote notes. Sometimes I doodled while I was on the phone. . . ."

Millard was talking about the words he used to document the financial crisis he faced when he returned from his February 1976 marketing trip. Millard wrote that Joe and Bruce's 1 percent of gross agreements (and Philip Reed's) "wipes out anything the company is able to do in the short run." MacGregor asked if changing their gross agreements to stock wasn't one of the first things Millard did upon his return.

Millard replied, "Well, first of all, I don't really remember the first thing I did when I got back from the trip. Whenever I would be gone, for me to be gone a whole month away from my company, I mean I typically came back and there was a deluge of sixty-second meetings and documents and paper all over the place, and like that, so . . ."

MacGregor forged ahead, and finally, after another five minutes, Millard answered his questions. ". . . The end result of our getting together was that we terminated the [1 percent] agreement, and I gave them an option to buy into the company up to five percent for each of them."

The end result. It was a phrase Millard would use repeatedly throughout the trial. He was interested in end results, and he still had one more to achieve.

The next morning little seemed to have changed. Millard sat in the witness chair, taking notes on his little yellow pads. As the jury filed in, Millard slipped the pad and pen into his jacket pocket and wished the jury a good morning.

During the breaks, Millard showed Giles his little notes. Giles straddled the banister and explained it all to Millard. Then, smiling to himself, Giles walked over to the wastebasket and tore the notes into tiny pieces. But not all of Millard's notes were notes. Sometimes they were just straight lines, drawn over and over again. And sometimes they were just doodles.

The following day MacGregor asked Millard if Joe and Bruce had asked for their stock during 1977. "I don't recall the delivery of the stock being any kind of an issue at all until December of '77...," answered Millard. "So, I would have told them when we—we were very close. When we got together, we just—we shared everything, really, and I would have told them had they asked.... See, there wasn't anything at risk for them. They weren't—you know, time didn't matter...."

Millard said that even he didn't really understand the complicated reorganizations that his lawyers had overseen. Did he feel a duty to inform them of those structural changes? MacGregor asked.

"I often shared with Joe and Bruce. We met often, spent a lot of time together—"

"Your Honor, may the witness be instructed to answer the question?" MacGregor asked.

"I felt that I had an obligation to tell them whatever I knew, at least whenever they asked. My real obligation I felt was to see to it that ultimately they had an opportunity to buy into IMSAI Manufacturing and that's what I felt so good about when I finally got to that result," Millard said.

"Your answer is you felt you had the duty to tell them only if they asked?" MacGregor said.

"I didn't say only if they asked," Millard insisted.

"What did you say, sir?" MacGregor asked.

"Well, let me just tell you. It would be, I felt I did not come and feel like I had an obligation to inform them of every little event that came along," Millard said.

"Did you think—" MacGregor started to say.

"But I certainly did feel always obligated to answer their questions and to see to it as I was able, that I would be able to do my part to see that the end result was possible."

There was no stopping Millard. He talked when he pleased, characterized previous testimony as he saw fit, answered questions not asked, and elaborated on questions he'd already answered. At times it seemed that Millard was asking the questions. Apparently, Millard wasn't sure what he had told Joe and Bruce, but as far as the "machinations that have been described in the trial," Millard hadn't understood all those corporate reorganizations himself.

MacGregor showed Millard another entry from his journal. Written a month before the June 1978 delivery of the stock certificates, the entry was a chart in Millard's handwriting showing the precise result of Millard's recent reorganizations. Millard had even labeled the companies IMSAI I and II, and IMS I and II.

"Did you tell them?" MacGregor asked.

Millard couldn't remember.

"Did you consider it important that they know or should have known at the time?" MacGregor asked.

"Well, I would have considered again the steps that we got there to be—were not as important to me by any means as the end result. So if we were together, and in a conversation, I expect I would have told them, and very likely could have and would, and did. When we did this—we were happy we got there. We got it done."

Intention was important to Millard. Sometimes it was difficult to make out whether he had really done something or just expected that he could have and would have. Soon, such intricate questions were forgotten.

Less than an hour remained in the day. Giles snapped his broad shoulders back, grabbed a yellow legal pad, and stepped forward: "Did you think it would have been appropriate in June thirtieth, 1978, to give Mr. Killian and Mr. Van Natta this five percent of the second IMS Associates that was now your holding company?"

"It would not have been appropriate because it was not the manufacturing company," said Millard.

Over and over again Millard and Giles used the word "appropriate." It symbolized Millard's beliefs and his case. Giles had done his job. He had asked Millard what was fair, right, and appropriate, and Millard had spoken simply and clearly.

All that remained were a few details to be cleaned up. MacGregor had demonstrated that the documents at Millard's companies weren't always created when they said they were.

Giles pulled out a large felt-tip pen and began listing the backdated documents on the posterboard. He had to ask Millard the date and subject of each document, so it took about twenty minutes before they were all up on the board. Then Giles said, "Is it fair to say if you look at the documents in chronological order there appear to be some contradictions?"

"Yes, there is," Millard said.

Giles had a solution. They would date different columns for when different documents were created. That way they could figure out which documents were actually created when they said they were, which documents were created when they were backdated, and which documents weren't created when they were created or when they were backdated but at another time.

Giles prepared to ask Millard when the first document was created. "Counsel, it's four-fifteen. Is this a good place to interrupt?" the judge asked.

Giles would have to wait until the next day before he could put each document in its proper column. But it all seemed to make sense the next morning once Giles had organized it all on the board. As Millard explained: "It was my understanding that it was important that as a sole stockholder of my own company that was appropriate to date the documents and the transactions dating from the date of the intention to establish a holding company for tax consolidation purposes."

Giles had one last point to make. During the reorganization, ComputerLand and IMSAI stock were in the same company. Giles asked Millard whether that fact entitled Killian and Van Natta to ComputerLand stock.

Millard replied, "No, sir, it did not. They were clear from the beginning and all the way along that there was no intention ever [that] they would be allowed to purchase any kind of a beneficial interest in ComputerLand."

It was amazing but true. In just a couple of days Giles had shown that Killian and Van Natta had got just what they asked for and Millard had been more than appropriate.

After six weeks of witnesses from the plaintiffs, Giles figured the trial was long enough. All those people he had told the jury about—Diane Hajicek, Rob Barnaby, Seymour Rubinstein, the alleged MicroPro conspirators—were never given a chance to answer his accusations.

In his two-day defense, Giles called neither Bill Millard nor Pat Millard, who, Giles had told the jury, would testify that "Bruce [Van Natta] was weird and odd-acting." Giles had told the jury a lot of things that he claimed people would testify to. Why did he need to call them to the stand when he had already spoken in their place?

Closing arguments would give Giles another chance to speak. Indeed, his opening and closing arguments would be more than twice as long as his defense.

MacGregor spoke first. He had looked a long time for the words that captured the essence of Millard and he had found them in *Alice in Wonderland*: "In the argument about the meaning of words, Mr. Millard wrote the word 'procure.' He didn't write 'option to buy.' He wrote 'procure.'

"Humpty-Dumpty and Alice are arguing about the word 'glory.' What does 'glory' mean? Humpty is on the wall. Alice is down below and Humpty is looking down in his rather scornful fashion, as Humpty used to look at those who dared to approach the wall. It was his citadel with the fortress, and Alice said, 'But glory, the word doesn't mean a nice knockdown argument,' Alice objected.

" 'When I use the word,' Humpty-Dumpty said, in a rather scornful tone, 'it means just what I choose it to mean. Neither more, nor less.'

" 'But,' Alice said, 'the question is whether you can make words mean so many different things.'

" 'No, no,' said Humpty-Dumpty, still on his perch on the wall. 'The question is—which is to be master. That's all.' " MacGregor had barely sat down before Giles popped up, his voice booming through the courtroom: "To quote Lewis Carroll, ' "The time has come," the Walrus said, "to talk of many things, of shoes and ships and sealing wax, of cabbages and kings and why the sea is boiling hot and whether pigs have wings." ' "

Giles seemed to have pulled the words out of the air. MacGregor's Humpty-Dumpty had been bumped by Giles' Walrus.

"You see, the Walrus in that book spoke about a lot of things, all disconnected, all irrelevant to one another. Never ties anything together, rather disjointed," claimed Giles. His voice was not nearly as deep or strident as it had been two months ago in his opening statement. He wore the strain on his face, blotchy from the hard work and lack of sleep.

But Giles grew calm as he talked about a courthouse, in London, "probably the most famous courthouse in the world." Giles had gone to Old Bailey and seen the lawyers dressed up in robes and wigs the same way they had for hundreds of years. There was a word they used in that ancient courtroom that Giles had hardly ever heard in the courtrooms of America—"truth."

Giles asked the jury to remember the instructions the judge had read. "In all the instructions I don't think the word 'truth' was used one time. Because we in American courts refer to evidence. . . . That doesn't mean we are not about truth here."

Truth was what Giles was about, and he started with his first truth: "You know, did any witness ever come in here and say Mr. Millard is a crook; he is a fraud; he is a cheat; he is a dishonorable guy, unworthy of trusting?" No, Giles answered himself. They all liked and trusted Millard.

But Giles said he knew the ugly truth behind Killian and Van Natta. "I think they are trying to steal a piece of ComputerLand. I don't think it's any different than if they walked into a 7-Eleven with a gun and held it up. . . . Does that make me mad? You bet it makes me mad. It makes me sick!"*

The Friday before Thanksgiving, 1986, the jury began deliberations. Raymond Brown, a mailman, was voted foreman. The jurors had been instructed to rule on the seventh question first: "Do you find that the March 3, 1976, oral agreement gave each of the Plaintiffs an immediate ownership interest in IMS Associates, Inc?"

A yes vote would appear to support Killian and Van Natta's claim that they owned stock in Millard's original company, IMS. A no vote would support Giles' claim that the 1976 agreement was only an option with no immediate ownership.

"Most of us didn't believe that part of Giles' case," said juror Tracy Ricketts. "We decided it was a binding contract," said juror Tina Dazhan.

Juror Ada Fernandez-Scott, however, was not ready to go with the majority until she knew the significance of a yes vote. "If I vote yes on this, does this mean that Joe and Bruce will get part of Computer-Land?" she asked.

Finally, late Friday afternoon, they voted 11 to 1 in favor of Killian and Van Natta's immediate ownership in IMS. On Monday, juror Pege Rankin, a high-school journalism teacher, and another juror

*Giles stood to earn a $1-million bonus for winning the case, or gaining an appeal without having to post bond, on top of his $1-million retainer.

changed their minds. Now, the vote was 9 to 3, still favoring Killian and Van Natta's immediate ownership in IMS.

The jurors turned their attention to the first three questions. Did Millard commit the fraud of intentional misrepresentation, concealment, and false promises? None of them thought Millard had committed intentional fraud. But they weren't so sure about the key words in the fourth question, "constructive fraud."

The judge had instructed them earlier on fiduciary duty and told them that the assets of one corporation could not be used for another. The key word was "used." "I took that to mean, and I think Tina [Dazhan] took that to mean, that you couldn't use them at all," said Brown. But the rest of the jury weren't bothered that Millard had used IMSAI's assets to benefit Computer-Land.

"It was all paid back," explained Ricketts.

"You have a perfect right to use your money for whatever you want to," explained Rankin.

As many of the other jurors argued, the money was used only if it *wasn't* paid back.

On Tuesday, a juror wrote a note to the judge asking whether one company could use the assets of another company. A dictionary was also requested. The judge, however, just reread his original instructions; there was no answer and no dictionary. But after lunch, the judge changed his mind. They could ask whatever they wanted—in open court!

Brown knew what he had to ask: "Should we then assume that we are to interpret the law . . . in a strict literal sense?"

The judge wasn't sure what to do. "Could you excuse me just a moment? I've got it back here," he said, slipping back into his chambers.

Four minutes later, the judge emerged with a law book. But the answer wasn't there. He said the answer all along was in the jury instructions: "The short answer is, no, you are not to take the literal interpretation of what I read. . . . Use your *common sense*, based upon your collective experiences."

Brown was floored. Dazhan couldn't believe it. They had wanted the judge to tell them that they had to take the law literally. "The other jurors weren't taking it literally, and Ray [Brown] and I were," recalled Dazhan. The shot had backfired. Said Brown: "That was the killer right there."

Once in the jury room, the voting was perfunctory. Nearly all the jurors were convinced that Giles' allegations about MicroPro and NED were true. "I thought that was very bad," said Rankin. "It bothered me that that happened."

Some were so convinced of Giles' allegations that they thought MicroPro and the other alleged conspiracy, Micro/Vest, were one and the same.

"I thought MicroPro sponsored Micro/Vest," said Brown. "I thought MicroPro had bought the rights [to the note] and was suing Millard and that end of the deal was Micro/Vest."

"I thought it was the same company. I thought they changed names like [what happened with] Computer Shack and ComputerLand," said Dazhan.

"I thought everybody thought the same way," said Brown.

Ricketts summed up the jury's verdict: "I thought Mr. Millard was real sincere in business. He is the kind of businessman I would go to work for—very open and honest." Before she could apply for a job, however, she and the other eleven men and women would have to decide whether the charges of fraud were false. Soon after they arrived the next morning at nine-thirty, they voted with a show of hands. It took about twenty minutes.

Brown handed the envelope to the court attendant, the court attendant handed the envelope to the judge, and the judge handed the envelope to the clerk. Brown was watching Giles as the clerk read the first vote. "All right!" Giles said softly, pumping his fist. After each vote, Giles cried louder and pumped his fist harder. The clerk read number four. "All right!" Giles exclaimed loudly, shaking Millard's hand vigorously.

It was just as Giles had predicted. The jury was there to decide the truth on this day before Thanksgiving. Giles had talked of a truth that spoke louder than the weight of evidence, facts, and numbers. Giles had asked them to look for that deeper truth within society, within themselves, and see if it wasn't also within Millard.

But the truth they found was different from the truth it might have been had the judge not let Giles blank out the last line of Millard's January 22, 1976, diary entry: "Don't know if IMS can last another 60 days. Order new Cadillac Seville today!!!!" In the Micro/Vest trial the jury had seen those words and had seen a different Millard. In that trial, the same judge, McCullum, had a different view of the role of "common sense." During the trial he had said to Hafif, "Common sense will not be in this case. We're dealing with evidence, facts and law. . . ."

A year and a half later in the Killian/Van Natta trial the judge was the same, but apparently the truth was not. This time, common sense was a part of the truth. And what about evidence, facts, and law? They would be carefully documented in an appeal that might take years and years.

But these were little things compared with Millard. The jury liked his clothes, liked his smiling wife, and liked him. In two days they would receive their invitations to Trader Vic's, and over free dinner, speeches, and an open bar they would like Millard even more.

PART
VI

IV

34

Death

and Taxes

After his Trader Vic's dinner for the jurors, Millard had returned promptly to Saipan. There was no reason to stay in California. "He was sick and tired of reading his name in the paper," said a friend who asked to remain anonymous. "He wanted to be somewhere where he didn't have to be harassed."

But Millard's propensity for trouble was unfailing. The requests for bribes began not long after his return to the island. For $1 million all of his tax troubles would be over, and as a bonus, the government would take those giant generators off his hands. "Goddamned if I'll pay!" Millard told family and friends. The men Millard claimed had made the offer had made a mistake. Another man might have ignored the incident and got on with his life. But Millard was a "global citizen." His principles left him no choice. Millard contacted the FBI and told them everything he knew—names, money, the works. "A few bad apples that ruined the barrel," as one of his lawyers said. It was up to Millard to shake the rotten cores out.

The Saipan Chamber of Commerce knew nothing of Millard's undercover activities when they graciously invited him to deliver the keynote address at their annual banquet. Although Millard accepted the invitation, he soon had misgivings about the task he faced. Almost every other waking hour he considered calling the Chamber to tell them they had the wrong man. He had been asked to talk about the future, but how could he speak about the future without dragging out the past and the present!

After much agonizing, Millard settled on a few words that he told the Chamber were "appropriate." Millard could be charming. They were eating dessert when he began to speak in his gentle voice of the good things on the island: "So when I talk about things that are possible that I see that could be different, I am speaking about the kind of things which you would hold truly could be different, meaning better . . . meaning more nurturing, more satisfying, and truly more valuable to yourself and to the other people on the island. I am also speaking as one who lives here and has no intention of living anywhere else—and I don't live here for tax reasons."

That done, he began to elaborate on those things that needed work: ugly telephone poles, unreliable power, undrinkable water, screwed-up sewers, and the government. Millard continued, looking straight into the eyes of the leading officials of Saipan: "I don't like being solicited for payoffs from government officials. . . . I don't like it and I don't think you should either. Saipan's future can be a replay of its past, or it can be different. I hope that it could be dramatically dramatic, more nurturing, more satisfying, and more valuable for everyone involved here. I'm leaving out the really tough stuff." But Millard did get to the tough stuff, and as always, the words came straight from his heart: "Now I believe that each person on this island—certainly every person in this room—is either part of the solution or we're part of the problem."

Millard was out when the calls began. Pat Millard and her pregnant daughter, Elizabeth, were there to hear the ringing that wouldn't stop. "Millard is gone . . . Danger time . . . You're history," was the message of the unidentified caller, said Pat Millard. The police, FBI, Attorney General's Office, and the Department of Public Safety were contacted and taps were placed on the Millards' three phones. But all they could trace was the prefix—the same prefix as Saipan's Capitol Hill. "Very interesting," was all Millard's lawyer would say. The ominous calls, which rang from morning till late at night, abruptly ended.

Then the government took action. Vice Speaker of the House Benigno Fitial introduced a resolution to declare Millard persona non grata in the Commonwealth. Other officials demanded more—an immediate investigation. "Mr. Millard has cast a cloud over our government that can only be removed by learning the facts of these allegations and taking appropriate action to restore public confidence in our government," said Speaker Joe R. Lifoifoi in a public statement. A subpoena was issued in the name of William H. Millard, and for a time it seemed he would have to name the alleged corrupt officials he had condemned in his dinner chat. But the Saipanese had underestimated Millard and his army of attorneys. Giles counterattacked, filing a flurry of motions that fought the constitutionality of the subpoena. Months went by and still Millard would not talk. And when the court upheld the legislature's power to subpoena Millard, his attorneys simply appealed, buying more time.

While Millard was defending himself in Saipan, he was both attacking and counterattacking in the U.S., delaying the opposition with an onslaught of briefs and motions. Micro/Vest had to spend millions of dollars and four years before they could force Millard before a jury. On appeal, the cycle was repeating itself. Millard's appellate attorney, Shirley Hufstedler, also understood the system, and few were surprised that she, too, was able to draw numerous delays out of the court. Two years had passed since Micro/Vest's trial victory, and another two years would pass before the matter would finally be decided. At that rate, Micro/Vest's investors would have to outlive the Reagan presidency to see if they had won anything on a simple contract, signed more than a decade before.

The plan Millard and his lawyers had sketched out in the summer of 1986 was beginning to take shape. They had won the Killian and Van Natta trial as Millard had always thought they would. Now Killian and Van Natta would live with the fear that "we can foreclose on their homes," said Giles, who warned of other threats. "The syndication [of the suit] was improper. They owe $300,000 [to their investors]." As if this weren't enough, Millard threatened suit against Killian and Van Natta, MacGregor, et al., charging abuse of process and infliction of emotional distress. Giles gave notice of the suit and dangled the possibility of filing it. "It's harassment," claimed MacGregor. "To try and scare us out of the appeal."

• • •

Millard's revenge was not limited to Killian and Van Natta. "It's exactly what we will do to Micro/Vest—later," Giles predicted. "We will make [Philip] Reed reimburse all the investors." Giles estimated that since Philip Reed had testified to earning more than $3 million from selling his shares in the note, Martin had pocketed double that windfall. Giles believed both men would have to give all the money back.

Millard wanted more. "We are going to bring a lawsuit against MicroPro!" Giles threatened. When Giles first made the charge in the Killian/Van Natta trial, MicroPro had dismissed it as an "absurd" threat, noting that the statute of limitations had long ago run out on the claim. Millard's revenge was not easily assuaged by such legal limits. "Conspiracy, fraud, and deceit" were the words Millard's attorney used in an attempt to avoid the statute of limitations. But strangely, Millard's name would be absent from the front of the complaint. The legal vendetta Millard planned against MicroPro, the creation of his old friend and employee Seymour Rubinstein, would technically be brought by IMSAI and all of its creditors.

Meanwhile, on a distant front of the legal offensive, Giles began seeking information about Marriner's lawsuit against Micro/Vest. "Marriner [in their suit against Micro/Vest] is making the perfect lawsuit for us against Marriner," believed Giles. "They are admitting the whole case—that Loring Reed was involved in a conspiracy to screw us out of twenty percent of the company." Giles and his associate, Tom Purcell, planned to attend the trial, set for the fall of 1987 in the Federal Court of Massachusetts. What did Millard's strategist have up his other litigious sleeve? If Marriner should emerge victorious, "we will sue Marriner's ass," threatened Giles. "Whatever they get we are going after it!"

Back at ComputerLand, Ken Waters was trying to make sure some "ass" would be left for the victor. Faber had returned to semiretirement, leaving the young executive with a heady burden. There seemed only two choices: selling shares of ComputerLand to the public or selling the company outright. But image and emotions made a public offering impossible. "People would have asked, 'Why should I be paying to buy him [Millard] out?'" recalled Waters. "It would have looked like we were spitting the company out to get rid of Millard."

To sell ComputerLand, Waters engaged the services of the San Francisco investment banking firm of Hellman & Friedman. The first responses were not encouraging. "Aren't you the ones with the lawsuits?" Waters recalled reading among the desultory letters. Other potential buyers raised the company's history of negative publicity and its nearly mutinous franchisees. Waters ignored the bad news and concentrated on the bottom line. He raised $15 million of subdebt with Drexel, reduced corporate expenses by 35 percent, cut the royalty rate another 1.5 percent to 5.5 percent, and by February of 1987 buyers were knocking on ComputerLand's door. Bottom-line improvements were not the only change. Explained insiders: "Millard was ready to get serious about the price." And that meant a meteoric fall from the billion-dollar dreams of years gone by.

Micro/Vest investors blanched when they saw the valuation for the sale. The financiers of the deal, Warburg of New York, put the price tag for 100 percent of ComputerLand at a little over $150 million: Millard wanted to sell 53 percent, and the financiers were prepared to buy Micro/Vest's shares at the same price. Micro/Vest investors couldn't help but think back to Martin's promises and Hafif's painting of Millard as a billionaire. They added up the figures. If Micro/Vest withstood Millard's appeal, its share of the company would be roughly 28 percent of ComputerLand. Twenty-eight percent of $150 million was $42 million. That meant that one percent of the note was valued at roughly $420,000. But Martin had sold single shares for nearly double that amount, one group of lawyers having paid nearly three-quarters of a million dollars for just 1 percent. Bill Agee and Mary Cunningham had paid $375,000 for a 1-percent interest. Could it be true? wondered some of the Micro/Vest investors. Six long years, and now after a stunning court victory, when they finally cashed in their lottery tickets, the investment was revealed to be not a bonanza but a bomb.

But hadn't the dream come true, hadn't they and that working-class Alameda jury destroyed Millard, heaped on the punitive damages and brought him to his knees? Newspapers had estimated the victory at over half a billion. Where had all the money gone, and how could it have been reduced to a paltry $42 million? When they saw how little money would be available, some Micro/Vest investors clamored to kill the impending sale. Waters worried that the clamor by Micro/Vest would kill the sale of Millard's 53-percent interest and perhaps endanger their own investment. "Personal greed and emotions had become a bigger issue than the survival of the company," he recalled. "They were willing to fight forever and not take money on the table." Waters threatened to quit, warning that if the sale didn't move quickly, ComputerLand might forever be haunted by the ghost of Millard.

Meanwhile, Hafif was pushing to sell Micro/Vest's 28-percent interest on appeal. "But I got so much horseshit," recalled Hafif. "Like, 'Who says you can do this?' Obviously I can't do it unless they agree to it. If the deal doesn't make sense, they don't have to sign it. They gave me all this crap. I could have put together a package where everybody would have gotten a lot of bucks." Reed, however, complained that "we were given one day to look over four hundred to eight hundred pages, with Terry Giles telling us what it said." Reed called this Hafif's mushroom method: "Keep them in the dark and feed them shit." But Hafif felt no better off, himself, and the frustrated attorney reluctantly abandoned his attempt to cash in Micro/Vest's hoped-for court victory.

Giles reveled in the infighting. "I predicted they'd opt for the stock because otherwise they'd have to start telling the truth," said Millard's negotiator. "They had to hold on to the stock and hope it goes through the roof to protect themselves from lawsuits amongst their group."

In the sale of Millard's 53-percent interest in ComputerLand, Giles and Hafif were allies more than enemies, crediting each other for saving the deal. "When we needed to sort through a lot of legal problems, to Herb's everlasting credit, he and I were able to work very well together," said Giles of the man he now considered a friend. "It would have been impossible if I didn't have Herb working to try to save the company." Waters offered similar praise for the attorney. He had watched Martin threaten the deal and seen Hafif balance the jealous groups. "Without Herb making the necessary moves ComputerLand wouldn't be here anymore," said ComputerLand's president. As far as John Martin was concerned those compliments were condemnations. Hafif had sold out to the enemy—and if Martin and his followers had their way, he would never represent Micro/Vest again.

Martin, however, was just getting warmed up. At his deposition in the impending Boston Marriner trial, upon being introduced to Bill Conway, Marriner's attorney, Martin shook the tall, older man's hand and proffered his own unique greeting: "I certainly hope you've got at least ten million dollars in liability insurance," Martin said, his gaze suddenly turning to a glare, "because I'm going to sue your ass!" Conway was dumbfounded: "He still had my paw!" Conway watched with amazement as the formal deposition continued in the same dramatic vein. Not long after his colorful introduction, Martin leaped up, screaming that he was being illegally taped. Later that day at lunch, when Conway discovered that his six-foot-three-inch partner had received a similar introduction from Martin, he couldn't resist the joke. "How'd you like little Napoleon?"

Martin's bravado proved to be empty. At first it even appeared Hafif would try the potentially explosive Marriner case. Hafif prepared for the trial and booked a flight to Boston. "Then, all of a sudden," as he recalled, "the other guys are going ahead with the case." But Phil Reed said Hafif's price had gotten too high: "He wouldn't do it without an awful lot of money." In truth, Hafif was tired of what he saw as Micro/Vest's unending demands, absence of gratefulness, and lack of trust. He did want to be paid, and he wanted $50,000 in expenses up front plus a quarter of a million advance for his work (or half-million if he won the case). "No more for free, guys," he said.

Without Hafif, Martin's initial threats of malpractice and bravado quickly petered out. Millard's attorneys sat in the back of the courtroom. Martin knew what was going on. "This guy's calling Millard at every break!" he said, panicking, sensing a grand conspiracy. "All you see is this guy," Martin told the Micro/Vest group anxiously, "but Millard paid these guys off—he's running the whole thing!" Unconvinced of conspiracy, Reed nevertheless saw a practical risk in the Marriner trial. "It appeared that whatever came out of it would just give Millard fodder," he recalled. "Just the fact that we were having a fight gave Millard energy."

Three days of testimony was all it took. "The team was afraid of the level of exposure that could be abused in settling Micro/Vest," remembered Martin's wife. "They knew they were risking things that might jeopardize Micro/Vest." The fraud trial abruptly stopped and the lawyers went into chambers and talked settlement. Ten percent of Micro/Vest's potential share in ComputerLand was the cost of silence. Micro/Vest's president, John Molinari, was stunned. He had been told there was nothing to the suit, and now every investor in Micro/Vest was being forced to contribute to the costly legal expenses and the settlement. To him it seemed a direct conflict between the original holders of the note and the investors. "If somebody sells something to me and later on Marriner proves they got it by fraud, what does that mean?" he asked rhetorically, providing the answer. "I [an investor] would have to sue."

The testimony and records were impounded, never to be revealed to the public. Martin never did get around to filing his threatened malpractice suit, and his wife recalled her husband's words, shortly before he agreed to the settlement to which every shareholder in Micro/Vest would have to contribute: "Phil and I did this."

Despite Martin's escapades, that summer of 1987 the sale of ComputerLand would eventually struggle toward conclusion. The meeting would take place at a suite at the Regency in Hong Kong. Nearly an entire day would be spent laying out the documents and signing the appropriate pages—an eighteen-inch stack of contracts and addenda. Representatives from Warburg and Hellman & Friedman would be present. Millard would receive $81 million for his 53-percent share in ComputerLand. Roughly 20 percent of the cash would be held back over a two-year period, pending financial performance requirements. Andrighetto and Faber would also sell their small stock holdings.

Warburg would control ComputerLand's destiny. Clauses prohibiting Millard from ever sitting on the board would be written into the tremendously complex contract. Warburg would not buy the 16 percent tied up in the Killian and Van Natta suit or the 28 percent involved in Micro/Vest's suit. If Millard should somehow win both appeals, he would own 44 percent of ComputerLand. It was a possibility that would give few franchisees comfort.

But for Bill Millard the day would be filled with magic and joy and celebration. He would finally get what he deserved, and he would be rewarded with an intimate family celebration in the Far East's capital of capitalism. "We had a wonderful time," said Giles. "A ton of fun."

Meanwhile, in Saipan, Millard was about to speak his mind before a government-convened committee investigating his tales of corruption. Saipan seemed an unlikely spot for anything quite so serious, boasting as it did the world's most perfect climate and the world's highest per capita consumption of Budweiser. Life on Saipan generally involved a can of Budweiser in one hand. "Even the women drink Bud," said Saipan assistant U.S. attorney George Proctor, who never doubted the island's reputation as the king of Bud. "There is a hell of a lot of beer-drinking on the beach." Cheap beer prices and a temperature range between seventy (at night) and the low nineties made nearly every day perfect for drinking Bud on the beach.

The living was easy on Saipan: plentiful fishing, tropical fruits, no snakes, spiders, or scorpions. Other than the ocean and the seasonal typhoons, there were no natural dangers. Children ran barefoot and free. These conditions helped make work unpopular among the Saipanese, who preferred to import laborers from the Philippines and other islands. In short, the Saipanese were a simple people from another time, blessed by a perfect environment and known for their gentle and peaceful ways. But one beautiful summer day, a new wind blew into paradise, and the little island would never be the same.

High on Saipan's Capitol Hill, graced by palm trees and lush lawns, stood the House Session Hall. Emblazoned at the front of the low-ceilinged building was the seal of the Commonwealth, and down the end of the shoebox-shaped room, lined next to each other behind a long table, sat the legislators of Saipan. Many of the men looked alike, not altogether surprising on an island where nearly everyone was related and tax rolls were indexed by first names.

The House Session Hall was jammed to the brim with legislators, government workers, native Saipanese, and every journalist on the island—all four of them. Many of the Saipanese stood by the door, chattering in their native Chamorro, straining to get a look. The once "instant billionaire" sat at a table just a few feet before his inquisitors, dressed in a tropical short-sleeve shirt, white trousers, and white shoes. There was nothing disrespectful about his attire because only the CIA and FBI wore suits on the island, and when one arrived at the airport, out went the call, "A suit has arrived!" Millard's laywer, Giles, wore a suit, and though he had done his job, keeping the subpoena of Millard "wrapped up in the courts for six months," the day had finally come for Millard to speak.

One of the first witnesses was a short, middle-aged man named Galen Mack, who had worked as a consultant for Bill Millard. The government's counsel queried Mack about payoffs.

"I heard rumors of it," Mack said, adding that his sources were individuals whose information had been good in the past.

"Who are those people?" asked the attorney.

"I would not want to reveal names," Mack said.

"I don't care whether you want to or not," the attorney demanded. "Who are those individuals?"

Mack hesitated, then named five men. Later, he would regret his candor, delivering a written retraction to the local paper, the *Marianas Variety*. "I did not wish to address the types of alleged crimes being currently investigated by various federal agencies because I had only bits and pieces of hearsay," wrote Mack. "... In retrospect, I suspect that I should have simply risked the threatened charge of contempt." The next day, and for the rest of the hearings, Mack sat at the back of the room and watched. Seeing was one thing, understanding was another. The legislators had decided to permit a key witness to testify in Chamorro. The man, who had also been employed by Bill Millard, began speaking in the jumbled mixture of Micronesian, Spanish, Japanese, and English. Some considered this a strange way to hold a hearing since Chamorros speak English. By the door the standing-room crowd of natives laughed at the colorful testimony, while English-speaking attendees had no idea what was so funny. "Hell, we didn't know what was going on," recalled one observer. Finally, the hearing was halted to translate the native testimony into English. That would take time: two weeks to translate one hour. But when the sixty minutes of Chamorro was finally translated, observers said it didn't match up.

Giles was no longer surprised by anything in Saipan. He had seen enough to know the island was "a bit like the wild West," untamed, rugged, and "a lazy society that has abused the privileges of U.S. citizenship." Since Millard's arrival there had even been talk about the island going communist—joining the Soviet Union! Giles saw a primitive people who had not evolved greatly from the basic South Pacific tradition of showering the island chief with gifts. "You'd land your boat and they'd expect you to give presents," said Giles, who wished the Saipanese had just been "up front about it."

All this incensed the attorney: "I was a locomotive out of control!" Hell-bent at venting the anger he felt for the improprieties Millard had suffered, Giles attacked the legislators. "Saipan is an island with many good things going for it," began the forceful attorney, much in the same manner Millard had nearly eight months before at his speech before the local Chamber of Commerce. Compliments completed, the lawyer pounced on the island's problems. "Then, public law No. 513 was enacted, without notice to Mr. Millard, and as far as we can tell, without the benefit of public debate. This law changed the tax structure in Saipan for one person and one person only . . . William H. Millard."

Giles explained his client's quandary. "If Mr. Millard was willing to give payoffs to certain key government officials, then 'the Millard Tax Bill,' as public law No. 513 had become known, would be repealed." The rumors were so persistent, said Giles, that "anywhere that Mr. Millard went on the island he would be given the message that if he would simply make the required payments, the law would change. . . . Mr. Millard came to understand that that was simply 'the way it is in Saipan.'"

Once the legislators began questioning Giles, the lawyer started shouting and gesticulating—or as he would say, "putting on the steam." Muscles built since meeting Millard had stayed firm, and Giles was solid and broad, and what with his fierce glare, he could intimidate the best of them. The former criminal lawyer was asked why Millard spilled the beans to the FBI and not local authorities. Giles really lost his temper. "Because [he shouted] . . . we don't trust you and we don't trust your committee! Now that's saying it just about as plain as I can say it."

But the legislators had another view of "the way it is in Saipan." When Millard finally testified they were curious as to why a computer billionaire from California would come to a tiny, obscure island in the Pacific called Saipan.

"That is personal!" objected Giles, pounding the table and leaping to his feet.

Millard, however, appeared unaffected by the obvious reference to the tax savings he reaped in moving to the island. He was forceful, and as one remembered, "like a man speaking from his convictions." Giles recalled his testimony as "lucid, concise, very calm." When Millard spoke, the hall grew silent. A lot of people thought the truth was finally going to come out.

Millard told of being solicited for bribes to sell his generators and change his tax law. "I said no, never—no way—not a dime." Millard's information, as the U.S. attorney in Guam, William O'Connor, had warned the legislature, was composed entirely of "hearsay." After all the legal motions to delay his testimony, after all of Giles' angry accusations, it seemed, at least as best Millard could recall, that the eccentric computer tycoon "had never been approached directly by any public official for a bribe."

The rulers of Saipan (who like their subjects also tended to have the same last names) did not take the allegations lightly, and as usual, Bruno Andrighetto, through his friend the governor, eagerly passed along Millard's predicament to Micro/Vest. "They're all cousins and he goes over and tells them they're assholes," said Andrighetto. "They're all fucking cousins. How can you do that!" During the hearings, one local newspaper labeled a photograph of Millard testifying in bold capital letters: "ACCUSER." Gov. Pedro P. Tenorio and Lt. Gov. Pedro A. Tenorio had another name for the man who had tried to take advantage of their island tax haven and then saw fit to slander the entire government. In a joint public statement they declared: "William Millard is a liar."

The officials portrayed a drastically different version of Millard's tale of government corruption. The computer tycoon had tried to pawn off four secondhand Arizona generators to Saipan's government for $8 million. Millard would not allow any inspection of the generators, claimed the officials, until he received an irrevocable letter of credit and irrevocable purchase order.

"To us it was an insult," Pedro A. told the *Marianas Variety* for publication. "He must be a nut, a complete nut."

It was a day like any other in Saipan, a day for drinking Budweiser and going to the beach. Millard's former consultant, Galen Mack, picked up a young woman by the name of Remedios Conley and began driving out of town. The woman's elderly husband was told that they were going to the store to buy some soap. It was about noon; the date was October 27, 1987.

That evening a friend of Mack's phoned David Hughes, the editor of the *Variety*, and asked if Mack had stopped by the newspaper. "There was supposed to be a letter for you," the man told the newspaper editor without explanation. Hughes told the man that nothing had arrived. Later it would be revealed that Mack had just made an appointment to meet with the island's assistant U.S. attorney.

Mack drove the woman down the crushed-coral roads to deserted Obyan Beach, a pristine hideaway not far from the airport and roughly four miles from Millard's home. By nightfall Mack's wife was worried. Her husband had not shown up for lunch, and when he failed to return for dinner, she called the police.

The following evening two boys walked near Obyan Beach, hunting for the small land crabs found underneath Saipan's coconut trees. They wandered onto a path through the boonies, the island name for the dense jungle vegetation. Facedown on the path, a few feet apart, lay the bodies of a man and a woman. Bullets fired point-blank from a .45 magnum pistol had shattered the backs of their skulls. Several hundred yards from the execution-style killings, Galen Mack's abandoned four-wheel-drive truck was found undisturbed.

Eyewitnesses to the scene told the *Variety* that "some valuable evidence could have been lost by the police" in the way the bodies were removed. "The odds-on bet of many Saipan residents is now that Galen Mack was the murder victim of someone who didn't want him talking to a federal grand jury, or the U.S. attorney, about possible corruption or crime in the Commonwealth," reported the newspaper. "That hypothesis has been heightened by the fact that the Federal Bureau of Investigation has now entered the picture. . . ."

35

The Sting

I t began without warning. They would come to the house when John Martin's wife was alone with the children, knock on the windows, and walk on the roof, almost as if they wanted to make noise. And there were the phone calls: odd, obviously phony phone calls. Women who said they were supposed to meet John Martin-Musumeci in distant places like Reno, Nevada. "John couldn't have affairs," remembered Martin's unbelieving wife, Susan Musumeci. "He was afraid of intimacy."

But still she wondered about the strangers, the calls, and the phone message her husband played for her: "You fucking son of a bitch . . . your time is coming . . . we will meet soon . . ." Men would follow her when she left work, and once she was nearly driven off the road. When she began divorce proceedings against her husband in 1987, Martin ripped out a black box from under the bumper of his car. "It's a sophisticated military tracking device," he told her after putting the ominous black box on the seat between them and warning her not to talk. "People bomb each other this way."

After nearly ten years of marriage to John Martin, Susan Musumeci knew the pattern well. Her husband would be fine for three weeks, then for a week or ten days he would fall under the spell. Martin was sure he was being watched. If his wife received a call from a friend, he was convinced they were talking about h:m. Martin would withdraw into isolation, refusing to go out for meals or other activities. He would carry his microwave dinner into a closed room, smoke marijuana, and watch television or movies on his VCR. Martin often smoked the drug throughout the day, storing joints over the visor of his red Italian sports car. He preferred old movies, especially those starring Humphrey Bogart. A favorite was *The Treasure of the Sierra Madre*. Martin felt the classic tale of greed, in which prospectors murder each other to protect their shares, had never gotten the recognition it deserved.

During these dark periods Martin ate chocolate incessantly and smoked forty to sixty cigarettes a day, often not waiting for one to burn out before he lit the next. He slept little, drinking several of his twenty to thirty daily cups of coffee in the middle of the night, an hour when his mind frequently turned to his hero, Howard Hughes. "When he spoke about Hughes, he would rise, straighten his spine, and breathe more deeply," remembered his wife, who was frightened by his reverence for the mad, drug-addicted billionaire. Martin told her not to worry. "He always said he would not be as insane as Howard Hughes."

The nights were endless. She would awake in the early morning hours to see Martin sitting in bed, smoking, drinking coffee, wringing wet in his own sweat, his face as white as the sheets. "I'm trying to let go of it," Martin would say, shivering. "He's trying to knock me off!" Martin's days and nights were consumed by his fear and hatred of Millard. There was no other way. He told his wife that if he didn't get Millard, Millard would strike first. "He considered Millard evil," remembered Susan Musumeci. "He was going to rid the world of evil."

Martin was obsessed with Millard. Always, always Martin "would think upon and look at any and all strategies to get Millard," recalled his wife. There was no time for rest. Martin had no real friends: the people in his life were lawyers or business associates, and when he came out of isolation, he would phone them and scream obscenities for hours on end. Often his body shuddered from the abuse. But Martin fed the hatred, channeling it into new strategies.

Martin's constant vigilance occasionally took on comic overtones. Like Millard, Martin's family life was dominated by women—usually friends of his wife. At Martin's home in Lafayette a woman medical student and a nun (studying drug treatment and counseling at nearby

Berkeley) helped with meals, ironed Martin's shirts, and cared for the children. The budding doctor gave Martin regular massages. Even as she dug her thumbs into his badly curved spine, Martin wouldn't stop talking. "He talked compulsively," she said, "about how he was going to get Millard and Herb Hafif."

Martin was always on "red alert." One day some neighborhood children were playing with BB guns. As the young boys approached the front door, Martin went into action. He flew out the back, leaped into his Cadillac, ducked down, and dialed the police on his car phone. Then, he slowly backed the car out, his head barely below the dashboard. The nun and the young woman had a good laugh. Martin ordered them to never tell anyone about his false alarm.

But finally, the threats, the bouts of self-imposed isolation, the drugs—all became overwhelming. It wasn't enough that every couple of months Martin would return from the East Cost victorious, flash thousands of dollars in hundred-dollar bills that he quickly stuffed back into his pocket, and then announce with a mischievous glint in his eye: "I had a successful trip!" It wasn't enough because everything was owned by Martin's corporations. Martin had no savings account and refused to pay the most ordinary bills: He owed doctors, dentists, utility companies, and of course, lawyers. Many found this habit puzzling as it was well publicized that Martin had made several millions of dollars selling shares in the ComputerLand note. But just before the Micro/Vest trial, Martin's wife came out to find her car gone. She called the police, thinking it was stolen. The BMW had merely been repossessed.

Over the years Susan Musumeci had tried to separate from Martin, but always he came back, wanting another chance. When she moved to Maui, he moved to Maui, moving his girlfriend into a half-million-dollar home just down the street, and installing five telephone lines and a fax machine. Martin's feverish energy had not mellowed under the Hawaiian sun. For nearly a year he had been flying to southern California on a secret mission. "I've got a major game plan," he told his wife. "Something that will blow everybody out of the water! We'll be able to go anywhere."

The day Susan Musumeci finally told him they were finished, Martin told her of another game plan. "I will destroy you if you leave me. Everyone will think you are crazy." At Susan Musumeci's first deposition in Maui, she saw the first act in Martin's new play. Martin sat across from his wife and her attorney, Ed Mason. The 250-pound, six-foot-three-inch attorney had practiced in Philadelphia and had earned a reputation in the islands as a skilled divorce attorney. His nickname was the "junkyard dog."

Susan Musumeci was trying to answer the questions, but Martin kept giving her the finger and screwing up his face into obscene expressions. He also kept whispering in his attorney's ear, telling him what to say. Martin began breaking in as she spoke. "You fucking slut, you fucking cunt." He also directed his expletives toward her attorney. "Shut this scumbag up or we are going to leave!" responded the gruff lawyer.

Martin's eyes swept from the table to Mason. The threat was clear. There was a tray with a stainless-steel coffeepot, a sugar bowl, coffee mugs, and a pitcher of water. Martin heaved the table forward in a mad thrust. Steaming-hot coffee splashed over Mason and Martin's wife. *

"You son of a bitch!" yelled the big attorney, charging after Martin. But the little man moved amazingly fast, churning down the hall and a small flight of stairs. Susan Musumeci hurried after the pair. Martin had run across the street, and behind the cushioning flow of traffic, he resumed his cursing. "You come back here and see if you can say that! I've met plenty like you!" bellowed the former Philadelphia attorney, coffee dripping from his suit. "You've met your match!"

But that was before Martin's grand strategy kicked into gear. The couple entered into mediation. Martin would pick up paperweights and other objects, toss them in the air, and glare at his wife. During the breaks he would whisper in her ear, "I want to mash your face in. I have fantasies of taking your head and beating it." And if that wasn't enough, Martin told the mother of his two children that he "had all of the money," and if she did not agree to solve all of the problems between them before the mediators, then he would "keep her in court forever."

Susan Musumeci began to fear for her and her children's lives. The bills Martin refused to pay were piling up, and she could no longer afford to pay Ed Mason's fees. She offered the case to seven lawyers

*In Mason's declaration before the bankruptcy court, he stated: "John Musumeci began threatening and verbally abusing . . . and concluded the meeting by throwing a coffee pitcher and other items from the deposition table. . . ."

throughout the islands, but Martin's reputation was already known and no one would touch it. And so, when Martin suggested that his trusty aide, Richard Bowman, help draft a settlement, Susan Musumeci finally saw there was no other way out. The curious document included her forfeiture of all alimony if she had a boyfriend (Martin already had a girlfriend), denied her any share in the note, and left no doubt about her husband's intentions: ". . . Both John and Susan fully release and discharge the other of and from all liquidated or unliquidated claims of any nature whatsoever, which the other may have had or may have as of this date against the other, *including fraud and fraud in the inducement regarding execution of this Agreement*, misrepresentation, full disclosure or lack thereof . . ."

Martin had figured it all out. In lieu of sharing his millions in Micro/Vest (and other family assets), Martin agreed to pay his wife a promissory note. The promises uncannily resembled those in the original Millard/Marriner note. The amount was $300,000. The terms were four years. The interest was 9 percent a year. But of course, unlike Bill Millard's promissory note, John Martin's gave himself a right of first refusal.

He was on the evening news. A whole one and a half minutes. Hundreds of thousands of people watched in the San Francisco Bay Area. John Martin had filed the largest bankruptcy in the history of Hawaii. The numbers were Herculean, fantastic, propelling him into the rare realm of his hero, Howard Hughes. For John Martin was now a billionaire—in debt.

Read the *San Francisco Chronicle*: "John Martin, a co-founder and frequent adversary of ComputerLand Corp., has filed a Chapter 11 bankruptcy petition in which he claims an astounding $1.6 billion in liabilities."

Few saw the dark genius of Martin's gargantuan move. By filing for bankruptcy Martin delayed paying the hundreds of thousands of dollars he owed to his wife, Bruno Andrighetto, Herb Hafif, law firms, and the accounting firm of Arthur Young. He also delayed a $400-million liability in a disputed case brought by his old company, $84 million in a disputed judgment brought by a Delaware corporation, a number of smaller claims, and $1.2 billion in the Marriner suit. Actually, the numbers were closer to $1.7 billion (Martin liked to quote the higher figure) and included about a million dollars owed in delinquent taxes and penalties.

Martin neglected to mention that several of the suits he listed as liabilities had been settled or dismissed. But the incredible figures looked impressive, and Martin had the original complaints to back up the fantastic numbers. Besides, who would dare question the bankruptcy: Martin had signed the petition under penalty of perjury.

The real strategy went much further than the notoriety of being over one and a half billion in debt. Buried in the bulky bankruptcy petition were two pages entitled Executory Contracts. Listed on those pages were $850,000, which Hafif had paid Martin for 3 percent of the note; $600,000, which the garbage men had paid for 2 percent of the note; $125,000 the Andrighetto Group 2 had paid for 6.67 percent of the note; 3 percent that Andrighetto held as collateral for a Martin promissory note; the 5 percent each that Hafif and Nachtrieb had earned for their legal efforts, as well as a number of smaller sales. The notation after Hafif's stock read simply, "RESCINDED"; after Andrighetto's stock, "RESCINDED/TERMINATED/DISPUTED"; and after the stock Hafif and Nachtrieb had earned for their legal work, "held pursuant to legal service agreement."

Martin, of course, wanted the stock all back—and more. Never mind that Martin had received nearly $2 million on those particular sales, and that Hafif had worked for years on the Byzantine case. Only weeks remained before the oral argument in the Micro/Vest appeal, which once and for all would decide the ownership of 28 percent of ComputerLand's stock. Martin believed his strategy would "blow them all away."

Investors who had paid millions of dollars or worked years had nothing but a promise. Martin claimed to have sold executory contracts, and if he deemed the contracts unperformed, he could collect the stock—and keep the money he had pocketed. Martin decided that Herb Hafif, Harold Nachtrieb, and an investor by the name of Harold Schwartz, among others, had not performed. He had demanded that they pay him for the legal expenses Micro/Vest was incurring and they had refused. There was a reason for their refusal. Martin was not paying his legal expenses, and besides, Philip Reed was the treasurer. "Martin was also behind in legal fees," Andrighetto said, laughing. "We should have taken the stock away from him, too!" Andrighetto estimated that Martin owed $400,000 in legal expenses.

Andrighetto thought he knew why Martin was filing for bank-ruptcy. "Why? Uncle Sam is on his ass and Uncle Sam doesn't get off," said Martin's friend. "He had to get all these guys off his back. The only thing that pissed us off is that he dragged Micro/Vest into it." But somehow even that violation didn't stop the produce man from admiring his friend's pluck. "He's a fucking fighter from the word go," said Andrighetto. "He's crazy!"

The Hawaiian bankruptcy judge knew nothing of this. Martin was in bankruptcy, creditors were clamoring to be paid, and some secre-tive corporation in California was refusing to turn over confidential agreements and stock that Martin claimed to have legitimately earned. Defying logic, Martin claimed to have increased his shares by selling pieces of the note. While Micro/Vest insiders put Martin's stake at between 3 and 8 percent, Martin declared that he owned 30.67 of the note, plus a 10-percent bonus for the legal fees he had paid. Martin may not have finished high school, but he counted his way up to owning more than 40 percent of the stock of Micro/Vest— more than when he first sliced up the pie with Andrighetto and Reed.

"I saw through his plan," said Micro/Vest's president, John Molin-ari. Martin had always been deferential around the elderly former appellate judge, addressing him as "Your Honor." Molinari was not easily fooled. He saw that Martin's scheme was to have the contracts declared executory so that he could "repudiate" them at a later date. "Martin says, 'I own!'" said Molinari, who had seen a similar ratio-nale in the man they were all supposedly fighting—Bill Millard.

On October 20, 1988, the state appellate court in San Francisco buzzed with spectators and members of the press. Herb Hafif stood just outside the doors, pacing in his ill-fitting suit and heavy brown shoes. Some saw his rough face through the glass, his dark eyes framed by thick bags that seemed more the scars of old fights than the long years before the jury. Behind the tough visage was a hint of nerves. The war against Millard had consumed eight long years, mil-lions of dollars of legal bills, and tens of thousands of hours of billable time, all simply to enforce one simple contract. One hour would decide the issue.

Hafif knew his greatest challenge was not the intricacies of law but the prestigious stature of Shirley Hufstedler's firm. Otto Kaus, a former California Supreme Court justice, was a partner, as well as Robert Thompson, a former associate judge in the California Court of Appeals. Two past presidents of the California State Bar were partners, and only a few years before, Hufstedler's husband had represented the Supreme Court on a critical case. Shirley Hufstedler herself, a former judge of the Ninth Circuit Court of Appeals, was no slouch. High on the list of nominees for the U.S. Supreme Court, she had been considered an intellectual equal to Sandra Day O'Connor and had served as U.S. Secretary of Education, from 1979 to 1981.

Hafif's successful firm had no such fine judicial breeding or reputation. Famous as a personal-injury lawyer, Hafif was no favorite of judges and certainly not of the more elite and intellectual appellate judges on the other side of the courtroom doors. Hafif figured that he was seen as flamboyant, successful, but at heart, a "slasher." Some of the Micro/Vest group had wondered whether Hafif was the right man for the appeal. Hafif knew exactly where those darts had come from, but he was not about to risk the case to some "appellate" lawyer. "It was a rumble that I had to face," recalled Hafif. "When I said there was no way, everybody said, 'Nobody really suggested that.'"

Besides, Hafif knew that his talents as an appellate attorney were secondary. Decades of trial work had taught him that the secret to a great appellate lawyer is to have a good trial lawyer try the case, "because there ain't going to be much there." Hafif's appeal work began years before in the courtroom during the Micro/Vest trial. Painstakingly he had avoided the shortcuts he sensed were fodder for appeal. He had made sure every argument was decided before the jury, even if they had earned a point before trial. "I didn't want an appeal based on a summary judgment," said Hafif, referring to the partial summary judgment Judge Kroninger had granted Micro/Vest back in 1982.

There were more subtle points. When an attorney on the Micro/Vest team suggested a jury instruction to which they might technically have been entitled, Hafif rejected it, not wanting to "take that extra bite out of the apple." Powerful and emotional as Hafif appeared in the courtroom, when the court transcript was read, the words themselves were surprisingly restrained. Even his punitive damages argument—which had incited the jury to punish Millard with the record judgment—when read, was relatively calm. Hafif knew that all of this might not be enough. He worried that every point Hufstedler made would be given "full credence because of who she was."

And Shirley Hufstedler's appeal gave plenty of cause for concern. Longer than the allowed limit, her brief was noteworthy for its creative arguments and fierce prose. Hufstedler had decided that IMS had indeed gone south, dissolving into the beaches and palm trees of Millard's great Panamanian tax-skirting scheme. And with that magic dissolution, Hufstedler waved her wand and made all of IMS's obligations go away—including the Marriner promissory note. The only difficulty with this argument was that there was no record of the dissolution in the Secretary-of-State records.

Hafif was furious at Hufstedler's argument. It was based on the absence of evidence in the trial that IMS was *not* dissolved, and the knowledge that, except in extraordinary cases, the appellate court would not admit evidence outside the record. Hafif argued that it was up to Millard to have proved the vanishing act. "First of all, it's such an absurdity to say that this company that signed an agreement didn't exist," said Hafif. "But to come up with it [the strategy] and it is dead flat wrong. The company does exist—it withdrew the dissolution and she knows it!"

In his reply brief, Hafif charged that the IMS dissolution argument was not made at trial because "with the contrary documentary evidence that exists, for Millard to have made such claim at trial or pretrial would have subjected him to criminal fraud sanctions..." To Hafif, Hufstedler's argument amounted to saying: "We took all your money, we got you to give up all your rights, but aha! We did not have a corporation at that time!" The argument would have been comic if not for the fact that the court seemed to be seriously considering Millard's latest maneuver. When Micro/Vest petitioned the appeals court to take judicial notice of IMS's existence, the court refused. Hafif was stunned. He had thought it was a matter of course.

Hafif's reasoning in trading the huge punitive damages for an additional 5 percent in ComputerLand had been to simplify the appeal—and, he hoped, insure that they collect. At the time, the highest punitive damages award upheld in California was just $3.5 million. Micro/Vest's $141-million punitive damage award was sure to be chopped down, or the case might be sent back for another round through the courts. As history had shown, that game could go on forever. By throwing out the monetary side of the punitive damages, Hafif had hoped to collect the judgment faster and eliminate one more potential opening in the appeal.

But to Hufstedler the partial settlement was a double-edged sword to be turned against Micro/Vest. "... The waiver of all monetary recovery is an admission that Micro/Vest had no tort case...," she wrote to the court, arguing that the mere waiving of monetary damages was in itself damning evidence of a poisoned trial: "Micro/Vest persuaded the jury and the trial court that the appellants were evil persons who should be severely punished by huge damages.... Why is Micro/Vest trying so desperately to prevent this court from examining its conversion case? The answer is abundantly clear. Micro/Vest never had a cause of action for conversion, and its successful use of that spurious tort was the means for its obtaining the whole judgment on appeal."

Hafif strode to the defendants table on the left of the courtroom, head down, locked in concentration, but for one nagging memory. On his right, curiously apart from the Micro/Vest group, sat John Martin, tanned and heavier, flanked by his girlfriend, lawyers, and entourage. Hafif glanced over and thought back to their first meeting, asking himself again why he had taken a case from a man he despised.

Time had only confirmed his initial impression of John Martin. It had seemed for a while that by keeping his "oar in the water" with him, Hafif could exercise some control over Martin for the benefit of the group. But the task wore on Hafif: Each time Hafif gave him something, Martin wanted more. Martin had told his wife that he now viewed Hafif as a greater nemesis than Millard. Hafif understood. "He sees me as somebody who has exposed him to this group [Micro/Vest], which was the only family he ever had," said Hafif. For years Hafif had been the only one "blowing the whistle" on John Martin. It was Hafif who explained to the unbelieving group that Martin was stirring up the ComputerLand franchisees, trying to goad Faber to head a rival chain under his command. Most Micro/Vest investors had thought it was a clash of egos, and some saw Martin and Hafif as cut from the same cloth. "They are the same type of person," said Andrighetto. "They always think they are right and they will never listen." When Hafif warned of the problems Martin was creating, many were convinced the overbearing attorney was simply pursuing his own agenda.

Martin had known that many would look the other way when he attacked Hafif's stock. Hafif's imperial style had offended others in the group, and some believed Martin was justified in wondering whether Hafif had sold out the group to secure his own best interest. Martin pointed to the 1.5 percent Hafif was guaranteed—even if he lost the appeal. Some seemed to savor the irony of Hafif's predicament. The man who had tried and won the largest punitive damages award in California history, the man who had made John Martin famous, the man who was owed nearly three-quarters of a million dollars in legal fees, was being sued because John Martin had decreed that Herbert Hafif's pension plan (which paid $500,000 for 2 percent of the note) had not paid its few thousand dollars share of Micro/Vest's attorneys' fees.

No one was safe from Martin's wrath. In his bankruptcy action, Martin filed a complaint against his own corporation, Micro/Vest, and against the court-appointed trustee, Spurgeon Avakian, demanding they turn over 40.67 percent of the shares that Martin claimed had already vested. Of course, Martin also demanded that the remainder of his 40.67-percent share be turned over upon the successful completion of the appeal. Micro/Vest and Avakian were also ordered to turn over all provisions of the Partial Settlement Agreements. Molinari and Avakian said no to Martin and hired lawyers.

Individual investors began to receive phone calls. Those unwilling to pay up were warned that their stock, too, might join Hafif's and the others marked for collection. And why not! Martin knew he was the creator! He had envisioned the grand concept, the map of the computer marketplace, and sold the first franchisees! In the beginning the ComputerLand note was his and his alone. The others had brought only money and opportunity. It was Martin who stalked the victim, preyed on its weakness, and now, anyone who dared to step in his path—even Phil Reed—would risk his vengeance.

The barrel-chested lawyer looked over at Shirley Hufstedler, her hair wrapped in a meticulous bun, and listened as she began to unravel her bizarre argument to the court. Presiding Judge Clinton White had announced that Judge Robert Merrill would write the opinion, an unusual move, since the court usually keeps such matters private. Hufstedler quickly advanced the impropriety of Hafif's tort argument and the subsequent punitive damages. Merrill interrupted. Had not Micro/Vest waived the monetary damages? he asked Hafif. The lawyer bowed in agreement. Hufstedler's frustration increased. Dead companies and extinguished options brought the hint of a smile to the well-prepared Justice Merrill. He was enjoying himself, dismantling the prestigious former judge with a volley of piercing questions. In response, a ruffled Hufstedler began making declarations of fact, as though she had written the note and been there a dozen years before: "Marriner never lent ComputerLand a cent!" she protested.

Hafif could smell victory but he knew the taste would be sour and empty of satisfaction. He had spent a lifetime fighting the rich and the powerful. His latest barrage of cases centered on whistle-blowers who had uncovered dangerous defects and gross mischarging in the MX missile and the Stealth bomber. Television's *60 Minutes* had twice featured Hafif, and Hafif made the national news. Compared to those battles, waged in the media and on Capitol Hill, what was the satisfaction in becoming an unwitting pawn in Martin's machinations, of rounding out the portfolios of a consortium of wealthy lawyers and speculators who viewed the whole battle as a good crap shoot. Hafif remembered why he took the case: "To show that no matter how much money you have, no matter how powerful your lawyers are, and no matter how much money you paid them, on down to the final appeal—you can be stopped." He remembered how he had placed that message above his personal disgust for Martin. But where was the satisfaction when Micro/Vest mimicked the enemy he set out to destroy, when they turned on one another like pirates, when he had warmer feelings for Bill Millard than his own client, and when he knew that Millard, for all his bullheadedness, for all his distorted, misguided principles, was not half the danger of a man like John Martin.

Hafif was nervous and angry. He attacked Hufstedler's argument, thrusting his big arm, spitting out fighting words like punches. The justices warned him to temper his histrionics, but Judge White's eyes sparkled. Hafif put on a good show.

Hafif threw himself into battle, combating Hufstedler, leaning his broad frame toward the bench. Legal points were avoided. Of all things, he concentrated on ethics, warning that lawyers, tarnished with a reputation equal to used-car dealers, were on the verge of sinking to the level of insurance companies. The judges cautioned him to temper his outrage and struggled to interrupt his outbursts, but before it was over and done, Hafif shouted what he truly thought of Hufstedler's argument and Millard's eight-year multimillion-dollar legal battle.

"It's all insanely about nothing, all of it!"

36

Spirits

It was a typical November day in Maui: bright blue sky softened by an occasional buoyant cloud. Outside the little courtroom, the gray-haired nun sat in the hallway and silently prayed for strength. Her only jewelry was her Daughters of Mary and Joseph Order pin and the gold cross that hung from her neck. She was slight, and though she measured but a few inches over five feet, she was taller than the man against whom she would soon testify.

John Martin sat at the small table before the judge. He wore light beige pants hiked up above his ankles, a short-sleeve shirt, and gray tennis shoes. His hair had grown long and disheveled, and some had seen him carry a black canvas bag that resembled a duffel bag into the court.

First on the witness stand in the custody hearing was the same young woman who not long before had been kneading Martin's back. She testified that Martin had promised to go to a recovery program "because he was smoking a lot of marijuana and there were shifts in his personality. Every three weeks they would come on where he was fine and then all of a sudden he started exhibiting paranoid behavior..." As the young woman continued to document Martin's habits, she felt his gaze and turned to face his taunting smile.

The next witness was nervous. Her voice wavered and she trembled a little. "Sister Mary Moran," she answered, steadying herself.

"Is it correct that you were born in Ireland?" asked attorney Ed Mason, back on the case.

"Yes."

"And you are a Catholic nun?"

"Yes."

"And the order that you belong to are the Daughters of Mary and Joseph?"

"Yes."

After telling of her nearly three decades in the service of the Lord, two decades of which she spent as a missionary in Uganda, the nun explained that she was currently working on a specialty in the diagnosis and treatment of drug abuse. ". . . I saw him [Martin] under the influence of drugs . . . I've seen the drugs in the bathroom and in the bedroom . . . I've seen the paraphernalia there."

The nun also testified that Martin called on the Berkeley and Emeryville police to enforce his court-ordered child custody.

"Did the person identify himself or herself?"

"Absolutely not . . . Two police were there. John [Martin] was there . . . I was in the apartment with another sister . . . and there was this constant knocking at the door and I was afraid to answer. . . ."

Martin had threatened the nun, as he had his wife, other friends of the family, and neighbors. Police reports were on file in two states, and one was headed "Terroristic Threatening." (Martin's favorite warning: "You better look over your shoulder!") After threatening to kill a man, Martin told him, "I am not the type of person you want for an enemy."

None of this stopped Sister Mary for a moment. Her testimony was clear and concise. She was even-tempered and resolute. But one last witness remained in the most important trial of John Martin's life.

"Tell us your name and address please."

"John Musumeci."*

It was true that Martin's attorney asked him questions, but John Martin had his own agenda. He had attended more trials than many trial lawyers, plotted with the best, and been sued for more millions that most major corporations in America. The lawyer was just for

*In this trial, unlike the Micro/Vest trial, John Martin used the name he was born with—John Musumeci.

appearances. Martin needed no one but himself to argue his case. "My business activities were overwhelming by my own choosing," he explained to the court. "The ten-week trial in 1985 was something that was very well publicized and gave me the reputation of being a big litigator."

Martin went on the attack. "In early 1987, Susan . . . had spirits tell her that California was going to be blown up and that she wanted to live in Maui and that she wanted a divorce." Then, he seemed to lose his target. He explained that the Micro/Vest victory put him under great pressure, and he had to tell the court about his unique predicament. ". . . It was such a visual sort of a thing and of course I had partners in it; this wasn't all my own doing . . . I individually got sued for a total of twenty lawsuits all related to the litigation. Kind of like the Howard Hughes will where two hundred people claimed they had the will, and I got sued for one point seven billion dollars. This is very, very time consuming . . . ," Martin fretted, later describing how onerous it was for him to schedule in his children: ". . . I have close to one hundred motions and trials in Honolulu . . ."

The former devotee of est sought to shoot down the allegations of drug abuse by saying it was simply a question of agreement. ". . . In my agreement with her I agreed not to smoke it at all, and in fact hadn't, although I do have to admit . . . in fact I did smoke a couple of, not joints, but a little bit of it. . . ." Martin knew what his ex-wife was up to. She, too, had a ploy, but soon everybody would know who and what she had become. "It seemed as though when I talked— when she did call me, she was kind of like leading me on to get certain types of answers regarding things. As though I was being taped. . . ."

Finally he leveled his main charge. One day he had discovered that Susan Musumeci had been transformed into a New Age channeler. Incredible as it sounded, Martin told the court how she would slump over, lose consciousness, twitch, and take on the voices of the spirits. "There are three spirits," Martin explained to the judge. "Two of them are Achmed and the other one is called Alexandria."

Susan Musumeci suffered from heart trouble and had to stay in the hospital for a few days, but Martin wasn't so easily fooled. ". . . The hospital thought that she was having a heart attack or something like that. In reality what she was doing was having these experiences." Growing excited, Martin then revealed in glowing detail how Susan

Musumeci left the world as we know it: "Her body went into a paralysis state and she went into this whale called Mica and went around the sea and the ocean and visited some special places in the ocean. It was an out-of-body experience. . . ." Martin's testimony was not altogether unexpected. Before the custody hearing Martin had called friends and business associates of his ex-wife and told them she was having sex with whales.

Before the spirits descended, Martin and his ex-wife had been "very good Christians." Clearly pained by the experience, Martin described how the New Age spirits intruded on his devout faith: ". . . And it's a Christian thing and it's where the Bible says that this is an evil thing. . . . That's where the thing about being possessed comes out. I believe that when this happens. It is eerie."

Martin eagerly offered to share his firsthand knowledge of the other world with the judge. "These channels have talked to me. And I'm happy to talk to you about some of my discussions I've had with them: Achmed. What he's told me about Susan. What he's told me about what can happen with my children." Martin had brought a pamphlet on demonism and possession onto the witness stand with him and began holding it up above his head. "Judge, if you'd only read this," he pleaded.

Dropping demonism, Martin launched into a long, dramatic account of how he had paid his alimony. He had created an automatic payment account for the monthly $2,500 payments. "Let me pull out the chart here . . . ," he said, holding out a computer printout. "She received a payment on nine/eighteen."

Mason was stunned. "Excuse me?"

"She received the payment on nine/eighteen."

For a brief moment the attorney sounded lost. Martin was emphatic. Spirits, channelers, and sex with whales notwithstanding, perhaps he did pay alimony. At the break Mason yelled at his client. "He lambasted me," said Susan Musumeci. "Did he pay you or what!" she remembered the attorney demanding.

Martin explained that because he had an automatic account, he didn't receive canceled checks. But of course he had evidence to prove that he had paid his ex-wife alimony.

"What indication do you have that such payment was in fact made and received by Susan?"

Martin looked up at the judge and began to sit up. "Um, can I be excused? I believe that there's some correspondence—can I be excused? I believe that there's some correspondence that would be helpful to me in resolving this with you."

Martin walked down to his black canvas bag as the court went on break. He had a lot of papers. He'd pull them out, place them on the table, look around suspiciously, and then stuff them back in. The tail of Martin's shirt was starting to hang out and he twitched nervously.

Finally, Martin returned to the witness stand, rattling some papers like a saber—much in the same manner he had trumpeted his pamphlet on demonism. "Yeah, I don't have the—all I have is one statement in here. What I have is a computer run of when the checks were paid. Would you like me to explain what I have?"

"Computer run from whom?" asked Mason.

"From my computer," replied Martin.

"Do you have any outside evidence at all that Susan Musumeci was paid any spousal support?"

"Outside evidence? I don't know what you mean."

"Evidence not created by you?"

"Other than the statement that I just went to look for and was unable to find in that file, no."

The judge attempted to introduce Martin's bank account number into evidence. "Your Honor, can I go look in my bag again?" Martin said anxiously. "I know I brought all that stuff."

"Yes, you may," said the judge.

It was painful for Susan Musumeci to watch. Martin rummaged through the bag like a squirrel, jerking things out, casting furtive glances around the room, and then stuffing the papers back. The twitches had worsened and his face was flushed red except for the drained pale streaks around his nose. His personality shifts had become more pronounced. On the breaks he had bounded gleefully into the hallway, flashing the okay sign to his girlfriend. Back in the courtroom Susan Musumeci watched him suddenly collapse, clutch his head, and moan.

"Excuse me. Mr. Musumeci, were you able to find anything when you looked in your records a few minutes ago?" asked Mason.

"No."

Martin pleaded for one more journey to his black bag. First he said that he had spousal support checks in his briefcase, then he said that the bank had made a mistake . . . finally, he declared, "That payment is in my briefcase!"

The judge had heard enough and asked the lawyers to clarify what exhibits had been entered into evidence. Susan Musumeci watched her ex-husband lose what little control he had left. He mumbled and alternately gripped his head and clenched his jaw. Susan Musumeci tried not to look, but she became afraid. She, too, had once believed her husband was all huff and puff, but it wasn't long ago that she had watched him kick the family dog across the room and heave a large ceramic bowl at her head and put a dent in a wall.

"This is not fair to take my children away from me! It's not fair!" exploded Martin.

The judge had not decided the custody case. At the time of the outburst there was no ongoing argument or testimony. "There was nothing that happened," remembered Susan Musumeci, who along with fear felt sympathy for the man she still loved. "He came un-glued."

"Stop it! Stop it!" warned Martin's attorney.

"It's just not fair! She won't let me see them! It's not fair, Your Honor! This is something that we *agreed* to!"

Sister Mary Moran was pacing in the hall just outside the court-room. Before she had testified, she had prayed for total honesty, a spiritual honesty. She was nervous. But a friend had reminded her, "All you have to do is tell the truth."

Martin stormed out of the courtroom, banging the doors open. Sister Mary's hands flew up.

"Oh, John!" she cried in horror. "He spat on me! John spat on me!"

The spittle ran down the nun's chin, seeped around her cross, and slid onto her blouse.* The frail, gray-haired woman shook like a leaf. "It was as if she had been violated," recalled Martin's mother-in-law, who watched the scene in disbelief. At that moment the elevator doors opened and Martin disappeared with his girlfriend.

Like nearly every act in John Martin's life, the bizarre assault had

---

*In her affidavit filed in Martin's bankruptcy, Sister Mary Moran declared: "With a hateful look on his face, John Musumeci then approached affiant and with malicious and virulent intent purposely spat. [Moran] was shocked and repulsed by John Musumeci's actions and felt spittal [sic] on her chin, neck and upper chest."

been premeditated. In the last minutes of the hearing, as the judge took away Martin's police-enforced custody and lectured him on the importance of being a good father, John Martin had worked up an oozing mouthful of saliva.

Sister Mary Moran was brought back into the same courtroom where her gentle testimony had helped unravel Martin. Still quavering from the attack, the nun would never forget the "hateful look" on Martin's face. He had threatened her before, and now she was certain he would come after her. Later, she would pull herself together and file a police report, even going so far as to alert the police in Berkeley when she returned home. But none of this could stop the strange phone calls she soon began receiving. And as they comforted her, and wiped the spittle from her face and blouse, the clerk came back with the news. It was John Martin's lucky day. The judge had left for the afternoon.

37
Treasure Island

"It's time to move ahead, John, stop the crap, drop the suit like you promised, pay your bills, and don't tell us how much Faber loves you." Two years had passed since Phil Reed had written those words to Martin. Time had done little to temper his old friend's fury or circumstances. Reed knew of Martin's problems and for a time he was "concerned for his sanity," but Reed, too, had endured a bitter divorce, barely fighting off his first wife's claims to a share of the note. To Reed, winning the court battle had been like winning the lottery and finding out the true meaning of money: "All of these people get their hooks into you."

While Reed certainly didn't "condone what he [Martin] did," he understood his frustration. And Reed was willing to be open-minded toward Martin's latest scheme. "He [Martin] was impressed with the apparent power of the bankruptcy court," remembered Reed, who half-believed it when Martin excitedly told him that his bankruptcy might help matters get settled faster. "Instead it turned out to be quite a mess," said Reed, who watched "distrust of John Martin" multiply as his friend "collected money that wasn't going toward legal fees." Reed knew what some of Micro/Vest's investors thought of Martin's motives. "Holy mackerel, this guy is trying to take it all!"

Numb from playing the peacemaker, tired of listening to Martin and Hafif paint each other as demons, Phil Reed didn't know whom to believe anymore. Like his diminutive friend, Reed had begun to question Hafif's motives. Years had passed, Millard was rich, and Micro/Vest was still fighting for a share in a closely held corporation. Reed wondered whether Martin had really been an unrecognized genius after all. He thought back to when Micro/Vest "had Millard in the corner and let him out." Perhaps they should have forced the bond, risked the survival of ComputerLand, and pushed Millard into bankruptcy? Reed pondered whether Martin's dark plan for pirating ComputerLand and then hoisting a new flag, under the leadership of Faber, might not have been in Micro/Vest's best interests.

Memories of Hafif's unfulfilled assurances that Millard would settle and never appeal clouded Reed's former feelings of gratitude for the attorney's success at trial. Visions of how Hafif was "close to Giles, close to Millard, and close to Barbara" only served to remind Reed how seldom the imperious attorney had conferred with his own clients. Few Micro/Vest investors had forgotten the first settlement agreement and the countless documents that Hafif rushed over. "We couldn't take them with us," recalled Reed. "Nobody was comfortable. Some businesspeople like Bill Agee thought it was horseshit— that he [Hafif] should have been canned."

When it came time to act and make decisions, Reed had believed that Micro/Vest's second president, John Molinari, was in control. Many assumed that only the elderly former appellate judge—as the sole shareholder and sole officer of Micro/Vest—had authority to make settlements for the group. Or did he? Molinari did not make the settlements and wasn't sure whether he should have. "A lot of things are not clear to me," said the former judge. "Herb said he had authority to do whatever he thought was proper. He believed he had authority." Perhaps Millard had been right all along. Micro/Vest was like no other corporation, unsure of its rightful leader, lacking rules, officers, and procedure. One small box contained its entire corporate history, and the entity's only purpose was to disappear, to distribute stock that it did not own, that was not even issued in its name.

Molinari had seldom been informed when Martin made a sale or pledged stock for a loan. In truth, those investors had only bought a promise and owned nothing but Martin's word. If only there had been a stock register, regretted Molinari, then he would have known exactly how much stock Martin did and did not own. Without any established procedure to follow, Molinari could only "suppose" that Martin and Reed represented the people they sold stock to. The lines of authority were equally nebulous. Molinari knew only where he had not stood; "Herb and Giles did all the settlements," said the judge. "I didn't sign any of those agreements, and neither were they signed by Mussman [Micro/Vest's first president]."

In the end, Hafif was formally told to make no settlements without Molinari's approval. But by that time some in Micro/Vest felt the damage was done. "Herb acted like he was God's gift," said Reed. "Like Micro/Vest was his personal playpen." And no matter how badly Hafif portrayed Martin to the group, Reed felt a deep obligation to Martin, the same unwritten debt that Andrighetto would never forget. No failing on Martin's part could dull that devotion: Martin had been the motivator, the unifying force that had aligned them against Millard. As Micro/Vest's unofficial treasurer, Reed knew better than anyone that Martin had been behind in his legal fees for the last few years. Always a religious man, Reed's faith had blossomed in the last ten years, and much of his free time and money went to the Christian organization World Vision. When Martin asked him to give testimony in support of his executory-contract strategy, Reed did not hesitate. "If I'm subpoenaed, I tell the truth, exactly the way I see it."

On November 28, 1988, in the county of King, in the state of Washington, Philip Reed executed an affidavit to be used in John Martin's bankruptcy petition seeking to rescind certain contracts for Micro/Vest stock. "Neither Mr. Harold Schwartz nor the Harold Schwartz group has ever sent any payment to me for any reason nor has either Mr. Schwartz or the Schwartz group ever asked me for any billing or itemization . . . accounting or description of any expenses whatsoever." Reed was not asked whether John Martin had paid his legal bills and he did not volunteer the information.

Issued in the last days before the New Year, the decision in ComputerLand's appeal was long, scholarly, and direct. Merrill did not mince his words, nor temper his distaste for Millard and his lawyers. He began his eighty-page decision by discrediting Millard's account of his oral agreement.

... The two Millard declarations are contradictory on their face. In the first one, Millard asserted that he had both long-distance and face-to-face discussions with Loring Reed in January 1976, which culminated in an "oral loan agreement" pursuant to which Marriner loaned IMS $250,000.... In the second declaration, Millard stated that all of the discussions... were between himself and Philip Reed only, and that he did not talk to or meet Loring Reed until *after* IMS had actually received the loan proceeds from Marriner.

Next Merrill did a little ghost-busting on Hufstedler's dead option:

... Appellants now contend that IMS, the entity which executed the Note... was dissolved sometime on or about February 17, 1977.... The bulk of appellants' argument on appeal is based on the contention that this alleged dissolution extinguished any conversion option contained in the Note.... Aside from the fact that appellants never advanced this argument before either Judge Kroninger or Judge McCullum... During trial, Millard himself testified that he did not think that IMS was ever liquidated.

Merrill then fired the damning condemnation that would be generously quoted in the newspapers:

... Millard was constantly tinkering with his various corporations, all owned entirely by himself and his wife. He was continuously engaged in a kind of shell game with them whereby one would be informally merged into another, and their purportedly separate and distinct individual identities treated as nonexistent.

He did not spare Millard's lawyers:

Appellants' contention that IMS's alleged death or merger destroyed the option, although sophisticated and speciously legalistic, flies in the face of the statements and behavior of the parties both before and during trial.

Merrill dubbed Hufstedler's numerous assertions a "laundry list" and dismissed her legal argument that Micro/Vest was a sham corporation violating "public policy and securities laws": "... The evidence is that the individuals who paid to be a part of Micro/Vest were investing in the anticipated ownership of the various corporations in which they

believed the conversion option gave Micro/Vest a 20 percent ownership interest. This is not the same thing as selling shares in litigation.... The rights and protections created by the federal and state
securities laws are for the benefit of purchasers of securities. Here, of
course, none of the purchasers of interest in Micro/Vest are being
heard to complain . . ." Micro/Vest's judgment was affirmed, and Millard was ordered to pick up the cost of Micro/Vest's defense.

Hafif didn't even have time to read the opinion. Thousands of
miles away, across an ocean of Pacific blue, a bankruptcy judge in
another case had ruled in favor of Martin's executory-contract strategy. Millions of dollars' worth of stock that Martin had sold might
soon be his again. Or so it seemed until Hafif had his say. Hurriedly,
the attorney sent off a long, angry letter to Phil Reed. Martin may
have moved first, but he had always known that the final challenge
would come from Herb Hafif, his new nemesis. Hafif's letter read:

> Bad results happen in bankruptcy courts with good lawyers and it only
> takes one or two small facts to twist it and Martin knows what those facts
> are and we may be playing into Martin's hands.
>
> We have a moral obligation to do what's right for everybody who had
> invested money . . . a deal is a deal. It's obvious knowing what I knew
> about Martin in '86, that he had tried to set up a competing Computer-
> Land, that he was violating every fiduciary duty in the world, that I wasn't
> going to pay him money so that he could *not* pay the money to Micro/
> Vest. And he was not my collection agent. I would deal directly with
> you . . . I doubt seriously that I wouldn't be able to send a bill for over $1
> million and what could my 2 ½ percent [the stock Hafif's pension plan
> bought from Martin for $500,000]—what cold my share of fees add up to.
> It was the best deal Micro/Vest ever had, and no wonder you and Bruno
> paid my share of attorney fees.
>
> The way it's going to work is very simple. One, I'm going to make a
> motion to move the whole thing back here. Apparently Molinari will join
> in that and Schwartz will join in that, and we'll get it back here and then
> we'll make a motion to put the son of a bitch into final bankruptcy,
> chapter 7, so we can get an independent trustee appointed, and fix his
> wagon good, and then I'm going to attack the bankruptcy itself, because
> he's lied about the obligations, he has no obligation of $1.2 billion, that
> case was settled. He really isn't bankrupt is what it amounts to. He has

enough stock left of his own to pay all of his debts without screwing anybody else—the only problem for the little bastard is that he won't have any left...

It was the letter of one confiding in a friend, but it may have been a mistake. The lines were no longer clear. Reed spoke frequently with Martin and no longer felt any loyalty to Hafif, who in his eyes had become just another attorney. The more Reed thought on it the more he saw—just as Andrighetto did—the two feuding men as one. "John and Herb to me are very, very much alike," said Reed. "They remind me a great deal of one another."

To be sure, Martin was pushing his luck with the bankruptcy, but Reed wondered whether Hafif wasn't trying to empty the pot while they weren't looking. Hafif's contract entitled him to 40 percent of punitive damages. Now the attorney was pressing to get 40 percent of the 5 percent of ComputerLand that he had traded for the punitive damages. Technically, not all of the $141 million traded for the 5 percent of stock were punitive damages (several million were legal fees, dividends, and compensatory damages). Some Micro/Vest investors, including John Martin, took that reasoning further, arguing that since Hafif threw out the punitive damages he was no longer entitled to any of the additional stock.

Hafif was unaware of how far his star had fallen, and his letters had the tone of pronouncements, of a captain still running the ship. Only weeks before he had written to Molinari, providing a progress report on what he assumed was the common enemy: "Our good friend John Martin has finally done it to himself," he wrote, describing Martin's Hawaiian exploits in graphic detail. "... In addition to everything else apparently the IRS is hot on his trail... his responses were that he wasn't getting any money, but the testimony in his trial was that he was getting cash from the companies..."

Martin's IRS troubles were no news to Molinari. "There is a big government tax lien against him," said Molinari. "I know because it's been served on me." But the steady former judge was unmoved by Martin's tax troubles or Hafif's inflammatory appeal. He had a fiduciary relationship to Martin as well as to Hafif. Sitting on the bench for fifteen years had taught him to be wary of fiery rhetoric, to overlook personalities and decide from a distance. Hafif's pleas only reminded Molinari that "even if I may think Martin is one hundred percent wrong and Hafif right, I can't do that openly, I've got a fiduciary duty to Martin."

Micro/Vest turned inward and investors began spending hundreds of thousands of dollars defending themselves against John Martin. Of course, in a sense Martin was suing himself, since he was a Micro/Vest investor, and thus if he ever did pay his legal fees, he would reach a landmark even more dubious than his billion-plus debt—the funding of the prosecution and the defense of himself. The irony wasn't lost on Molinari. "I thought all of these people were fighting Millard, and once we disposed of Millard we'd cut up the pie. Now the people are fighting amongst themselves."

While Martin and Micro/Vest fought over the elusive pot of gold, Hufstedler worked furiously to find an opening. She petitioned the court for a rehearing, attacking the nonpublication of the appeal— the formal procedure by which appeals become precedent—as a "serious abuse of the nonpublication rule" and a fundamental weakness of Micro/Vest's case. "Even if the option was alive, ComputerLand was not subject to it," Hufstedler declared.

To Hafif, her arguments seemed less designed to persuade Merrill of the nearly impossible—a rehearing—than to protect the image of Millard and tarnish Micro/Vest's victory. "These arguments including oral arguments before this court have been characterized by virulent attacks on Mr. Millard personally...," argued Hufstedler. "Micro/Vest's hands are unclean... Micro/Vest has again filed a scurrilous brief... Micro/Vest's answer... follows its usual briefing recipe: miscitation of authorities, distortion of the record, attacks on petitioners and their counsel..."

In the spring of 1989, the flurry of briefs finally came to a halt. The appellate court denied a rehearing and the California Supreme Court, unmoved by Hufstedler's arguments or her reputation, refused to hear the matter, and it seemed, after more than eight years, Millard had finally lost. Rumor had it that Hufstedler earned three-quarters of a million dollars for the appeal.

In one of her final petitions a frustrated Hufstedler had written: "This court is the petitioner's last hope of obtaining redress." For a time there was talk of appealing to the U.S. Supreme Court, or as

Giles had promised, suits against individual Micro/Vest investors. Terry Giles did not give up easily. His contingency plan had included the possibility of losing the Micro/Vest suit, and months before he had begun preparing for the worst. There were other courts, other means of legal revenge. Giles was ready for the challenge: he had sold his car dealership and other businesses and taken a public vow to lead Millard's legal crusade full time. And in his opinion, Micro/Vest's 10 percent settlement with Marriner had been a critical first step toward a second chance. Giles wasted no time immediately threatening suit against Marriner's attorney, Bill Conway. But Conway threatened right back with federal sanctions against frivolous suits. Giles explained the theory of his lawsuit in a letter to Conway on May 4, 1988.

I appreciate your view of Federal Rule of Procedure 11 and your nicely worded warning, however, you and I both know your clients have significant exposure.

In the Boston case where your clients sued Micro/Vest, a letter document was introduced whereby the Gerritys indicated to Loring Reed, just a few months after he had sold the note to Micro/Vest, that "they didn't blame the other guy for being upset." It was related in trial that the other guy was a reference to Bill Millard and that the Gerritys had written this letter after they had found out that Loring Reed had sold the note to John Martin and his son. That letter, which I lovingly refer to as the "smoking gun . . . " should make things very interesting in Federal Court.

Your clients knew that Loring Reed had done the wrong thing to Bill Millard. They failed to act appropriately in accordance with their fiduciary duties to the man that they lent money to . . . lying and concealing documentation that should have rightfully been testified to and turned over in discovery in Micro/Vest. Only their incredible greed in their case against Micro/Vest has brought the truth to the surface.

Because of our dealings over the last couple of years I have a great deal of admiration and respect for you as an attorney. I do not know what your opinion of me is but I can assure you that filing unjustified and unwarranted law suits is not a part of my repetoire.

Five months later, United States District Judge William W. Schwarzer wrote a terse order:

> The Millards raised and lost essentially the same conspiracy theory in the Micro/Vest action. Therefore, they are precluded from relitigating it. . . . At best, the so-called new evidence is only conclusory allegations of what the Millards hope to discover if the Court gives them another opportunity to litigate their claims . . . the Millards contend that the Court has specific personal jurisdiction over Liz Corporation because it is the alter ego of Loring Reed, Jr. . . . The Millards have not produced any evidence to support their alter ego theory. On the contrary, according to the declaration of its president, Philip Reed, Loring Reed, Jr. is only an eight per cent owner of Liz Corporation . . ."

Marriner's motion for summary judgment was granted and Millard's suit was dismissed for lack of jurisdiction. Conway quickly made good on his promise to request sanctions under Rule 11. Wrote Judge Schwarzer in his Memorandum of Opinion and Order: "Defendants now move the Court for sanctions pursuant to Federal Rule of Civil Procedure 11 and 28 United States Code section 1927, and under the Court's inherent power to discipline attorney misconduct. . . . The rule is violated by the filing of a pleading that is 'frivolous, legally unreasonable, or without factual foundation.' Under this standard, the First Amended Complaint and the Millards' opposition to summary judgment are both sanctionable."

Judge Schwarzer was clear about the legal and moral significance of Millard's transgression. ". . . The essential elements of a claim for abuse of process are (1) that the plaintiff was motivated by an improper ulterior purpose, and (2) that he intentionally committed some act not proper in the regular conduct of the process." Concluded the judge: "For the reasons stated, the Millards' complaint and their opposition to summary judgment were wholly 'frivolous, legally unreasonable, and without factual foundation' . . ."

The court gave Millard ten days to pay approximately $150,000 in legal fees.* Millard's plans for revenge appeared to be backfiring. He was paying double to hear a distinguished judge describe his motives as "ulterior," his rationale as "improper," and worst of all, his conduct, or as Millard would call it, integrity, as "wholly frivolous."

In response, Giles filed a declaration in opposition to the defendants' motion for sanctions. The long, zealous document, punctuated

---

*At the time of this writing, several months after the order, Millard had still not paid the legal fees.

by frequent headings and underlinings, and filed under penalty of perjury, seemed more designed to appease Millard than to sway the court:

> There is not one single shred of evidence placed before this Court to even suggest that Mr. and Mrs. Millard are frequent litigants, that they or their lawyers rush into the filing of lawsuits, or that they engage in abusive or harassing tactics once involved in litigation . . . I know that this Court cannot "step into my mind" and appreciate the reason why I came back to the practice of law to represent their interests. However, I can say without qualification that I was impressed with Mr. and Mrs. Millard, I perceived a degree of integrity and honesty that I had previously not encountered. Since I undertook their representation, Mr. and Mrs. Millard have brought and prosecuted only one lawsuit, and that is this case . . . For two individuals who are supposedly *so litigious* and *so prone* to use their resources to bring meritless cases, Mr. and Mrs. Millard have filed but not served an abuse of process action . . .

> Other than the abuse of process action in Killian, Mr. and Mrs. Millard *are not pursuing any litigation against anyone* at this point in time. Further, to the best of my personal knowledge, they have not brought any lawsuit other than this case since April, 1985. One of Mr. and Mrs. Millard's former companies, IMSAI Manufacturing Corporation, through a *Trustee* and by Order of the United States Bankruptcy Court has brought an action . . . The point is that the Defendants' representation to this Court that Mr. and Mrs. Millard are litigious or prone to abuse their resources to engage in harassing litigation is *flat out wrong*. Mr. and Mrs. Millard, like everyone else, have disputes with third parties, but the *record is clear* that any charge of their being litigious is a sham.

> I can, and want to, personally state that I have never encountered two individuals of greater honesty or personal integrity than Mr. and Mrs. Millard.

In fact, a suit against MicroPro had been been filed in the name of IMSAI by James H. Riggs as trustee. "Attorneys for Millard uncovered new evidence and called me," said Riggs, an attorney in Oakland. "I reopened the bankruptcy. The legal costs are on a contingency basis and the firm of Terry Giles has done all the legal work."

MicroPro had no doubt about the origin of the case. "You quickly come to the conclusion that Millard is behind it," said MicroPro's counsel Jay Jones. By the time of Giles' plea to Judge Schwarzer, the suit against MicroPro had already been thrown out of court under the statute of limitations. But Millard wasn't finished. IMSAI filed a petition to appeal.

Meanwhile, Martin was back in California. His bankruptcy petition had been moved to Alameda, but on a June day in 1989, Martin was in Oakland to give a deposition in his ongoing divorce. It seemed there was now some question about the settlement agreement Richard Bowman had written and his wife had signed. New legal heat was being brought to bear on John Martin.

Robert Kilbourne (Martin's ex-brother-in-law and the man who introduced Martin to his boss, Hafif) entered the room. Kilbourne watched Martin turn white. "Kilbourne's the one who thought all this up," screamed Martin, "and he's working with Mason and Hafif and they're all in it together and they're out to get me!"

Before anyone could react, Martin grabbed Kilbourne's legal documents and ran. Martin's lawyer tried to hold Kilbourne back. "Get control over your client!" shouted Kilbourne. "Either give me my documents back or I'm calling the police!"

Martin stormed around in the foyer, not ready to leave and not ready to return. When he heard the police had been called, he decided to call off his great escape. The deposition was adjourned, but he was ready to talk about settling his divorce: four and a half hours of talk—man to man. Kilbourne had once been Martin's friend and known him for nearly a decade, but he had never seen him so close to the edge, so ready to burst: "John looks like I would imagine anyone would feel who was fighting everyone on the face of the planet."

But Martin had new allies and a new strategy. A few weeks before he had filed an application with the bankruptcy court to authorize the spending of $25,000 to determine the viability of suing Herb Hafif. Long before Martin had threatened Hafif with a suit: it had only been a question of the proper time and the proper place. By making the claim while he was in bankruptcy, creditors of Martin might be inclined to see Hafif as a new revenue stream.

In the application, Martin accused Hafif of not giving him copies of any of the partial settlement agreements that waived the bond requirement and substituted 5 percent in ComputerLand stock for the punitive damages. This, of course, argued Martin, "resulted in material erosion and depreciation of the value of the judgment."

Martin also blamed Hafif for forcing him to drop his proposed malicious prosecution case against Millard as part of the partial settlement. Martin believed this put him in the unenviable position of having to turn on himself and those who invested with him. Martin claimed that he "was forced by Hafif into the position of suing his own fellow investors and himself, *should he prosecute his claim for malicious prosecution and abuse of process.*"

Martin also sought to rescue the $11,250,000 plus interest of attorneys' fees that had been waived in the partial settlements: ". . . debtor [Martin] was and is entitled to that entire amount. . ." Martin also wanted a share of the $8-million-plus cash dividends and the "shares in various other corporations" awarded by the trial court that were waived by Hafif.

But these were only minor grievances. Martin claimed that Millard had been willing to pay more than 5 percent of the stock of ComputerLand for the waiver of the bond and punitive damages.

> . . . The additional shares which the Micro/Vest beneficiaries were to receive by reason of the first settlement were apparently given up, or somehow disappeared.

> This exchange is significant because Hafif claims his legal fee, which *fee* by contract is 40% of any punitive damages, applies to the 5%, which is the fruit of punitive damages awarded. The result to Micro/Vest, however, is that Micro/Vest ends up with fewer shares and owes (according to Hafif) a much larger legal fee to Hafif. The debtor claims a material interest in said punitive damages or in the excess fee claimed by Hafif. *

The bankruptcy judge authorized the spending of $25,000 to investigate suing the man responsible for Micro/Vest's historic court vic-

---

*Of course no one—including John Martin—had ever considered the possibility of punitive damages until Hafif took over the case and unveiled his bold tort argument.

tory.* "I don't think the case would have been settled without Hafif," said one investor at the time of the investigation. "With his vendetta, Martin by himself would have blown it." Nevertheless, Martin's investigation of Hafif would be professional and comprehensive, and according to the court would include the "compilation, review and analysis of hundreds of documents, preparation of a chronology and legal research." One Micro/Vest investor summed up the group's feeling: "Everybody says what the hell. What can you lose? If he [Martin] gets anything, we get a piece."

None of this surprised Hafif greatly. Many of Micro/Vest's investors had been motivated by speculation, the promise of making millions on a few hundred thousand dollars' investment. They saw no moral or social message in defeating Millard and holding him to his word. Neither did they join together against Martin's attempts to get more money. "We figured we'd rather not get in this hassle so we paid the twenty thousand dollars," said one Micro/Vest investor. "I think Martin was wrong, but rather than spend more money [fighting him] we decided, 'Let's pay the goddamned thing!'" As Martin investigated suing Hafif, the little investors sat back and, as one said, watched the "cockfight" commence. High-priced lawyers or wealthy speculators, they were in it for the money and some figured "anything Martin does is going to benefit them."

Hafif held another view. He believed Martin's ultimate strategy was to "huff and puff and bluster" into some kind of a deal with Micro/Vest. But the attorney swore that he would never approve of any deal with John Martin. He would make no compromises and was ready to litigate if it came down to a fight. And Hafif had spent fortunes in the courtroom before. If it cost him a million to make sure everything was fair—for every Micro/Vest investor—he'd spend a million. "I don't mind going to court," Hafif said, smiling. "It's like throwing the rabbit into the briar patch. It doesn't bother me."

"Bill has come out of this with lots of cash, more cash than you probably could spend in a lifetime," enthused Terry Giles in the sum-

*Ironically, Martin's first lawyer on Micro/Vest, Charles Dell'Ario, had sued Martin for nonpayment of fees, declaring in his suit, "the numerous lawsuits and pending actions against Defendants [Martin] . . . quite often arose out of Defendants' inability to pay their bills."

mer of 1989, tanned from a recent trip to Saipan. In two years Millard's man claimed to have doubled the pot of gold from the sale of ComputerLand and stock. Millard's holdings were estimated at $200 million—not including an additional 16 percent if he prevailed in the Killian/Van Natta appeal. Even Millard's follies returned a profit. Those used generators he couldn't unload on Saipan were peddled by his son-in-laws to an Indian reservation in the "central western" United States for a cool $1.5-million profit.

Giles was Millard's voice, his eyes, his ears, and even his legs. When Millard felt anger, Giles voiced his wrath—in legal complaints or island tribunals. Always Millard remained cool, calm, principled, and distant. Now that Millard's legal vendetta had backfired, Giles launched a new crusade: the accumulation of money. Six months a year the former car dealer flew the international skies, traveling the world to run Millard's numerous new businesses and monitor his countless investments. Rumors had Millard money in South Africa, Asia, and Europe. Giles told his wife, Patty, that Millard was his last job. "He's my best friend, he's the learning curve."

What did Millard do with his hundreds of millions and time? Tired of island electricity, Millard had taken one of his used generators and created his own power plant to power his computers and run the software with which the self-taught architect electronically designed his coral compound. Workers were brought in from the Philippines and the States. Perched on a bluff, on the edge of the jungle, the two-story residence included a pool, tennis court, and "condos" for Millard's two daughters and their husbands (Barbara had left for Canada soon after Millard gave her money from the sale of ComputerLand).

Not satisfied with the shiplike portals typically found in Saipan homes, Millard put in giant typhoon-proof windows, specially constructed "to withstand coconuts flying at 120 miles an hour." Around this Xanadu, Millard built a thirty-foot wall that soon earned the nickname "The Wall of China." The formidable fortification drew the animosity of virtually the whole island, including Millard's rich American neighbors. In addition to concrete walls, Millard had the latest in electronics. "Of course it's got real good security," noted Giles.

Few knew what Millard actually did behind those walls. He seldom left the island and never traveled for business. Giles spoke of the Micro/Vest case as a catharsis that tore Millard from the world of computers and opened him to a whole new world of opportunities. How you lived life meant more than anything else to Millard. "Would the Millards be living any differently if Micro/Vest hadn't come along?" asked Giles. "No, you can't live a better lifestyle. Has he allowed it to affect his sanity? Not at all."

As Giles added things up, Millard had capital, experience, and the inner wisdom of knowing that he didn't compromise his morals or principles. "I'd also like to think he's got some new relationships in his life—me and some other people: his son-in-laws. Bill's always been a family man. Family is number one in his life."

Meanwhile, the family known as Micro/Vest was in turmoil. And Millard and Giles also had the satisfaction of knowing that even if Micro/Vest someday patched up its differences, the payoff might prove illusory.

ComputerLand had failed to go public and create a ready market for its stock. The investment bankers had taken the story of the company's improved earnings and prospects abroad and throughout the U.S. to surprisingly good reviews. But investors felt the price was too high, and when Businessland's stock plummeted a few weeks before the planned 1988 offering, ComputerLand's public hopes were dashed. One board member doubted the company would venture back to Wall Street before 1990 or 1991. Timing was everything, and it seemed more than ever that the best time to take ComputerLand public had been half a decade before, in the boom times of 1983 and 1984.

All of this appeared to give Millard and Giles great satisfaction. Soon a decade would pass since the "conspiracy" of John Martin and Phil Reed. But what had they won? What would they do with 28 percent of the stock of a privately held company? "There's no one who's going to want to buy twenty-eight percent," asserted Giles. "They're not going to make that sizable investment without any control, right?"

And Giles predicted that was only the beginning of Micro/Vest's woes. While the battle raged between Martin and Hafif over Micro/

Vest, he believed taxes were already becoming due. Giles did some rough calculations. Based on the $150-million valuation of ComputerLand, Micro/Vest's 28-percent share had a minimum value of $42 million. "That means they'll be facing about fifteen million dollars in taxes come April 1990," said Giles. "No market for the stock and a fifteen-million-dollar tax bill."*

The real catch-22 that made Giles' eyes sparkle was that Micro/Vest had always trumpeted its corporate status. It was no sham corporation as Millard had always charged, but a true corporation with a president and a corporate record. If that was indeed true, said Giles, then the tax man would call twice: "They'll have a corporate tax, and when they distribute the stock out to them [investors], the individuals will have to pay [personal] taxes."

Such thoughts brought joy to Giles and Millard. Every snag Micro/Vest hit tore a new hole in John Martin's legacy, adding new proof that Martin couldn't possibly have been the creator. Bill Millard had always known the real John Martin: the man who had begun life as John Joseph Musumeci, and under Hafif's magic wand had briefly seemed the source, the one, the only originator of ComputerLand. But now Martin had turned upon himself and Millard could rest easily for it was clear that Martin would be remembered as a bankruptcy artist, a man who sued for profit and threatened a gray-haired nun.

While Martin fought evil spirits, Millard had followed his principles and cried out for justice. Nor did he run for cover when disaster loomed. The walls around his castle were big, true enough, but he could have fled the island and sought sanctuary in another retreat, perhaps one with equal tax advantages. They couldn't intimidate Bill Millard. Standing up before his accusers, Millard had testified before the government and the grand jury—and he had his supporters. Many of the est employees at ComputerLand not fired in the overhaul of the company were still doggedly loyal to Millard and his memory. They would not stand for those who dared criticize the Chairman. A similar loyal minority appeared to be evolving in Sai-

---

*Despite the "Millard Tax Bill," Millard had managed to avoid millions of dollars of capital gains taxes.

pan: one article in the local papers was entitled, "Millard is an honest man."

There was some relief when an island convict finked on a fellow prisoner and the murder of Galen Mack appeared to be solved. But even before, when rumor swirled around the execution-style killings, the Millards did not temper their righteous ways or hold back their principles. And when all the government hearings and grand juries boiled down to one man and one trial, Pat Millard sat on the jury in judgment. Of course, she was essentially the only person on the jury not related in some way to the man. When the votes were cast and the man went free, Pat Millard stood alone with her principles, as her husband would have wanted, casting her solitary vote for conviction.

After the Micro/Vest trial victory, Saipan had seemed a perfect escape, an island paradise without equal. Then, Millard found himself ensnared in his own "personal" tax bill, tagged as persona non grata and besieged by death threats and ominous murders. But the ultimate challenge to Millard's self-imposed isolation was found in the local constitution—Article XII, Section 1, to be exact: ". . . the acquisition of permanent and long term interests in real property within the Commonwealth shall be restricted to persons of Northern Marianas descent." Section 3 continued: "any land transaction in violation of this provision shall be void."

Millard had engaged a native agent to secure him a long-term lease "in contravention of the restrictions or alienation of land contained in Article XII of the Commonwealth Constitution," alleged a Saipan complaint. The suit further charged that Millard had taken advantage of the ignorance of the previous owners of the land as to "what the entire scheme was about." And what did the lawyer who represented the previous landowner want? "Of all of Millard's follies this is the greatest," said Theodore Mitchell, a Saipan lawyer, given to sudden bouts of anger, who figured to take 50 percent of Millard's land as his fee if his ongoing suit prevailed. "Millard's Wall of China will have to come down. He'll have to tear it all down."

But the real walls had crumbled much earlier. Millard had spent a lifetime building a labyrinth of policies and practices and principles, regimenting work into a neat package that he claimed was the essence of life. He never saw himself as a computer entrepreneur, but rather as a philosopher king: his call was not to technology or fame or even money. People followed because he was the father who would make the rules that would not be broken. And no one would fail for lack of talent or initiative.

Back in the heady days of Luxembourg, when IMSAI was churning out paper sales and ComputerLand was siphoning off its capital and resources, Millard stood before his great empire and saw no limits. Flying into the future in his Learjet, in 1978, Millard wrote in his diary his thirteen-year goal to "make a difference worldwide in business, applied science, politics and peace."

Twelve years later, stripped of his company and legacy, Millard's time was running out. There had been nothing wrong with his dream. For a brief moment he had danced with the computer revolution and led it into the homes and businesses of America. His mistake was that he imagined he had sculpted the dancing figures from clay. And when he saw them stretch and think beyond his control, he struck out with vengeance and every lawyer money could buy.

In his little poem read to the Micro/Vest jury, Harold Nachtrieb had written the last act to the play:

The hardest to take from Big Bill Millard
Is the way he has treated his friends . . .

I ask for your verdict against this man,
With his billions and "stonewall" defense.
The truth hoists Millard on his selfish petard
All the "proof" in his case makes no sense.

Sometimes in life the tables are turned
So the evil themselves learn the blues.
The evidence here is abundantly clear
That the fate for Millard is to lose.